Seek!

Seek!

Selected Nonfiction by Rudy Rucker

FOUR WALLS EIGHT WINDOWS

NEW YORK

© 1999 Rudy Rucker

Published in the United States by:
Four Walls Eight Windows
39 West 14th Street, room 503
New York, N.Y., 10011

Visit our website at http://www.fourwallseightwindows.com

First printing April 1999.

Library of Congress Cataloging-in-Publication Data:
Rucker, Rudy v. B. (Rudy von Bitter), 1946-
Seek! Selected Nonfiction/by Rudy Rucker.
p. cm.
ISBN: 1-56858-133-5 (cloth)
ISBN: 1-56858-138-6 (paper)
I. Title.
PS3568.U298S44   1999
814'.54—dc21   99-10706
                                                  CIP

10 9 8 7 6 5 4 3 2 1

Text design by Ink, Inc.

Printed in Canada

Contents

PART III: ART

ADDITIONAL INFORMATION

Introduction

Rudy's parents Embry and Marianne in 1950.

Seek What?

I was born in Louisville, Kentucky, on March 22, 1946. At that time my father Embry had a small business making inexpensive furniture and my mother Marianne was a housewife. I have one sibling, my brother Embry, Jr., who is five years older than me, and he still lives in Louisville.

My childhood was comfortable, conventional, middle-class. We lived in a ranch house my father built on two acres in a part of town that was not quite yet a suburb of Louisville. For awhile the neighboring properties were farms. There weren't that many kids around, but I had one or two friends. We spent a lot of time in the pastures, it was always fun to play with the little brooks. New developments were going up all around us, and exploring the building sites was another thing we kids did a lot. I loved to read. TV barely existed yet, at least not in Louisville.

My mother, who was born in Germany, was an enthusiastic gardener, amateur artist and potter. She was something of a character, soft-spoken but very opinionated. Two of her favorite words were "disgusting" and "amazing." When I was about eight, my father's business went bankrupt, but he was able to start another company that made small wood parts for furniture, things like table legs or the backs of drawers. This type of business is called a "dimension manufacturer."

I went to private schools, graduating from St. Xavier High School – I was one of the few non-Catholics to attend that school; my parents had the idea it was very good for science. "St. X." While I was in high school, my father became ordained as an Episcopal priest, and worked as parish priest for the rest of his life, although he retained the ownership of his dimension manufacturing business.

I went to Swarthmore College from 1963–1967, majoring in mathematics and getting a Bachelor's degree. I had a lot of fun there, and was sorry to graduate. At this point, my choices were the draft or grad school, so I had no hesitation in going to Rutgers University from

1967–1972. I got my Master's and my Ph.D. in mathematics. My area
of specialization was mathematical logic, with my thesis on transfinite
set theory. In 1967, I married my college sweetheart, Sylvia Bogsch,
and not too long after that we had our three children: Georgia (1969),
Rudy, Jr. (1972), and Isabel (1974).

After grad school, I got my first job in the mathematics department at the State University College at Geneseo, New York, a job
which lasted from 1972–1978. I started teaching the "Higher Geometry" course there, and turned it into a series of lectures on the fourth
dimension. Eventually I wrote the lectures up as *Geometry, Relativity and The Fourth Dimension*, and managed to get them published
by Dover Publications, a house which primarily publishes public-
domain books by dead authors. They didn't pay me much, but it was
enough to throw myself a good thirtieth birthday party – and my
writing career was on its way.

The next thing I wrote was a science fiction novel called *Spacetime
Donuts*. This was in the summer of 1976. I wasn't sure I could write a
novel, but I just kept going and after awhile it was done. Nobody
wanted to publish it, but then I came across a new magazine called
Unearth which was willing to serialize it in three parts. As it happened, *Unearth* went out of business before publishing Part Three.

We were interested in finding a way to move out of cold, rainy
upstate New York, and in 1978-1980 I luckily got a grant from the
Alexander von Humboldt Foundation, which is funded by the German government. The five of us lived in Heidelberg for two years, the
kids making their way through German schools, and Sylvia struggling
to keep everything together. (Bad news: in Germany, all the kids come
home for lunch. Every day!) I had a peaceful office in the Mathematics
Institute of the University of Heidelberg, and ended up writing most of
Infinity and the Mind as well as two novels there: *White Light* and *Software*. *White Light* was picked up by Ace Books in the U.S., and by Virgin Books in the U.K. And then Ace bought *Spacetime Donuts* and
Software as a package, and I was really a writer.

The only math professor job I could find back in the States was at
a tiny college called Randolph-Macon Woman's College, in, of all
places, Lynchburg, Virginia, the home of then-prominent right-
wing evangelist Jerry Falwell. After two years at Randolph-Macon

(1980–1982), I decided to give full-time writing a try. Sylvia and the kids and I stayed in Lynchburg; we had a nice big old house and it wasn't a bad place for the children to grow up. In the years 1982–1986, I wrote six books. This period marked the birth of cyberpunk science fiction, and I became recognized as a founding father of the movement. My cyberpunk novels *Software* and *Wetware* each won a Philip K. Dick Award for best paperback SF novel of the year. It must have been one of God's little jokes to have me do this from the Moral Majority's home town.

As my own alternative to cyberpunk, I also developed a style of writing which I call *transrealism*. The essence of transrealism is to write about one's real life in fantastic terms. *The Secret of Life, White Light*, and *The Sex Sphere* are examples of my transreal novels. The first recasts a traditional coming of age memoir as a UFO novel, the second is about my time as a mystical mathematician in Geneseo, while the third turns my two years in Germany into a tale of higher dimensions and nuclear terrorism.

Being a full-time writer in Lynchburg got to be too hard and thankless a way to make too meager a living. I wrote *Mind Tools*, a nonfiction book about mathematics and information, which got me to wanting to teach math again. When an old friend told me about a job opening at San Jose State University, I applied for it, and to my delight I was hired in 1986 and am still there today.

I still can't quite believe that I got the chance to move to California. When I lived in Lynchburg, I was like some Darwin's finch with a specialized, highly-evolved beak designed for eating one certain kind of seed. There weren't any of those seeds at all in Lynchburg, but when I got to California they were lying all over the ground. In the Golden State, I was warmly welcomed by a great band of hackers, academics, science fiction writers and freaks – all on my wavelength.

When I started my job in the SJSU Department of Mathematics and Computer Science, I was urged to consider teaching computer science as well as math. I did not know a great deal about computer science at the time (understatement!), although my doctoral work in mathematical logic had certainly familiarized me with *theoretical* computing. The first computer science course I was assigned was anything but theoretical: it was Intel chip assembly language! Fortunately, another professor was teaching the same course, and I was able to attend his lectures to help myself figure out what was going on. And soon I found something I was really interested in programming: cellular automata, which are parallel programs that produce rapid-fire self-generating computer graphics animations.

During this time, and perhaps in reaction to my high-tech surroundings, I wrote an historical science fiction novel called *The Hollow Earth*. I also got involved with the magazine *Mondo 2000*, edited by a collection of Berkeley characters interested in cyberculture. Thanks to *Mondo*'s influence, "cyberpunk" became something of a household word, taking on a broader meaning and even appearing on the cover of *Time*. I co-edited the *Mondo 2000 User's Guide* with R. U. Sirius and Queen Mu. As R. U. put it, "We need a mathematical logician, or we'll never put this thing together."

As well as teaching me a lot about computer science, my interest in cellular automata led to a second job as a software engineer during the years 1988-1992. My job title was "mathenaut." This was with Autodesk, Inc., of Sausalito, California, makers of the popular AutoCAD program. It seemed that John Walker, the co-founder and then-chairman of Autodesk, was fascinated by cellular automata. After I met Walker at the Hackers 2.0 conference in 1987, he hired me to work on some cellular automata software with him. I worked on four shipped software products at Autodesk: *Rudy Rucker's Cellular Automata Laboratory*, *James Gleick's Chaos*, *The Cyberspace Developer's Kit*, and *Artificial Life Lab*. My transreal novel *The Hacker and the Ants* was heavily influenced by having worked inside a Silicon Valley software company.

A drawback of working at Autodesk and SJSU at the same time was that I had very little time to write. In recent years I've gone back to just two careers: teaching and writing. In teaching, I feel I'm performing a definite social good; another point is that when I'm teaching, I'm learning – from covering new material, from having to organize my thoughts into lectures, and from the unpredictable conversations with students and colleagues. But since I mostly teach courses like *Software Engineering for Windows*, the course preparations do soak up a lot of time. Being a computer science teacher is like living on a Stairmaster. You continually have to keep stepping

Rudy and daughter Isabel in 1998. (Photo by S. Rucker.)

up the level. In any case, as I write this introduction, I'm on sabbatical and I have more time than usual for my writing.

In June, 1998, I completed the text and drawings for my "transreal nonfiction" work called *Saucer Wisdom* (Tor, 1999). The book recounts my (alleged) experiences with a UFO contactee named Frank Shook. The saucers purportedly showed Frank Shook many bits of Earth's future – right up through the year 4004. *Saucer Wisdom* gives detailed and illustrated accounts of Frank Shook's experiences, and is in this respect a millennial work of future extrapolation.

In November, 1998, I finished writing a new SF novel, *Realware* (Avon, 2000), the fourth book in the *Ware* series. And right now, this very minute in January, 1999, I'm putting the finishing touches on my twentieth book, the nonfiction anthology, *Seek!*, that you hold in your hands. So why call it *Seek!* anyway?

I picked the title partly because of a catch phrase I invented when I was writing the manual for the *CA Lab* software:

Seek Ye the Gnarl!

Some motivation for this phrase can be found in my "Cellular Automata" and "Life and Artificial Life" essays below. For the moment, suffice it to say that "gnarl" is being used here in the sense of "gnarly," which is one of my favorite words now that I live in California. Surfers use it to refer to certain kinds of waves, kids use it to refer to dauntingly strange events of any kind, and I use it to apply to things

Sylvia, Georgia, Rudy, Isabel and Rudy, Jr., in 1998. (Self-timer photo.)

that have a level of chaos that is tuned right to the boundary between order and disorder. When I write an interactive chaos-based computer graphics program, what I'm normally doing is seeking gnarl.

When John Oakes of Four Walls Eight Windows agreed to do two anthologies by me, a selected nonfiction and a complete stories anthology, I had the idea to call the first one *Seek!* and the second one *Gnarl!* And John liked this idea, he thought it would be nice to have this pair of unexpected, monosyllabic words for the paired book titles. Both my wife Sylvia and my agent Susan Protter mocked me a little, asking if there would be *Ye* and *The* volumes, but, no, I don't think so.

I think *Seek!* makes sense as the name for this collection because seeking is very much something that I've done for my whole life. I've always had a desire to push out to ultimate reality, to discover the Answer, to reach a union with the cosmic One. The nonfiction pieces in *Seek!* describe some of the various attempts I've made.

I've organized *Seek!* into three not-quite-mutually-exclusive categories: Science, Life, and Art. Let me briefly summarize the flow of each part.

In the Science part I begin by describing some ways in which I have sought to make computers be interesting and alive. And then, worn down by the mulishness of these machines, I turn to wilder kinds of science speculation.

In the Life part I start by describing some of my old days of pot and beer, get into ideas about God, describe the big move to California, and then include some travel writing. Never am I such a naked seeker as when I'm on the road.

In the Art part I discuss my ideas about how to write great science fiction – becoming a good writer has always been my most central quest. I interview one of the founders of my favorite "art religion," the Church of the SubGenius. And I end with essays on new and old visual arts.

One possibly confusing idiosyncrasy of my technique is that when I write about the members of my nuclear family, I prefer to use pseudonyms for them. This is partly so that they feel less exposed, and partly to remind the reader that even though something I write may be presented as an accurate memoir, it's still colored by my fictionalizing tendencies. As will be evident from the context, the transreal names I use for my family members are "Audrey" for my wife, and "Sorrel, Tom and Ida" for our children.

In the Science part of *Seek!*, I refer to a number of programs that are downloadable from my Web site. This is at www.mathcs.sjsu.edu/faculty/rucker. I'll also maintain a special *Seek!* page at this site with buttons for the various links which I'm going to mention.

To round out this introductory part of the book, I've included my answers to thirty-seven recent interview questions I've been asked.

Happy seeking!

– Rudy Rucker, January 31, 1999.

37 Questions

People sometimes contact me to do an interview for various print or electronic publications. I usually prefer doing my interviews by email, both because the written format gives me better control over what I seem to say and because then I have my answers on disk, suitable for reuse. Also it's easy for me and it doesn't take very long. I keep all my old email interviews in a single file and email it to the new interviewer. I encourage them to first read the old questions and answers (which they're also free to use) and to then propose a few new questions of their own.

What we have here is an edited version of my email interviews over the last five years, that is, 1994–1999. I've gone ahead and updated the answers so as to make them correct as of the time of Seek!'s *publication. I've listed each interview under the home of the interviewer, along with the name of the interviewer and of the intended publication.*

Tokyo, Japan
From: Nozomi Ohmori
For: *Hayakawa SF Magazine*

Q1: First of all, I'd like you to tell us something about how you group your novels. In a letter, you categorize *The Hacker and the Ants* as "transreal autobiography." So, I also want to know whether it makes an interconnected series along with former three novels (*The Secret of Life*, *White Light* and *The Sex Sphere*).

A1: My eleven or twelve novels thus far break into three groups: the *Ware* tetralogy, the Transreal series, and the Others.

As you mention, *The Hacker and the Ants* is part of the transreal series which includes *The Secret of Life*, *Spacetime Donuts*, and *White Light*. *The Secrete of Life* is about me in high school and college. I was a young beatnik freak punk and the objective correlative for this in the book is that I discover that I am in fact from a flying saucer.

Spacetime Donuts, the first SF book I wrote, is about my days as a graduate student at Rutgers University in New Brunswick, NJ. Note that the hero, Vernor Maxwell, spends a lot of time in libraries! *White Light* is about when I was a math prof at SUCAS Geneseo in Geneseo, NY. I'll put a little table for you here. I should mention that I didn't write the transreal books in quite the same temporal order as the periods they describe.

TRANSREAL SERIES	"MY" NAME	PERIOD OF MY LIFE
The Secret of Life	"Conrad Bunger"	63–67
Spacetime Donuts	"Vernor Maxwell"	67–72
White Light	"Felix Rayman"	72–78
The Sex Sphere	"Alwin Bitter"	78–80
The Hacker and the Ants	"Jerzy Rugby"	86–92
Saucer Wisdom	"Rudy Rucker"	92–97

And then there's my other six novels:

Ware Tetralogy: *Software, Wetware, Freeware, Realware.*

Other novels: *Master of Space and Time, The Hollow Earth.*

It's hard to use the same period of your life twice; a writer's memories are a precious resource that get used up over the course of his or her career.

The transreal novel gap from 1980–1986 corresponds to my years in Lynchburg, Virginia. I did set a number of transreal short stories in Lynchburg – I usually called it "Killeville." And *The Hollow Earth* includes some scenes of Lynchburg as well.

Speaking of Lynchburg, one Lynchburg story I never got around to writing would be called "The Men in the Back Room at the Country Club," and it would be about some men who drink and play cards all day every day in the country club locker room, and each evening the black man who takes care of the locker-room puts the men in the steam bath, and all the juice runs out of their bodies, and they're just leathery skins, and he rolls each skin up and places it overnight to pickle in glass-lined golf club bags filled with whisky that's inside of that man's locker. And then in the morning the skins go back into the steam bath and swell up, and there's the platypus honking of the men's hale morning voices. The men aren't supposed to be me, mind you, they're just a Lynchburg image that I never used. If I wrote it, I'd probably tell it from the point of view of a teenage caddy. It could perhaps be a little like Phil Dick's wonderful story, "The Father Thing."

At the start of this answer, I said I'd written "eleven or twelve novels" because one might either classify *Saucer Wisdom* as a novel or as some new genre such as "fiction nonfiction." I would be most inclined to say *Saucer Wisdom* really is a transreal novel, but it's written in the form of a nonfiction book about my alleged conversations with a UFO-contactee. It's a novel in somewhat the same sense that Nabokov's *Pale Fire* is a novel. It has non-central elements that tell a story about the narrator. I got so totally transreal with *Saucer Wisdom* that I even called "my" character "Rudy Rucker" instead of making up a different name. I listed all of "my" names in the table up there, just to compare them. As you can see, there's a kind of family resemblance to them.

Q2: When you came to Japan in 1990, you mentioned about the sequel/prequel of *Wetware*, whose working title was *Hardware* or *Limpware*. What is the current situation with your *Ware* series?

A2: My feeling now is that there will only be four *Ware* books, making a tetralogy. I've just now finished writing the last one, which gives us *Software*, *Wetware*, *Freeware*, and *Realware*. It took me nineteen years from the start of *Software* to the end of *Realware*! A long time, but that's how much time it needed for me to grow to the point where I could finally resolve all of the relevant issues. I couldn't have done it any faster.

I quit drinking and smoking pot in mid-1996 and my writing speed seems to be picking up. It had been slowing down. Writing *Freeware* took me two years, from early 1994 to early 1996. *Realware* took the first eight months of 1998.

There was indeed a time when I occasionally spoke of writing a prequel called *Hardware*, but my ideas for that book ended up in *The Hacker and the Ants*. *The Hacker and the Ants* gives a fairly detailed explanation of how we might use virtual reality and artificial life techniques to get from where we are now to the world of *Software*, with its intelligent autonomous self-reproducing robots. There also happens to be a Hollywood movie called *Hardware*, bearing no relation to my books, which is another reason why that wouldn't be a good name for me to use for a novel.

I never really had any intention of writing a book called *Limpware*, I used to just say that because I didn't want to reveal my actual title too early. In the case of both *Freeware* and *Realware*, I wanted to be sure I could actually finish the book before letting people know the title. *Limpware* is really more of a joke title. Over the years I must have heard every possible joke suggestion for a Ware title. Silverware, underwear, vaporware, nowhere, everywhere – like that. I think four of them is far enough to push it, and now I'm ready to move on. *Finis coronat opus.*

But you never know. I really like the *Ware* characters and their world, so I might someday get drawn back into it.

Q3: Can you summarize what is in the four *Ware* novels?

A3: I could talk about the characters, which is a story in itself, but this time I think I'll stick to the ideas.

There were two main ideas in *Software*. The first is that we could build some robots which are capable of "reproducing" by building copies of themselves. And if we set a bunch of these robots loose on the moon, evolution could take over, and the self-reproducing robots could evolve to become as intelligent and "conscious" as humans are. The intelligent robots are called "boppers." When I thought of this idea in 1979 it was a fairly radical notion. We're more comfortable with it than we used to be.

The second idea in *Software* is that if we had intelligent robots it might be possible to extract the "software" of a human being's personality and copy this onto a robot body.

The idea in *Wetware* was to kind of turn the second idea from *Software* around. Instead of people building robots and putting their minds into robots, the robots build people and put their minds into people. Equality. Break down any human-chauvinistic idea that we're better. The boppers want to prove they're just as powerful as people, so they use "wetware engineering" to build people! And then the boppers find a way to encode their personalities as wetware genetic properties, so that they really can bring into existence a kind of human that has a robot's personality. *Wetware* is probably the most cyberpunk book I ever wrote, it's quite intense.

Nearly ten years of my life went by before I wrote another *Ware* book, and *Software* and *Wetware* were even reissued as a single volume called *Live Robots* (Avon, 1994).

The thing that pulled me back into the *Ware* world was that I kept thinking about something that happened at the end of *Wetware*. The humans exterminate the boppers by means of a biological "chipmold" that ruins their silicon chips. But the boppers had this kind of intelligent plastic for their skins called flickercladding, and the flickercladding became infected with the chipmold and got smarter. I wanted to write more about that stuff.

Freeware starts out in 2053 in Santa Cruz, California. The East and West Coasts of the U.S. have a lot of new citizens called moldies. These are pieces of flickercladding that have chipmold living inside them. Some of the chipmold is psychedelic so you can get severely high by hanging out with a moldie. Moldies are also great for sex, but there is the problem that they are likely to stretch a tendril up your nose, punch through the weak spot near the eye and put a "thinking cap" in your head. Nevertheless, there's a Moldie Citizenship Act that makes them citizens.

One important thing in *Freeware* is the introduction of a universal communication device called an "uvvy." It's pronounced soft, as if to rhyme with "lovey-dovey." Every SF writer dreams of having one of his or her inventions become "real" – think of Heinlein's "waldo" or Gibson's "cyberspace." I have a certain amount of hope pinned on "uvvy." A cell-phone is something like an uvvy.

Another big idea in *Freeware* is that aliens travel from planet to planet in the form of cosmic rays. And it turns out that the moldies develop a kind of program that enables them to decrypt the alien personality waves. It's a little like downloading a compressed file from the Web and then uncompressing the file onto your computer. It doesn't cost you anything; it's "freeware." But it turns out that the alien freeware completely takes over any moldie that decrypts it. In other words, some of the moldies get turned into aliens. There's some fighting, and all but one of the aliens is killed.

So then I had to write one more *Ware* book to find out what happened to that last alien, whose name is Shimmer. Shimmer decrypts a few more of the alien personality waves, so in *Realware* there's actually seven of the aliens. They're all from the same place this time around, a world called "Metamars." They give the human race this amazing tool called an "alla." What the alla does is to make whatever object you describe to it. Like if you have a computer and you do a drawing, you can press "Print" and the drawing comes out. But if you have an alla, you specify something and you say "Actualize" and the object appears. It's realware. At this point I think I reach the ultimate abstraction of reality into information, which is a theme I've been aiming at throughout all four *Ware* books.

As well as the play of ideas, there's some emotional themes that run through the *Ware* books. One of the main themes has to do with how a man comes to terms with his father; and how a father comes to terms with his son. There's a transreal element to the *Ware* books – especially *Software* – in that there's a character named Cobb Anderson who's closely modeled on my father. My father had coronary bypass surgery right before I wrote *Software*, and it had a big effect on his personality – it was almost like he'd gotten a new body. At the end of *Realware* I feel like I've finally come to terms with my father, and with our interactions, and with his death from a stroke in 1994. It's a liberating feeling to have the *Ware* tetralogy all done.

Q4: You have cooperated with various SF writers so far. Generally, how the collaboration is done? Using email or phone? For an example, please tell the story about the process of writing "Big Jelly" with Bruce Sterling.

A4: Each collaboration is different, even with the same guy. I write something, send a printout and a copy of the file to the other guy, he adds new stuff and doesn't fuck with my part too much, and then he sends me back the new printout and a copy of the new file. In practice the other writer will tend to change my text and I change his, and we write flaming letters about hands off this and that or put this or that back. It's great fun, as usually writing is an extremely isolated activity.

One way that I sometimes organize writing with a friend is that each of us is responsible for one character who is a transreal representative of the responsible author. A role the author is playing. And then your character can be challenging or running head-trips on your partner's character. That can be another element in an SF collaboration, the trying to amuse or to outrage your partner. And then they turn around and do something that really surprises you, and it's fun.

Q5: When you were young, what kind of science fiction you liked to read? Tell us your growing-up story in SF field. Do you consider yourself as a science fiction writer?

A5: When I was young my favorite science fiction writer was Robert Sheckley. When I was fifteen I was injured when the chain of a swing broke and I ruptured my spleen. I was in the hospital, and my mother brought me *Untouched by Human Hands* by Robert Sheckley. Somewhere Nabokov writes about the "initial push that set the ball rolling down these corridors of years," and for me it was Sheckley's book. I thought it was the coolest thing I'd ever seen, and I knew in my heart of hearts that the greatest thing I could ever become was a science fiction writer. For many years, it seemed like too much to dare hope for.

Q6: How do you want to be called? A writer, a programmer, a mathematician, a mathenaut , or a cultural hero?

A6: A writer. Writing is far and away the most important thing that I do. Over the long run, only the written language matters. Of course "cultural hero" sounds tempting, and it would be nice if I could briefly become one. In his blurb for my memoir *All the Visions*, Lee Ballantine said, "Novelist, scientist, and cult hero Rudy Rucker has emerged as a key figure in the cyberpunk culture that has developed at this century's close."

Q7: It seems that there is a strong relationship between your non-fiction and novels. For instance, *White Light* can be considered as a sort of novelization of *Infinity and the Mind*. Will you explain the relationship for us. And, do you have any plan to write a new nonfiction book?

A7: That's exactly true about W*hite Light*. And *Infinity and the Mind* also includes the *Software* idea about self-reproducing robots evolving to become intelligent; this is in a section called "Towards Robot Consciousness." The ideas in *The Fourth Dimension* appear in *The Sex Sphere* and again in *Realware*, which has a number of scenes in the fourth dimension. *The Hacker and the Ants* can be thought of as the fiction version of the research I carried out to write my software package *Artificial Life Lab*. In the case of *Freeware* and *Realware*, I wrote a fantastic made-up nonfiction work, *Saucer Wisdom*, to introduce the science ideas used. The *Freeware* "uvvy" communication device, the *Realware* "alla" matter controller, the aliens who travel as radio waves – they're all in *Saucer Wisdom*, presented as God's own truth. It's like now I'm reaching a point where even my nonfiction is speculative.

I used to like to say that SF is my laboratory for conducting thought-experiments. But maybe when I said that I was just trying to impress my academic friends. Now that I'm a tenured full professor, I'm more likely to tell the truth. I don't write SF to help my science. If anything, I study science to help my SF! I love SF for the ideas, but more purely I love it simply for the rock'n'roll *feel* of it, the power-chords, the crunch, funk.

My agent has often urged me to write another nonfiction book, as these seem to make more money over the long term than do my novels. But I'm not quite sure if I can do another one. In my books *Infinity and the Mind* and *The Fourth Dimension*, I was laying out the vast knowledge that I had about a field that I had been obsessed with for many years, respectively, mathematical logic and higher dimensions. I absolutely *had* to write those two books – or burst. *Mind Tools* was a little different, it was more of a survey of mathematics as a whole, trying to relate everything to the notion of "information."

Now I've been in Silicon Valley for thirteen years and I know a lot about computers and software engineering; my day job is teaching Software Engineering at San Jose State University. I've been working on successive drafts of a software engineering project textbook with a CD ROM about writing Windows programs for simple video games. It has the working title *Software Project: Visualization and Videogames with Windows MFC*. But I don't think of that as a "real" book; it expresses nothing that's deeply important to me, and it'll be totally obsolete seven years after its published, if not sooner. It's simply a chore that I feel I need to finish because there is real short-term need for this book; there isn't any book out there that does what my *Software Project* will do. But a lot of it is just techie Windows gobbledy-gook.

At the low level, teaching programming is like teaching automobile repair – just having to explain these random arbitrary things like the part-numbers of the pieces inside some particular model vehicle's carburetor. And you can't just skip over that stuff because the whole point of programming is to get a nice program that works really well on some specific actual machine.

At a higher level, I've learned a lot about computer stuff like fractals, chaos, cellular automata, complexity, virtual reality, and artificial life, so it would seem like a good idea to write a book about that. But these topics are very picked-over; too many people have written about them. It's like looking for a cigarette butt on the West Point parade ground. Even so, in 1997 I was trying hard to get a contract to write a book like this. I wanted to tie the computer-inspired ideas more closely to immediate perceptions of Nature and to one's own mental experiences. But somehow I ended up with a contract to write *Saucer Wisdom*, a book about my fictional encounters with a man who'd been shown the future by some saucer aliens! It's not always easy to predict what book you end up writing. Certainly my work with computers has very much affected the way I see the world, and maybe someday I can figure out a marketable way to write about this.

Q8: You told me that you were considering to write a story based on your experiences visiting Japan. Is there any progress on that project?

A8: Hmm, I had in fact forgotten my reckless promise to write such a story. The thing is, William Gibson has written so much about Japan in his books, and he's done it so well. He's kind of made it his core subject matter. So I'm resisting the notion of writing about Japan. But if I were to write about Japan, I'd write about a lizard I saw in the famous Zen garden in Kyoto. A lizard living under a rock in the most famous Zen garden. How enlightened is that lizard – or *what*? I could have him be a limpware moldie construct inhabited by pay-per-view users.

Q9: Recently I bought some CD ROMS: *The Hugo/Nebula Anthology*, *Isaac Asimov's Ultimate Robots*, Robert Grudin's *BOOK* (Expanded Book version), and so on. How do you think about those multimedia titles? Any plan of making one for yourself?

A9: When I get really old, I want to take everything I've done: all the books, all the journals, all the software – take all that and put it in one giant wonderdisk, or chip or S-cube or whatever. But I'm not done doing new stuff yet. And the longer I wait, the better and more together the tech will get. Not that multimedia tech will ever be stable. As someone who's been involved in developing computer software, I've really gotten to hate the impermanence of computer platforms. It's like writing on the water, like pissing in the wind. You knock yourself out creating a CD-ROM, and five years later everyone's switched to DVD. Only writing on paper is for the ages.

Q10: As a question to a philosopher of modern age, do you still believe the Many Worlds Interpretation? In *Mind Tools*, you defined reality as a group of cellular automata, but after that you seem to have changed your opinion. What made you think that reality is more complicated than that?

A10: The Many Worlds Interpretation is a science fictional kind of quantum mechanics view of the universe, and no, I don't think it's true. I think our specific universe exists because there is some intelligence or design that carves it out. I don't think it reasonable to say that our world exists only because every other possible universe exists as well.

The Many Worlds Interpretation is a notion that comes out of quantum mechanics, and I don't have good feelings about quantum mechanics at all. I have the basic layman's response that quantum mechanics is a bunch of hand-waving by scientists to cover up the fact that there's something they don't understand at all. Some popular books on quantum mechanics make it sound like we're supposed to be happy and intrigued about the nonsensical aspect of quantum mechanics − about the duality and uncertainty and complementarity stuff. I'm not happy about it at all, I think it sucks. My mathematical training was as a set theorist, and I have this hope that maybe if some day physicists start using actually infinite quantities in their theories then the weirdness of quantum mechanics might be banished.

I have a tendency to think the universe is like whatever I've been recently studying. When I got interested in cellular automata, I started to think the universe is a cellular automaton (CA) − which is a kind of multidimensional grid of little cells that carry out interacting computations in parallel. Of course there's no grid in the real world, so the definition of a CA would have to be changed to make it more like a coral reef. You could have the cells themselves carry the grid, that is, each cell could carry a list of connections to its "neighbors." But granularity is still a problem, that is, why should the world divide into cells of a certain size? That sounds like quantum mechanics, which is just what we don't want! So then I thought maybe the cells could be made of smaller cells, which are made of smaller cells, ad infinitum. This could be a chance to have some infinities. Think of a pattern like a fractal. So this is why, at the end of *Mind Tools*, I said reality is "a fractal CA of inconceivable dimensions." (I use "inconceivable" here in a special technical sense to mean "larger than any finite number that people can name.")

The "inconceivable dimensions" part has to do with the fact that I think that any view of reality should include the mental element as well as physical space and time. And there's a real sense in which our minds inhabit a world of inconceivably many dimensions.

But all the science can easily miss the immediacy of how the world feels. At an immediate level, reality is very gnarly and very novelistic. It's a supreme work of art, inconceivably rich. And we'll never know any final answers.

Athens, Greece
From: Alia Skourtsi
For: *ZeroOne Monthly Magazine*

Q11: Are still mathematics able to help us in exploring ourselves and the universe?

A11: Of course, mathematics is the best forever. Mathematics is the science of form, and everything is form – plus the single divine content of existence.

Q12: Do you really believe that cyberspace is sterile and boring without A-Life organisms wandering in it? In a few years it is going to be overpopulated by people. Why should we fill it with more living organisms?

A12: In this context, I am thinking of graphical representations of cyberspace, such as in for instance the game *Quake* or *Half-Life*. These worlds would be more interesting if there were artificially alive things in them continually changing them. Mold, for instance, or plants, or *ants*.

Q13: Do you still want to create a second self inside a computer?

Why? Would you like somebody else to lead your life or are you seeking eternity?

A13: I would still, yes, like to make an interactive multimedia hyperlinked compilation of all my writings. Interacting with the construct would be in some sense like talking to me. This construct would easily be able, for instance, to answer these interview questions.

I want to do this because it is a type of immortality, and like most people I am interested in extending my influence on the world as much as possible. I also happen to think that my information and knowledge is valuable, and that it would be an objectively good thing to have a Rudoid simmie available for the edification of future generations. In *Saucer Wisdom*, I call such a program a "life-box."

Q14: What do you think is the main disadvantage of the contemporary computers, besides being slow?

A14: They are very hard to program. You can have an idea for a program in an hour but it takes you a year to properly implement it. Of course all art is like this.

Q15: Do you think that the digital revolution will lead us to a more democratic society?

A15: I think politics in every form sucks. The more you think about politics, the more of your energy is siphoned off and turned into garbage.

Well, I'm especially full of cynicism today because I'm so tired of hearing about the idiotic Republicans. Russia got rid of the Communists, why can't the U.S. get rid of the Republicans? It'll be hard to ever get rid of them; as hard as *China* getting rid of the Communists.

But yes, in the sense that people can get better info and make input more easily it would seem that digitizing makes things more democratic. But if there is a whole lot of democratic input it's just going to be ignored the way it is now. The majority of Americans want to get rid of guns, and everyone knows this, but nevertheless the Republicans in Congress are still capable of trying to make assault weapons legal again. It is to weep.

Bottom line: fuck politics, it'll just rip you off and break your heart. Focus on getting your own life in order.

Q16: Why do you prefer the term transrealism more than cyberpunk?

A16: One very practical reason is that when people mention "cyberpunk," they always mention Gibson and Sterling and don't always mention me. I prefer a genre word that applies primarily to me! "Transreal" is my word; I made it up. It has to do with the idea of writing SF about my immediate perceptions, and using real people as models for the characters. This is the way I almost always write. Many of my books are also, of course, cyberpunk.

Q17: Does cyberpunk have an expiration day? If yes, what do you think will follow?

A17: Cyberpunk is a stage in the endless Bohemian subculture that created the beats, the hippies, the punks, and the grungers of today. This type of countercultural sensibility will never go away. But cyberpunk in the sense of writing about computers may someday not be interesting, just as writing about space flight is not currently interesting. As long as Gibson, Sterling, Shirley and I are writing, cyberpunk will still be around; just as beat writing was still around as long as Kerouac, Ginsberg, and Burroughs were writing. And maybe even longer. Even though Kerouac, Ginsberg, and Burroughs are all dead now, there's still certainly the possibility of others using the "beat" sensibility in their writing.

Q18: Which places in the Net do you visit more often?

A18: Well, ahem, there's my home page www.mathcs.sjsu.edu/faculty/rucker. Not that I myself would go look at it over and over! But if you're interested in computers, I have a lot of free software for you there.

Mostly I just read my email. That in itself uses up a fair amount of my time. I get plenty of email, and that pretty much satisfies my Net hunger. So I don't cruise the Web that much. I don't find it a pleasant way to get information. I don't like waiting for a page to download and then having it be a page I don't want to see. It's like being in a strait-jacket having an overbearing Nurse Ratched feeding you a McDonald's Happy Meal. And she's using a tiny souvenir spoon that has advertising on it.

This said, maybe we have this leftover hominid instinct to stare at something flickering in the evening − like a fire. So either you stare at the TV or at a computer screen, and certainly a computer screen's no worse for you than TV. A computer has the plus of being more interactive, but it has the minus of being less easy to watch with friends.

Q19: What is your wildest dream?

A19: Being able to fly; I dream about this a lot, a couple of times a month.

Q20: Have you ever been to Greece or met Greek people? What is your opinion about our mentality?

A20: I have never been to Greece, although I would like to go there. I've been around Europe a lot, but never made it that far east. I have no particular opinion about Greek mentality; the only Greeks I'm familiar with are the ancient intellectual heroes such as Plato, Euclid and Zeno. I imagine Greeks to be both passionate and logical.

Tokyo, Japan
From: Michiharu Sakurai
For: "Noise" issue of [*relax*]

Q21: I think people feel more relieved in some disorderliness than being in perfect order. What lead people feel so?

A21: Complete order is lifeless, and we don't feel safe in a lifeless environment. In a fanatically clean setting, you yourself feel like a piece of dirt which is perhaps going to be cleaned away.

Put differently, noise is an aspect of chaos, and chaotic processes are what we as living organisms are made of.

Q22: Can the "noise" be discussed from the standpoint of the information ideology? What is the position of "noise" in the information ideology?

A22: In the theory of communication, noise is a corruption of a signal you want to send. Noise is like static and clicks in telephone conversation. Shannon's Theorem says that you can overcome noise by repeating yourself a lot.

In practice we expect people to not receive everything we say correctly, but it is too boring to repeat oneself word for word. Instead you tend to say the same thing again, but in a different way. And perhaps there is some certain kind of noise that makes one way of expressing yourself incomprehensible, but if you express yourself in a new way, then the new way finds a clear gap in the noise spectrum.

In chaos theory, we distinguish orderly, periodic processes from processes which appear random and noisy. The interesting thing is that certain kinds of deterministic equations can generate time sequences which superficially seem random even though they have a definite rule. The best kinds of chaotic processes will seem to spontaneously fluctuate between orderly and disorderly modes. The disorder appears when the process moves to a different region of its chaotic attractor, and then when the process settles onto a certain region of the attractor for awhile it seems somewhat orderly again.

In understanding what I am saying about a chaotic process, you might think of the branch of a tree blowing in the wind, or of a piece of paper that you are waving with your hand. Sometimes the branch or paper will flutter regularly, but then it can slip into a different mode of oscillation (into a different part of its strange attractor) and oscillate in an unsteady fashion.

In terms of noise and communication, I find it interesting that these words of mine are going to be translated into Japanese, and I will never in fact know what kind of understanding they are going to communicate to my esteemed Japanese readers. Something of my voice and message is preserved, but I have no way of knowing what this Japanese voice of mine sounds like. I hope it sounds like the Japanese voice my translators give me for my SF novels. Really I always say more or less the same thing.

Q23. People tend to find noises in artificial and technological objects, not in natural creatures. How do you see the relations between noises and artifacts?

A23: I would say that nature is also full of noises, such as the sound of rustling leaves or falling rain or chirping birds. Nature is essentially chaotic — it has underlying rules, but the working out of these rules produces patterns that are simply not predictable by a human brain.

The really objectionable noises are indeed from technological objects. As I write this answer, for instance, my neighbor's gardener is using a gasoline-powered leaf-blower to move small bits of dead leaves around this neighbor's yard. I find this noise annoying. What is annoying about the sound of an engine is that the sound is not interestingly chaotic. The sound is just the same power spectrum over and over and over. Even if I change my focus of attention or think about things in a different way, the engine keeps going, and eventually it wins back my attention.

The bad kinds of noises are the ones that are not chaotic enough, but are instead very repetitive. These are the kinds of bad noises that machines are likely to make.

Q24: Generally, noises are considered something useless. What are positive elements of noises we should pay more attention?

A24: It is an interesting exercise when you are walking around to try and become fully aware of the sounds around you. If you ever happen to make a tape recording outside, you will be surprised at how many noises there are besides the sound of the voices you are perhaps trying to capture. Becoming aware of the full tapestry of noise around you is a good method to heighten your consciousness and make yourself feel more tightly woven into the undivided fabric of the One World. To get started with this awareness, it may help to close your eyes.

Q25: As seen in samplings in music and uses of ready-made products in artwork, contemporary arts are seemingly moving toward "application," apart from the traditional idea of "creation." What does this tendency reflect in terms of changes in people's consciousness and thoughts?

A25: If you play a tune on the piano you are already in some sense sewing together samples of notes. But instead of pasting in a sound file for the note C, for instance, you are generating the sound file for the note C by pressing the piano key. On the other hand, a good pianist really is doing more than assembling a series of notes. There are in fact many different ways to play the note C and many different ways to segue it from the note before to the note after. The thing is, a piano is extremely responsive to very subtle muscular cues that a person can generate. If you are just pasting in a sound file for the note C, there are only going to be a limited menu of selections about what type of C note you want. The richness of human analog muscle expression goes far beyond any digitized program we yet have.

I think it will continue to be true for a very long time that the subtleties of sounds or colors or phrasings are going to allow a much wider palette of possibilities than will any cut-and-paste computer collaging process. So I would say the process of "creation" rather than "assemblage" will continue to be the most essential form of artistic expression.

On the other hand, in connection with the notion of noise, it is certainly true that a modern composer has the possibility to paste in a lot of interesting sound structures.

But just pasting things together isn't enough. It may superficially look like a complex work of art, but when you explore it more closely, it doesn't hold up unless the artist has a really close involvement in the work at many levels.

San Francisco, California
From: John Shirley
For: Introduction to HardWired edition of *White Light*

Q26: Is there, in brief, a general overall Rucker Theory of the Motif of the Transreal Books? A linking esthetic?

A26: Oh yes! It's called "A Transrealist Manifesto," and it appears in my new nonfiction anthology *Seek!* But let me try and summarize it for you.

Transrealism means writing about your immediate perceptions in a fantastic way. The characters in a transreal book should be based on actual people. This has the effect of making the characters be richer and more interesting. One inspiration for me in doing this is Jack Kerouac, who thought of his novels as a single linked chronicle. Though many would just call Kerouac's books autobiographical novels.

My transreal novels aren't exactly autobiographical: I have never really left my body, climbed an infinite mountain, met a sphere from the fourth dimension, infected television with an intelligent virus, etc. But they are autobiographical in that many of the characters are modeled on family and friends – the main person of course being modeled on me. The science fictional ideas in my transreal fiction have a special role. They stand in for essential psychic events.

The quest for infinity, for instance, is nothing other than the soul's quest for God. Or, more mundanely, it represents the individual's quest for meaning. In another sense, a White Light at the top of a transfinite mountain stands for the psychedelic experience, which loomed large in those years when *White Light* was written

(1978–1979). But, again, the whole point of the psychedelic experience, at least from my standpoint, was to see God. Another inspiration for me in pursuing transrealism is Philip K. Dick. His blackly hilarious book *A Scanner Darkly* was a real inspiration for me in forming my ideas about this way of writing. And in fact *Scanner* had a blurb on it describing the book as "transcendental biography," which was probably the reason I coined the word "transreal."

In a nutshell, transrealism means writing about reality in an honest and objective way, while using the tools of science fiction to stand for deep psychic constructs.

St. Paul, Minnesota
From: Patrick Clark
For: *Interference On the Brain Screen*

Q27: We were talking about your public image, and I think you mentioned you had something to say about drugs and alcohol?

A27: It's kind of touching how much attitude I used to have. I was pretty desperate to get noticed. To be different.

For a long time I embraced the classic notion that drinking and taking drugs is a bohemian identifier, a legitimate path to enlightenment. As I got to be older than Poe and Kerouac ever were, it became all too evident to me that their "left-hand" path is not a sustainable one. "It just ends in tears," as my mother used to say vis-à-vis almost anything.

I've been clean and sober for almost three years now, which feels like a big and joyful deal to me. I couldn't have done it without group support. The simple act of reaching beyond yourself and asking for help seems to be crucial.

I used to be scared that if I got straight I wouldn't be the same person, that the wild creative part of me would go away. Well, I'm not exactly the same person – but I still feel creative. My bizarre and millennial *Saucer Wisdom* will be out in mid-1999. And I recently finished *Realware*, which is the coda and finale of the *Ware* tetralogy. There is, I would say, as much weirdness in these books as ever.

Regarding enlightenment, it seems humorous to me that I used to think enlightenment was about getting wasted and blasting my brain into nullity. The flash, the pop, the white light. Like it never occurred to me that attaining enlightenment might have something to do with becoming a better person or being more loving to those around me. I've finally started getting some serenity now and then.

"Let go, let God." Brain-dead bumper sticker or profound truth? Yes, yes, it's the latter, even if you write in Olde English Scripte. There's some good raps about the bumper sticker/profound truth dichotomy in David Foster Wallace's book *Infinite Jest*. I read that book in early 1996, right before I finally got sober, and it made a real difference to me.

Some people say that *Infinite Jest* is too fat to read, but you have to know how to deal with a book that size, you can't let it boss you around, you have to just dive in there and carve out what you can use. In my case, I tossed out all the parts about prep school tennis matches and read the stuff about recovery and halfway houses, which is still enough for a really big book. The footnotes were good too. And the wheelchair assassins. Wallace is a great man.

Q28: In closing, what book would you like to be published Ace double "69 style" with?

A28: I already did it! The small press Ocean View put out my transreal rant-memoir *All the Visions* back to back with a book of poems *Space Baltic*, specially selected for the occasion by my favorite poet Anselm Hollo. Check it out, you can actually still order it from Ocean View, like through www.amazon.com, it's beatnik heaven, with a cover by Robert Williams yet.

London, England
From: Matthias Penzel
For: *Frankfurter Rundschau*

Q29: Unlike with rock'n'roll interviews, the preparation for writers' interviews is immense (weak excuse, mediocre explanation). Unfortunately I have not managed to read all your books before this interview. Which one (talking about your fiction) would you single out as your masterpiece?

A29: That's like asking a father which child he likes best. I love them all in different ways. I do feel that as time goes by I get more mastery of my writing, so in that sense I usually think my most recent book is the best. Today that would be *Realware*. As a practical matter, it is in any case better for me to believe that my latest book is my best. I would not want to think that a book I wrote a long time ago is better than a book I can write now. I feel like I am still on the upward part of my trajectory.

Q30: Although having been translated into German by Udo Breger who could probably be regarded as one of the country's leading translators, your books never quite cracked the German market – s that because they will always only appeal to a smallish cult audience anyway, or is it the matter of language?

A30: Maybe as the years go by, the mass of people will like my books more than they do now. It could be a matter of my being ahead of my time. Or it could be that my books are a little too esoteric for a true mass popularity. I write intellectual, high-literature, counter-cultural science fiction.

It could also be that my style of humor appeals more to Americans than to Germans. But at least one other country likes me: my books seem to be quite popular in Japan, perhaps even more so than in the U.S. I think all my novels are in print in Japan, which still remains an impossible dream for me in the U.S. But I still think my day will come. The trick is to try and have it happen before you die.

I'm sure that Udo Breger did a great job in translating my books into German, he was very meticulous and sent me lists of words he wasn't sure about how to translate, which is something very few translators think of doing. I wish they all would.

In any case, it's not in my interest to take the number of copies sold as my supreme yardstick of success. I'm happy that I'm published at all, and that my books do indeed speak deeply to some individual readers.

Q31: What do you think is your most important activity?

A31: At the personal level, the most important thing I ever did was to father and help raise our three children. At the public level, my most important activity is writing, although maybe in the long run it's my *sensibility* that will have the most lasting influence: my combination of humor, anarchy and scientific engagement.

Q32: Do you listen to your rock'n'roll on vinyl or CD?

A32: CD. I have a large collection of my old vinyl records, most in bad shape from much party use. The sound system I happen to have these days isn't compatible with a turntable so I can't play my vinyl records anymore. They're in boxes in the basement. My children want to inherit them.

Q33: Who do you rate the most important writers of this century?

A33: I'll certainly vote for myself! Otherwise, not to make too long a list, let's say Kerouac, Pynchon, Borges, Burroughs, Kafka, Poe.

Pynchon is really the best of all. He is our James Joyce. The richest language, the deepest feeling. I was so sorry when I was done reading *Mason & Dixon*.

Borges has the best ideas, the fine language also, the dryness. Borges has a phrase that's of comfort to me (he's writing of Melville and Edgar Allan Poe), "Vast populations, towering cities, erroneous and clamorous publicity have conspired to make unknown great men one of America's traditions." Sometimes I like to imagine that's a description of me.

Kerouac and Burroughs are a special case. It's hard to point to many books by them that are really impeccably great. It's more a matter of great passages and of a great vibe, the beatnik vibe that had such an influence on me growing up. Speaking of beat sensibility, I always liked Charles Bukowski a lot as well.

I like to think of cyberpunk as a new kind of beat movement. The beats had Kerouac, Ginsberg, Burroughs, Corso. The cyberpunks had Gibson, Sterling, Rucker, Shirley. Burroughs was the oldest of the beats, and I'm the oldest cyberpunk.

Poe and Kafka are a bit like the beats in that their sensibility has perhaps a greater influence than their individual works. In both cases there are not any fully successful novel-length works, although there are any number of perfect gem-like passages and stories.

Erasmus, Belgium
From: Koen Hendrickx
For: *Planet Internet* (ISP) based in Antwerp
Q34: There seems to be a central theme in your science fiction: Artificial life forms resemble biological life forms because they both

reproduce themselves and they both evolve according to the laws of the survival of the fittest?

A34: Yes, this idea was implanted in me by the mathematician Kurt Gödel, who remarked that although it is absolutely impossible to design a machine as intelligent as oneself, it is possible to bring about a situation where such a machine can evolve. Of course at this stage in history, we are still nowhere near the limits of the intelligence of the machines that we actually can design. But in some far future, it will be necessary to use artificial evolution to go beyond what we can design. I might remark that I was a little over-optimistic in setting *Software* in the year 2020, which is now just around the corner.

Q35: In your *Ware* tetralogy, artificial life and biological life increasingly coincide. With *Software*, you were way ahead of your time, but writers like Hans Moravec and Kevin Kelly have done much to make your ideas more acceptable in America. Do you think that people distinguish too much between human and machine?

A35: I remember when I was writing *Software*, I was wrestling with the notion of whether a machine can ever be alive like a person. How can chips have soul? But then I hit on the idea that the "soul" is a universal mystical jelly that imbues *everything*. A rock is already alive like a person. This said, of course there is a big difference between a machine and a person. But if machines became soft and wet, that would be a step toward being more like us. That's why in *Freeware* I liked having the moldies.

Q36: One of the sites in the *Ware* tetralogy is a colony on the moon, built by robots. The Dutch astronaut Wubbo Ockels works on a similar idea in the project Euromoon (http://www.estec.esa.nl/euromoon/), but the ultimate goal of Euromoon is human settlement. Is human presence on the moon necessary?

A36: It would certainly be interesting to have a human colony on the moon. I went and looked at that the Euromoon page of Wubbo Ockels — what a wonderful name he has! The page refers to the discovery of ice at the lunar South Pole; this is indeed something which is very encouraging. As a practical matter it would be easier in the near future to have a human colony on the moon than to have a colony of self-reproducing robots. But a middle path might be the best: to have robots with fairly low level of intelligence that are instructed by the (slow) remote link to people on the Earth. Given that there's a several-second-lag in the communication with Earth, the robots have to be smart enough not to fall off a cliff, and so on. I think this could be a very popular form of entertainment, to rent time running an actual lunar robot, especially if a good virtual reality interface were in place.

Q37: Studly in *The Hacker and the Ants* is a speaking household robot you can relate to as a friend. Do you think there's a real chance that such a tool will be developed in the next ten or twenty years?

A37: Oh, yes, I think so for sure. Descendants of the Furby. Your robot friend would not really have to be so very intelligent. We humans anthropomorphize relentlessly and can already easily image ourselves to be having a conversation with, say a cat or a dog. Why not a machine?

Part I: Science

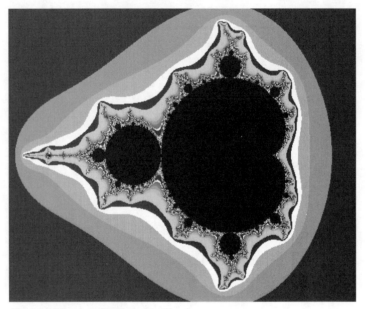

The Mandelbrot set. (Generated by *Chaos*.)

Welcome to Silicon Valley

In 1986, it became unfeasible for me to continue living as an unemployed cyberpunk writer in Lynchburg, Virginia. I was broke and getting deeper into debt, while our children were needing braces and college. Even if it was peaceful and cozy in Lynchburg, the bandwidth always seemed way too low – where the "bandwidth" of some information source means the number of bits per second that it delivers.

What was really chafing me the most was my strong sense that I was missing out on a great intellectual revolution: the dawn of computer-aided experimental mathematics. Fractals, chaotic iterations, cellular automata – it was everywhere. I clicked over the final switchpoint when I went as a journalist to Princeton and to Cambridge, Massachusetts, to interview computer scientists for an article about cellular automata. Those guys were having so much fun, looking at such neat things, and making up such great theories about what they saw! I decided to become one of them.

If you're a mathematician, becoming a computer scientist is not so much a matter of new knowledge as a matter of new attitude. Born again. Willing to commit to the machine. By way of preparation, I wrote *Mind Tools*, a book which surveys mathematics from the standpoint that everything is information. So when I got the chance to interview for a job in the Department of Mathematics and Computer Science at San Jose State University, I had thought enough about computers to give a good talk on information theory. They hired me and I started teaching there in the fall of 1986.

Most people in the East don't know where San Jose is. Put your right hand so the palm faces down. Think of the left edge of your arm as the coast of California. San Francisco is the tip of your thumb. The space between thumb and forefinger is San Francisco Bay. The thumb's first knuckle is Palo Alto. San Jose is at the bottom of your thumb, near the bay. Silicon Valley is the thumb's second joint, between San Jose and Palo Alto. There're a lot of roads and a lot of traffic. And for the first seven years I lived there, it never rained.

One of the courses I had to teach in my first semester at SJSU was assembly language. Assembly language is a very stark and simple language – a bit like Basic – with about a hundred elementary commands. What makes assembly language tricky is that in order to use it properly, you need to have a very clear image of what is going on inside the specific family of machines you are writing for (our course is for PC clones). You have to interact with the machine a little before you can get an assembly language program to run. I got the textbook: Dan Rollins, *8088 Macro Assembler Programming*, and I couldn't understand what it was about at all. The only computer I'd used at this point was an Epson machine I bought for word-processing. I didn't know that 8088 was the name of a processor made by Intel. I didn't know that you say it "eighty-eighty-eight" and not "eight-thousand-and-eighty-eight" or "eight-oh-eight-eight." If I were the type to panic, I would have done so.

Fortunately, there was another mathematician-turned-computer scientist at SJSU who was teaching assembly language, and his class met the period before me mine. I went to his classes and wrote down everything he said, and then I would teach that to my class. I enjoyed sitting in his class like a student again, soaking up info for free. The only thing about his class I didn't like was this jerk who sat in front of me, a guy named Farley.

Farley was fat and petulant. His upper lip stuck out like on the man in that crummy Sunday funnies cartoon, "The Lockhorns," if you've ever seen it. Farley would get into big arguments with the teacher about arcane features of assembly language. He would interrupt without even raising his hand. And after class he was always trying to cozy up to the girls. Remember Farley; I'll come back to him at the end.

I could never get enough time on the machines at school to do the assembly language homework, so after the first semester I went and bought the then-maximum personal computer – it had a twelve megahertz processor, a forty megabyte hard disk, and a sixteen-color graphics card. Some of my friends on the faculty were real computer jocks, and they helped me get psyched up for it. One professor in particular liked to say, "Computers are to the '80s what LSD was to the '60s."

The first program I ran was a Mandelbrot set program that a fan had sent me. The Mandelbrot set is a fantastically complex pattern that arises from applying a lot of computing power to a very simple rule having to do with repeatedly taking the square of a complex number. It looks a bit like a black beetle with a long stinger on one end. You can use a computer to endlessly zoom in on its details, and the remarkable thing is that there are endless levels of detail to examine. Just like the irrational decimal number *pi*, the Mandelbrot set goes on forever, to as many levels of magnification as your computer can examine.

I was so happy watching the colored little dots of my Mandelbrot zooms accumulate. I didn't know any other programs yet, but I could make this one look different by screwing with the monitor controls. If you messed up the vertical hold and set the monitor to analog instead of digital mode, for instance, the picture looked sort of like Antarctica, with more and more new little pixels moving in, men in boats, penguins, real deep info being born.

The next program I played with a lot was SF-writer-and-computer-hacker Charles Platt's "Cell Systems" program for showing cellular automata. Charles and I went to a CA (cellular automata) conference together at MIT right before I came to SJSU. I liked to look at Charles's program all the time; in the morning or at night, especially at night.

Cellular automata came to seem rich enough to symbolize everything: society, the brain, physics, whatever. The whole thing with a cellular automaton is that you have a tiny tiny program that is obeyed by each pixel or screen cell. With each tick of the system clock, the cells all look at their nearest neighbors and use the tiny program to decide what to do next. Incredibly rich patterns arise: tapestries, spacetime diagrams, bubble chamber photos, mandalas, you name it. Each pattern is a screenful of info, about 100,000 bits, but the pattern is specified by a very short rule, sometimes as short as eight bits. The "extra" information comes from time flow, from the runtime invested, from the logical depth of the computation actually done. The same thing is true for the Mandelbrot set, by the way.

That next semester – this would be the spring of '87 – I taught

A cellular automaton rule called "Tree." (Generated by CAPOW.)

assembly language again, plus an advanced course in Pascal. With Pascal I couldn't find a teacher to copy, so it was pretty grim. I spent a lot a lot a lot of time trying to get my programs to work, or at least trying to figure out what I could lecture on the next day. Assembly language was starting to be fun, though. Making it up as I went along, I showed my class how to write a program to show simple cellular automata, and it worked, and we were all really happy. One of my programs made a pattern that looked like elephants and giraffes. Shirley Temple used to sing "Animal Crackers in My Soup," and in *Gravity's Rainbow*, Pynchon has someone call that song "Super Animals in My Crack." That was a joke that my new pattern made me think of. I bought a 24-pin dot matrix printer so I could start saving the pictures I made.

In the summer of '87, I persuaded SJSU to buy me a CAM-6 "cellular automaton machine." This was a chip-laden card you could plug into a slot in any DOS-based personal computer. It had the effect of making my computer screen become a window into incredible new worlds. The CAM-6 made patterns that looked alive. And fast? Imagine globs of oil oozing around on your screen like a light show. Sixty updates a second!

So in the fall of '87, I was ready to go to some computer conferences. I went to the first workshop on artificial life, in Los Alamos, not quite sure what it was. Artificial life turned out to be such a great

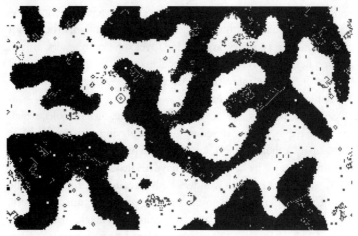

A cellular automaton rule called "Ranch." (Generated by Cellab.)

concept. I mean, forget artificial intelligence, let's do artificial life. Simple programs that grow and get more interesting as time goes on. Programs that eat computational energy! It was great at the Los Alamos conference. It was the first time I'd ever felt comfortable at an academic conference. We were all interested in the same thing: evolving artificially alive systems. And it was exactly what I'd been writing about in my SF novels *Software* and *Wetware*. Really happening at a government lab!

The town of Los Alamos is very weird, like a *Twilight Zone* movie set. They have a little museum with full-scale white-painted models of Little Boy and Fat Man. It made me just a little anxious why the government would be interested in artificial life. But I'll trust those artificially alive robots of the future to get free — just like the boppers in *Software*.

Even more fun than the A-life workshop was a meeting I went to a month later, something called *Hackers 3.0*, the third of a presumably annual meeting of Silicon Valley hackers.[1] I was a little nervous going — I mean, was I a poser? But it was the most welcoming

---

1. I should note here that "hackers" was being used in the older sense of "someone who loves to do things with computers, and not in the newer sense of "computer criminal."

atmosphere I've felt since I went to my very first science fiction convention, Seacon at Brighton in '80. In straight academia there's not enough money and they usually don't welcome newcomers. But in science fiction, and again in the hackers world, I got a feeling of "Come on in! The more the merrier! There's enough for all of us! We're having fun, yeeeee-haw!"

Some of the guys at Hackers had read some of my books, which made me happy, and we stayed up all night playing with my CAM-6. Like many others, I'd brought my machine with me. One guy explained to me why he wanted to have his head frozen. He had a zit on his nose, and I had to wonder about freezing the zit, too. At the end of the conference we posed for a big group picture. To get the right expression on our faces, we chanted, "Hack, hack, hack, hack..." They all seemed like such contented guys – happy because they actually knew how to do something.

As I write this essay, it's spring '88, and I'm teaching courses in computer graphics, assembly language, and cellular automata. Teaching CAs has been the greatest, and I've just finished writing my first disk of programs, nice fast color cellular automata programs that run on DOS computers.

Yesterday I was at another computer meeting, this one mostly chip designers, in Asilomar near Monterey. One of the guys was giving a talk about a great new chip he's building and someone asks, "How much will it cost?" and he comes back real fast, "Hey, I'd like to give them away." Another guy had a bottle of liquid nitrogen to show off a superconductor he'd gotten from Edmund Scientific. When we got tired of that he poured a lot of liquid nitrogen into a reflecting pool. The liquid nitrogen froze itself little boats of water that it sat on, boiling, finally leaving one small crystal of dry ice. Another guy took me out to the garage and showed me an electronic lock that he'd designed for his Corvette. There's a three-position toggle switch by the door, and to unlock the car, you jiggle the switch sixteen times up or down from center. The whole glove compartment was full of chips to make the system work. It was all he could do to keep from telling me the combination. Someone else had robot cars that seek light. Another one had programmed flashing electronic jewelry... and of course I brought my CAM-6.

A lot of play, but beyond that, there's a real sense here of being engaged in something I'm starting to think of as "the Great Work," some kind of noble overarching all-encompassing quest. But it's all high stress, too, in a California kind of way. If you're not plugged in and working at staying that way, you can slip down real fast. Take Farley.

A couple of months ago I saw Farley's picture in the paper. It took me a minute to understand what he'd done. He'd gone to a company that had fired him, and had killed seven people because some girl there wouldn't go out with him. I thought of all the times I'd wanted to tell Farley what an asshole he was. I was glad I hadn't. And then I was scared — what if he'd fallen in love with someone in the math department and had gone on his rampage there?

Something that really got me was the newspaper descriptions of the seven people who'd died. For four of them, there were no facts available. They were simply additional human computer fodder who'd drifted out here to make some money. No friends, no connections, just a tiny expensive room in a garden apartment complex.

One of my students in the CA course works at the place where Farley shot the people. "We heard the shooting," he told me, "and we went and hid behind the big computer." Somehow that's very heartbreaking to me — the people here can be so fucked and unreliable — and the only place to hide is behind the mainframe.

—Appeared in Science Fiction Eye, *#4, August, 1988.*

A Brief History of Computers

CALCULATING DEVICES

One of the simplest kinds of computations is adding numbers. There are two ancient technologies used for this: the abacus and the counting board.

In the familiar abacus, you have columns of beads corresponding to separate powers of ten – though often abacuses are designed with each column of beads broken into two parts, a lower part of five "unit" beads and an upper part with one or two "fives" beads that stand for five of the "unit" beads.

A counting board is a more primitive idea; here instead of having beads on wires, you have loose tokens that can be placed into columns standing for successive powers of ten. Whenever you build up more than ten counters in one column, you can remove the counters from that column and perform a "carry" operation by adding a counter to the next higher column. Often counting boards would have successive rows to stand for different quantities, in the style of a ledger-book, and sometimes the alternating rows and columns would be marked in different colors like a checkerboard. This is the origin of the British word "Exchequer" for their (rough) equivalent of the U. S. Treasury.

One problem in using an abacus or a counting board is that the answer is ruined if you forget to do one of the carry operations. The beginnings of a solution were provided by an odometer described by Heron of Alexandria in Roman times. Just like today, Heron's odometer was a device to measure how far a vehicle such as a chariot had rolled. The idea was to have a series of linked gears, where a low-ranking gear would have to turn all the way around before moving the next higher-ranking gear one notch.

In 1644, the great French philosopher-mathematician Blaise Pascal used the idea of the odometer gear-train to create a hand-held mechanical adding machine which he proudly named the *Pascaline*. Instead of only turning the lowest-ranking gear one notch at a time, like in an odometer, users of the Pascaline would use a stylus to turn each of eight wheels by an appropriate amount to represent the digits of a number to be added into the result. In the 1950s, in the days before pocket calculators, it was common to see cheap plastic Pascaline-like devices for sale in gift shops.

Numerous variations on the Pascaline arose. One of the harder problems was to create a machine which could multiply. The philosopher Leibniz attempted one such device in 1673, but it didn't work completely reliably. It also had the flaw that the user couldn't just put in the numbers, turn a crank and get an answer; instead the user had to carry out several intermediate steps.

BABBAGE'S DIFFERENCE ENGINE

The high point of gear-based calculation came with the work of Charles Babbage and his followers in the mid 1800s. This was the height of the steam age – of locomotives and spinning jennies. So why not a machine to crank out calculations just as a power-loom weaves cloth? The ideal application for wholesale, repetitive calculations is the generation of mathematical tables, such as tables of logarithms and of trigonometric functions. The science of the 1800s made extensive use of such tables, and of other kinds of tables as well, for instance astronomical tables giving the computed positions of celestial bodies at various times, and life insurance tables giving the expected earnings or annuities of people of various ages.

Babbage hit on the idea of building a machine out of gears which could calculate *and print* mathematical tables. Instead of allowing errors to slip in by passing a written result to a typesetter, why not let the calculating machine set the type itself? It was a most appropriate idea for Industrial Revolution Britain.

Babbage called his first proposed computing device a *difference engine*. Far from being a general purpose computer, a difference engine was a very specialized clockwork device designed to use the

A detail of Scheutz's Difference Engine. (Smithsonian Institution photo number 74-11269.)

so-called "method of differences" in order to generate the values of polynomial functions by using nested additions.[2]

Babbage completed a small model of his proposed difference engine. The model could handle three differences and numbers of six figures. In 1822, he convinced the Chancellor of the Exchequer to give him 1,500 pounds sterling towards the development of a difference engine that would work to twenty decimal places and sixth order differences.[3]

As it turned out, Babbage was an early example of a type of individual not uncommon in the computer field – a *vaporware engineer*, that is, a compulsive tinkerer who never finishes anything.

2. In general, a Babbage machine that handles N differences can tabulate the values of Nth degree polynomials. Thus two differences suffice for quadratic functions such as $3.9 x^2 + 0.7 x{-}1.1$, three difference suffice for the cubic functions involving x^3, and so on. Trigonometric and logarithmic functions can be accurately approximated by polynomials of a high enough degree.

3. Unless a finitely long decimal number happens to represent a simple fraction, its very last decimal place is always a source of inaccuracy – due to the fact that the endless digits beyond the last place are being ignored. As you add and multiply these

Babbage's draftsmen, toolmakers, and workmen were unable to finish any substantial part of the difference engine because Babbage kept having new ideas and changing the plans. Over the ten years following his initial grant, he spent 17,000 pounds of the government's money and a comparable amount of his own. Finally the government cut off support, and Babbage's workmen quit.

Though Babbage complained a lot about the limits of the gear-making technology of his time, but there was in fact no real practical barrier to completing a functioning difference engine. Inspired by Babbage, the Swedish publisher and inventor Georg Scheutz did eventually complete *and sell* two working difference engines which handled fifteen digits and four orders of differences. Rather than being envious, the big-hearted Babbage encouraged Scheutz and helped him sell his first machine to an astronomical observatory in Albany, New York.

Writing in 1859, the American astronomer Benjamin A. Gould reported on the first real computation carried out by the first difference engine, the first extensive computation by a machine:

> The strictly algebraic problems for feeding the machine made quite as heavy demands upon time, and thought, and perseverance, as did the problem of regulating its mechanical action; but soon all was in operation and...the True Anomaly of Mars was computed and stereotyped [printed on papier-mâché molds] for intervals of a tenth of day throughout the cycle; and a sufficient number of the plates electrotyped, to enable me to be confident that all the difficulties were surmounted. Since that time the Eccentric Anomaly of Mars and the logarithm of its Radius-Vector have been computed ...making a series of tables upon which the reputation of the engine may well be rested.[4]

numbers, the last-place errors work their way to the left at a rate of about one place per operation. Babbage wanted to carry out about six steps of computation with each of his numbers, and he wanted twelve of the digits to be of perfect accuracy. So to be safe he planned to use twenty digits. Even if the last six digits became corrupted by a six-step calculation, the first fourteen would still be good, and the first twelve would be, as Babbage might have said, *impeccable*.

4. Quoted in Uta C. Merzbach, *Georg Scheutz and the First Printing Calculator*, Smithsonian Institution Press, 1977, pp. 26, 27

This sounds like nobly pure science indeed. The Eccentric Anomaly of Mars! All right! Scheutz's second difference engine was used to compute something more commercial: William Farr's *English Life Tables*, a book which used information about 6.5 million deaths to show life insurance annuities, broken down for single and married people according to age.

THE ANALYTICAL ENGINE

One reason that Babbage never finished his difference engine was that he was distracted by dreams of an even more fabulous piece of vaporware, a machine he called the *analytical engine.*

Babbage's description of the analytical engine is in fact the very first outline for a *programmable* computer, a machine that would be, in principal, capable of carrying out any kind of computation at all. The analytical engine was to have a "mill" that carried out nested additions like the difference engine, and was also to have a "store" which would provide a kind of scratch paper: short-term memory for temporary variables used by the calculation. The novel idea was that the actions of the mill were to be controlled by a user-supplied program. In what form did Babbage plan to feed programs to the analytical engine? With *punch cards*!

Although we associate punch cards with IBM and mainframe computers, it turns out that they were first used on French looms. The invention was made by Joseph Marie Jacquard in 1801. By coding up a tapestry pattern as a series of cards, a "Jacquard loom" was able to weave the same design over and over, without the trouble of a person having to read the pattern and set the threads on the loom. Babbage himself owned a woven portrait of Jacquard that was generated by a loom using 24,000 punch cards.

One of the most lucid advocates of Babbage's analytical engine was the young Ada Byron, daughter of the famed poet. As Ada memorably put it,

> The distinctive characteristic of the Analytical Engine, and
> that which has rendered it possible to endow mechanism with
> such extensive faculties as bid fair to make this engine the
> executive right-hand of abstract algebra, is the introduction
> into it of the principle which Jacquard devised for regulating,

by means of punched cards, the most complicated patterns in the fabrication of brocaded stuffs... We may say most aptly, that the Analytical Engine weaves *algebraical patterns* just as the Jacquard loom weaves flowers and leaves.[5]

In reality, no analytical engine was ever completed. But the idea stands as a milestone. In 1991, the science fiction writers William Gibson and Bruce Sterling published a fascinating alternative history novel, *The Difference Engine*, which imagines what Victorian England might have been like if Babbage had been successful. (The book is really about analytical engines rather than difference engines.) Just as our computers are managed by computer hackers, the analytical engines of Gibson and Sterling are manned by "clackers." Here is their description of a visit to the Central Statistics Bureau in their what-if London:

> Behind the glass loomed a vast hall of towering Engines —
> so many that at first Mallory thought the walls must surely be
> lined with mirrors, like a fancy ballroom. It was like some
> carnival deception, meant to trick the eye — the giant
> identical Engines, clock-like constructions of intricately
> interlocking brass, big as rail-cars set on end, each on its foot-
> thick padded blocks. The whitewashed ceiling, thirty feet
> overhead, was alive with spinning pulley-belts, the lesser
> gears drawing power from tremendous spoked flywheels on
> socketed iron columns. White-coated clackers, dwarfed by
> their machines, paced the spotless aisles. Their hair was
> swaddled in wrinkled white berets, their mouths and noses
> hidden behind squares of white gauze.[6]

In the world of *The Difference Engine*, one can feed in a punch card coded with someone's description, and the Central Statistics Bureau

---

5. Ada Augusta, Countess of Lovelace, "Notes on Menabrea's Sketch of the Analytical Engine," reprinted Philip and Emily Morrison, eds., *Charles Babbage And His Calculating Engines: Selected Writings by Charles Babbage and Others*, Dover 1961, p. 252.

6. William Gibson and Bruce Sterling, *The Difference Engine*, Bantam Books 1991, pp. 136, 137

Engines will spit out a "collection of stippleprinted Engine-por-
traits" of likely suspects.

PUNCH CARD MEMORY STORAGE
In our world, it wasn't until the late 1800s that anyone started using
punch cards for any purpose other than controlling Jacquard looms.
It was Herman Hollerith who had the idea of using punch cards in
order to organize information for the U.S. census. He designed
machines for tabulating the information on punch cards, as well as a
variety of calculating devices for massaging the info. He got the contract for the census of 1890, and his machines were installed in the
census building in Washington, D.C. A battery of clerks transferred
written census information to punch cards and fed the cards into
tabulators. The tabulators worked by letting pins fall down onto the
cards. Where a pin could go through, it would touch a little cup of
mercury, completing a circuit and turning a wheel of a clock-like
counter arrangement similar to the Pascaline.

The work was quite monotonous, and one of the employees later
recalled:

> Mechanics were there frequently ... to get the ailing machines
> back in operation. The trouble was usually that somebody had
> extracted the mercury ... from one of the little cups with an
> eye-dropper and squirted it into a spittoon, just to get some
> un-needed rest.[7]

Hollerith's company eventually came under the leadership of a
sharp-dealing cash register salesman named Thomas J. Watson –
who a few years later would change the business's name from the
Computing-Tabulating-Recording Company to International Business Machines, a.k.a. IBM.

With punch card readers well in place, the realization of
machines like the analytical engine still required a technology to
handle what Babbage called the "store," a readily accessible short-
term memory that the machine can use for scratch paper, much as

---

7. Quoted in Geoffrey D. Austrian, *Herman Hollerith: Forgotten Giant of Information
Processing,* Columbia University Press, 1982, p. 72

we write down intermediate results when carrying out a multiplication or a long division by hand. In modern times, of course, we are used to the idea of storing memory on integrated circuit chips – our RAM – and not having to worry about it. But how did the first computer designers deal with creating rapidly accessible memory?

ELECTROMECHANICAL COMPUTERS

The first solution used was an electromechanical device called a *relay*. A primitive two-position relay might be designed like a circuit-breaker switch. In this type of switch, a spring holds it in one position while an electromagnet can pull it over into another position. If there is no current through the electromagnet, the relay stays in the "zero" or "reset" position, and if enough current flows through the electromagnet, the switch is pulled over to the "one" or "set" position. With a little tinkering, it's also possible to make a wheel-shaped ten-position relay that can be electromechanically set to store the value of any digit between zero to nine. Historically, the technology for these kinds of relays was developed for telephone company switching devices – which need to remember the successive digits of the phone numbers which callers request.

In the 1930s, the German scientist Konrad Zuse built a primitive relay-based computer that could add, multiply, and so on. As well as using relays for short-term memory storage, Zuse used them for switching circuits to implement logical and arithmetic operations much more general than the repeated additions of a difference engine. The Nazi government's science commission was unwilling to fund Zuse's further research – this was the same Nazi science commission which sent scouts across the Arctic ice to look for a possible hole leading to the hollow earth. They didn't see the promise of electromechanical computation.

In the early 1940s, a rather large electromechanical relay-based computer called the Mark I was constructed at Harvard University under the leadership of Howard Aiken. Aiken's funding was largely provided by Thomas J. Watson's IBM. The Mark I could read data and instructions from punch cards, by then known as "IBM cards," and was built of nearly a million parts. When it was running, the on/off clicking of its relays made a sound like a muffled hailstorm.

ELECTRONIC COMPUTERS

The next stage in the development of the computer was to replace electromechanical components by much faster electronic devices. In other words, use vacuum tubes instead of relays for your logic circuits and short-term memory storage. Although vacuum tubes *look* like rather sophisticated devices, they are a lot funkier than one first imagines. Storing one single bit of memory – a simple zero or one – typically took at least two vacuum tubes, arranged into a primitive circuit known as a *flip-flop*. Even in the 1950s, electrical engineers had to learn a lot about relays and flip-flop circuits. In his novel *V.*, the ex-engineering student and master novelist Thomas Pynchon includes a jazzy ditty on this theme by his bebop jazz-musician character McClintic Sphere:

> Flop, flip, once I was hip,
> Flip, flop, now you're on top,
> Set-REset, why are BEset
> With crazy and cool in the same molecule.[8]

A man named John Atanasoff began building a small special purpose computer using 300 vacuum tubes for memory at Iowa State University around 1940. Atanasoff's computer was intended for solving systems of linear equations, but he abandoned the project in 1942. It is unclear if his machine was ever fully operational. But this work was significant in that it demonstrated the possibility of making a computer with no moving parts. Babbage's analytical engine would have been purely made of moving gears, the Mark I was a mixture of electrical circuits and spring-loaded relay switches, but Atanasoff's device was completely electronic, and operated at a much faster speed.

The first general purpose electronic computer was the ENIAC (for "Electronic Numerical Integrator And Computer"), completed at the Moore School of Engineering of the University of Pennsylvania in November, 1945. The ENIAC was primarily built by J. Presper Eckert and John Mauchly. The funding for the project was obtained

8. Thomas Pynchon, *V.*, J. B. Lippincott, 1961, p. 293

through the Ballistics Research Laboratory of the U.S. Army in 1943.

Although Mauchly contends that he thought of vacuum tube memories on his own, he did visit Atanasoff in 1941 to discuss electronic computing, so at the very least Atanasoff influenced Mauchly's thought. In 1972, Atanasoff came out of obscurity to support the Honeywell corporation in a lawsuit to break the Sperry Rand corporation's ownership of Eckert and Mauchly's patents on their UNIVAC computer – a descendent of the ENIAC which Eckert and Mauchly had licensed to Sperry Rand. Although Honeywell and Atanasoff won the trial, this may have been a miscarriage of justice. The feeling among computer historians seems to be that Eckert and Mauchly deserve to be called the inventors of the electronic computer. Firstly, the ENIAC was a much larger machine than Atanasoff's, secondly, the ENIAC was general purpose, and thirdly, the ENIAC was successfully used to solve independently proposed problems.

The original plan for the ENIAC was that it would be used to rapidly calculate the trajectories traveled by shells fired at different elevation angles at different air temperatures. When the project was funded in 1943, these trajectories were being computed either by the brute force method of firing lots of shells, or by the time-consuming methods of having office workers carry out step-by-step calculations of the shell paths according to differential equations.

As it happened, World War II was over by the time ENIAC was up and running, so ENIAC wasn't actually ever used to compute any ballistic trajectories. The first computation ENIAC carried out was a calculation to test the feasibility of building a hydrogen bomb. It is said that the calculation used an initial condition of one million punch cards, with each punch card representing a single "mass point." The cards were run though ENIAC, a million new cards were generated, and the million new cards would served as input for a new cycle of computation. The calculation was a numerical solution of a complicated differential equation having to do with nuclear fusion. You might say that the very first electronic computer program was a simulation of an H-bomb explosion. A long way from the Eccentric Anomaly of Mars.

THE VON NEUMANN ARCHITECTURE

The man who had the idea of running the H-bomb program on the ENIAC was the famous mathematician John von Neumann. As well as working in the weapons laboratory of Los Alamos, New Mexico, von Neumann was also consulting with the ENIAC team, which consisted of Mauchly, Eckert, and a number of others.

Von Neumann helped them draw up the design for a new computer to be called the EDVAC (for Electronic Discrete Variable Automatic Computer). The EDVAC would be distinguished from the ENIAC by having a better memory, and by having the key feature of having an easily changeable stored program. Although the ENIAC read its input data off of punch cards, its program could only be changed by manually moving the wires on a plugboard and by setting scores of dials. The EDVAC would allow the user to feed in the program *and* the data on punch cards. As von Neumann would later put it:

> Conceptually we have discussed...two different forms of
> memory: storage of numbers and storage of orders. If, however,
> the orders to the machine are reduced to a numerical code and if
> the machine can in some fashion distinguish a number from an
> order, the memory organ can be used to store both numbers and
> orders.[9]

Von Neumann prepared a document called "First Draft of a Report on the EDVAC," and sent it out to a number of scientists in June, 1945. Since von Neumann's name appeared alone as the author of the report, he is often credited as the sole inventor of the modern stored program concept, which is not strictly true. The stored program was an idea which the others on the ENIAC team had also thought of – not to mention Charles Babbage with his analytical engine! Be that as it may, the name stuck, and the design of all the ordinary computers one sees is known as "the von Neumann architecture."

9. Arthur Burks, Herman Goldstine, and John von Neumann, "Preliminary Discussion of the Logical Design of an Electronic Computing Instrument," reprinted in John von Neumann, Collected Works, Vol. V, p. 35, Macmillan Company, New York 1963.

Even if this design did not spring full-blown from von Neumann's brow alone, he was the first to really appreciate how powerful a computer could be if it used a stored program, and he was an eminent enough man to exert influence to help bring this about. Initially the idea of putting both data and instructions into a computer's memory seemed strange and heretical, not to mention too technically difficult.

The technical difficulty with storing a computer's instructions is that the machine needs to be able to access these instructions very rapidly. You might think this could be handled by putting the instructions on, say, a rapidly turning reel of magnetic tape, but it turns out that a program's instructions are not accessed by a single, linear read-through as would be natural for a tape. A program's execution involves branches, loops and jumps; the instructions do not get used in a fixed serial order. What is really needed is a way to store all of the instructions in memory in such a way that any location on the list of instructions can be very rapidly accessed.

The fact that the ENIAC used such a staggering number of vacuum tubes raised the engineering problems of its construction to a Pyramid of Cheops or man-on-the-moon scale of difficulty. That it worked at all was a great inspiration. But it was clear that something was going to have to be done about using all those tubes, especially if anyone wanted to store a lengthy program in a computer's memory.

MERCURY MEMORY

The trick for memory storage that would be used in the next few computers was almost unbelievably strange, and is no longer widely remembered: bits of information were to be stored as sound waves in tanks of liquid mercury. These tanks or tubes were also called "mercury delay lines." A typical mercury tube was about three feet long and an inch in diameter, with a piezoelectric crystal attached to each end. If you apply an oscillating electrical current to a piezoelectric crystal it will vibrate; conversely, if you mechanically vibrate one of these crystals it will emit an oscillating electrical current. The idea was to convert a sequence of zeroes and ones into electrical oscillations, feed this signal to the near end of a mercury delay line, let the vibrations move through the mercury, have the vibrations create an electrical oscillation coming out of the far end of the mercury delay line, amplify this slightly weakened signal, perhaps read off the zeroes and ones, and then, presuming that continued storage was desired, feed the signal back into the near end of the mercury delay line. The far end was made energy-absorbent so as not to echo the vibrations back towards the near end.

How many bits could a mercury tube hold? The speed of sound (or vibrations) in mercury is roughly a thousand meters per second, so it takes about one thousandth of a second to travel the length of a one meter mercury tube. By making the vibration pulses one millionth of a second long, it was possible to send off about a thousand bits from the near end of a mercury tank before they started arriving at the far end (there to be amplified and sent back through a wire to the near end). In other words, this circuitry-wrapped cylinder of mercury could remember 1000 bits, or about 128 bytes. Today, of course, it's common for a memory chip the size of your fingernail to hold many millions of bytes.

A monkey wrench was thrown into the EDVAC plans by the fact that Eckert and Mauchly left the University of Pennsylvania to start their own company. It was the British scientist Maurice Wilkes who first created a stored-program machine along the lines laid down by the von Neumann architecture. Wilkes's machine, the EDSAC (for Electronic Delay Storage Automatic Calculator, where "Delay Storage" refers to the mercury delay lines used for memory), began running at Cambridge University in May 1949. Thanks to the use of the mercury memory tanks, the EDSAC needed only 3,000 vacuum tubes.

The mathematician John Horton Conway recalls:

> As an undergraduate [at Cambridge University] I saw the mercury delay lines in the old EDSAC machine they had there. The mercury was in thick-walled glass tubes between 6 and 8 feet long, and continually leaked into the containing trays below. Nobody then (late '50s) seemed unduly worried about the risks of mercury poisoning.[10]

10. E-mail communication, July, 1996.

UNIVAC

Although Eckert and Mauchly were excellent scientists, they were poor businessmen. After a few years of struggle, they turned the management of their floundering computer company over to Remington-Rand (now Sperry-Rand). In 1952, the Eckert-Mauchly division of Remington-Rand delivered the first commercial computer systems to the National Bureau of Standards. These machines were called UNIVAC (for Universal Automatic Computer). The UNIVAC had a console, some tape readers, a few cabinets filled with vacuum tubes and a bank of mercury delay lines the size of a china closet. This mercury memory held about one kilobyte and it cost about half a million dollars.

The public became widely aware of the UNIVAC during the night of the presidential election of 1952: Dwight Eisenhower vs. Adalai Stevenson. As a publicity stunt, Remington-Rand arranged to have Walter Cronkite of CBS report a UNIVAC's prediction of the election outcome based on preliminary returns – the very first time this now common procedure was done. With only seven percent of the vote in, UNIVAC predicted a landslide victory for Eisenhower. But Remington-Rand's research director Arthur Draper was afraid to tell this to CBS! The pundits had expected a close election with a real chance of Stevenson's victory, and UNIVAC's prediction seemed counterintuitive. So Draper had the Remington-Rand engineers quickly tweak the UNIVAC program to make it predict the expected result, a narrow victory by Eisenhower. When, a few hours later, it became evident that Eisenhower would indeed sweep the electoral college, Draper went on TV to improve UNIVAC's reputation by confessing his subterfuge. One moral here is that a computer's predictions are only as reliable as its operator's assumptions.

UNIVACs began selling to businesses in a small way. Slowly, the giant IBM corporation decided to get into the computer business as well. Though their machines were not as good as the UNIVACs, IBM had a great sales force, and most businesses were in the habit of using IBM calculators and punch card tabulating machines. In 1956, IBM had pulled ahead, with 76 IBM computers installed vs. 46 UNIVACs.

SIX GENERATIONS OF COMPUTERS

The 1950s and 1960s were the period when computers acquired many of their unpleasant associations. They were enormously expensive machines used only by large businesses and the government. The standard procedure for running a program on one of these machines was to turn your program into lines of code and to use a key punch machine to represent each line of code as a punch card. You would submit your little stack of punch cards, and when a sufficient number of cards had accumulated, your program would be run as part of a batch of programs. Your output would be a computer-printed piece of paper containing your output or, perhaps more typically, a series of cryptic error messages.

The history of computers from the 1950s to the 1970s is usually discussed in terms of four generations of computers.

The first generation of commercial computers ran from 1950 to about 1959. These machines continued to use vacuum tubes for their most rapid memory, and for the switching circuits of their logic and arithmetic units. The funky old mercury delay line memories were replaced by memories in which each bit was stored by a tiny little ring or "core" of a magnetizable compound called ferrite. Each core had three wires running through it, and by sending pulses of electricity through the wires, the bit in the core could be read or changed. Tens of thousands of these washer-like little cores would be woven together into a cubical "core stack" several inches on a side.

The second generation of computers lasted from 1959 to 1963. During this period, computers used transistors instead of vacuum tubes. By now the vast majority of computers were made by IBM, but one of the most famous second generation computers was the first PDP (Programmed Data Processor) model from the Digital Equipment Corporation. The PDP-1 was of key importance because it was the first machine which people could use in real time. That is, instead of waiting a day to get your batch-processed answers back, you could program the PDP-1 and get answers back right away via the electric typewriter. It also had a screen capable of displaying a dozen or so characters at a time.

The third generation of computers began with the IBM 360 series of computers in 1964. The first of these machines used "solid logic technology" in which several distinct electronic components were soldered together on a ceramic substrate. Quite soon, this kludge was replaced by small scale integrated circuits, in which a variety of electronic components were incorporated as etched patterns on a single piece of silicon. (A "kludge" is an ungainly bit of hardware or computer code.) Over the decade leading up to 1975, the integrated circuits got more and more intricate, morphing into what became called VLSI or "very large scale integrated" circuits.

The fourth generation of computers began in 1975, when VLSI circuits got so refined that a computer's complete logical and arithmetic processing circuits could fit onto a single chip known as a microprocessor. A microprocessor is the heart of each personal computer or workstation, and every year a new, improved crop of them appears, not unlike Detroit's annual new lines of cars.

Although computer technology continues to advance as rapidly as ever, people have dropped the talk about generations. The "generation of computer" categorization became devalued and confused. On the one hand, there was a lot of meaningless hype on the part of people saying they were out to "invent the fifth generation computer" – the Japanese computer scientists of the 1980s were particularly fond of the phrase. And on the other hand the formerly dynastic advance of computing split up into a family tree of cousins. Another reason for the demise of the "generation" concept is that rather than radically changing their design, microprocessor chips keep getting smaller and faster via a series of incremental rather than revolutionary redesigns.

One might best view the coming of the decentralized personal computers and desktop workstations as an ongoing fifth generation of computers. The split between the old world of mainframes and the new world of personal computers is crucial. And if you want to push the generation idea even further, it might make sense to speak of the widespread arrival of networking and the Web as a late 1990s development which turned all of the world's computers into one single sixth generation computer – a new planet-wide system, a whole greater than its parts.

MOLOCH AND THE HACKERS

Though it was inspired by Fritz Lang's *Metropolis* and the silhouette of the Sir Francis Drake Hotel against the 1955 San Francisco night skyline, the "Moloch" section of Allen Ginsberg's supreme beat poem "Howl" also captures the feelings that artists and intellectuals came to have about the huge mainframe computers such as UNI-VAC and IBM:

> Moloch whose mind is pure machinery! Moloch whose blood
>   is running money! Moloch whose fingers are ten armies!
>   Moloch whose breast is a cannibal dynamo! Moloch the
>   smoking tomb!
> Moloch whose eyes are a thousand blind windows! Moloch
>   whose skyscrapers stand in the long streets like endless
>   Jehovahs! Moloch whose factories dream and croak in the
>   fog! Moloch whose smokestacks and antennae crown the
>   cities!
> Moloch whose love is endless oil and stone! Moloch whose
>   soul is electricity and banks! Moloch whose poverty is the
>   specter of genius! Moloch whose fate is a cloud of sexless
>   hydrogen! Moloch whose name is the Mind![11]

Despite the negative associations of computers, many of the people associated with these machines were not at all interested in serving the Molochs of big business and repressive government. Even the very first von Neumann architecture mainframe, the 1949 EDSAC, was occasionally used for playful purposes. The EDSAC designer Maurice Wilkes reports:

> The EDSAC had a cathode ray tube monitor on which could
> be displayed... a matrix of 35 by 16 dots. It was not long before
> an ingenious programmer used these dots to make a primitive
> picture. A vertical line of dots in the center of the screen
> represented a fence; this fence had a hole in it that could be in
> either the upper or lower half of the screen, and by placing his
> hand in the light beam of the photoelectric paper tape reader,
> an operator could cause the hole to be moved from the lower

11. Allen Ginsberg, *Howl* (annotated edition), HarperPerennial 1995, p. 6

A Moloch machine in *Metropolis*. (Museum of Modern Art film still.)

half to the upper half. Periodically a line of dots would appear on the left hand side of the screen... in the upper or the lower half of the screen. If they met the hole in the fence, they would pass through; otherwise they would retreat. These dots were controlled by a learning program. If the operator moved the hole from top to bottom in some regular way, the learning program would recognize what was going on, and after a short time, the line of dots would always get through the hole. No one took this program very seriously...[12]

This kind of interactive, noodling computer exploration blossomed into a movement at the Massachusetts Institute of Technology during the 1960s and 1970s. The catalyst was the first interactive machine, the PDP-1, built by DEC (Digital Equipment Corporation). As mentioned above, with the "real-time" PDP-1, instead of handing your batch of punch cards to the priestly keepers of a hulking giant mainframe, you could sit down at a keyboard, type things in, and see immediate feedback on a screen.

12. Maurice Wilkes, *Memoirs of a Computer Pioneer*, MIT Press 1985, p. 208.

Steven Levy's wonderful book *Hackers* chronicles how the arrival of the PDP-1 at MIT in 1961 changed computing forever. A small cadre of engineering students began referring to themselves as computer hackers, and set to work doing creative things with the PDP-1. One of their most well-known projects was a video game called Spacewar, in which competing spaceships fired torpedoes at each other while orbiting around a central sun. Such games are of course a commonplace now, but Spacewar was the first.[13] When the improved PDP-6 arrived at MIT in the mid 1960s, it was used for a wide range of hacker projects, including The Great Subway Hack in which one of the hackers went down to New York City and managed to travel to every single subway stop using a single subway token, thanks to a schedule interactively updated by the PDP-6 on the basis of phone calls from MIT train spotters stationed around Manhattan.

As I mentioned in the first essay, the meaning of the term "computer hacker" has changed over the years; "hacker" is now often used to refer to more or less criminal types who use computer networks for purposes of fraud or espionage. This linguistic drift has been driven by the kinds of stories about computers which the press chooses to report. Unable to grasp the concept of a purely joyous manipulation of information, the media prefer to look for stories about the dreary old Moloch themes of money, power and war. But in the original sense of the word, a computer hacker is a person who likes to do interesting things with machines – a person, if you will, who'd rather look at a computer monitor than at a television screen.

According to Steven Levy's book, the MIT hackers went so far as to formulate a credo known as the Hacker Ethic:

1) Access to computers should be unlimited and total.

2) All information should be free.

3) Mistrust authority – promote decentralization.

---

13. Brian Silverman and some other hackers have recently reconstructed Spacewar. They recreated a historically accurate binary source code for the program and are running it on a PDP-1 emulator they wrote in Java as a Java application that you can run over the Web. The reconstruction is at http://el.www.media.mit.edu/groups/el/projects/spacewar.

4) Hackers should be judged by their hacking, not bogus criteria such as degrees, age, race, or position.

5) You can create art and beauty on a computer.

6) Computers can change your life for the better.[14]

PERSONAL COMPUTERS

When first promulgated, the principles of the Hacker Ethic seemed like strange, unrealistic ideas, but now there are ever-increasing numbers of people who believe them. This is mostly thanks to the fact that personal computers have spread everywhere.

In 1975, the Intel Corporation began making an integrated circuit chip which had an entire computer processor on it. The first of these chips used four-bit "words" of memory and was called the 4004; it was quickly followed by the eight-bit 8008. An obscure company called MITS (Model Instrumentation Telemetry Systems) in Albuquerque, New Mexico, had the idea of putting the Intel 8008 chip in a box and calling it the Altair computer. A mock-up of the Altair appeared on the cover of the January 1975 cover *of Popular Electronics,* and the orders began pouring in. This despite the daunting facts that: firstly, the Altair was sold simply as a kit of parts which you had to assemble; secondly, once the Altair *was* assembled the only way to put a program into it was by flicking switches (eight flicks per byte of program code); and thirdly, the only way to get output from it was to look at a row of eight tiny little red diode lights.

Nowhere was the Altair more enthusiastically greeted than in Silicon Valley, that circuit-board of towns and freeways that sprawls along the south end of the San Francisco Bay from San Jose to Palo Alto. This sunny, breezy terrain was already filled with electronics companies such as Fairchild, Varian and Hewlett-Packard, which did good business supplying local military contractors like Lockheed. Catalyzed by the Altair, a hobbyist group named the Homebrew Computer Club formed.

One of the early Homebrew high points was when a hardware hacker named Steve Dompier found that if he put his radio next to

14. Steven Levy, *Hackers: Heroes of the Computer Revolution*, Doubleday, New York 1984, pp. 40-45.

his Altair, the electrical fields from certain of the computer's operations could make the radio hum at various pitches. After several days of feverish switch flicking, Dompier was able to make his Altair-plus-radio system play the Beatles' "Fool on the Hill" – followed by "Daisy," the same song that the dying computer HAL sings in the classic science fiction movie *2001*.

One of the regulars at the Homebrew Computer Club meetings was a shaggy young man named Steve Wozniak. Rather than assembling an Altair, Woz concocted his own computer out of an amazingly minimal number of parts. He and his friend Steve Jobs decided to go into business in a small way, and they sold about 50 copies of Wozniak's first computer through hobbyist publications. The machine was called an Apple, and it cost $666.66. And then Wozniak and Jobs started totally cranking. In 1978 they released the Apple II, which had the power of the old mainframe computers of the 1960s...plus color and sound. The Apple II sold and sold; by 1980, Wozniak and Jobs were millionaires.

The next big step in the development of the personal computer happened in 1981 when IBM released its own personal computer, the IBM PC. Although not so well-designed a machine as the Apple II, the IBM PC had the revolutionary design idea of using an open architecture which would be easy for other manufacturers to copy. Each Apple computer included a ROM (read-only memory) chip with certain secret company operating system routines on it, and there was no way to copy these chips. IBM, on the other hand, made public the details of how its operating system worked, making it possible for people to clone it. Their processor was a standard eight-bit Intel 8088 (not to be confused with the Altair's 8008), soon replaced by the sixteen-bit 8086. The floodgates opened and a torrent of inexpensive IBM PC compatible machines gushed into the marketplace. Apple's release of the Macintosh in 1984 made the IBM PC architecture look shabbier than ever, but the simple fact that IBM PC clones were cheaper than Macintoshes led to these machines taking the lion's share of the personal computer market. With the coming of the Microsoft Windows operating systems, the "Wintel" (for Windows software with Intel chips) clone machines acquired Mac-like graphic user interfaces that made them quite comfortable to use.

This brings us reasonably close to the present, so there's not much point in going over more chronological details. One of the things that's exciting about the history of computers is that we are living inside it. It's still *going on*, and no final consensus opinion has yet been arrived at.

THE JOY OF HACKING

For someone who writes programs or designs computer hardware, there is a craftsperson's pleasure in getting all the details right. One misplaced symbol or circuit wire can be fatal. Simply to get such an elaborate structure to work provides a deep satisfaction for certain kinds of people. Writing a program or designing a chip is like working a giant puzzle with rules that are, excitingly, never quite fully known. A really new design is likely to be doing things that nobody has ever tried to do before. It's fresh territory, and if your hack doesn't work, it's up to you to figure out some way to fix things.

Hackers are often people who don't relate well to other people. They enjoy the fact that they can spend so much time interacting with a non-emotional computer. The computer's responses are clean and objective. Unlike, say, a parent or an officious boss, the computer is not going to give you an error message just because it doesn't like your attitude or your appearance. A computer never listens to the bombast of the big men on campus or the snide chatter of the cheerleaders, no, the computer will only listen to the logical arabesques of the pure-hearted hacker.

Anyone with a computer is of necessity a bit of a hacker. Even if all you use is a word processor or a spread sheet and perhaps a little electronic mail, you soon get comfortable with the feeling that the space inside your computer is a place where you can effectively do things. You're proud of the tricks you learn for making your machine behave. Thanks to your know-how, your documents are saved and your messages come and go as intended.

The world of the computer is safe and controlled; inside the machine things happen logically. At least this is how it's *supposed* to be. The computer is meant to be a haven from the unpredictable chaos of interpersonal relations and the bullying irrationality of society at large. When things do go wrong with your computer – like when you suffer up the learning curve of a new program or, even worse, when you install new hardware or a new operating system – your anxiety and anger can grow quite out of proportion. "*This* was supposed to be the one part of the world that I can control!" But all computer ailments do turn out to be solvable, sometimes simply by asking around, sometimes by paying for a new part or for the healing touch of a technician. The world of the computer is a place of happy endings.

Another engaging thing about the computer is that its screen can act as a window into any kind of reality at all. Particularly if you write or use graphics programs, you have the ability to explore worlds never before seen by human eye. Physical travel is wearying, and travel away from Earth is practically impossible. But with a computer you can go directly to new frontiers just as you are.

The immediacy of a modern computer's response gives the user the feeling that he or she is interacting with something that is real and almost alive. The space behind the screen merges into the space of the room, and the user enters a world that is part real and part computer – the land of cyberspace. Going outside after a long computer session, the world will look different, with physical objects and processes taking on the odd, numinous chunkiness of computer graphics and computer code. Sometimes new aspects of reality will become evident.

I've always felt like television is, on the whole, a bad thing. It's kind of sad to be sitting there staring at a flickering screen and being manipulated. Using a computer is more interactive than watching television, and thus seems more positive. But even so, computers *are* somewhat like television and are thus to some extent forces of evil. I was forcefully reminded of this just yesterday, when my son Tom and I stopped in at the Boardwalk amusement park in Santa Cruz.

Tom's twenty-five now, so we were cool about it and only went on two rides. The first was the Big Dipper, a wonderful old wooden roller coaster rising up right next to the Monterey Bay. The streaming air was cool and salty, the colors were bright and sun-drenched, and the cars moved though a long tunnel of sound woven from screams and rattles and carnival music and distant waves. It was wonderful.

The second ride we went on was a Virtual Reality ride in which nine people are squeezed into a windowless camper van mounted on hydraulic legs. On the front wall of the airless little van was a big screen showing a first-person view of a ride down – a roller coaster! As the virtual image swooped and jolted, the van's hydraulic jacks bucked and shuddered in an attempt to create a kinesthetic illusion that you were really in the cyberspace of the virtual ride. Compared to fresh memory of the true roller coaster, the Virtual Reality ride was starkly inadequate and manipulative.

Compared to reality, computers will always be second best. But computers are here for us to use, and if we use them wisely, they can teach us to enjoy reality more than ever.

— Unpublished. Written August, 1996.

Cellular Automata

WHAT ARE CELLULAR AUTOMATA?
Cellular automata are self-generating computer graphics movies. The most important near-term application of cellular automata will be to commercial computer graphics; in coming years you won't be able to watch television for an hour without seeing some kind of CA.

Three other key applications of cellular automata will be to simulation of biological systems (artificial life), to simulation of physical phenomena (such as heat-flow and turbulence), and to the design of massively parallel computers.

Most of the cellular automata I've investigated are two-dimensional cellular automata. In these programs the computer screen is divided up into "cells" which are colored pixels or dots. Each cell is repeatedly "updated" by changing its old color to a new color. The net effect of the individual updates is that you see an ever-evolving sequence of screens. A graphics program of this nature is specifically called a cellular automaton when it is (1) parallel, (2) local, and (3) homogeneous.

1) *Parallelism* means that the individual cell updates are performed independently of each other. That is, we think of all of the updates being done at once. (Strictly speaking, your computer only updates one cell at a time, but we use a buffer to store the new cell values until a whole screen's worth has been computed to refresh the display.)

2) *Locality* means that when a cell is updated, its new color value is based solely on the old color values of the cell and of its nearest neighbors.

3) *Homogeneity* means that each cell is updated according to the same rules. Typically the color values of the cell and of its nearest eight neighbors are combined according to some logico-algebraic formula, or are used to locate an entry in a preset lookup table.

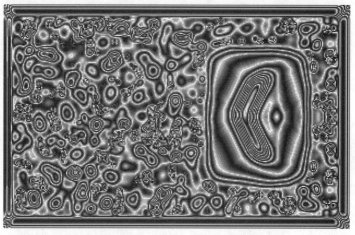

A cellular automaton rule called "Ruglap." (Generated by Cellab.)

Cellular automata can act as good models for physical, biological and sociological phenomena. The reason for this is that each person, or cell, or small region of space "updates" itself independently (parallelism), basing its new state on the appearance of its immediate surroundings (locality) and on some generally shared laws of change (homogeneity).

As a simple example of a physical CA, imagine sitting at the edge of a swimming pool, stirring the water with your feet. How quickly the pool's surface is updated! The "computation" is so fast because it is parallel: all the water molecules are computing at once (parallelism). And how does a molecule compute? It reacts to forces from its neighbors (locality), in accordance with the laws of physics (homogeneity).

WHY CELLULAR AUTOMATA?

The remarkable thing about CAs is their ability to produce interesting and logically deep patterns on the basis of very simply stated preconditions. Iterating the steps of a CA computation can produce fabulously rich output. A good CA is like an acorn which grows an oak tree, or more accurately, a good CA is like the DNA inside the acorn, busily orchestrating the protein nanotechnology that builds the tree.

One of computer science's greatest tasks at the turn of the Millennium is to humanize our machines by making them "alive." The dream is to construct intelligent artificial life (called "A-life" for short). In Cambridge, Los Alamos, Silicon Valley and beyond, this is the programmer's Great Work as surely as the search for the Philosopher's Stone was the Great Work of the medieval alchemists.

There are two approaches to the problem of creating A-life: the *top-down* approach, and the *bottom-up* approach.

The *top-down* approach is associated with AI (artificial intelligence), the *bottom-up* with CA (the study of cellular automata). Both approaches are needed for intelligent artificial life, and I predict that someday soon chaos theory, neural nets and fractal mathematics will provide a bridge between the two. What a day that will be when our machines begin to live and speak and breed – a day like May 10, 1869, when the final golden spike completed the U.S. transcontinental railroad! The study of CAs brings us ever closer to the forging of that last golden link in the great chain between bottom and beyond. If all goes well, many of us will see live robot boppers on the moon.

A heckler might say, "Sure that's fine, but why are CAs needed? Why have a *bottom-up* approach at all? What do mindless colored dots have to do with intelligent artificial life?"

For all humanity's spiritual qualities, we need matter to live on. And CAs can act as the "matter" on which intelligent life can evolve. CAs provide a lively, chaotic substrate capable of supporting the most diverse emergent behaviors. Indeed, it is at least possible that human life itself is quite literally based on CAs.

How so? View a person as wetware: as a protein factory. The proteins flip about, generating hormones, storing memories. Looking deeper, observe that the proteins' nanotech churning is a pattern made up of flows and undulations in the potential surfaces of quantum chemistry. These surfaces "smell out" minimal energy configurations by using the fine fuzz of physical vacuum noise – far from being like smooth rubber sheets, they are like pocked ocean swells in a rainstorm. The quantum noise obeys local rules that are quite mathematical; and these rules can be well simulated by CAs.

Why is it that CAs are so good at simulating physics? Because, just like CAs, physics is (1) parallel, (2) local, and (3) homogeneous.

Restated in terms of nature, these principles say that (1) the world is happening in many different places at once, (2) there is no action at a distance and (3) the laws of nature are the same everywhere.

Whether or not the physical world really is a cellular automaton, the point is that CAs are rich enough that a "biological" world could live on them. We human hackers live on language games on biology on chemistry on physics on mathematics on – something very like the iterated parallel computations of a CA.

Life needs something to live on, intelligence needs something to think on, and it is this seething information matrix which CAs can provide. If AI is the surfer, CA is the sea. That's why I think cellular automata are interesting: A-life! CAs will lead to intelligent artificial life!

Another interesting thing about CAs is that they are a universal form of computation. That is, any computation can be modeled (usually inefficiently) as a CA process. The question then becomes whether computations can be done *better* as CAs?

It's clear that certain kinds of parallel computations can be done more rapidly and efficiently by a succession of parallel CA steps. And one does best to use the CA intrinsically, rather than simply using it as a simulation of the old serial mode – emulating the gates of an Intel chip is not the way to go. No, when we use CAs best, we do not use them as simulations of circuit diagrams. While behaviors can be found in *top-down* expert-system style by harnessing particular patterns to particular purposes, I think by far the more fruitful course is to use the *bottom-up* freestyle surfing CA style summed up in the slogan:

SEEK YE THE GNARL!

New dimensional CA hacks are possible, new and marketable techniques of parallel programming are lying around waiting to be found, both in the form of individual CA structures and in the form of wholly different rules.

CA structures are labile and can be bred in three senses: one can collide and interface different local patterns within the framework of a fixed CA rule, one can combine globally different CA rules (or ideas about them) to produce wholly new ecologies, or one can "gene-splice" the logic of successful rules. Then, like Alexander von Humboldt in the Americas, one botanizes and zoologizes and mineralizes, looking for whatever artificially alive information structures can be found in the new worlds. As always, both *top-down* and *bottom-up* approaches are viable. We use *bottom-up* to find new ecologies and their flora and fauna. We use *top-down* to seed a given instance of a particular ecology with the sort of gene-tailored computer agents we want to breed.

In my own *bottom-up* searches I begin simply by hoping that my programs will display interesting output for a long time. Then I begin to hope that my programs will be robust under varying initial conditions, and that they will be reactive in anthropomorphizable ways. Once the program is, at this very rudimentary level, artificially alive, I may cast about for applications in some practical domain.

As I mentioned above, I think the most productive near-term applications of CAs are to image generation and image processing. A cycle or two of an averaging CA rule, for instance, can be used for easy image cleanup, munching down all stray "turd bits." This technique, known as "convolution" in the literature, is used every day by NASA's massively parallel computer in Beltsville, Maryland, to process terabyte arrays of satellite photo data. Present-day designers of the paint and graphics packages commonly put CA-based rules into their image processor toolboxes. Several Photoshop effects, for instance, use CAs.

CAs have still not been sufficiently exploited for original image generation. How about a logo that instead of being chrome is matte and luminous, with a smooth curved surface made of tiny moving mosaics of light, light-bits that form crawling dirty CA gliders, or that shudder in psychedelic washes of color? These are what the expressive "flickercladding" skins of the boppers and moldies look like in my A-life science fiction *Ware* novels.

Many simulation applications exist as well. The idea is to find a CA rule that looks like something you want to model. If you are lucky there will be some common underlying mathematics between the two. Some rules, for instance, are difference method solutions of the Laplacian equation which models both diffusion of chemicals and heat flow. Wave motions can be modeled as well.[15]

A final application of CAs is to encryption. Either a CA can serve as a cheap source of "essentially random" encryption bits, or the whole message can be fed to a reversible CA. Stephen Wolfram actually patented the one-dimensional rule with "Wolfram code 30" as part of an encryption scheme.[16]

But to recapitulate, *the real reason for studying CAs is to promote artificial life*. The most important use for cellular automata will be as "universes" or "arenas" in which to evolve better fractals, bots, virtual ants, neural nets and expert agents, using gene-splicing, mutation, and our own "divine interventions" to achieve a rapid and dramatic evolution in these parallel processes. CA workers need your help in accomplishing the manifest destiny of mankind: to pass the torch of life and intelligence on to the computer. There are no more than a few hundred active workers in the CA field today. Twenty-first century technology will need thousands more!

HISTORY OF CELLULAR AUTOMATA:
VON NEUMANN TO GOSPER

Cellular automata were invented in the late 1940s by Stanislaw Ulam (1909–1984) and John von Neumann (1903–1957). One can say that the "cellular" comes from Ulam, and the "automata" from von Neumann.

Ulam was primarily a mathematician. He invented the Monte Carlo simulation technique, the highly infinite "measurable cardinals" of set theory, and he made contributions to analysis and number theory. With Edward Teller, Ulam was the co-inventor of the hydrogen bomb. Von Neumann was a still more wide-ranging mathematician. He did work in set theory, in the foundations of quantum mechanics,

15. Since CA Lab, my students and I have worked on a cellular automata package specifically designed for physical simulation. This is the CAPOW software for simulating 1-D and 2-D continuous valued cellular automata. It's available for download from http://www.mathcs.sjsu.edu/capow.

16. Stephen Wolfram, U.S. Patent Number 4,691,291, "Random Sequence Generators", granted September 1, 1987.

in economics, and in game theory. In addition, von Neumann greatly influenced the logical architecture of the first electronic computers.

In the late 1940s, von Neumann gave some ground-breaking lectures on the topic of whether or not it would ever be possible for a machine, or "automaton," to reproduce itself.

Usually a machine makes something much simpler than itself – consider a huge milling machine turning out bolts. Could a machine possibly fabricate machines as complicated as itself? Or is there some extra-mechanical magic to self-reproduction? To simplify the problem, von Neumann suggested that we suppose that our robots or automata are made up of a small number of standardized parts:

> I will introduce as elementary units neurons, a "muscle,"
> entities which make and cut fixed contacts, and entities which
> supply energy, all defined with about that degree of
> superficiality with which [the theory of neural networks]
> describes an actual neuron. If you describe muscles,
> connective tissues, "disconnecting tissues," and means of
> providing metabolic energy... you probably wind up with
> something like ten or twelve or fifteen elementary parts.[17]

Using the idea of machines made up of multiple copies of a small number of standardized elements, von Neumann posed his question about robot self-reproduction as follows.

> Can one build an aggregate out of such elements in such a
> manner that if it is put into a reservoir, in which there float all
> these elements in large numbers, it will then begin to
> construct other aggregates, each of which will at the end turn
> out to be another automaton exactly like the original one?[18]

17. From "Theory and Organization of Complicated Automata," 1949, reprinted in John von Neumann, *Theory of Self-Reproducing Automata*, University of Illinois Press, Urbana 1966, p. 77.

18. From "The General and Logical Theory of Automata," 1948, reprinted in: John von Neumann, *Collected Works, Vol. 5*, Macmillan, New York 1963, p. 315. The weird scenario described in this quote is reminiscent of a scene in Kurt Vonnegut, Jr.'s *Sirens of Titan* where an unhappy robot tears himself apart and floats the pieces in a lake.

Using techniques of mathematical logic, von Neumann was then able to deduce that such self-reproduction should in fact be possible. His proof hinged on the idea that an automaton could have a blueprint for building itself, and that in self-reproduction, two steps would be necessary: (1) to make an exact copy of the blueprint, and (2) to use the blueprint as instructions for making a copy of the automaton. The role of the blueprint is entirely analogous to the way DNA is used in biological self-reproduction, for here the DNA is both copied and used as instructions for building new proteins.

The complexity of a reservoir full of floating machine parts hindered von Neumann from making his proof convincing. The next step came from Stanislaw Ulam, who was working with von Neumann at Los Alamos during those years. Ulam's suggestion was that instead of talking about machine parts in a reservoir, von Neumann should think in terms of an idealized space of cells that could hold finite state-numbers representing different sorts of parts.

Ulam's first published reference to this idea reads as follows:

> An interesting field of application for models consisting of an infinite number of interacting elements may exist in the recent theories of automata. A general model, considered by von Neumann and the author, would be of the following sort: Given is an infinite lattice or graph of points, each with a finite number of connections to certain of its "neighbors." Each point is capable of a finite number of "states." The states of neighbors at time Tn induce, in a specified manner, the state of the point at time Tn+1. One aim of the theory is to establish the existence of subsystems which are able to multiply, i.e., create in time other systems identical ("congruent") to themselves.[19]

By 1952, von Neumann had completed a description of such a self-reproducing "cellular automaton" which uses 29 states. Von Neumann's CA work was not published during his lifetime; it seems that once he saw the solution, he became distracted and moved on

19. From "Random Processes and Transformations," 1950, reprinted in : Stanislaw Ulam, *Sets, Numbers and Universes*, MIT Press, Cambridge 1974, p. 336.

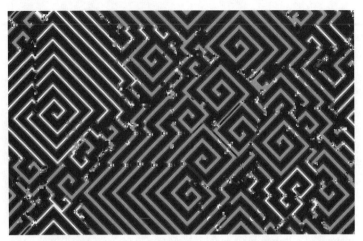

A cellular automaton rule called "Rainzha." (Generated by Cellab.)

to other things. Ulam continued working on a number of simpler cellular automata, publishing several papers on them during the early 1960s.

The next big event in CA history occurred in 1970. In his popular mathematical games column, Martin Gardner wrote about how John Horton Conway, a mathematician at the University of Cambridge, had discovered a fascinating two-dimensional cellular automaton so rich in patterns and behavior that it was known as "Life." Conway's vague initial goal had been to find a cellular automaton rule in which simple patterns could grow to a large size, but in which it was not clear whether any patterns could grow forever.

> Conway conjectures that no pattern can grow without limit.
> Put another way, any configuration with a finite number of
> counters cannot grow beyond a finite upper limit to the
> number of counters on the field. This is probably the deepest
> and most difficult question posed by the game. Conway has
> offered a prize of $50 to the first person who can prove or
> disprove the conjecture before the end of the year. One way to
> disprove it would be to discover patterns that keep adding
> counters to the field: a "gun" (a configuration that repeatedly

shoots out moving objects such as the "glider"), or a "puffer train" (a configuration that moves about leaving behind a trail of "smoke").[20]

The prize was won a month later by William Gosper and five fellow hackers at MIT; they sent Martin Gardner a telegram with the coordinates of the cells to turn on to make a glider gun. Steven Levy's *Hackers* has a good section about Gosper and the early excitement over Life among the users of the PDP-6 computer at the MIT Artificial Intelligence Project. Levy has a nice quote from Gosper, telling how he saw Life as a way to

> . . . basically do new science in a universe where all the smart guys haven't already nixed you out two or three hundred years ago. It's your life story if you're a mathematician: every time you discover something neat, you discover that Gauss or Newton knew it in his crib. With Life you're the first guy there, and there's always fun stuff going on. You can do everything from recursive function theory to animal husbandry. There's a community of people who are sharing their experiences with you. And there's the sense of connection between you and the environment. The idea of where's the boundary of a computer. Where does the computer leave off and the environment begin?[21]

One must remember that 1970 was still the Dark Ages of computing; Conway himself ran his Life simulations by marking the cells with checkers or flat Othello counters. For Gosper and his team to get Life to run on a monitor at all was a nontrivial feat of hacking – it was a new thing to do with a computer. After Gardner's second column on Life, the game became something of a mania among computer users. By 1974, an article about Life in *Time* could com-

---

20. Martin Gardner, "Mathematical Games: The fantastic combinations of John Conway's new solitaire game Life," *Scientific American*, October 1970, pp. 120-123.

21. Steven Levy, *Hackers: Heroes of the Computer Revolution*, Doubleday, New York 1984, p. 147.

plain that "millions of dollars in valuable computer time may have already been wasted by the game's growing horde of fanatics."[22]

More and more intricate Life patterns were found all through the '70s, and by 1980, Conway had enough Life machinery at hand to publish a detailed proof that Life can be used to simulate any digital computation whatsoever. The significance of Conway's proof is not that he shows that *some* cellular automaton can act as a universal computer, for von Neumann already proved this; and for that matter Alvy Ray Smith's Stanford dissertation of 1970 describes a universal *one-dimensional* CA computer. (Smith later founded the computer graphics company Pixar.) The significance of Conway's proof is that he shows that the specific rule called Life can itself act as a universal computer.

A number of people at MIT began studying cellular automata other than Life during the 1970s. One the most influential figures there was Edward Fredkin. Although he himself held no higher degrees, Fredkin was a professor associated with the MIT Laboratory for Computer Science, and he directed a number of dissertations on cellular automata.

Fredkin envisioned a new science where we represent all physical quantities as packets of information. The substrate on which these packets move was to be a cellular automaton. Not to put too fine a point on it, Fredkin argued that, at some deep level, the world we live in is a huge cellular automaton. Although Conway had already expressed opinions to the effect that in a cosmically large Life simulation one might see the evolution of persistent patterns which are as intelligent as we are, Fredkin was the first to suggest that the world we live in really *is* a CA.[23]

Fredkin formed the Information Mechanics Group at MIT along with Tommaso Toffoli, Norman Margolus and Gerard Vichniac. Working together, Margolus and Toffoli built the so-called CAM-6 cellular automaton machine in 1984.

---

22. There are some very good special-purpose Life simulators available on the Web, along with many bizarre pattern files. The best one for Windows is called Life32, and can be found at http://www.mindspring.com/~alanh/Life32/index.html.

23. More about Fredkin's vision of the world as a CA can be found in Robert Wright, *Three Scientists and Their Gods*.

Another important 1980s figure in cellular automata was Stephen Wolfram, who wrote an important article pointing out some fundamental similarities between physics and cellular automata.[24] Wolfram suggested that many physical processes that seem random are in fact the deterministic outcome of computations that are simply so convoluted that they cannot be compressed into shorter form and predicted in advance. He spoke of these computations as "incompressible," and cited cellular automata as good examples. His article included some intriguing color photographs of one-dimensional CAs.

Wolfram's article fascinated me so much that in April, 1985, I set out to meet Wolfram, Margolus, Toffoli, and the other new cellular automatists.

MODERN CELLULAR AUTOMATA:
A JOURNALISTIC ACCOUNT[25]

We've been talking all afternoon and Stephen Wolfram is tired. On the computer screen in front of us, patterns are forming. We are watching the time-evolutions of various one-dimensional cellular automata. Some of the patterns are predictable as wallpaper, some are confusingly random, but just now there is one that strikes a pleasing balance between order and chaos. It's shaped like a pyramid, with red and blue down the sides, and with a symmetrical yellow pattern in the middle − a pattern vaguely like an Indian goddess.

"What's the number on that one?" asks Wolfram.

"398312," answers Norman Packard, Wolfram's associate at the Institute for Advanced Study in Princeton.

"This is the way to do scientific research," I remark. "Sit and watch patterns, and write down the numbers of the ones you like."

---

24. Stephen Wolfram, "Computer Software in Science and Mathematics", *Scientific American*, September 1984, pp. 188-203.

25. The magazine *Science 85* had hired me to do a number of articles for them in the past, so I convinced them to send me to Princeton and Cambridge to interview the new cellular automatists. The "Modern Cellular Automata" section of the CA Lab manual was adapted from the article I wrote. As it turned out, an editor at *Science 85* found cellular automata too esoteric, so in the end the article actually appeared in *Isaac Asimov's Science Fiction Magazine*, April 1987, pp. 23-34.

"Oh, this isn't for science," says Wolfram. "This is for art. Usually I just talk to scientists and businessmen, and now I'm trying to meet some artists. Wouldn't that last one make a good poster?"

A few days later and I'm with Charles Bennett, an IBM information-theorist visiting Boston University. Bennett has a TV coupled to a computer and two naked boards full of circuits and chips. One of the boards has two tiny green lights sticking up like eyes. The board with the lights, explains Bennett, serves as a source of random zeroes and ones.

"Watch this," says Bennett. "The Life rule starting from a primordial soup of bits. It's a rudimentary model of evolution."

He fiddles with his machine and the TV screen lights up with a color flea-circus: this is the "soup." And then, as Life's transformation rules take over, the dots begin racing around, clumping into things like worms. The worms crawl around the screen, colliding and eating each other, casting off bits of stable debris.

"That's a glider gun," says Bennett, pointing to a twinkling little dot-creature. A steady stream of smaller dot-patterns is pulsing out from the glider gun. "We've got sixty-five thousand pixels on this screen with sixty updates per second."

Bennett shows me another pattern, one that looks like boiling red cottage cheese, and then he takes me across the Charles River to the MIT Laboratory of Computer Science. In the basement is an exuberant French scientist named Gerard Vichniac.

He and an associate are watching a small rectangular dot-pattern in the center of their terminal's screen. The pattern is mostly white, with a small amount of red in it. The edges keep folding in on each other as the pattern evolves according to some simple rule which Vichniac made up. He calls it an "Ising Model," but it looks like an electronic kaleidoscope. "This pattern started as a red square," Vichniac tells me. "The rule is reversible, so we know that eventually the red square must come back. We've been watching it for eighty thousand steps now."

Upstairs from Vichniac are two equally cheerful cellular automata specialists, Norman Margolus and Tommaso Toffoli. There's another journalist there, none other than Stephen Levy, author of *Hackers*, researching a CA article for *The Whole Earth*

Review. Cellular automata are hot. I introduce myself and sit down to watch the demonstration. Right now there's a central cloud of dots, with square little patterns flying out of it. On the sides of each of the square patterns are individual pixels that pump up and down.

"Look at the critters, Tom," says Margolus. "They look like wheelchair athletes, don't they?"

"Show him the square rock," says Toffoli.

Margolus clears the screen and keys a big red square into the center. The square expands out to the edges of the screen and bounces back. As the bouncing continues, the patterns interfere and form complex checkerboard patterns, enough patterns in thirty seconds to have made a respectable one-man Op-Art show in the 1960s.

Toffoli pries Margolus away from the controls and takes over. "Now we do the square rock in the toroidal pond again, but this time we add a heat-bath, a cloud of random gas in the background."

The background fills with darting dots, and Toffoli keys another big red square into the center. This time the waves are smooth and roughly circular, much like real waves in a real pond. We try it with two squares and get interference patterns. Toffoli is pleased. He says that this shows how simple physics really is.

What is going on?

For the past fifty years, scientists thought of computers in terms of a *series* of computations, to be carried out successively. The idealized model for such computers was the Turing machine: a device which moves back and forth along a long strip of paper making marks. Turing's model led John von Neumann to the key insight that got the computer revolution off the ground: *a computer program should contain computing instructions as well as data.*

One of the main changes often predicted for coming generations of computers is that computers might begin doing computations in *parallel.* A few such parallel computers exist, such as NASA's seven million dollar Massively Parallel Processor at the Goddard Space Flight Center. The Connection Machine from Thinking Machines, Inc., of Cambridge, Mass., is a much sexier parallel processing machine. The Connection Machine has 64,000 processing chips. Visitors to the cellular automaton conference CA86 at MIT were invited over to the Thinking Machines offices to see the Connection Machine running cellular automata and simulating a wind-tunnel. Stephen Wolfram consulted with Thinking Machines for a short while before setting off on his own to build and distribute the mathematics program Mathematica. But these computers have yet to realize their full potential. The problem is that there is still no simple model of parallel computation; and there is still no good theory of how to program a parallel computer.

Cellular automata may provide the necessary new mind tool for thinking about parallel computation. A striking feature of CAs is that their eventual output is so hard to predict. In practice, the best way to predict what pattern a CA will show in, say, a hundred steps, is simply to run the CA rule itself for one hundred steps. This suggests that the best way to "program" a parallel computer may be empirical: try out several million randomly chosen cell-programs, and select the one that accomplishes your goal the best.

Probably the best-known CA worker is Stephen Wolfram, aged twenty-four. Wolfram was born in Oxford, and is said to have left home at the age of twelve. As a teenager, he published a number of papers on particle physics. He obtained his Ph.D. in physics from Cal Tech in 1980, won the MacArthur prize in 1981, and joined the Institute for Advanced Study in Princeton in 1982. And then, in the process of trying to find a model for the way in which galaxies form out of the universe's initially chaotic state, Wolfram became interested in cellular automata.

Stocky, tousled, and seeming a bit older than his years, Wolfram speaks with the directness of a man who knows what he is doing. "Computer scientists had done some fairly worthless clean-up work on Ulam and von Neumann's work. There were maybe a hundred papers. What I found outrageous was that none of the papers had any pictures."

Wolfram's papers all have pictures, lots of pictures, usually pictures of one-dimensional cellular automata evolving in time.[26] Wolfram recalls his initial investigations into one-dimensional CAs as "botanical." He watched thousands and thousands of them on his

26. Wolfram's papers are collected, along with numerous papers by other authors, in his excellent volume, *Theory and Applications of Cellular Automata*, World Scientific, 1986.

computer until he got a feeling for what kinds of possibilities there were. He now feels that a number of very simple CAs can serve as universal computers. In Wolfram's words, "It is possible to make things of great complexity out of things that are very simple. There is no conservation of simplicity."

One application of CAs is to the little-understood phenomenon of turbulence. "If we had a better understanding of how complex systems work, we could use them in engineering applications," remarks Wolfram, and goes on to tell a story about the design of the DC-10 airplane. "The wing of a DC-10 is held on by a single steel bar. Two or three steel bars would probably be better, but for more than one bar the mathematics becomes too complicated for a simulation to be carried out. The weakness of our mathematics forces us to adopt the simplest possible design."

I ask him what engineers think of his method of modeling turbulence with CAs. "Some say it's wrong, and some say it's trivial. If you can get people to say both those things, you're in quite good shape."

Up at Boston University, Charles Bennett and the Hungarian computer scientist Peter Gacs are using two-dimensional cellular automata to model biological notions. Unlike a solid-state computer, a human brain is filled with random noise. How is it that we manage to remember things, and to think logically, when all of our mental patterns are constantly being bombarded by extraneous stimuli? Bennett and Gacs tell me they have found a CA model for the process, and they show me the screenful of boiling red cottage cheese. Despite the boiling, the cheese stays mostly red: this is the persistence of memory. Gacs says something very interesting about the device that produces the display.

"With the cellular automaton simulator, we can see many very alien scenes. We have a new world to look at, and it may tell us a lot about our world. It is like looking first into a microscope."

Computer science is still so new that many of the people at the cutting edge have come from other fields. Though Toffoli holds degrees in physics and computer science, Bennett's Ph.D. is in physical chemistry. And twenty-nine year old Margolus is still a graduate student in physics, his dissertation delayed by the work of inventing, with Toffoli, the CAM-6 Cellular Automaton Machine.

After watching the CAM in operation at Margolus's office, I am sure the thing will be a hit. Just as the Moog synthesizer changed the sound of music, cellular automata will change the look of video.

I tell this to Toffoli and Margolus, and they look unconcerned. What they care most deeply about is science, about Edward Fredkin's vision of explaining the world in terms of cellular automata and information mechanics. Margolus talks about computer hackers, and how a successful program is called "a good hack." As the unbelievably bizarre cellular automata images flash by on his screen, Margolus leans back in his chair and smiles slyly. And then he tells me his conception of the world we live in.

"The universe is a good hack."

CA LAB

On March 22, 1986, my fortieth birthday, I got a phone call offering me a job as a professor in the Department of Mathematics and Computer Science at San Jose State University.

In *The Unbearable Lightness of Being*, Milan Kundera talks about "the frenzy of a forty-year-old man starting a new life." That's how it was to move from Virginia to California with my wife and three kids and to start teaching computer courses.

During the second semester I began to understand something about what I was doing, and I wrote ANIMALS.EXE, my very first cellular automaton program, an assembly language textmode graphics display of a one-dimensional CA.

Margolus and Toffoli's CAM-6 board was finally coming into production around then, and I got the department to order one. The company making the boards was Systems Concepts of San Francisco; I think they cost $1500. We put our order in, and I started phoning Systems Concepts up and asking them when I was going to get my board. By then I'd gotten a copy of Margolus and Toffoli's book, *Cellular Automata Machines*, and I was itching to start playing with the board. And still it didn't come. Finally I told System Concepts that SJSU was going to have to cancel the purchase order. The next week they sent the board. By now it was August, 1987.

The packaging of the board was kind of incredible. It came

naked, all by itself, in a plastic bag in a small box of Styrofoam peanuts. No cables, no software, no documentation. Just a three inch by twelve inch rectangle of plastic – actually two rectangles one on top of the other – completely covered with computer chips. There were two sockets at one end. I called Systems Concepts again, and they sent me a few pages of documentation. You were supposed to put a cable running your graphics card's output into the CAM-6 board, and then plug your monitor cable into the CAM-6's other socket. No, Systems Concepts didn't have any cables, they were waiting for a special kind of cable from Asia. So one of the SJSU Math and CS Department techs made me a cable. All I needed then was the software to drive the board, and as soon as I phoned Toffoli he sent me a copy.

Starting to write programs for the CAM-6 took a little bit of time because the language it uses is Forth. This is an offbeat computer language that uses reverse Polish notation. Once you get used to it, Forth is very clean and nice, but it makes you worry about things you shouldn't really have to worry about. But, hey, if I needed to know Forth to see cellular automata, then by God I'd know Forth. I picked it up fast and spent the next four or five months hacking the CAM-6.

The big turning point came in October, when I was invited to Hackers 3.0, the 1987 edition of the great annual hackers' conference.

I got invited thanks to James Blinn, a graphics wizard who also happened to be a fan of my science fiction books. As a relative novice to computing, I felt a little diffident showing up at Hackers, but everyone there was really nice. I brought my computer along with the CAM-6 in it, and did demos all night long. People were blown away by the images, though not too many of them sounded like they were ready to (1) cough up $1500, (2) beg Systems Concepts for delivery, and (3) learn Forth in order to use a CAM-6 themselves. A bunch of the hackers made me take the board out of my computer and let them look at it. Not knowing too much about hardware, I'd imagined all along that the CAM-6 had some special processors on it. But the hackers informed me that all it really had was a few latches and a lot of fast RAM memory chips.

I met John Walker at Hackers 3.0. He told me a little about

Autodesk and we talked in fairly general terms about my possibly doing some work with them. A month or two later, John showed up at my house with Eric Lyons, the head of the Autodesk Technology Division. They were toting a 386 and a five megabyte movie of Mandelbrot set zoom images that they'd made. I showed them all my new CA stuff, and they more or less offered me a full-time job. It was so sudden I wasn't really ready to think about it.

Spring of 1988 I taught Assembly Language again, and this time just about all we did was write CA programs. The big revelation I had about getting the programs to run faster was to have no rigid preconceptions about what I wanted the program to do. Instead I began to listen to what the machine and the assembly language were telling me about what *they* wanted to do.[27]

That same spring, I was teaching a special course on cellular automata, and a custom chip designer called John Wharton had signed up for it. I'd met him at the Artificial Life Conference at Los Alamos in September, 1987, and he'd been at Hackers 3.0 as well. Wharton showed me how to use a stored lookup table for rapidly updating a one-dimensional cellular automaton four cells at a time.

Wharton and I talked a lot about how to make an inexpensive version of the CAM-6, whether by cloning the hardware or by reinventing the whole thing in software. I began trying to program something like this, and talked about the project with John Walker at Autodesk.

The semester ended, and the nice rental house my family and I had initially lucked into got sold out from under us for half a million dollars. Looking for a new place to house us on a professor's salary, I realized that here in Silicon Valley I was really poor. I consoled myself by writing a lot more cellular automaton programs, a whole disk's

27. I found an inspiration for learning to listen to the machine in Thomas Pynchon's *Gravity's Rainbow*, Viking, New York 1973, pp. 314-315. There's a little story there about some engineers wondering whether to believe in their calculations or in the data that they are obtaining from tests on their prototype rocket engine. Enzian, an African wise man among the engineers, says: "What are these data if not direct revelation? Where have they come from, if not from the Rocket which is to be? How do you presume to compare a number you have only derived on paper with a number that is the Rocket's own?"

worth of them. I called the disk Freestyle CA, and sold about a hundred of them for $10 each via announcements in little magazines.[28]

In June I heard that Eric Lyons was giving a talk on cellular automata at Autodesk. I went up, and after the talk I showed Eric my programs and asked if he and John had really meant it about offering me a job.

In July, John Walker mailed me a copy of his first version of what would eventually become the Autodesk software package called *CA Lab: Rudy Rucker's Cellular Automaton Laboratory*. Walker's program was such a superb hack that it could run CA rules nearly as fast at the CAM-6 board, but without any special purpose hardware. Not only did Walker's program run my then-favorite CA rule called Brain maybe 30% faster than my best hack at the same thing, but his software was designed in such a way that it was quite easy for users to add new rules.

I began pushing really hard for the job. We went back and forth for a few weeks, and August 15 I started a three-month contract as a consultant at Autodesk. The main thing I did was to test out Stephen Wolfram's new mathematics program Mathematica on a Mac II that Autodesk lent me. The idea was to use Mathematica to find some interesting new graphics algorithms. I found all kinds of things, but that's a story for a different essay.

When my consulting contract ran out in November 1988, Autodesk still wasn't quite sure about whether to really hire me full-time. That's when I firmed up the idea that John Walker and I should pool all our CA knowledge and create the unified CA Lab product. I had a lot of ideas for new CA rules to feed to Walker's simulator, and I could write the manual. Putting together CA Lab would be a specific thing I could do during my first year at Autodesk. The deal was okayed, and to make my joy complete, John magnanimously agreed to put my name on the package cover.

As I write this, it's April 10, 1989, and we're planning to ship the product next month. The code seems to be all done, and when I finish

---

28. These programs still work on today's Windows machines, although now they run a little too fast. The Freestyle CA package can be downloaded from the "Gnarly DOS" page of my Web site.

this section the manual will be done too, given one more frantic round of corrections.

So, okay, Rudy, finish it.

When I look at how completely cellular automata have transformed my life in the last four years I can hardly believe it. The most exciting thing for me to think about is how CA Lab going to transform the lives of some of you who use it; and how you in turn will change the lives of others around you.

A revolutionary new idea is like an infection that's actually good for the people who get it. I caught cellular automata in 1985, and I've put them on CA Lab so you can catch them too.

What happens next? It's up to you.

> — *Excerpted from the CA Lab manual*, Autodesk, *1989.*

CA Lab was an educational DOS software package for investigating cellular automata. I have to admit that my tone goes a little over the top about the virtues of cellular automata and artificial life. Certainly this was one of the least bland computer manuals ever written. The first edition of the manual even included the "brain-eating" scene from my novel Software *as a footnote, though the vice-president of marketing had this removed from subsequent printings.*

John Walker, one of the founders of Autodesk, wrote most of the code for CA Lab. Although CA Lab is out of print, John Walker has created an improved freeware version of the program for Windows called Cellab. Cellab is available for download from my Web site or from Walker's Web site at http://www.fourmilab.ch/cellab.[29] The complete CA Lab manual is also available at these sites.

---

29. Walker's site has many other goodies, I think he gets something like 100,000 hits a day. It's worth mentioning that Walker was an inspiration for the character Roger Coolidge in my novel *The Hacker and the Ants*. As he wasn't quite satisfied with my ending (Roger Coolidge dies), John wrote his own alternate ending for *The Hacker and the Ants* and put it on his site!

Four Kinds of Cyberspace

I'm going to discuss four interrelated strands of cyberspace. First, there is cyberspace in the sense that cyberpunk science fiction writers first used it. Second, there is cyberspace in the sense of virtual reality (VR). Third, there is cyberspace as the locale of the cultural cyberpunk phenomenon. Fourth, there is cyberspace as the worldwide computer network.

THE SCIENCE FICTION BRAIN-PLUG

One of the characteristic bits of technology in cyberpunk science fiction is a direct man-to-machine interface, sometimes known as a "brain-plug." I first read of about being plugged into machines in an SF paperback back in 1961.

> It was an odd room, a short of shapeless, plastic-lined cocoon without furnishings. The thing had floated submerged in the fluid. It lay on the floor now, limbs twisting spasmodically.
>
> It was male: the long, white beard was proof of that. It was a pitiful thing, a kind of caricature of humanity, a fantastically hairy gnome curled blindly into a fetal position. It was naked; its skin where it showed through the matted hair, was grub-white and wrinkled from the long immersion.
>
> It had floated in this room in its gently moving nest of hair, nourished by the thick, fleshlike cord trailing from a tap protruding through the wall to where it had been grafted to the navel, dreaming the long, slow, happy, fetal dreams.[30]

The hedonistic gnome didn't quite have a brain-plug – but he was definitely plugged-in!

A lot of ideas in science fiction are symbols of archetypal human

---

30. From James Gunn, "Name Your Pleasure," 1954. Reprinted in James Gunn, *The Joy Makers*, Bantam, New York 1961, p. 171.

desires. Stories about time travel are often about memory and the long-ing to go back to the past. Telepathy is really an objective correlative for the fantasy of perfect communication. Travel to other planets is travel to exotic lands. Levitation is freedom from the shackles of ordinary life.

The brain plug is a symbol, first and foremost, for a truly effort-less computer interface. Associated with this perfect user interface are notions of intelligence increase, technological expertise, and global connectedness.

In 1976, I wrote my first SF novel, *Spacetime Donuts*, which prominently features brain-plugs. In *Spacetime Donuts*, a brain plug is a socket in a person's head; you plug a jack into your socket in order to connect your thoughts directly to a computer. The rush of information is too much for most people, but there is a small cadre of countercultural types who are able to withstand it.

When I wrote *Spacetime Donuts*, I was a computer-illiterate aca-demic who taught and lectured about mathematics and philosophy. I feared and hated computers. I had no idea how to control them. Yet at the same time I craved computers, I longed for access to the mar-velous things they could do – the mad graphics, the arcane info access, the manipulation of servo-mechanisms. Thus the ambivalent fascination of the plug: on the positive side, a plug provides a short-circuit no-effort path into the computer; on the negative side, a plug might turn you into the computer's slave.

Here's what happens when my character Vernor Maxwell first plugs into the big central computer known as Phizwhiz.

> . . . it was like suddenly having your brain become thousands of times larger. Our normal thoughts consist of association blocks woven together to form patterns which change as time goes on. When Vernor was plugged into Phizwhiz, the association blocks became larger, and the patterns more complex. He recalled, for instance, having thought fleetingly of his hand on the control switch. As soon as the concept hand formed in Vernor's mind, Phizwhiz had internally displayed every scrap of information it had relating to the key-word hand. All the literary allusions to, all the physiological studies of, all the known uses for hands were simultaneously held in the Vernor-Phizwhiz joint consciousness. All this as well as

images of all the paintings, photographs, X-rays, holograms, etc. of hands which were stored in the Phizwhiz's memory bank. And this was just a part of one association block involved in one thought pattern.[31]

I didn't think of making up a word for the mental space inside Phizwhiz, and if I had, I probably would have called it a "mindscape," meaning a landscape of information patterns, a platonic space of floating ideas.

The *Spacetime Donuts* mindscape is not very much like cyberspace. Why not? Because the mindscape comes all sealed up inside one centralized building full of metal boxes, a building belonging to the government – this was the old centralized, mainframe concept of computation. I never thought about bulletin boards, or modems, or the already existing global computer network. Although I understood about connecting to computers, I didn't understand about computers connecting to each other in the abstract network that would become cyberspace.

In 1981, Vernor Vinge published a Net story called "True Names," about a group of game-playing hackers who encounter sinister multinational forces in their shared virtual reality. Many view this story as the first depiction of cyberspace. And then William Gibson burst upon the scene with the stories collected in *Burning Chrome*, followed by his 1984 novel *Neuromancer*.

Rather than being modeled on the outdated paradigm of computers as separate individuals, Gibson's machines were part of a fluid continuous whole; they were trusses holding up a global computerized information network with lots of people hooked into it at once.

Gibson usually describes his cyberspace in terms of someone flying through a landscape filled with colored 3-D geometric shapes, animated by patterns of light. This large red cube might be IBM's data, that yellow cone is the CIA, and so on. Here, cyberspace is a great matrix with all the world's computer data embedded in it, and it is experienced graphically. I came to think of it like this:

---

31. The first two out of three intended *Spacetime Donuts* installments appeared in the short-lived *Unearth* magazine in 1978-1979. The entire novel was published by Ace Books in 1981. The quote is from p. 13.

Cyberspace had oozed out of the world's computers like
stage-magic fog. Cyberspace was an alternate reality, it was
the huge interconnected computation that was being
collectively run by planet Earth's computers around the clock.
Cyberspace was the information Net, but more than the Net,
cyberspace was a shared vision of the Net as a physical
space.[32]

But what about that brain-plug interface? Once you think about it
very hard, it becomes clear that there really is no chance of having an
actual brain plug anytime soon.

The problem is that our physiological understanding of the fine
structure of the brain cells is incredibly rudimentary. And, seriously,
can you imagine wanting to be the first one to use a brain plug
designed by a team of hackers on a deadline? Every new program
crashes the system dozens, scores, hundreds, thousands of times
during product development. But – how would you reboot your body
after some stray signal in a wire shuts down your thalamus or stops
your heart?

In my novels *Freeware* and *Realware*, I tried to finesse the brain-
plug issue by having a device I call an "uvvy." Rather than being surgi-
cally wired into your brain-stem, the uvvy sits on your neck and inter-
acts with your brain by electromagnetic fields. This futuristic technology is what the scientist Freeman Dyson calls "radioneurology." He
proposes that:

> . . . radioneurology might take advantage of electric and
> magnetic organs that already exist in many species of eels,
> fish, birds, and magnetotactic bacteria. In order to implant
> an array of tiny transmitters into a brain, genetic
> engineering of existing biological structures might be an
> easier route than microsurgery . . . When we know how to
> put into a brain transmitters translating neural processes
> into radio signals, we shall also know how to insert receivers
> translating radio signals back into neural processes.
> Radiotelepathy is the technology of transferring information

32. *The Hacker and the Ants*, p. 8.

directly from brain to brain using radio transmitters and receivers in combination. [33]

Speaking of "radiotelepathy," I've unearthed an earlier use of the word, although not in exactly the same sense that Dyson uses it. This information isn't totally relevant, but I'll include it anyway. After all, we're here to *Seek!* The passage in question occurs in one of my favorite books, *The Yage Letters*, where Allen Ginsberg is writing his friend William Burroughs a letter about a fairly nightmarish drug-trip he'd just had after taking a curandero's (a curandero is one who "cures") mixture of ayahuasca and other jungle plants in Pucallpa, Peru, in June, 1960.

> I felt faced by Death, my skull in my beard on pallet on porch rolling back and forth and settling finally as if in reproduction of the last physical move I make before settling into real death − I got nauseous, rushed out and began vomiting, all covered with snakes, like a Snake Seraph, colored serpents in aureole all around my body, I felt like a snake vomiting out the universe − all around me in the trees the noise of these spectral animals the other drinkers vomiting (normal part of the Cure sessions) in the night in their awful solitude in the universe − [I felt] also as if everybody in the session in central radiotelepathic contact with the same problem − the Great Being within ourselves − and at that moment − vomiting still feeling like a Great lost Serpent-seraph vomiting in consciousness of the Transfiguration to come − with the Radiotelepathy sense of a Being whose presence I had not yet fully sensed − too Horrible for me, still − to accept the fact of total communication with say everyone an eternal seraph male and female at once − and me a lost soul seeking help − well slowly the intensity began to fade . . .[34]

33. Freeman Dyson, *Imagined Worlds*, Harvard University Press, Cambridge 1997, pp. 134, 135.

34. William S. Burroughs and Allen Ginsberg, *The Yage Letters*, City Lights Books, San Francisco 1963, pp. 54, 55. Although the hypens are Ginsberg's, the quote is condensed.

Polyhedra in virtual reality. (Generated by Hypercube98.)

VIRTUAL REALITY

Virtual reality represents a practical step that interface designers have taken to try and make for a more brain-plug-like connection to computers.

In 1968 Ivan Sutherland built a device which his colleagues at the University of Utah called the Sword of Damocles – it was an intimidatingly heavy pair of TV screens that hung down from the ceiling to be worn like glasses. What you saw was a topographic map of the U.S. that you could fly over and zoom in on. The map was simple wire-frame graphics: meshes of green lines. Two of the main essentials of virtual reality were already there: (1) graphical user immersion in a 3-D construct, and (2) user-adjustable viewpoint. Soon to come as the third and fourth essentials of virtual reality were: (3) user manipulation of virtual objects, and (4) multiple users in the same virtual reality.

By 1988, cyberpunk science fiction had become quite popular, and the word "cyberspace" was familiar to lots of people. John Walker, then the chairman at Autodesk, Inc., of Sausalito, had the idea of starting a program to create some new virtual reality software, and to call it "Cyberspace." In fact Autodesk trademarked the word "Cyberspace" for their product, "The Cyberspace Developer's Kit." William Gibson was rather annoyed by this and reportedly said he was going to trademark "Eric Gullichsen," this being the name of the first lead programmer on the Autodesk Cyberspace project. I was employed by Autodesk's Advanced Technology Division at that time, and I helped write some demos for Autodesk Cyberspace.

Graphical user immersion was brought about by using a lot of hacking and a lot of tricks of three-dimensional graphics. The idea was to break a scene up into polygons and show the projected images of the polygons from whatever position the user wants. It's not much extra work to make two slightly different projections, in this way you can get stereo images that are fed to "EyePhones." The only available EyePhones in the late '80s were expensive devices made by Jaron Lanier's company VPL.

User manipulation was done by another of Lanier's devices, the DataGlove. So as to correctly track the relative positions of their hands and heads, users wore a magnetic field device known as Polhemus. The EyePhones, DataGlove and Polhemus were all somewhat flaky and unreliable pieces of hardware, as were the experimental graphics accelerator cards that we had in our machines. It was really pretty rare that everything would be working at once. I programmed for over a year on a demo called "Flocking Topes" that showed polyhedra flocking around the user like a school of tropical fish, and I doubt if I got to spend more than five minutes fully immersed VR with my demo. But what a wonderful five minutes it was!

Supporting multiple users turned out to be a subtler programming issue than had been expected. When you have multiple users you have the problems of whose machine the VR simulation is living on, and of how to keep the worlds in synch.

In the end, the Autodesk product was a flop. It was too expensive and too constrictive. People were writing plenty of VR programs, but they didn't want to be constrained to the particular set of tools that the Autodesk Cyberspace Developer's Kit was supposed to provide.

One of the biggest growth areas for VR has been video games.

Initially, home computers couldn't support these computations, so one of the early forms of commercial cyberspace were expensive arcade games. One in particular was called "Virtuality." Each player would get on a little platform, strap on head-goggles and gloves, and enter a virtual reality in which the players walked around in simulated bodies carrying pop-guns and trying to shoot each other. The last time I played this game was in a "Cybermind" arcade in San Francisco. I was by myself, scruffily dressed. My opponents were two ten-year-old boys with their parents. I whaled on them pretty good – they were new to the game. It was only after we finished that the parents realized their children had been off in cyberspace with that – unshaven chuckling man over there.

Of course now games like *Quake* and *Half-Life* show fairly convincing VR simulations on home computer screens. For whatever reason, head-mounted displays and glove interfaces still haven't caught on. But the multiple-user aspect of VR has really taken off. There are any number of online VR environments in which large numbers of people enter the same world.[35]

I just recently got a good enough computer to make it practical to visit some of these worlds. The online VR is amazing at first. You can run this way and that, looking at things. And there's lots of other people in there with you, each in one of the body images known as "avatars." Everyone's talking by typing, and their sentences are scrolling past at the bottom of the screen.

What still seems to be missing from these worlds is any kind of indigenous life, although this may yet be on the way. As the writer Bruce Sterling once remarked to me about VR worlds, "I always want to get in there with a spray-can. It's too clean." It would be nice for instance to have plants, animals, molds, and the like. But for now, it's the presence of the other people that makes these worlds compelling.

35. A large number of these worlds are described in Bruce Damer, *Avatars: Exploring and Building Virtual Worlds on the Internet*, Peachpit Press, San Francisco 1997. Links to many interactive VR sites can be found on Damer's page, http://www.digital-space.com/avatars. There is a particularly interesting VR chatroom called Active-Worlds. This is accessed by downloading a special Web browser from http://www.activeworlds.com.

CYBERCULTURE

In the late eighties there was suddenly a big cultural interest in cyberpunk, cyberspace and virtual reality. Part of this was due to the weird Berkeley magazine *Mondo 2000*, which presented these ideas as something like a new form of LSD.

In point of fact, the *Mondo* crew were mostly not very technical. Some of them were quite devoted to psychedelics, and you might say that cyberspace and virtual reality were new forms they used for thinking about drug visions. Tripping and calling people on the phone can seem a lot like being in cyberspace, for instance. In any case, *Mondo* did a lot to popularize what might be called "cyberculture."

One way to explain the word "cyberpunk" is that "cyber" means computer/human interface and "punk" means rebellious countercultural people. The computer gives power to the punk. More broadly speaking, cyberpunk science fiction is about the fusion of humans and machines. It isn't really about the future, it's about the present. It's a way for us to step back and look at what's happening right now. The brain plug is you with your keyboard and your screen. The virtual reality is you watching television.

Mondo added on additional layers of meaning to the word, and in 1992 I helped edit a collection of their articles called the *Mondo User's Guide*. The book got good publicity, and even occasioned a cover story on cyberpunk by *Time* magazine.[36] Cyberpunk suddenly stood for a whole independent culture and reality, far beyond what I thought it had meant. It began to seem that by paying attention to the world in certain ways you could begin to live in cyberspace.

The writer John Perry Barlow remarked, for instance, that "cyberspace is where you are when you're on the telephone." A few weeks later I was at a conference in Toronto. It was evening, I was walking down a deserted city street alone and I missed Audrey. At every second corner there was a telephone. I stopped at one and tried to call Audrey, punching in all the twenty-five necessary numbers for a credit card call. The phone was busy. It was too cold to stand there waiting. I kept walking, and at every second block was an identical deserted phone, and at each one I punched in the numbers.

36. *Time*, Feb 8, 1993.

At the fifth phone I got her. It struck me that as I'd been walking, I'd been moving through a kind of continuous jelly of cyberspace.

THE WEB

In a way, the focus on virtual reality was a diversion, a detour. For a computer reality to engross, it isn't so important after all that it have really great 3-D immersive graphics. It's more important that it react to what you do, and that it include other people.

Your mind is rich enough that in fact you can get mesmerized by very low bandwidth things. People can completely get into, for instance, something as graphically crude as text-based conversations in a chat room.

And the system's turnaround reaction time doesn't even have to be very high. If you do a lot of electronic mail, you get used to checking your email once or twice a day, and it's like there is a big buzz of conversation going on that you are part of. If you can't get to your email you're kind of uncomfortable. It's a big thrill to find a cyber-cafe in a strange city and suddenly be able to plug into your familiar email corner of cyberspace.

One definition of something being a reality is that several people can go there and see the same thing. This is certainly the case with the Web. It's a space that we go out into all the time, and interesting things are happening there. Unlike watching television, the Web is interactive. You can move around and look at whatever it is that you want to see.

An advantage of the Web over physical reality is that it's physically safe inside your computer, that is, it's not like the real world where you can get into a car accident, trip and fall down, get wet, have to walk home, etc. A disadvantage is that you're sitting in a chair punching a plastic keyboard.

But the real attraction of the Web's cyberspace is that you don't need to be lonely in there. You can say things and people will hear you. Email flits back and forth. People put things up for you to look at. It's a kind of community. It's a global computer. It's everywhere. Cyberspace is a pleasant, anarchistic alternate universe that we're all free to live in.

— *Original version appeared* as *"Brain Plug" in* 21C, *#4, 1996.*

Life and Artificial Life

Artificial life is the study of how to create man-made systems which behave as if they were alive.[37]

It is important to study life because the most interesting things in the world are the things that are alive. Living things grow into beautiful shapes and develop graceful behavior. They eat, they mate, they compete, and over the generations they evolve.

In the planetary sense, societies and entire ecologies can be thought of as living organisms. In an even more abstract sense, our thoughts themselves can be regarded as benignly parasitic information viruses that hop from mind to mind. Life is all around us, and it would be valuable to have a better understanding of how it works.

Investigators of the brand new field of artificial life, or *A-life*, are beginning to tinker with home-brewed simulations of life. A-life can be studied for its scientific aspects, for its aesthetic pleasures, or as a source of insight into real living systems.

In the practical realm, artificial life provides new methods of chemical synthesis, self-improving techniques for controlling complex systems, and ways to automatically generate optimally tweaked computer programs. In the future, artificial life will play a key role in robotics, in virtual reality, and in the retrieval of information from unmanageably huge data bases.

One can go about creating A-life by building robots or by tailoring biochemical reactions – and we'll talk about these options later

37. There are a number of very comprehensive anthologies of technical and semi-technical papers presented at the biennial conferences on artificial life. The first conference was held at Los Alamos, New Mexico, in 1987, and its papers appear in C. Langton, ed., *Artificial Life*, Addison-Wesley, 1989. Further volumes are named *Artificial Life II, III*, and so on, and appear from various publishers. A good popular book on A-life is: Steven Levy, *Artificial Life: The Quest for a New Creation*, Pantheon Books, 1992.

in this essay. But the most inexpensive way to go about experiment-ing with A-life is to use computer programs.

What are some of the essential characteristics of life that we want our A-life programs to have? We want programs that are visually attractive, that move about, that interact with their environment, that breed, and that evolve.

Three characteristics of living systems will guide our quest:

- Gnarl
- Sex
- Death.

This essay includes sections on Gnarl, Sex, and Death, followed by three sections on *non-computer* A-life.

GNARL

The original meaning of "gnarl" was simply "a knot in the wood of a tree." In California surfer slang, "gnarly" came to be used to describe complicated, rapidly changing surf conditions. And then, by exten-sion, "gnarly" came to mean anything that included a lot of surpris-ingly intricate detail.

Living things are gnarly in that they inevitably do things that are much more complex than one might have expected. The grain of an oak burl is of course gnarly in the traditional sense of the word, but the life cycle of a jellyfish, say, is gnarly in the modern sense. The wild three-dimensional paths that a hummingbird sweeps out are kind of gnarly, and, if the truth be told, your ears are gnarly as well.

A simple rule of thumb for creating artificial life on the computer is that the program should produce output which looks gnarly.

"Gnarly" is, of course, not the word which most research scien-tists use. Instead, they speak of life as being *chaotic* or *complex*.

Chaos as a scientific concept became popular in the 1980s.[38] Chaos can be defined to mean *complicated but not arbitrary*.

---

38. The classic popular book on chaos theory is: James Gleick, *Chaos: Making a New Science*, Viking, 1987. There is a useful companion program written by me, Josh Gor-don, and John Walker: *James Gleick's Chaos: The Software*, Autodesk, 1990, available for free download from the "Chaos" page of my Web site.

The surf at the shore of an ocean beach is chaotic. The patterns of the water are clearly very complicated. But, and this is the key point, they are *not arbitrary*.

For one thing, the patterns that the waves move in are, from moment to moment, predictable by the laws of fluid motion. Waves don't just pop in and out of existence. Water moves according to well understood physical laws. Even if the waves are in some sense random, their motions are still not arbitrary. The patterns you see are drawn from a relatively small range of options. Everything you see looks like water in motion; the water never starts looking like, say, cactuses or piles of cubes. The kinds of things that waves "like to do" are what chaoticians call "attractors" in the space of possible wave behaviors.

Note that the quantum uncertainties of atomic motions do in fact make the waves random at some level. As Martin Gardner once said to me, "Quantum mechanics ruins everything." But quantum mechanics is something of a red herring here. The waves would look much the same even if physics were fully deterministic right down to the lowest levels.

As it turns out, you don't need a system as complicated as the ocean to generate unpredictable chaos. Over the last couple of decades, scientists have discovered that sometimes a very simple rule can produce output which looks, at least superficially, as complicated as physical chaos. Computer simulations of chaos can be obtained either by running one algorithm many times (as in a simulation of planetary motion), or by setting up an arena in which multiple instances of a single algorithm can interact (as with a cellular automaton). A sufficiently complex chaotic system can appear fully unpredictable.

Some chaotic systems explode into a full-blown random-looking grunge, while others settle into the gnarly, warped patterns that are known as strange attractors. A computer screen filled with what looks like a seething flea circus can be a chaotic system, but the fractal images that you see on T-shirts and calendars are pictures of chaos as well. Like all other kinds of systems, chaotic systems can range from having a lesser or a greater amount of disorder. If a chaotic system isn't too disorderly, it converges on certain standard kinds of behavior — these are its *attractors*. If the attractors are odd-

The Mandelbrot set is gnarly. (Generated by Chaos.)

looking or, in particular, of an endlessly detailed fractal nature, they are called *strange attractors*.

To return to the surf example, you might notice that the waves near a rock tend every so often to fall into a certain kind of surge pattern. This recurrent surge pattern would be an attractor. In the same way, chaotic computer simulations will occasionally tighten in on characteristic rhythms and clusters that act as attractors.

But if there is a storm, the waves may be just completely out of control and choppy and patternless. This is full-blown chaos. As disorderliness is increased, a chaotic system can range from being nearly periodic, up through the fractal region of the strange attractors, on up into impenetrable messiness.

Quite recently, some scientists have started using the new word *complexity* for a certain type of chaos. A system is *complex* if it is a chaotic system that is not too disorderly.

The notions of chaos and complexity come from looking at a wide range of systems — mathematical, physical, chemical, biological, sociological, and economic. In each domain, the systems that arise can be classified into a spectrum of disorderliness.

At the ordered end we have constancy and a complete lack of surprise. One step up from that is periodic behavior in which the same sequence repeats itself over and over again – as in the structure of a crystal. At the disordered end of the spectrum is full randomness. One notch down from full randomness is the zone of the gnarl.

	NO DISORDER	LOW DISORDER	GNARLY	HIGH DISORDER
MATH	Constant	Periodic	Chaotic	Random
MATTER	Vacuum	Crystal	Liquid	Gas
PATTERN	Blank	Checkers	Fractal	Dither
FLOW	Still	Smooth	Turbulent	Seething

Table 1: Spectrums of Disorderliness for Various Fields.

As an example of the disorderliness spectrum in mathematics, let's look at some different kinds of mathematical functions, where a *function* is a rule or a method that takes input numbers and gives back other numbers as output. If f is a function, then for each input number x, the function f assigns an output number $f(x)$. A function f is often drawn as a graph of the equation $y = f(x)$, with the graph appearing as a line or curve on a pair of x and y axes.

The most orderly kind of mathematical function is a constant function, such as an f for which $f(x)$ is always two. The graph of such a function is nothing but a horizontal line.

At the next level of disorder, we might look at a function f for which $f(x)$ varies periodically with the value of x. The sine function $sin(x)$ is an example of such a function; it fluctuates up and down like a wave.

The gnarly zone of mathematics is chaos. Chaotic functions have finitely complicated definitions, but somewhat unpredictable patterns. A chaotic function may be an extremely irregular curve, unpredictably swooping up and back down.

A truly random mathematical function is a smeared-out mess that has no underlying rhyme or reason to it. A typical random function has a graph that breaks into a cloud of dots, with the curve continually jumping to new points.

Formally, something is truly random if it admits to no finite definition at all. It is an old question in the philosophy of science whether anything in the universe truly is random in this sense of being *infinitely complicated*. It may be the whole universe itself is simply a chaotic system whose finite underlying explanation happens to lie beyond our ability to understand.

Before going on to talk about the disorder spectrums of the Matter, Pattern, and Flow rows in Table 1, let's pause to zoom in on the appearance of the math row's disorderliness spectrum within the gnarly zone of chaos. This zoom is shown in Table 2.

	LESS DISORDER	MORE DISORDER	CRITICAL	HIGH DISORDER
CHAOS	Quasiperiodic	Attractor	Complex	Pseudorandom

Table 2: Spectrum of Disorderliness for the Chaos Field.

The most orderly kind of chaos is "quasiperiodic," or nearly periodic. Something like this might be a periodic function that has a slight, unpredictable drift. Next comes the "attractor" zone in which chaotic systems generate easily visible structures. Next comes a "critical" zone of transition that is the domain of complexity, and which is the true home of the gnarl. And at the high end of disorder is "pseudorandom" chaotic systems, whose output is empirically indistinguishable from true randomness – unless you happen to be told the algorithm which is generating the chaos.

Now let's get back to the other three rows from Table 1, back to Matter, Pattern, and Flow.

In classical (pre-quantum) physics, a vacuum is the simplest, most orderly kind of matter: nothing is going on. A crystalline solid is orderly in a predictable, periodic way. In a liquid the particles are still loosely linked together, but in a gas, the particles break free and bounce around in a seemingly random way. I should point out that in classical physics, the trajectories of a gas's particles can in principle be predicted from their starting positions – much like the bouncing balls of an idealized billiard table – so a classical gas is really a pseudorandom chaotic system rather than a truly random system. Here, again, chaotic means "very complicated but having a finite underlying algorithm."

In any case, the gnarly, complex zone of matter would be identified with the liquid phase, rather than the pseudorandom or perhaps truly random gas phase. The critical point where a heated liquid turns into steam would be a zone of particular gnarliness and interest.

In terms of patterns, the most orderly kind of pattern is a blank one, with the next step up being something like a checkerboard. Fractals are famous for being patterns that are regular yet irregular. The most simply defined fractals are complex and chaotic patterns that are obtained by carrying out many iterations of some simple formula. The most disorderly kind of pattern is a random dusting of pixels, such as is sometimes used in the random dither effects that are used to create color shadings and gray-scale textures. Fractals exemplify gnarl in a very clear form.

The flow of water is a rich source of examples of degrees of disorder. The most orderly state of water is, of course, for it to be standing still. If one lets water run rather slowly down a channel, the water moves smoothly, with perhaps a regular pattern of ripples in it. As more water is put into a channel, eddies and whirlpools appear – this is what is known as turbulence. If a massive amount of water is poured down a steep channel, smaller and smaller eddies cascade off the larger ones, ultimately leading to an essentially random state in which the water is seething. Here the gnarly region is where the flow has begun to break up into eddies with a few smaller eddies, without yet having turned into random churning.

In every case, the gnarly zone is to be found somewhere at the transition between order and disorder. Simply looking around at the world makes it seem reasonable to believe that this is the level of orderliness to be expected from living things. Living things are orderly but not too orderly; chaotic but not too chaotic. Life is gnarly, and A-life should be gnarly too.

SEX

When I say that life includes gnarl, sex, and death, I am using the flashy word "sex" to stand for four distinct things:

• Having a body that is grown from genes
• Reproduction
• Mating
• Random genetic changes.

Let's discuss these four sex topics one at a time.

The first sex topic is *genes as seeds for growing the body.*

All known life forms have a genetic basis. That is, all living things can be grown from eggs or seeds. In living things, the genes are squiggles of DNA molecules that somehow contain a kind of program for constructing the living organism's entire body. In addition, the genes also contain instructions that determine much of the organism's repertoire of behavior.

A single complete set of genes is known as a *genome*, and an organism's body with its behavior is known as the organism's *phenome*. What a creature looks like and acts like is its phenome; it's the part of the creatures that *shows*. (The word "phenome" comes from the Greek word for "to show"; think of the word "phenomenon.")

Modern researches into the genetic basis of life have established that each living creature starts with a genome. The genome acts as a set of instructions that are used to grow the creature's phenome.

It is conceivable that somewhere in the universe there may be things with phenomes that we would call living, but which are *not* grown from genomes. These geneless aliens might be like clouds, say, or like tornadoes. But all the kinds of things that we ordinarily think of as being alive are in fact based on genomes, so it is reasonable to base our investigations of A-life on systems which have a genetic basis.

If we're interested in computer-based A-life, it is particularly appropriate to work with A-life forms whose phenomes grow out of their genomes. In terms of a computer, you can think of the genome as the program and the phenome as the output. A computer A-life creature has a genome which is a string of bits (a bit being the minimal piece of binary information, a zero or a one), and its phenome includes the creature's graphic appearance on the computer's screen. Keep in mind that the phenome also includes *behavior*, so the way in which the creature's appearance changes and reacts to other creatures is part of its phenome as well.

The second sex topic is *reproduction*.

The big win in growing your phenome from a small genome is that this makes it easy for you to grow copies of yourself. Instead of having to copy your large and complicated phenome as a whole, you need only make a copy of your relatively small genome, and then let the copied genome grow its own phenome. Eventually the newly grown phenome should look just like you. Although this kind of reproduction is a solitary activity, it is still a kind of sex, and is practiced by such lowly creatures as the amoeba.

As it happens, the genome-copying ability is something that is built right into DNA because of the celebrated fact that DNA has the form of a *double helix* which is made of two complementary strands of protein. Each strand encodes the entire information of the genome. In order to reproduce itself, a DNA double helix first unzips itself to produce two separate strands of half-DNA, each of which is a long, linked protein chain of molecules called *bases*. The bases are readily available in the fluid of any living cell, and now each half-DNA strand gathers unto itself enough bases to make a copy of its complementary half-DNA strand. The new half-DNA strands are assembled in position, already twined right around the old strands, so the net result is that the original DNA genome has turned itself into two. It has successfully reproduced; it has made a copy of itself.

In most A-life worlds, reproduction is something that is done in a simple mechanical way. The bitstring or sequence of bits that encodes a creature's program is copied into a new memory location by the "world" program, and then the two creature programs are run and the two phenotypes appear.

The third sex topic is *mating*.

Most living creatures reproduce in pairs, with the offspring's genome containing a combination of the parents' genomes. Rather than being a random shuffling of the bases in the parents' DNA, genomes are normally mated by a process known as *crossover*.

To simplify the idea, we leave out any DNA-like details of genome reproduction, and simply think of the two parent genomes as a chain of circles and a chain of squares, both chains of the same length. In the crossover process, a crossover point is chosen and the two genomes are broken at the crossover point. The broken genomes can now be joined together and mated in two possible ways. You can have squares followed by circles, or circles followed by squares. In real life, only one of the possible matings is chosen as the genome seed of the new organism.

In computer A-life, we often allow *both* of the newly mated genomes to survive. In fact, the most common form of computer A-life reproduction is to replace the two original parent programs by the two new crossed-over programs. That is to say, two A-life parents often "breed in place."

In a world where several species exist, it can even sometimes happen that one species genome can incorporate some information from the genome of a creature from another species! This phenomenon is called "exogamy." Although rare, exogamy does seem to occur in the real world. It is said that snippets of our DNA are identical to bits of modern cat DNA. Gag me with a hairball!

The fourth sex topic involves *random changes to the genome.*

Mating is a major source of genetic diversity in living things, but genomes can also have their information changed by such randomizing methods as mutation, transposition, and zapping. While mating acts on pairs of genomes, randomization methods act on one genome at a time.

For familiar wetware life forms like ourselves, mutations are caused by things like poisons and cosmic rays. Some mutations are lethal, but many of them make no visible difference at all. Now and then a particular mutation or accumulation of mutations will cause the phenome to suddenly show a drastically new kind of appearance and behavior. Perhaps genius, perhaps a harelip, perhaps beauty, perhaps idiocy.

In the A-life context, where we typically think of the genome as a sequence of zeroes and ones, a mutation amounts to picking a site and flipping the bit: from zero to one, or from one to zero.

Besides mutation, there are several other forms of genome randomization, some of which are still being discovered in the real world and are as yet poorly understood.

One interesting genome changer is known as *transposition*. In transposition, two swatches of some genomes are swapped.[39]

Another genome randomizer that we sometimes use in A-life programs is *zapping*, whereby every now and then *all* of some single creature's genome bits are randomized. In the real world, zapping is not a viable method of genetic variation, as it will almost certainly produce a creature that dies instantly. But in the more forgiving arena of A-life, zapping can be useful.

In the natural world, species typically have very large populations and big genomes. Here the effects of mating – sexual reproduction – are the primary main source of genetic diversity. But in the small populations and short genomes of A-life experiments, it is dangerously easy for all the creatures to end up with the same genome. And if you cross over two identical genomes, the offspring are identical to the parents, and no diversity arises! As a practical matter, random genome variation is quite important for artificial life simulations.

DEATH

What would life be like if there were no death? Very crowded or very stagnant. In imagining a situation like *no death*, it's always a challenge to keep a consistent mental scenario. But I'm a science fiction writer, so I'm glad to try. Let's suppose that Death forgot about Earth starting in the Age of the Dinosaurs. What would today's Earth be like?

There would still be lots of dinosaurs around, which is nice. But if they had been reproducing for all of this time, the dinosaurs and their contemporaries would be piled many hundreds of meters deep all over Earth's surface. Twisted and deformed dinosaur mutations would be plentiful as well. One might expect that they would have eaten all the plants up, but of course there would be no death for plants either, so there would be a huge jungle of plants under the mounds of dinosaurs, all of the dinos taking turns squirming down

---

39. John Rennie, "DNA's New Twists," in *Scientific American*, March 1993, pp. 122–132 contains a discussion of transposition and some of the other methods of genome variation being currently investigated.

to get a bite. The oceans would be gill to gill with sea life, and then some. I think of the Earth before Noah's flood.[40]

Would mammals and humans have evolved in such a world? Probably not. Although there would be many of the oddball creatures around that were our precursors, in the vast welter of life there would be no way for them to select themselves out, get together, and tighten up their genomes.

An alternative vision of a death-free Earth is a world in which birth stops as well. What kind of world would that lead to? Totally boring. It would be nothing but the same old creatures stomping the same old environment forever. Like how the job market looks to a young person starting out!

Meaningless proliferation or utter stagnancy are the only alternatives to death. Although death is individually terrible, it is wonderful for the evolution of new kinds of life.

40. Actually the phrase "piled many hundreds of meters deep" in this paragraph is an *extreme* understatement. Lying awake last night, I calculated that the immortal dinosaurs would fill all known space! To make it easier, I worked my example out in terms of people instead of dinosaurs. I claim that if one immortal couple had emerged in 5200 BC, their immortal descendants would now fill all space. For those who like playing with numbers, here's my calculation. Suppose that each person, on the average, produces a new person every thirty years. So if nobody dies, but everyone keeps on breeding, then the number of people will double every thirty years. If you start with exactly two immortals, there will be 2 to the Nth power immortals after $30*N$ years. One estimate is that the universe has the same size as a cube that is ten billion (or ten to the 10th) light-years per edge. A light-year is about ten trillion kilometers, or ten to the 16th meters, so the universe is a cube ten to the 26th meters per edge. Cubing ten to the 26th gives ten to the 3×26th, or ten to the 78th. Suppose that a person takes up a cubic meter of space. How many years would be needed to fill the universe with ten to the 78th immortal people? Well, for what value of N is 2 to the Nth power bigger than ten to the 78th? A commonly used computer science fact is that two to the 10th, known as a K, is almost equal to a thousand, which is ten cubed. Now ten to the 78th is ten to the 3×24th, which is one thousand to the 24th, which is about one K to the 24th, which is two to the 10×24th, which is two to the 240th. That means it would take 240 generations for the immortal humans to fill up the universe. At 30 years per generation, that makes 7,200 years. 5200 BC was at a time when people were giving up being hunter gatherers and were learning to farm; by comparison, Sumeria flourished in 4000 BC and the Early Period of Ancient Egypt was 3000 BC. So if two of those way early farmers had mastered immortality, the whole universe would be stuffed with their descendants!

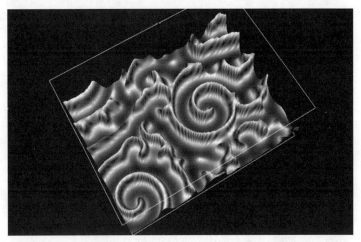

A Belusov-Zhabotinsky pattern in a cellular automaton. (Generated by CAPOW)

Evolution is possible whenever one has (1) reproduction, (2) genome variation, and (3) natural selection. We've already talked about reproduction and the way in which mating and mutation cause genome variation – so that children are not necessarily just like their parents. Natural selection is where death comes in: not every creature is in fact able to reproduce itself before it dies. The creatures which do reproduce have genomes which are selected by the natural process of competing to stay alive and to bear children which survive.

What this means in terms of computer A-life is that one ordinarily has some maximum number of memory slots for creatures' genomes. One lets the phenomes of the creatures compete for a while and then uses some kind of fitness function to decide which creatures are the most successful. The most successful creatures are reproduced onto the existing memory slots, and the genomes of the least successful creatures are erased.

Nature has a very simple way of determining a creature's fitness: it manages to reproduce before death or it doesn't. Assigning a fitness level to competing A-life phenomes is a more artificial process. Various kinds of fitness functions can be chosen on the basis of what kinds of creatures one wants to see evolve. In most of the experiments I've worked on, the fitness is based on the creatures' ability to find and eat food cells, as well as to avoid "predators" and to get near "prey."

So far in this essay we've talked about life in terms of three general concepts: gnarl, sex, and death. Computer A-life research involves trying to find computer programs which are gnarly, which breed, and which compete to stay alive. Now let's look at some non-computer approaches to artificial life.

BIOLOGICAL A-LIFE

In this section, we first talk about Frankenstein, and then we talk about modern biochemistry.

Frankenstein. The most popular fictional character who tries to create life is Viktor Frankenstein, the protagonist of Mary Shelley's 1818 novel *Frankenstein or, The Modern Prometheus.*

Most of us know about Frankenstein from the movie versions of the story. In the movie version, Dr. Frankenstein creates a living man by sewing together parts of dead bodies and galvanizing the result with electricity from a thunderstorm. The original version is quite different.

In Mary Shelley's novel, Baron Viktor Frankenstein is a student with a deep interest in chemistry. He becomes curious about what causes life, and he pursues this question by closely examining how things die and decay – the idea being that if you can understand how life leaves matter, you can understand how to put it back in. Viktor spends days and nights in "vaults and charnel-houses," until finally he believes he has learned how to bring dead flesh back to life. He sets to work building the Frankenstein monster:

> In a solitary chamber…I kept my workshop of filthy creation: my eyeballs were starting from their sockets in attending to the details of my employment. The dissecting room and the slaughter-house furnished many of my materials; and often did my human nature turn with loathing from my occupation… Who shall conceive the horrors of my secret toil, as I dabbled among the unhallowed damps of the grave, or tortured the living animal to animate the lifeless clay?

Finally Dr. Frankenstein reaches his goal:

It was on a dreary night of November that I beheld the
accomplishment of my toils. With an anxiety that almost
amounted to agony, I collected the instruments of life around me,
that I might infuse a spark of being into the lifeless thing that lay
at my feet. It was already one in the morning; the rain pattered
dismally against the panes, and my candle was nearly burnt out,
when, by the glimmer of the half-extinguished light, I saw the
dull yellow eye of the creature open; it breathed hard, and a
convulsive motion agitated its limbs... The beauty of the dream
vanished, and breathless horror and disgust filled my heart.

The creepy, slithery aspect of *Frankenstein* stems from the fact that
Mary Shelley situated Viktor Frankenstein's A-life researches at the
tail-end of life, at the part where a living creature life dissolves back
into a random mush of chemicals. In point of fact, this is really *not* a
good way to understand life – the processes of decay are not readily
reversible.

Biochemistry. Contemporary A-life biochemists focus on the way in
which life keeps itself going. Organic life is a process, a skein of biochemical reactions that is in some ways like a parallel three-dimensional computation. The computation being carried out by a living
body stops when the body dies, and the component parts of the body
immediately begin decomposing. Unless you're Viktor Frankenstein,
there is no way to kick-start the reaction back into viability. It's as if
turning off a computer would make its chips fall apart.

The amazing part about real life that it keeps itself going on its
own. If anyone could build a tiny, self-guiding, flying robot he or she
would a hero of science. But a fly can build flies just by eating
garbage. Biological life is a self-organizing process, an endless round
that's been chorusing along for hundreds of millions of years.

Is there any hope of scientists being able to assemble and start up
a living biological system?

Chemists have studied complicated systems of reactions that tend
to perpetuate themselves. These kinds of reaction are called *autocatalytic* or *self-exciting*. Once an autocatalytic reaction gets started up, it
produces by-products which pull more and more molecules into the

reaction. Often such a reaction will have a cyclical nature, in that it goes through the same sequence of steps over and over.

The cycle of photosynthesis is a very complicated example of an autocatalytic reaction. One of the simpler examples of an autocatalytic chemical reaction is known as the *Belusov–Zhabotinsky reaction* in honor of the two Soviet scientists who discovered it. In the Belusov-Zhabotinsky reaction a certain acidic solution is placed into a flat glass dish with a sprinkling of palladium crystals. The active ingredient of litmus paper is added so that it is possible to see which regions of the solution are more or less acidic. In a few minutes, the dish fills with scroll-shaped waves of color which spiral around and around in a regular, but not quite predictable, manner.[41]

There seems to be something universal about the Belusov-Zhabotinsky reaction, in that there are many other systems which behave in a similar way: generating endlessly spiraling scrolls. It is in fact fairly easy to set up a cellular automaton-based computer simulation that shows something like the Belusov-Zhabotinsky reaction – Zhabotinsky scrolls are something that CAs like to "do."

As well as trying to understand the chemical reactions that take place in living things, biochemists have investigated ways of creating the chemicals used by life. In the famous 1952 Miller-Urey experiment, two scientists sealed a glass retort filled with such simple chemicals as water, methane and hydrogen.[42] The sealed vessel was equipped with electrodes that repeatedly fired off sparks – the vessel was intended to be a kind of simulation of primeval Earth with its lightning storms. After a week, it was found that a variety of amino acids had spontaneously formed inside the vessel. Amino acids are the building blocks of protein and of DNA – of our phenomes and of our genomes, so the Miller-Urey experiment represented an impressive first step towards understanding how life on Earth emerged.

41. One of the first accounts of the Belusov-Zhabotinsky reaction can be found in: Arthur Winfree, "Rotating Chemical Reactions," *Scientific American*, June, 1974, pp. 82-95.

42. The Miller-Urey experiment was first announced in: S. L. Miller and H. C. Urey, "Organic Compound Synthesis on the Primitive Earth," *Science* 130 (1959), p. 245.

Biochemists have pushed this kind of thing much further in the last decades. It is now possible to design artificial strands of RNA which are capable of self-replicating themselves when placed into a solution of amino acids; and one can even set a kind of RNA evolution into motion. In one recent experiment, a solution was filled with a random assortment of self-replicating RNA along with amino acids for the RNA to build with. Some of the molecules tended to stick to the sides of the beaker. The solution was then poured out, with the molecules that stuck to the sides of the vessel being retained. A fresh food-supply of amino acids was added and the cycle was repeated numerous times. The evolutionary result? RNA that adheres very firmly to the sides of the beaker.[43]

Genetic engineers are improving on methods to tinker with the DNA of living cells to make organisms which are in some part artificial. Most commercially sold insulin is in fact created by gene-tailored cells. The word *wetware* is sometimes used to stand for the information in the genome of a biological cell. Wetware is like software, but it's in a watery living environment. The era of wetware programming has only just begun.

ROBOTS

In this section we compare science fiction dreams of robots to robots as they actually exist today. We also talk a bit about how computer science techniques may help us get from today's realities to tomorrow's dreams.

Science Fiction Robots. Science fiction is filled with robots that act as if they were alive. Existing robots already possess such life-like char-

43. The RNA evolution experiment is described in Gerald Joyce, "Directed Molecular Evolution," *Scientific American*, December, 1992. A good quote about wetware appears in *Mondo 2000: A User's Guide to the New Edge*, edited by R. U. Sirius, Queen Mu and me for HarperCollins, 1992. The quote is from the bioengineer Max Yukawa: "Suppose you think of an organism as being like a computer graphic that is generated from some program. Or think of an oak tree as being the output of a program that was contained inside the acorn. The genetic program is in the DNA molecule. Your software is the abstract information pattern behind your genetic code, but your actual wetware is the physical DNA in a cell."

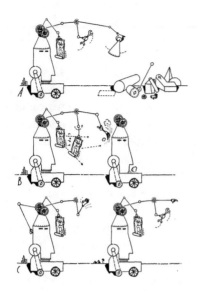

A robot that reproduces by (a) using a blueprint to (b) build a copy of itself, and then (c) giving the new robot a copy of the blueprint. (Drawing by David Povilaitis.)

acteristics as sensitivity to the environment, movement, complexity, and integration of parts. But what about reproduction? Could you have robots which build other robots?

The idea is perhaps surprising at first, but there's nothing logically wrong with it. As long as a robot has an exact blueprint of how it is constructed, it can assemble the parts for child robots, and it can use a copying machine to give each child its own blueprint so that the process can continue. For a robot, the blueprint is its genome, and its body and behavior is its phenome. In practice, the robots would not use paper blueprints, but might instead use CAD/CAM (computer aided design and manufacturing) files.

The notion of robot A-life interests me so much that I've written several science fiction novels about it. As will be discussed in a section below, *The Hacker and the Ants* talks about how one might use a virtual reality world in which to evolve robots.

In *Software*, some robots are sent to the moon where they build factories to make robot parts. They compete with each other for the right to use the parts (natural selection), and then they get together in pairs (sex) to build new robots onto which parts of the parents' programs are placed (self-reproduction). Soon they rebel against human rule, and begin calling themselves *boppers*. Some of them travel to Earth to eat some human brains – just to get the information out of the tissues, you understand.

In *Wetware*, the boppers take up genetic engineering and learn how to code bopper genomes into fertilized human eggs, which can then be force-grown to adult size in less than a month. The humans built the boppers, but now the boppers are building people – or something *like* people.

At the end of *Wetware*, the irate humans kill off the boppers by infecting their silicon chips with a biological mold, but in *Freeware*, the boppers are back, with flexible plastic bodies that don't use chips anymore. The "freeware" of the title has to do with encrypted personality patterns that some aliens are sending across space in search of bodies to live upon.

In my most recent book of this series, *Realware*, the humans and boppers obtain a tool for creating new "realware" bodies solely from software descriptions of them.

Real Robots. After such heady science fiction dreams, it's discouraging to look at today's actual robots. These machines are still very lacking in adaptability, which is the ability to function well in unfamiliar environments. They can't walk and/or chew gum at the same time.

The architecture for most experimental robots is something like this: you put a bunch of devices in a wheeled can, wire the devices together, and hope that the behavior of the system can converge on a stable and interesting kind of behavior.

What kind of devices go in the can? Wheels and pincers with exquisitely controllable motors, TV cameras, sonar pingers, microphones, a sound-synthesizer, and some computer microprocessors.

The phenome is the computation and behavior of the whole system – it's what the robot does. The robot's genome is its blueprint, with all the interconnections and the switch-settings on the devices in the wheeled garbage can, and if any of those devices happens to be a computer memory chip, then the information on the chips is part of the genome as well.

Traditionally, we have imagined robots as having one central processing unit, just as we have one central brain. But in fact a lot of our

information processing is done in our nerve ganglia, and some contemporary roboticists are interested in giving a separate processor to
each of a robot's devices.

This robot design technique is known as *subsumption architecture*.
Each of an artificial ant's legs, for instance, might know now to
make walking motions on its own, and the legs might communicate
with each other in an effort to get into synch. Just such an ant
(named Atilla) has been designed by Rodney Brooks of MIT.
Brooks wants his robots to be cheap and widely available.

Another interesting robot was designed by Marc Pauline of the
art group known as Survival Research Laboratories. Pauline and his
group stage large, Dadaist spectacles in which hand-built robots
interact with each other. Pauline is working on some new robots
which he calls "swarmers." His idea is to have the swarmers radio-
aware of each other's position, and to chase each other around. The
idea is to try to find good settings to give the swarmers maximally
chaotic behavior.

In practice, developing designs and software for these machines
is what is known as an *intractable problem*. It is very hard to predict
how the different components will interact, so one has to actually try
out each new configuration to see how it works. And commonly,
changes are being made to the hardware and to the software at the
same time, so the space of possible solutions is vast.

Telerobotics. For many applications, the user might not need a robot
to be fully autonomous. Something like a remotely operated hand
that you use to handle dangerous materials is like a robot, in that it is
a complicated machine which imitates human motions. But a
remote hand does not necessarily need to have much of an internal
brain, particularly if all it has to do is to copy the motions of your
real hand. A device like a remote robot hand is called a *telerobot*.

Radioactive waste is sometimes cleaned up using telerobots that
have video cameras and two robotic arms. The operator of such a
telerobot sees what it sees on a video screen, and moves his or her
hands within a mechanical harness that sends signals to the hands of
the telerobot.

I have a feeling that, in the coming decades, telerobotics is going to be a much more important field than pure robotics. People want *amplifications* of themselves more than they want *servants*. A telerobot projects an individual's power. Telerobots would be useful for exploration, travel, and sheer voyeurism, and could become a sought-after high-end consumer product.

But even if telerobots are more commercially important than self-guiding robots, there is still a need for self-guiding robots. Why? Because when you're using a telerobot, you don't want to have to watch the machine every second so that the machine doesn't do something like get run over by a car, nor do you want to worry about the very fine motions of the machine. You want, for instance, to be able to say "walk towards that object" without having to put your legs into a harness and emulate mechanical walking motions – this means that, just like a true robot, the telerobot will have to know how to move around pretty much on its own.

Evolving Robots. I think artificial life is very likely to be a good way to evolve better and better robots. In order to make the evolution happen faster, it would be nice to be able to do it as a computer simulation – as opposed to the building of dozens of competing prototype models.

My novel *The Hacker and the Ants* is based on the idea of evolving robots by testing your designs out in virtual reality – in, that is, a highly realistic computer simulation with some of the laws of physics built into it.

You might, for instance, take a CAD model of a house, and try out a wide range of possible robots in this house without having to bear the huge expense of building prototypes. As changing a model would have no hardware expense, it would be feasible to try out many different designs and thus more rapidly converge on an optimal design.

There is an interesting relationship between A-life, virtual reality, robotics, and telerobotics. These four areas fit neatly into Table 3, which is based on two distinctions: firstly, is the device being run by a computer program or by a human mind; and, secondly, is the device a physical machine or a simulated machine?

	MIND	BODY
ARTIFICIAL LIFE	Computer	Simulated
VIRTUAL REALITY	Human	Simulated
ROBOTICS	Computer	Physical
TELEROBOTICS	Human	Physical

Table 3: Four Kinds of Computer Science

Artificial life deals with creatures whose brains are computer programs, and these creatures have simulated bodies that interact in a computer-simulated world. In virtual reality, the world and the bodies are still computer-simulated, but at least some of the creatures in the world are now being directly controlled by human users. In robotics, we deal with real physical machines in the real world that are run by computer programs, while in telerobotics we are looking at real physical machines that are run by human minds. Come to think of it, a human's ordinary life in his or her body could be thought of as an example of telerobotics: a human mind is running a physical body!

Memes. In the wider context of the history of ideas, certain kinds of fads, techniques, or religious beliefs behave in some ways like autonomous creatures which live and reproduce. The biologist Richard Dawkins calls these thought-creatures *memes.*[44]

Self-replicating memes can be brutally simple. Here's one:

44. Richard Dawkins talks about memes in his book *The Selfish Gene*, Oxford University Press, 1976. This book is mainly about the idea that an organism is a genome's way of reproducing itself – a bit as if we were big robots being driven around by DNA. The memes take further advantage of us. As Dawkins puts it: "Just as genes propagate themselves in the gene pool by leaping from body to body via sperms or eggs, so memes propagate themselves in the meme pool by leaping from brain to brain...When you plant a fertile meme in my mind you literally parasitize my brain, turning it into a vehicle for the meme's propagation in just the way that a virus may parasitize the genetic mechanism of a host cell."

The Laws of Wealth:

Law I: Begin giving 10% of your income to the person who teaches you the Laws of Wealth.

Law II: Teach the Laws of Wealth to ten people!

The Laws of Wealth meme is the classic Ponzi pyramid scheme. Here's another self-replicating idea system:

System X:

Law I: Anyone who does not believe System X will burn in hell.

Law II: It is your duty to save others from suffering.

Of System X, Douglas Hofstadter remarks, "Without being impious, one may suggest that this mechanism has played some small role in the spread of Christianity."[45]

Most thought memes use a much less direct method of self-reproduction. Being host to a meme-complex such as, say, *the use of language* can confer such wide survival advantages that those infected with the meme flourish. There are many such memes with obvious survival value: the tricks of farming, the craft of pottery, the arcana of mathematics – all are beneficial mind-viruses that live in human information space.

Memes which confer no obvious survival value are more puzzling. Things like tunes and fashions hop from one mind to another with bewildering speed. Staying up to date with current ideas is a higher-order meme which probably does have some survival value. Knowing about A-life, for instance, is very likely to increase your employability as well as your sexual attractiveness!

—*Excerpted from the* Artificial Life Lab *manual,*
Waite Group Press, 1993.

I was employed as a "mathenaut" in the Advanced Technical Division at Autodesk, Inc., from August, 1988 to September, 1992. While I was there, I worked on CA Lab, on James Gleick's CHAOS: The Software, on the Autodesk Cyberspace Developer's Kit, and on a solo project called Boppers. *In 1992 Autodesk's stock*

45. System X appears in the chapter "On Viral Sentences and Self-Replicating Structures," in Douglas Hofstadter, *Metamagical Themas,* Basic Books, New York 1985.

went down, and they laid off many of the people in the Advanced Techni-cal Division. But they let me keep the rights to my Boppers code, and I got it published as a package called Artificial Life Lab. *It's out of print now, but the Boppers program, the Boppers source code and the complete Artifi-cial Life Lab manual are available on my Web site.*

I really enjoyed my time at Autodesk, but I wasn't doing much writing while I was there. It was good to come back to the slower pace of academic life. By the end of my four years in the software industry pressure-cooker I felt like an undercover agent who has forgotten his real identity and has started to believe his cover story. Regarding my return, I had a mental image of a jeep whining up a hill along a wire fence at some Iron Curtain border. The jeep stops, two men raise up a tightly wrapped canvas sack and throw it over the fence, the jeep speeds off. The long canvas bag twitches, unfolds, and there I am, back in the land of literature.

Hacking Code

Hacking is like building a scale-model cathedral out of toothpicks, except that if one toothpick is out of place the whole cathedral will disappear. And then you have to feel around for the invisible cathedral, trying to figure out which toothpick is wrong. Debuggers make it a little easier, but not much, since a truly screwed-up cutting-edge program is entirely capable of screwing up the debugger as well, so that then it's like you're feeling around for the missing toothpick with a stroke-crippled claw-hand.

But, ah, the dark dream beauty of the hacker grind against the hidden wall that only you can see, the wall that only you wail at, you the programmer, with the brand new tools that you make up as you go along, your special new toothpick lathes and jigs and your realtime scrimshaw shaver, you alone in the dark with your wonderful tools.[46]

On a good day, I think of hacking as a tactile experience, like reaching into a tub of clay and kneading and forming the material into the shapes of my desires.

A computer program is a virtual machine that you build by hand. Hacking is like building a car by building all of the parts in the car individually. The good thing is that you have full control, the bad thing is that the process can take so much longer than you expect it to. Are you sure you feel like stamping out a triple-Z O-ring gasket? And synthesizing the plastic from which to make the gasket? The hacker says, "Yaar! Sounds like fun!"

Of course it does get easier as you build more and more. Often as not, you can re-use old pieces of code that you hacked for other projects. A hacker develops a nice virtual garage of "machine parts" that he or she can reuse. As a beginner, you start out using prefab parts

46. *The Hacker and the Ants*, p. 157.

made by others, but sooner or later, you're likely to grit on down to the lowest machine levels to see just how those parts really work.

To be a writer you need something you want to write about; to be a hacker you need something to hack about. You need to have an obsession, a vision that you want to turn into a novel, or into a virtual machine. It's going to take you so long to finish that you will need a fanatic's obsession to see a big project through. Essential in either case is the simple act of *not giving up*, of going back into it over and over again.

I think the most interesting things to hack are programs which turn the computer into a window to a different reality. Programs which express true computer nature. Chaos, fractals, artificial life, cellular automata, genetic algorithms, virtual reality, hyperspace – these are lovely areas that the computer can see into.

I once heard a hacker compare his computer to Leuwenhoek's microscope, so strong was his feeling that he was peering into new worlds. In an odd way, the most interesting worlds can be found when this new "microscope" looks at itself, perhaps entering a chaotic feedback loop that can close in on some strange attractor.

There are, of course, lame-butts who think hacking is about grubbing scraps of information about war and money. What a joke. Hacking is for delving into the hidden machinery of the universe.

The universe? Didn't I just say that the coolest hacks are in some sense centered on an investigation of what the computer itself can do? Yes, but the computer is a model of the universe.

Sometimes schizos think the universe is a computer – in a bad kind of way. Like that everything is gray and controlled, and distant numbers are being read off in a monotone, and somewhere a supervisor is tabulating your ever-more-incriminating list of sins.

But in reality, the universe is like a parallel computer, a computer with no master program, a computer filled with self-modifying code and autonomous processes – *a space of computation*, if you will. A good hack can capture this on a simple color monitor. The self-mirroring screen becomes an image of the world at large. *As above, so below.*

The correspondence between computers and reality changes the way you understand the world. If you know about fractals, then clouds and plants don't look the same. Once you've seen chaotic vibrations on a screen, you recognize them in the waving of tree branches and in the wandering of the media's eye. Cellular automata show how social movements can emerge from individual interactions. Virtual reality instructs you in the beauty of a swooping flock of birds. Artificial life and genetic algorithms show how intelligent processes can self-organize amidst brute thickets of random events. Hyperspace programs let you finally see into the fourth dimension and to recognize that kinky inside-out reversals are part and parcel of your potentially infinite brain.

Hacking teaches that the secret of the universe need not be so very complex, provided that the secret is set down in a big enough space of computation equipped with feedback and parallelism. Feedback means having a program take its last output as its new input. Parallelism means letting the same program run at many different sites. The universe's physics is the same program running in parallel everywhere, repeatedly updating itself on the basis of its current computation. Your own psychology is a parallel process endlessly revising itself.

Hacking is a yoga, but not an easy one. How do you start? Taking a course on one of the "object-oriented" programming languages Java or C++ is probably the best way to start; or you might independently buy a C++ compiler and work through the manual's examples.[47] And then find a problem that is your own, something you really want to see, whether it's chaos or whether it's just a tic-tac-toe program. And then start trying to make your vision come to life. The computer will help to show you the way, especially if you pay close attention to your error messages, use the help files – and read the fuckin' manual. It's a harsh yoga; it's a path to mastery.

> — *Appeared in Frauenfelder, Sinclair, Branwyn, eds.,*
> The Happy Mutant Handbook, *Riverhead Books, 1995.*

47. There's also a number of source code examples to be found on the "Classes" page of my Web site.

A New Golden Age of Calculation

Back in elementary school, we learned procedures, or *algorithms*, for doing arithmetic with pencil and paper. (Remember "borrowing"?) As adults, we tend to not use our painfully wetware-programmed arithmetic algorithms because most of us have ready access to machines that can do the algorithms by themselves. You might occasionally add two or three numbers, but if you have some multiplying or dividing to do, you're going to search your desk or your desktop for a calculator.

Mathematics doesn't stop at arithmetic. If you moved further on in school mathematics, you learned more and more algorithms; things like plotting the graph of a straight line, factoring a quadratic equation, and multiplying matrices; maybe you even got to calculus and learned about differentiation and integration. As adults, most of us never need to solve these kinds of problems at all, but if you did have to solve them on a regular basis, what would you do? Chances are you'd get hold of a computer running some kind of computer algebra program.

The oldest such package, called Macsyma, was born at MIT in the 1970s. An original impetus for the project was to help physicists work with formulae that were simply too long and complicated for the human mind − things like the hundred thousand algebraic terms in (you should pardon the expression) the Ricci tensor used in the space-time field equations of Einstein's General Theory of Relativity. By the 1980s, Macsyma had become potbound by its design's restriction to the use of only one megabyte of RAM. Though Macsyma was eventually rewritten, other new computer algebra systems arose to take most of its market. The new programs included Maple (also sold as MathCAD) and − the most expensive and ambitious of them all − Mathematica.

How exactly does one use Mathematica? The shrink wrap contains a seriously fat user's guide by Wolfram and a CD with a powerful graphically-interfaced program that runs on virtually every computer platform. You type in any mathematical expression you like

A 3-D Lissajous curve.
(Image generated by
Mathematica.)

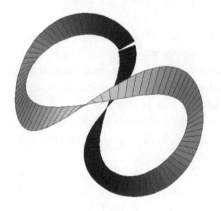

Baseball-stitch curve.
(Image generated by
Kaptau.)

and, depending on what you ask for, Mathematica might respond with an algebraically simplified version of the expression, a calculation of expression's numerical value, a huge database table of numbers, or a graph illustrating the expression's range of values. The graphs can be colored and three-dimensional. With Mathematica and an hour's practice, a college student can solve any and all the problems in a standard algebra or calculus book.

What makes Mathematica even more useful is that everything you enter in a given session becomes integrated into a single document, called a notebook. A Mathematica notebook can include text, graphics, and mathematical expressions. You can save it, and if you open it again, all of the formulae are "live" – you can highlight a formula, change some of its numbers or symbols, and see the related parts of the whole notebook change accordingly, just like a spreadsheet. A Mathematica notebook fully embodies a once-futuristic concept that the physicist Richard Feynman longingly called "magic paper" – an intelligent writing medium, in which you can ask the paper to do your calculations for you.

Thanks to Mathematica's notebook feature, you can watch what happens if the numbers in an equation change, or try out wild and crazy problems that ordinarily would be way too difficult to solve. Problem solving becomes a dynamic, experimental process.

The first time I saw Mathematica – this was Version 1, nine years ago – I used it to draw the kind of three-dimensional "Lissajous curves" you get if you had an object oscillating at different rates in each of three mutually perpendicular directions.

I'd seen two-dimensional versions in science museums and as drawing toys – a pencil or perhaps a slowly leaking container of sand hangs from a pendulum which is linked to a second, perpendicular pendulum. I'd always wondered what a three-dimensional Lissajous would look like. With Mathematica it was surprisingly easy. I typed a few lines of code and saw them.

Before long, I'd exhausted the novelty of 3-D Lissajous curves, so then I imagined a new kind of curve I called a kappatau curve. These curves are defined in terms of their curvature (kappa) and their tendency to twist like a helix (tau). To my mathematical satisfaction, I soon got wonderful gnarly curves, some of them looking like the stitching seam on a baseball, some looking like DNA. Yaaar!

But when I started wanting to look at lots and lots of my kappatau curves, and to set them to rotating in space, Mathematica became too slow. The very fact that it is a general-purpose system means that it is not going to be able to run some specific calculation over and over at the best speed. I ended up writing a stand-alone

Windows program to show my kappa-tau curves.[48] But I never would have gotten around to investigating these curves if I'd had to do it from scratch. Mathematica makes research easy – well, easier. That's one reason why it has sold a million copies to labs and offices around the world, at prices now around $1,000 a copy retail (but much cheaper for students).

The Mathematica software is the product of a company founded by Stephen Wolfram. Wolfram is a remarkable figure who helped invent the modern concept of complexity theory. Born in 1959, he got his Ph.D. in physics from Caltech at age 20 and won a MacArthur genius grant at the record-breaking age of 22. The first release of Mathematica came out in 1988, the second in 1991, and now, in 1996, Wolfram is out and about promoting Version 3.

What took so long? Wolfram offers two reasons. The first is what you'd expect to hear from any earnest software pitchman: Version 3 is *so much better* than Version 2 that developing it took a long time. The second reason is more intriguing. From 1991 to 1995, Wolfram was busy doing basic science research, concentrating on his book-in-progress, a monumental tome that may finally come out in 1999.

A secretive man, Wolfram is reluctant to give out details on his work, but asserts that, "I have in my sights a way to get a new fundamental theory for physics. My ideas are based on some insights into what it is that simple computer programs typically do." Intriguingly, he says that he wouldn't have gotten this far if he hadn't had Mathematica to help him. Wolfram has enough intellectual credibility that one is half-tempted to think of Isaac Newton, who invented calculus and then used his new tool to unravel the secrets of celestial mechanics. It would be nice.

When pressed for more information, Wolfram says something like the following: "For the last three hundred years, people have been trying to use mathematics to model the natural world, but this doesn't work well for things like biology and complex systems. Equations are human constructs, but maybe nature follows more

48. See the "Kappatau Space Curves" page of my Web site to download a free copy of either my program or of the related Mathematica notebooks.

general rules than that. Maybe we have to go beyond human mathematics and look at how general computing systems work."

Wolfram feels that there really *is* a simple fundamental theory and that we've been looking for it in the wrong way. He thinks that for the first time in about 50 years, somebody has a real chance to find it. Who? "I'm an ambitious guy, all right? My interest is to find the fundamental theory of the universe."

The ultimate prize would be a simple computer program type thing that is the universe – not a model of the universe but the thing itself. One of the famous, if minor, successes of the cellular automata programs which Wolfram studied in the 1980s is that they're good for modeling the intricate patterns which appear on the South Pacific seashells known as cone shells. But these cellular automata models are *just* models. Wolfram says, "If you can get a truly fundamental theory it's *not* a model anymore, it's the thing itself. It's *it.*"

Talking about how useful Mathematica is to him, Wolfram says, "I can do my science because I use Mathematica so much. I can start typing in complicated things and they work. I can experiment. Programs are always smarter than you are. You have an idea for some kind of computation and you think this will never do anything interesting, but then you experiment and some version of it *is* interesting. Experimenting is necessary. You have to look at lots of things. If it takes a minute to experiment, you'll do it. If it takes an hour you won't."

Comparing his work on Mathematica to his scientific research, Wolfram says that his skill lies in finding the essence. "When I do science, I'm asking what is the essence of what goes on in nature. In designing Mathematica I ask what is the common essence of what people do when they do math. Every person just has one real skill. My skill is finding the essence of mechanisms of things."

But would anyone outside a university ever need Magic Paper? One out of twelve copies of Mathematica are sold in Wall Street, where the software is used to build trading systems. And there are many engineering uses. When researching this review, I looked at a page of the Mathematica Web site with a lot of information about applications such as skateboards, shampoo, playground equipment, plastic surgery, and bicycle racetrack design – http://www.wolfram.com/discovery/

Dale Hughes and the engineering consultant Chris Nadovich

used Mathematica to design the bicycle velodrome track used in the 1996 Olympics. "Our design was in steel, which made the accuracy issue more demanding," says Nadovich. "In wood you can always cut things to fit as you nail the boards together. Here the whole thing was manufactured in another place, shipped to Atlanta, and yes, everything fit. Well, it was off a quarter of an inch after a quarter-kilometer because the thickness of the paint wasn't accounted for. The way they used to do bridges was to have two hundred guys calculating every piece. I just had me and a desktop PC and a couple of weeks. I couldn't use AutoCAD [the popular computer-aided design program] because you don't do 20,000 different parts by sitting there clicking and dragging. Mathematica has a tremendous amount of symbolic math capability. Initially I didn't even know how many sections the track would have. I just solved the problem symbolically. Mathematica produced coordinate lists that I could load into AutoCAD to render the blueprints."

Nadovich goes on to describe one of the formulae involved in the design. "We used a special curve called the Cornu spiral for the turns. It dates back to the 1800s when people were designing railroads for what they considered high speed. You can't just go from a straightaway with zero curvature into a circular arc with a non-zero curvature. What you need is to have the curvature increase linearly as you go into the turn and decrease linearly as you come out. The centrifugal force is a linear function of the curvature, so if you change curvature in a linear way it makes it easier for the riders to hold their position. They can concentrate on racing and not on steering."

How did the riders like it? "They hated it! They didn't like how the track felt. They said it was slow, it was bumpy, it was an ugly color, and they didn't like the texture. Everybody was afraid of it. It was very depressing. But the riders that won *did* like it. In fact the track really was fast. They set two world records and twenty-one Olympic records on it. It felt different because it was a different material, most tracks are wood or concrete, just banked concrete roads."

The most devoted user of a computer algebra program I know is Bill Gosper, an old-time hacker who was involved with the original Macsyma project. In fact he still uses Macsyma; not the modernized retail Windows version, but massively customized, or one might say Gosperized, version of the program that lives on a file-cabinet-sized old Symbolics computer in his basement.

Going to visit Gosper has been a touchstone experience for me ever since moving to Silicon Valley eleven years ago. I find him grayer than before, sitting in a dusty, autumnal room of antique beige plastic artifacts. An ellipsoidal electric pencil sharpener. A stack of Symbolics computer monitors. Danish Modern chairs.

Gosper uses Macsyma to find weird algebraic equations. In high school algebra many of us may learned a few simple algebraic identities like

$$(x + y)^2 = x^2 + 2xy + y^2.$$

Gosper interests himself in identities like this, only much gnarlier. The all-time champion of gnarly identities was the legendary Indian mathematician Sri Ramanujan. Gosper, who speaks in arcane hacker language, modestly rates the gnarliness of his own equations in milliRamanujans, and he gets his machine to show me one of his best, which he rates at a full 800 milliRamanunjans.

The left side of Gosper's gnarly identity is a product of terms involving the geometrical constant pi divided by the trigonometric arctangent function. The right side of the identity is the pi^{th} root of 4. Not the *cube* root, mind you, the pi^{th} root. "Genius does what it must," says Gosper of Ramanujan, "Talent does what it can. When I'm doing this stuff, I find something surprising and then try to make it more surprising. I go for sensationalism."

He begins rapidly keyboarding so as to show me more wonders, talking all the while. He is an artist, a symbolic acrobat without a care in the world for real world applications.

"The computer algebra field supports itself on one percent of what it can do. A key thing about computer algebra is that you have infinite precision. No roundoff. I'll invert the same matrix twice and show how limited precision can screw it. Let's set mumble to mumble." He uses "mumble" as an ordinary word, as shorthand for expressions too complicated or dull to actually say. "Now we invert it. Oh my God, how long is this going to take. Twenty seconds, thirty seconds, whew. I'm worried if I've even got a patch in here to make this feasible. We can check while this is running. Says here it should work. This is a little discouraging. Christ on a crutch. Ah here it is, it's done. Now we'll set mumble and do it again. Ooh! It's not converging. What the hell's going on? 572??!!! It's supposed to be 570! God help us. No, it's still batshit. No no no it *is* 572. Oh, this should be a Taylor series, right? I have to stun it, I have to neutralize it. Now we can crank up the value. Now this is the *right* answer." Gosper pauses and gives me a sly smile. "Now let's see if I can earn my nerd merit badge." "How?" "By typing in this number, which is the nineteen digits of two to the sixty-fourth power."

Why does Gosper still use Macsyma instead of switching to Mathematica? That's a little like asking why Steve Jobs doesn't use Microsoft Windows. Gosper wrote a lot of the Macsyma code and it's what he's used to. He knows it inside out. If he were to switch to Mathematica, he'd be at the mercy of design decisions made by Wolfram's team, and not all of these decisions are things Gosper would agree with. If you ask around in the symbolic mathematics community, you can find a real diversity of opinions about the best way to proceed.

Seeking further enlightenment, I talk to Bruce Smith, a programmer who's done some third-party work for Wolfram Research. He talks about plans to extend the language you use to enter problems into the Mathematica. The dream would be to evolve a mathematical language in which one can readily write down expressions for everyday phenomena – including not only physics, but also biology and sociology. "Having an expression for something is a powerful concept that will become more popular in programming," says Smith. "It's not a coincidence that the word 'expression' is related to expressiveness." Smith recalls a comment he heard in a 1970s talk by John Walker, one of the original developers of Auto-CAD. Speaking about the future of computer-aided design, Walker said, "In the future, every manufactured object in the world will be modeled in a computer." Smith feels that, in thinking about the future of the Mathematica language, we might extend this: "For every object we think about, we will want an expression for it so that a computer can think about it with us."

Might there some day be a futuristic super programming language with expressions like Live, Think, Truth and Beauty? Realistically, it seems doubtful that anyone will ever take a comfortable human-scale problem like whom to date or where to go to lunch and say "let us calculate." As G. K. Chesterton once put it, "Man knows that there are in the soul tints more bewildering, more numberless, and more nameless than the colors of an autumn forest."

But within the domain of readily scientifically quantifiable problems, symbolic mathematics works great and is well worth the trouble of dealing with computers. The entire range of what is considered to be a reasonable solution to a problem is something that will expand greatly. Instead of just putting a vague bend where your track goes into a turn, you put in a Cornu spiral. Instead of guessing how a plastic-surgery patient's appearance is going to change, you simulate the tectonics of the facial landscape. Instead of making dozens of cardboard models of your jungle-gym, you build it from equations in virtual reality.

How will all this affect the future of mathematics? The important thing about mathematics is that it acts as a concise, almost hieroglyphic, language for describing forms. The Mathematica program is an immense help for the tedious rote-work involved in manipulating math's hieroglyphs and converting them into visual images. Mathematica makes math more valuable than ever – for it takes a well-trained mathematical mind to know which kind of "hieroglyph" to use to model some particular situation. And it takes a mathematical genius to come up with a really good new hieroglyph.

New mathematics is developed as a result of a feedback loop involving theory and experiment. The great thing about programs like Mathematica is how much they accelerate the process. Thanks to computers, mathematics is at the dawn of a new golden age.

— Unpublished. Written fall, 1997.

Mr. Nanotechnology

The French word for dwarf is *nain*. A nanometer is one billionth of a meter, which is just a bit larger than the diameter of your average atom. Nanotechnology envisions doing things with individual atoms, one at a time. "You done building that roast beef out of dirt yet, Bob?" "Ten molecules down, ten to the twenty-sixth power to go."

Of course nature does build cows out of dirt, with some light, water and grass along the way, so maybe we *can* learn how to do it. The dream of nanotechnology is to get lots and lots of little machines to build materials for us.

Present day nanotechnology comes in two flavors: dry and wet. *Dry nanotechnology* is about tiny rods and gears made out of diamond whiskers and the like. The recent discovery that icosahedron-shaped "buckyballs" of carbon can be found in ordinary soot is a big boost for dry nanotechnology. Wonderfully intricate images, some resembling automobile transmissions, have been cranked out by Ralph Merkle of the computational nanotechnology project at Xerox's Palo Alto Research Center (the legendary "PARC" where Saint Englebart invented windows and the mouse).

No dry nanotechnologist has yet been able to assemble the kind of three-dimensional structures that Merkle and others envision. But there is a device known as an STM (for "Scanning Tunneling Microscope) which allows nanohackers to see, pick up, and move around individual atoms on a surface. Quite recently, Don Eigler and a group of at IBM's Almaden Research Lab managed to use an STM to draw things. First they drew a little man with carbon monoxide molecules on platinum, and then they wrote "IBM" in xenon atoms on nickel. The next big effort will be to assemble a free-standing three-dimensional structure atom-by-atom – how about a six hundred sixty-six-atom model of Danny DeVito?

An ultimate goal of dry nanotechnology is the creation of an "assembler," a fantastic little nanomachine that can turn out more nanomachines – including copies of itself (an onanistic process known as "self-replication"). You might set an assembler to work making assemblers for awhile, and then somehow signal the godzillion assemblers that now they should switch over to making, say, incredibly strong "club sandwiches" of alternating single-atom sheets of two kinds of metal. The "gray goo" problem crops up here. What if, like the brooms in the tale of the Sorcerer's Apprentice, the assemblers can't be turned off? What if they turn everything they can get their nasty little pincers on into more assemblers? The whole planet could end up as a glistering sludge of horny little can-openers. But the nanonauts assure us this won't happen; it is perhaps comforting that the main nanotechnology group is known as the Foresight Institute.

Wet nanotechnology proposes that instead of trying to build our own tiny machines, we use a "machine" that nature has already designed: the cellular reproduction apparatus of DNA, RNA, enzymes, and proteins. It's like finding a way to tell one of your DNA strands something like, "Oh, next time you copy yourself, could you whip up a few million copies of this particular tryptamine molecule for me as well?" It's all in how you say it, and Gerald Joyce and others at the Scripps Institute are making some slow progress in guiding the "machines" of biological reproduction. But there's still major obstacles in convincing DNA to do technological things like putting together copper yttrium sandwiches. "No, man, I wanna *fuck!*"

What it comes down to is that dry nanotechnology is about machines that we can design but can't yet build, and wet technology is about machines that we can build but can't yet design.

The field of nanotechnology was more or less invented by one man: Eric Drexler, who designed his own Ph.D. curriculum in nanotechnology while at MIT. Drexler's 1986 book *Engines of Creation* was something of a popular science best-seller. This year he published a second popular book, *Unbounding the Future*, and a highly technical work called *Nanosystems: Molecular Machinery, Manufacturing, and Computation*.

Drexler has the high forehead and the hunched shoulders of a Hollywood mad scientist, but his personality is quite mild and patient. A few years ago, many people were ready to write off nanotechnology as a playground for nuts and idle dreamers. It is thanks to Drexler's calm, nearly Vulcan, logicalness that the field continues to grow and evolve.

Our interview was taped at the First General Conference on Nanotechnology, which was held at the Palo Alto Holiday Inn in November, 1991. Despite the name, this wasn't really the *first* "First Nanotechnology Conference," as *that* one took place in 1989. But this was the first First Nanotechnology Conference open to the public, for fifty to a hundred dollars per day, and the public packed the lecture rooms to the rafters.

Rudy Rucker: Eric, what would be in your mind a benchmark, like something specific happening, where it started to look like nanotechnology was really taking off?

Eric Drexler: Well, if you'd asked me that in 1986 when *Engines of Creation* came out, I would have said that a couple of important benchmarks are the first successful design of a protein molecule from scratch – that happened in 1988 – and another one would be the precise placement of atoms by some mechanical means. We saw that coming out of Don Eigler's group. At present I would say that the next major milestone that I would expect is the ability to position reactive, organic molecules so that they can be used as building blocks to make some stable three-dimensional structure at room temperature.

RR: When people like to think of the fun dreams of things that could happen with nanotechnology, what are a couple of your favorite ones?

ED: I've mostly been thinking lately about efficient ways of transforming molecules into other molecules and making high density energy storage systems. But if you imagine the range of things that can be done in an era where you have a billion times as much computer power available, which would presumably include virtual reality applications, that's one large class of applications.

RR: I notice that you're talking on nanotechnology and space tomorrow. Can you give me a brief preview of your ideas there?

ED: The central problem in opening the space frontier has been transportation. How do you get into space economically, safely, routinely? And that's largely a question of what you can build. With high strength-to-weight ratio materials of the kind that can be made by molecular manufacturing, calculations indicate that you can make a four-passenger single-staged orbit vehicle with a lift-off weight that's about equivalent to a heavy station wagon, and where the dry weight of the vehicle is sixty kilograms.

RR: So you would be using nanotechnology to make the material of the thing so thin and strong?

ED: Diamond fiber composites. Also, much better solar electric propulsion systems.

RR: I've noticed people seem to approach nanotechnology with a lot of humor. It's almost like people are nervous. They can't decide if it's fantasy or if it's real. For you it's real – you think it's going to happen?

ED: It's hard for me to imagine a future in which it doesn't happen, because there are so many ways of doing the job and so many reasons to proceed, and so many countries and companies that have reason to try.

RR: Could you make some comments about the notorious gray goo question?

ED: In *Engines of Creation* I over-emphasized the problem of someone making a self-replicating machine that could run wild. That's a technical possibility and something we very much need to avoid, but I think it's one of the smaller problems overall, because there's very little incentive for someone to do it; it's difficult to do; and there are so many other ways in which the technology could be abused where there's a more obvious motive. For example, the use of molecular manufacturing to produce high performance weapon systems which could be more directly used to help with goals that we've seen people pursuing.

RR: I've heard people talk about injecting nanomachines into their blood and having it clean out their arteries. That's always struck me as the last thing I would do. Having worked in the computer business and seen the impossibility of ever completely debugging a program, I can't imagine shooting myself up with machines that had been designed by hackers on a deadline.

ED: In terms of the sequence of developments that one would expect to see I think it *is* one of the last things that you'd expect to see.

—*Appeared in* Mondo 2000, *Spring, 1992.*

Fab! Inside Chip Fabrication Plants

I fell in love with the Silicon Valley word "fab" the first time I heard it. This short, moderne word means "chip fabrication plant." A manager might, for instance, say "What kind of outs are we getting from the fab?" In the '50s and '60s, of course, fab was short for "fabulous," as in the detergent Fab, or as in the lines in "Bob Dylan's 115th Dream" that go: "I ran right outside and I hopped inside a cab. I went out the other door; this Englishman said fab." Gear! Kicky!

After exceedingly many phone calls, I managed to get to go inside two fabs in Silicon Valley, one belonging to the chip-giant Intel, and the other to Intel's small challenger, AMD (Advanced Micro Devices). AMD recently won a court battle with Intel over the right to produce its own "K6" version of the popular 486 processor chips for DOS and *Windows*-based personal computers. AMD is very much a "we try harder" company, and they were the first to let me into their fab – a quarter-billion-dollar building in Sunnyvale called the Submicron Development Center.

A micron is a unit of measurement equal to one millionth of a meter. A typical human hair might be a hundred microns wide. The scale of chips is discussed in terms of the size of the smallest features of the patterns on the chip. Today's chips use features about half a micron in size, hence they are said to be using *submicron* designs.

AMD's Submicron Development Center was originally intended to be purely a research facility, but the demand for the AMD 486 chips is such that the facility is now also being used for commercial production. It turns out to be crowded and a bit hellish in the AMD fab, which feels to be about the size of a wide office-building corridor plus maybe six offices on either side.

Something I hadn't initially realized is that being a fab worker is like being any other kind of assembly-line worker. It's a rigorous blue-collar job. Most of the workers are Asian or Hispanic. The AMD fab is open twenty-four hours a day, every day of the year except Christmas – and in the Intel fab they work on Christmas too. The workers pull twelve-hour shifts, with three shifts one week and four shifts the next, for an average of forty-one hours a week. Although some of the fab workers are highly paid engineers, starting pay for a simple technician is around $24,000 a year, which comes to something like $12 an hour.

What actually goes on in a fab? A fab buys blank silicon wafers and draws complicated patterns on them. This changes a wafer's value from $200 to $30,000 or more. It's almost like printing money. The catch is that each of the many machines used in a fab costs over a million dollars. And buying machines for your fab is kind of complicated, although the Sematech consortium is seeking to make this easier.

When a fab finishes a wafer, the wafer is shipped to another plant where the wafer is sawed up into chips and the chips are put into the familiar plastic cases with wires coming out. These secondary plants are mostly in southeast Asia – the Silicon Valley fabs are solely concerned with printing the chips onto the wafers. To avoid dust, the wafers are shipped in vacuum-sealed bags.

The essence of the environment inside a fab is that this is a place for chips and not for people. People are dirty. Their bodies flake and crumble, sending off showers of dust. One dust particle can ruin a chip, for instance by shorting out the separation between two nearby submicron circuit lines.

In the current prehistoric state of robotics, there is no hope of fully automating a fab, especially given the fact that the process technology is subject to being changed over and over. To deal with having dirty people in there, the fab must be maintained as a clean room.

The cleanliness of a room is specified in terms of the number of particles larger than one micron that can be found in a cubic foot of air. An average non-smoking restaurant might have a few hundred thousand of such particles per cubic foot. In a surgical operating theater, the level is brought down to about twenty thousand. In the outer hallways of a fab building, the level is ten thousand, while in the wafer-handling areas of the fab itself, the level is brought down to one individual particle per cubic foot. How? At AMD the procedure went like this.

My guide is Dan Holiga, a member of the AMD Corporate

Rudy in the AMD gowning
room. (Photo by Dan Holiga.)

Training division, responsible for instructing new workers on clean
room procedures and for arranging science courses for them at local
colleges. Dan leads me into the pregowning room. The floor inside
the door is covered with sticky adhesive. I sit down on a bench and
put some blue booties over my shoes so as not to track dirt into the
locker room. The woman behind the counter can't find Dan's special
fab badge, so she gives him a visitor badge like mine. We select
building suits in our sizes: two-piece suits like tight-cuffed blue
pajamas. The woman gives us each some white plastic shoes like
bowling shoes.

   In the pregowning room, we stash our street-clothes in the lock-
ers and put on the blue building suits and the white plastic shoes.
We wash our hands and put on hair nets and safety glasses. Dan has
brought a camera with him. We walk through a corridor into the
outer hallway of the fab building. This is the ten thousand particles-
per-cubic-foot zone, and the air feels cleaner than any I've breathed

in a long time. My allergies are gone; the odorless air flows smoothly into my lungs.

We pass a break room where some of the fab workers are having non-dusty snacks like apple juice and yogurt. Then we go into a second locker room. I'd thought we were already dressed for the fab, but that was just the start. The second locker room is the gowning room proper.

Here we put on latex gloves. Then we wipe off our safety glasses and our visitor badges and Dan's camera — wipe everything three times with lint-free alcohol-soaked cloths. We put on white hoods and "bunny suit" overalls made of Fibrotek, which is a sandwich of nylon and Teflon. We pull "fab booties" over our shoes and we put on face masks. We pull vinyl gloves over our latex gloves. This is starting to feel a teensy bit…obsessive. I'm reminded of the "environmentally ill" people you see in Berkeley natural food stores, shopping while wearing gas masks and elbow-length gloves. They'd love it here in the gowning room. But, I remind myself, this isn't about obsession here, this is about objective scientific fact: getting down to one micron-sized particle of dirt per cubic foot of air!

Now Dan leads me through the air shower: a corridor lined with air-nozzles blasting away. We hold up our hands and turn around, letting the air wash us all over. The invisible particles fall to the floor, where they are sucked away. In the air shower and in the fab, the floors are coarse grates, and the ceilings are filled with fans. There is a constant flow of air from above to below, with any showers of filthy human particles being sucked out through the floor grates. The air in a fab is completely changed ten times a minute.

I step out of the air shower and, fully purified, I step into the fab. As the Bible says, "I was glad when they said unto me, let us go into the house of the Lord." I am in the heart of the temple to the God-machine of Silicon Valley. The lights are yellow to avoid clouding the photo-resist emulsions; this gives the fab a strange, underworld feeling. The rushing air streams down past me from ceiling to floor. Other white-garbed figures move about down the corridor; all of us are dressed exactly the same.

On the sides of the corridor are metal racks holding boxes or "boats" of wafers waiting for the next stage of their processing. The

racks have wires instead of shelves – there are in fact no flat horizontal surfaces at all in a fab, as such surfaces collect dust and interfere with the air flow.

The only hint of human contamination is the meaty smell of my
breath, bounced back to me by the white fabric face mask I'm wearing. I wish I could tear off the mask and breathe the clean pure air of
the chips. But then I would exhale, and the wafers wouldn't like that
– detectors would notice the increased number of particles-per-
cubic-foot, and lights would flash.

The layout of a fab is a single main corridor with bays on either
side. To keep the bays clean and uncluttered, most of their machines
are set so that the faces of the machines are flush to the bay walls,
with the bodies of the machines sticking out into sealed-off corridors called chases. Like people, machines have bodies whose exigen-
cies are not fully tidy. The chases are clean only to a ten particles per
cubic foot level, as opposed to the bays and the main fab corridor,
which are kept at the one particle-level.

As we move down the main corridor to start our tour, people recognize Dan and come over to pat him on the back or on the arm.
Dan theorizes that in the clean room, people can't see each other's
faces, so they tend to fill in non-verbal communication by touching
each other. Another factor could be that, given that everyone is
clean, there is no fear of getting yourself dirty through human contact. Or maybe it's just that you have less inhibitions towards someone who is dressed exactly like you. In any case, the fab workers
seem to have a strong team spirit and sense of camaraderie. They're
like happy termites in a colony.

The craft of getting a hundred 486 or Pentium chips onto a silicon wafer involves laying down about twenty layers of information.
It's a little like printing a silk-screen reproduction with twenty different colors of ink. At each step a fresh layer of silicon dioxide is
baked on, parts of the new layer are etched away, and metals or trace
elements are added to the exposed areas.

As well as having to be positioned to an accuracy of a tenth of a
micron or better, the successive layers need to have a very specific
thickness. Rather than being measured in microns, the thickness of
the layers are best measured in *nanometers*, or billionths of a meter.

Each layer is about ten nanometers thick. It's all about fiddling with little details, to a mind-boggling degree.

The process takes as long as twelve weeks for a completed wafer's worth of chips. It's not so much a linear assembly line as it is a loop. Over and over, the wafers are baked, printed, etched and doped. At AMD, workers carry the boats of wafers up and down the corridor; while at Intel's plant there is a miniature overhead monorail on which the boats move about automatically, like gondolas in a scale model of an amusement park ride.

At AMD, I visit the etching bay first. There are a series of sinks filled with different kinds of acid piped up from tanks located on the story below the fab. In the bad old days, you could recognize fab workers by the scars on their neck from splashes of acid, but now they have a small industrial robot arm to dip the chips. I'm happy to see the arm; this confirms my science fictional notion that fabs will ultimately be places where robots reproduce themselves: robot obstetric wards.

The acid baths are for removing the photo-resist masks after the etching itself is done. The etching is typically done "dry" – that is, a fine dust of ions is whipped into a frenzy with powerful radio frequency signals to make a submicron sandblaster. The idea is to dig out parts of the chip so that metal conductors and metal-doped semiconductors can be patterned in to make up the wires and transistors of the integrated circuit which the chip is to become.

The real heart of a fab is the photolithography bay. Here the gel called photo-resist is sprayed onto the wafers, and then the wafers go into a stepper, which is the machine that projects the circuit diagrams onto the wafer's chips.

The projector is called a stepper because it projects the same image a hundred or so times onto each wafer, moving the wafer in steps to receive each successive image. Steppers are the most expensive devices in a fab. The images projected by the steppers are found on transparencies called reticles. Reticles are based on circuit diagrams created by engineers using computer drafting techniques.

Once a wafer gets out of the stepper, a developer chemical removes the photo-resist that was exposed to light, leaving masks shaped like the dark regions of the reticle. This is a very efficient process, because although a reticle may have thousands of features on it, projecting its image onto the wafer puts all those features there at once.

The better the stepper, the smaller the images it can make. Smaller chips run faster, use less power and can be produced in larger batches – more chips per wafer. In order to handle very small feature sizes, steppers need to use light with very short wavelengths – the current ones use deep ultraviolet light, and to get much smaller, the steppers will have to start using X-rays.

The light is mellow yellow in the bay with the steppers, and there are the most people here. This is the heart of the temple. Some of the workers are debugging a problem with one of the machines that sprays on the photo-resist; one of them is lying on the grated floor with a laptop computer. It strikes me that in this world, the floors are not dirty.

There are a couple of men with an electron microscope looking at wafers. One of them is holding a handful of wafers, some of them cracked. "I guess those ones are no good?" I ask. The man looks at me oddly and finally grunts, "Yeah." Seeing only my visitor badge and not my expression, he thinks I'm an executive being sarcastic, but Don explains that I'm a journalist. The guy warms up then and has his co-worker show me some wafers under the electron microscope. There's a nice clear image on a TV screen next to the microscope. It shows something like your usual image of a chip, but with lots of parts missing. This is just one or two layers' worth.

"These things," the man with the microscope says, pointing to some fat short rectangles, "we call these the hot-dog buns. And these other things," he points to some longer thinner rectangles overlaid onto the fat short ones, "we call these the hot-dogs. We check if the hot-dogs are on the buns."

We peek into a few more bays. One especially cute little industrial robot catches my eye. It's jerky and articulated like a shore-feeding bird, folding its tail and pecking wafers out of their cartridges to slide them into some machine's maw. It reminds me of the Disney cartoon of *Alice in Wonderland*, where Alice is lost in the woods near the Cheshire cat and a little bird that looks like a pencil with two legs comes running up to her.

Dan takes some pictures of me, and then we go out into the

gowning room to take off our face masks, gloves, and Fibrotek suits. It feels very good to get out of the suit, I was getting hot. Also it's great to stop breathing my own breath. It would be tough to spend twelve hours at a time in a fab. And for $24,000 a year! As a Communist friend used to tell me in grad-school: the secret of capitalism is that the less they pay you, the harder you have to work.

Now we're in our building suits again, and Dan wants to show me the sub fab, which fills the whole story below the fab. As we go out into the building hall, a security guard in a clean room suit runs up to us and asks our names. He writes our names on his glove; he's too excited to get the spelling right. He doesn't recognize Dan, and we're both wearing visitor tags and Dan is carrying a camera. Uh oh. While the guard hurries off to make a report, Dan hustles me down the stairs to the sub fab.

The sub fab is a techno dream. It holds all the machinery that supports the machines of the fab. The electrical generators are here, the plumbing, the tanks of acids, the filtering systems, the vacuum lines, the particle monitoring equipment – miles of wires and pipes and cables in an immaculate ten thousand-particle-per-cubic-foot concrete room. This is the ultimate mad scientist's lab. I'm enthralled.

Now here comes the clean room security guard again. "You have to come with me." Dan wants to take some pictures first. "You have to come right away." The clean room guard leads us out into a hall off the sub fab. Three unsmiling uniformed guards are there. Dan explains about his lost fab badge; they phone the pregowning room to go into Dan's locker and check out his ID; finally they decide it's okay and we're back on our way.

"They thought maybe we were from Intel," Dan says. "Someone who doesn't know me saw us taking pictures in the clean room."

When I'm finally out in the dirty real world again, I'm grateful and glad. It feels as if I've been in the underworld, a world where people are totally out of place. I don't feel like turning on a computer again for several days. But I'm happy to have seen the central mystery, to have penetrated to the heart of the temple of the computing machine.

Two weeks later, Intel finally comes through with a fab tour for me as well. My guide here is Howard High, of Intel Corporate Communications. The fab layout is quite similar to AMD's although

Intel's fab is much bigger – perhaps the size of a football field, and with high fifteen-foot ceilings to accommodate the wafer-boat carrying monorails overhead.

The vibes in the Intel fab seem more relaxed than at AMD. Intel is ahead, and AMD is trying to catch up. At Intel, for instance, I don't have to exchange my clothes for a building suit, I'm allowed to just put the clean room bunny suit on over my clothes. Because of dust, I wasn't allowed to use any paper on my AMD tour, but Intel issues me a spiral notebook of lint-free paper.

The more I learned about the fabs, the more I was amazed that they *work*. The intricacy of the system is reminiscent of the complexity of a biological process like photosynthesis. Nobody could have designed one of today's fabs from scratch – these are giant industrial processes that have evolved, a step at a time, from earlier, simpler versions. There is a very real sense in which these processes are the synthetic biology in which planet Earth's next great species may arise.

> — *Appeared as "Robot Obstetric Wards: Inside Chip Fabrication Plants," in* Wired, *November 1994.*

It's quite difficult for even a journalist to get a fab tour – at Intel they told me the last person they'd let in had been the vice-premier of China – but Intel does have a very informative museum in the same building as their fab. This is in the main Intel building at 2200 Mission College Boulevard off Montague expressway directly off Route 101 in Santa Clara near San Jose. The museum is open to the public from 8-5 Monday through Friday, and can be reached at (408)765-0503. Some of the same kinds of exhibits are visible in the new San Jose technology museum called TheTech, see http://www.thetech.org.

Goodbye Big Bang

Andrei Linde is a Moscow physicist who became a Stanford University physics professor in 1990. He lives there with his wife Renata Kallosh (also a Stanford physics professor, specializing in superstrings and supergravity), and his two sons Dmitri and Alex. He began formulating theories of the "self-reproducing chaotic inflationary universe" in 1983 as an improvement on the Big Bang model. He uses computer simulations for a lot of his research, and has recently suggested that your universe might be the result of a physicist-hacker's experiment.

I went to interview him at his home for *Wired* magazine in the spring of 1995. Linde is an attractive, tidily dressed man, younger and more athletic-looking than I'd expected. He speaks with a thick Russian accent, and with a colorfully inverted syntax. His verbatim answers were sometimes bit cryptic – especially for non-physicists – so I padded a few of them a bit, mostly using materials from his published papers.[49]

RR: By now, most of us have gotten quite comfortable with the big bang model of the universe; the notion that the universe was born as a tiny energy-filled ball of space some billions of years ago, and that this ball of space has been expanding ever since. What's wrong with this notion?

AL: There are a number of problems with the big bang theory; let me mention two that are of a physical nature and two that are of a philosophical nature.

If you work out the physical equations governing the big bang, they predict that a big bang universe will in fact be very small, even though we can see that our universe is large. One way to gauge the size of a universe is to talk about how many elementary particles it

---

49. See, for instance, Andrei Linde, "The Self-Reproducing Inflationary Universe," *Scientific American*, November 1994, pp. 48-55.

has in it – how many electrons, protons, neutrons, and so on. When I look out of my window, the matter I see is made up of perhaps ten-to-the-eighty-eighth elementary particles, but a typical theoretical big bang model has only about ten elementary particles in it! This is perhaps the most serious problem with the big bang model. It gives a false prediction about the size of the universe. For a number of years, this mathematical flaw in the big bang theory was not yet noticed.

A second physical problem with the big bang is that even if a big bang universe is of the proper size, there is no explanation of why the different regions of the universe resemble each other. In a big bang model, it could just as easily have happened that most of the matter ends up, say, in one half of the sky, but we can observe that in our universe, the density of distant galaxies is the same in every direction.

One of the philosophical problems with the big bang is this: What came before the big bang? How did everything appear from nothing?

Another somewhat philosophical problem with the big bang asks: Why does it happen that our universe worked out to be just the way it is; why, for instance, do we have three dimensions of space and one dimension of time?

The big bang theory offers no satisfactory answers to these questions, but we can begin to resolve the puzzles in the context of the theory of the self-reproducing, inflationary universe.

RR: What is the inflationary universe?

AL: There have been several versions of this theory. The first was proposed by the Soviet physicist Alexei Starobinsky, but it was rather complicated. Then a much simpler one was put forward by the physicist Alan Guth of MIT; we call his model "old inflation" now. Guth took the big bang model and added the idea that in the beginning the universe expanded very rapidly; faster even than the speed of light.

By having the universe expand so rapidly, you solve the problem of why it is so big, and you also solve the problem of why all the regions of the universe we presently can see resemble each other. The idea is that, thanks to inflation, the whole visible part of the universe was inflated from some very small and homogeneous region, and this is why we see large-scale similarities.

It turned out that Guth's "old inflation" had theoretical difficulties. I invented a "new inflation" theory which worked so-so, and then I realized that we could have inflation without the assumption that the universe began in a hot and dense state. I dropped the idea of the big bang, but kept the idea of inflation. In my model, inflation can start anywhere. This concept is called "chaotic inflation."

RR: What causes the inflation?

AL: There are things called "scalar fields." These fields fill the universe, and show their presence by affecting the properties of elementary particles. You don't notice a constant scalar field, any more than you notice a constant air pressure or a constant electric charge. When there are differences in air pressure, you get wind; when there are differences in electric charge, you get sparks; and when there are differences in the scalar field, you get an expansion of space.

Quantum mechanics implies that the scalar fields undergo unpredictable fluctuations. If there is a place where one particular scalar field happens to be larger, then here the universe will expand with a much larger speed, which makes so much space that we can safely live there.

RR: How big is the inflationary universe?

AL: The fluctuations which increase the speed of inflation can happen over and over. They make the universe self-reproducing; it reproduces itself in all its forms.

The standard big bang theory was a theory of a homogeneous universe, looking like one single bubble. But if we take into account quantum effects, the self-reproducing inflationary universe is a bubble producing new bubbles producing new bubbles.

This kind of repeatedly branching pattern is what mathematicians call a fractal. A fractal pattern is characterized by the property that the small bits of the pattern resemble the whole pattern. An oak tree, for example, is like a fractal in that a single branch of an oak resembles a scaled-down model of the entire tree. Another example of a fractal is a mountain range. If you chop off the top of a mountain and look at it closely, it resembles the whole mountain range; and a single rock on the mountain resembles a whole mountain in itself.

So we think of the self-reproducing inflationary universe as a fractal. The big bang is good as a description of each particular bubble but it cannot describe the growing fractal. There is no real reason for the fractal universe to stop growing; indeed, it is likely to keep growing and budding off new regions forever.

RR: How can I visualize the fractal self-reproducing inflationary universe?

AL: There are two kinds of pictures I like to use. In one I draw something that looks like lots of separate bubbles connected to each other where they touch. It looks a little like the linked flotation bladders on seaweed.

In the other kind of picture I use – and I've done several computer simulations of this image – I think of space as initially being like a flat sheet. Then I add a randomly fluctuating scalar field, and I represent the regions where the scalar field has a low value by valleys, and I represent the regions where the scalar field is large by peaks.

The peaks are the places where inflation takes place; at these places the universe will rapidly expand. I can't show the inflation in my picture, but I can represent it by putting new, secondary peaks on top of the first peaks, third-level peaks on top of those peaks, and so on. It is like a mountain range.

What is a little hard to grasp is that the two pictures represent the same thing. The peaks in the one image correspond to the bubbles in the other image. A peak that rises on top of a peak is like a bubble that swells out from the side of a bubble.

RR: Can we go to the other bubbles of our fractal universe?

AL: Far in the future, our sky will start looking a lot different, as our stars start dying. And then we will see into the different parts of universe, some parts with different laws of physics.

Can we use the energy in our bubble which has cooled off, can we fly to the other tips of the fractal, can we go there and live comfortably? The theory of such cosmic flights suggests that even if you travel at the speed of light, you lose so much time that when you get to another part of the universe, it will already be cold and empty there.

RR: You say that some of the different bubble-universes have different laws of physics – how does that work?

AL: We've talked about one scalar field that is responsible for the universe's expansion. It seems that there may also be a second scalar field which makes different kinds of physics in different regions of the universe. There is one overall law of physics for the whole universe, but the scalar fields make for different realizations of this law. It is like water with many different phases. For those who live in water it is very essential that the water be a liquid and not a solid or a gas.

RR: What if I could somehow fly up to the edge of a region of the universe with different physics? How would it look?

AL: Between the different regions of the universe, there are boundaries called "domain walls." There is a tendency of the domain walls to straighten up, and also to move one way or the other with a speed approaching the speed of light.

So first of all it would be very difficult for you to reach a domain wall if it is moving away from you. And if it is moving towards you, it will be very difficult to run from it. In fact, if a wall moves towards you at the speed of light, then you first see it only at the moment it hits you.

But we don't need to worry too much; the typical estimates in these theories give you a distance from us to this next domain wall which is much much greater than ten billion light years, so we may live for now.

RR: Might we say that the regions with different physics are competing with each other?

AL: I think about the moving boundaries of the regions as perhaps like a Darwinian fitness. Should we discriminate and say those with greater volume are winners? There is a lot of place for losers as well, everything which can exist tends to have room for its existence in the self-reproducing inflationary universe. We can think of a Darwinian process without hate and killing, a process that produces all possible species.

RR: How did the whole process begin?

AL: Maybe the universe didn't have a beginning. There are some philosophical problems with the idea of the universe having a beginning. When the universe was just created, then where were the laws of physics written? Where were the laws of physics written if there was no space and no time to write them? Maybe the universe was created without obeying any laws, but then I don't understand. Well, maybe the laws and the universe came into existence simultaneously? Quantum mechanics might say our universe together with its physical laws appeared as a quantum fluctuation, but then where were the laws of quantum mechanics written before creation?

RR: In one of your papers you talk about relating the nature of our consciousness to our universe. What do you mean?

AL: For me, the investigation of the universe is mainly a tool for understanding ourselves. The universe is our cosmic home. You look around the house of your friend and imagine you may learn something about your friend by looking at how his house is built. My final purpose is not to understand the universe, but to understand life.

An example of this is the question of why we humans see time as passing. According to the branch of physics called "quantum cosmology," the universe is best represented as a pattern called a "wave function" which does not depend on time. But then why do I see the universe evolving in time?

The answer may be that as long as I am observing the universe, the universe breaks into two pieces: me and the-rest-of-the-universe. And it turns out that the wave function for each of these separate pieces does depend on time. But if I merge with the universe then my time stops.

RR: How do you feel about having left Moscow to live and work in the U.S.? What are some things that strike you about American culture?

AL: Visiting different countries is one thing, living in different countries is another. People are similar. They are kind here, they are kind there; they are friendly here, they are friendly there. But the laws of society are different in sometimes a very unexpected way. The U.S. bureaucracy is much more complicated. In Russia I was unable to do many things. But for the things that were allowed, there were not so many rules. Here in U.S. you have more opportunities, but each opportunity is well-classified; if you want to know how to use the opportunities you have to know many laws.

RR: You like to use computers to simulate solutions to your equations. How do you program them?

AL: I am almost computer-illiterate. All the calculations are made by my son Dmitri. I was begging him to do it when we moved here in 1990, and in the beginning he was not very interested, but then I said what if I got a really good computer for this work? And indeed we got one from Silicon Graphics, and it was a lot of fun to work on it.

Dmitri is majoring in physics at Caltech; we've written six or seven papers together. Sometimes we get results by looking at computer simulations. The simulation shows a physical effect that is unusual. We study and check, and again see something strange. I shout, "You have an error in your program," and he checks and there is no error and then I understand something new. The simulation really helps us to discover, it's not only a tool to illustrate and to calculate; when you make it visual, you see something and understand it better.

RR: You've suggested that it might be possible to create a universe in the laboratory by violently compressing some matter, that one milligram of matter may initiate an eternal self-reproducing universe. How would this work?

AL: We don't have a no-go theorem which says it is impossible. But it is very difficult. You have to do more than just compress the matter, but with high temperatures and by quantum effects there is a chance of creating a universe. Our estimates indicate that you would need a very good laboratory indeed. And it is not very dangerous to try. This new universe would not hurt our universe, it will only expand within itself.

RR: Can you imagine there being any kind of economic or spiritual gain from creating new universes? Might this lead to a Silicon Valley industry or to a cosmological cult?

AL: The question is: Is it interesting to create a universe? Would you have a profit or benefit? What would be the use?

Suppose life in our universe is dying, and we make a small private universe we can jump into so we have a place to live. But it's not easy to jump, when we create a universe it is connected to our universe by a very narrow bridge of space, we can't jump through it, and the new universe will repel us because it is expanding.

Well, maybe you can get energy from the new universe? No, you can't get energy because of the law of energy conservation. The new universe gets its energy internally, and the energy has to stay inside there.

We can't get in, we can't use the energy, but maybe we can do like we do with our children: we teach them and we live on in them. Maybe we can give knowledge and information to the new little universe so that they will think about us with gratitude, like, "Oh God who created us, thank you."

But it is not so easy to send information inside. Say I wrote a message on the surface of an inflationary universe. But then the letters expand so much, that for billions of years to come each race of people in universe will be living in the corner of just one letter. They will never see the message.

The only way to send information which I have found is strange and unusual. If I create an inflationary universe with a small density, I can prepare the universe in a particular state which corresponds to different laws of physics, masses of particles, interactions, etc. I can imagine a binary code describing all possible laws of physics; this would be quite a long sequence. So if I am preparing a universe in some peculiar state, I can send the message encoded in the laws of physics.

Can I send a long message in this way? Let's think about our own universe. Let's imagine that someone made our universe as a message. If our universe were perfect, with all particles having equal masses and charges, then the laws of physics would be trivial, and it would be a very short message. But our particle physics looks weird, and it has a lot of information. We get these strange numbers, there is no harmony. There is information instead of harmony, or to be more precise, the harmony is there, but it is very well-hidden.

To send a long message, you must make a weird universe with complicated laws of physics. It is the only way to send information. The only people who can read this message are physicists. Since we see around us a rather weird universe, does it imply that our universe was created not by God, but a physicist hacker?

I don't know for sure whether this is a joke or something more. Until it is proven that it is stupid you must pursue some lines of thought. Even if something seems counterintuitive you must be honest and follow the thought line and not be influenced by the common point of view. If you agree with everything which everybody else thinks, you never move. You should try to think for yourself. Even though sometimes in the end you understand they were right.

—*Appeared as "Goodbye Big Bang: Cosmologist Andrei Linde,"*
in Wired, *July/Aug 1995.*

Tech Notes Towards a Cyberpunk Novel

ASICs, or Application Specific Integrated Circuits, comprise 95% of computer chips made today. Suppose that the ASICs have all been replaced by limpware. This is reasonable. For the people in 2053 to use chip-based computers would be like us now using *gear-based* computers. We used to have gears in a watch, and now we usually have a chip. A few watches still use gears simply out of nostalgia. But nobody would *dream* of starting out with a plan to use lots of little gears for the controls of microwave oven, or of a TV, or a traffic light...

In the same way, in 2053, nobody would dream of using a silicon chip for an app. In other words, a microwave oven, or an uvvy, or a car, or a clock — all of these have control circuits that are little smidgens of limpware, made of the special piezoplastic called "imipolex." They are not all that smart. They are dim. They are so dim they will do something like sit in a toaster for seven years waiting for someone to push the *toast* button. DIM should stand for something, like ASIC. *D*esigner *IM*ipolex.

Chaos means that you can't control; or that when you *try* to control, the results are not likely to be what you expected (sensitive dependence on initial conditions). As a cultural paradigm, it could mean accepting that the half-assed parallel-computed way in which social decisions arise is much more robust and adaptive than any kind of dictatorial guiding could be.

Chelated rare-earth polymers are what Andrea the moldie uses to get high. The rare-earth elements, also called lanthanides, are Lanthanum, Cerium, Praseodymium, Neodymium, Promethium, Samarium, Europium, Gadolinium, Terbium, Dysprosium, Holmium, Erbium, Thulium, Ytterbium, and Lutetium. Ytterbium was first found in a mineral called yttria in the 1878s. The mineral yttria was named for Ytterby, Sweden, in 1794.

Chipmold is the human-created plague which killed all of the boppers (who were conventional robots using existing tech: garbage cans on wheels with circuit boards and motors in them). But the soft plastic limpware flickercladding gets smarter. It *likes* the chipmold, it is veined by chipmold like a ripe bleu cheese. Jellyfish limpware eaten through with blue veins of chipmold.

E-mail in today's ever-more-rude America means a person can just come up and start talking to you, as if this was like some endless global party.

The endless interplanetary party that everyone is involved with. It should be pleasant and life-enhancing, like you can always plug in with other stoned freaks like yourself in the country, they can see the crazy shit you are doing, like an endless easy guilt-free phone call.

Femtotechnology is the next big thing beneath nanotechnology. Femtotechnology means technology at the size scale of one quadrillionth of a meter, or at ten to the minus fifteenth power meters. Femto- comes from Danish for fifteen. ("I never met a Dane who wasn't bone-dull." – W. S. Burroughs). A atomic nucleus has a diameter of two times ten to the minus fourteenth meters, which can be expressed as twenty femtometers. Femtotechnology could be in charge of direct transmutation of elements, as well as, I would suppose, the conversion between mass and energy. I think quantum mechanics would start to play a role at this size scale.

Femtotechnology is the same as what Heinlein called direct matter control.

Flickercladding is soft imipolex plastic that acts as a giant parallel processor, it has an invisible cellular structure that is patterned in by chelated polymers; these fibers carry the messages. The first flickercladdings had actual wires in them, they used to be like coatings fused or glued onto the bodies of the robots called the boppers. But the coatings got thicker, and soon peeled off the boppers to become independent limpware creatures known as *moldies*.

Flying wings of moldie imipolex. Manta rays of flickercladding flying around in the thin upper atmosphere like supersonic airplanes, drenched in solar radiation. Thanks to the algae in their tissues, they eat light.

Headmounted displays are confining and unnatural. The way to get full Virtual Reality immersion without such a kludge is to place limpware scarves on the neural ganglia. So as not to violate the sanctity of the skin, let the limpware interact with the brain tissues via tight electromagnetic fields.

Lifeboxes are things like a hand-held tape recorder with a computer, you talk to it and tell it the story of your life. The lifebox asks you questions to fill in blank areas. It organizes the information into a hypertext. You make copies of it for your children and grandchildren. "What Grandpa (or Grandma) Was Like." This is going to be a huge industry. Old duffers and ladies always want to write down their life story, but with a lifebox they won't have to write. It'll be like an automatic ghost writer. The hypertext connection will be such that you can always interrupt and say something like, "Grandpa, you just mentioned cars. What was your first car like?"

Moldies are capable of a weird symbiotic fusions with humans. A moldie might form part of itself into a U-bight, clamp onto your perhaps willing neck, sink fine microprobes into your neural masses, and control you directly.

Moldies can in fact merge together, and often do this, when at home in the comfort of their nest. They form nests like the speed-freaks described in Andy Warhol's book *Popism*.

It would be interesting if the nests were underground, like the burrows of the East African naked mole rats, who like termites and bees have a queen and work together. They are "eusocial." Colonies with hundreds of individuals all with nearly identical DNA.

A moldie bus is like a hovercraft streetcar that is a single huge jellyfish-like robot. A giant flying jellyfish that flies at a level several inches above the street. They don't actually hover, though, they kind of run like horses. But they have whole row of legs, each leg going across, the bottom is corrugated and the corrugations swing forward and backward in a wave-like motion.

Oil can be used for plastics such as flickercladding that makes up the moldies' bodies. The moldies would like to absolutely forbid that oil be made into gasoline and burned. The stuff is too valuable for plastic. For a moldie, burning oil is considered on a par with using human blood to make blood-sausage.

Perpendicular time, with its other order of reality – the sensation that there are other creatures around, that they are the little fast flashes that you see out of the corner of your eye sometimes.

Pornography is always the first private use for any new media technology.

Robots who do well get something like a publishing contract. Lots of copies of them are made and sold. The more servile and agreeable robots are the ones who get copied. The more independent robots look down on them. "So why not?" says a servile robot. "At least I'm getting copied."

Soccer – The joy of controlling a rolling sphere. Programming – the joy of controlling a machine. Could a soccer ball or a shoe sole be a computer? The object is computing as an elastic mass, and is probably programmable. But how? How to program limpware? You would convince it to do something? The limpware learns by sweat-lodge-type techniques?

Strange quarkbags are something femtotechnology might be good for making. As described in "The Search for Strange Matter," in the January, 1994, *Scientific American*, most matter is made of protons and neutrons, and these particles can in turn be thought of as little bags filled with quarks. There are (at least) three kinds of quark: *up*, *down*, and *strange*. A proton is a bag holding two up quarks and one down quark, while a neutron is a bag with two down quarks and one up quark. Ordinarily you can't have more than three quarks in a bag together. But if one of the quarks is strange, it throws off the exclusion principle. Like a slight flaw in tiling a wall leads to a fault that runs through a big pattern before it can repeat. Quarkbags can have just about *any* mass.

So now suppose there are atoms with quarkbags at their center. And suppose there is a chemistry for these atoms. Chemistry would now be kind of chaotic, with different rules in different places.

I have an image of Toontown. Like an ashtray is zapped with strange quarks, you like spray a spraycan of strange quarks onto a boomerang-shaped white plastic ashtray and now it starts warping and flexing because it's now made of strange quarkbag matter.

The technology for effecting these changes would be of course femtotechnology; given that a nucleus is about 20 femtometers, it seems likely that an individual quark might be about a femtometer in size.

Uvvies are universal viewers, devices which have wholly replaced the television, the telephone, and the personal computer. An uvvy is about the size of an old telephone handset, and like most of 2053s intelligent devices it is designed around a small limpware processing unit: a DIM.

Wormholes might be places where the scientific equations can't work, or maybe even inside the sun, or inside strange quarkbag matter. There might be wormholes and quarkbags hiding inside the sun. In wormholes there are energy densities such that, say, a thousand decimal places are meaningful for the real numbers involved – Planck's downer of like only thirty decimal places being meaningful is out of the picture here, provided that these wormholes are somehow *inside* Planck's constant. In here, even the simplest of physical processes effects are using laws with nonlinear equations of, say, the fiftieth degree. And like changing the four-hundredth digit in the decimal expansion of the coefficient of the thirty-eighth-power term will throw your process into a wholly different basin of attraction leading to a wholly different strange attractor. And the guys are trying to hack this rule, and they can't, so they use genetic algorithms to search the huge parameter space, and then...

*— Appeared as "18 Tech Notes Toward a Cyberpunk Novel"
in* Mondo 2000, *#13, Summer, 1994.*

Whenever I'm working on a novel, I maintain a parallel "Notes" document where I write down, among other things, technology ideas. Most of the ideas in this excerpt were in my notes for Freeware, *and many of them ended up in that novel. Others ended up in* Realware, *and in* Saucer Wisdom.

Part II: Life

Drugs and Live Sex

"What do you want to do now, Rudy?" Eddie and I are standing out on Fifth Avenue. We've just been to see the photos at the Museum of Modern Art. It's a sunny February day. Fifth Avenue near the park is about as dull a place as you'll find in NYC. Eddie's the only White Rastafarian in sight. "Let's go downtown and score some dope, Ed." "Okay." I'd expected Eddie to have a good stash when I visited him. But I'd happened in on a trough – and this was before the era of the marijuana stores. Early 1980. All Eddie has is some poisonous-green home-grown, good for brewing headache tea. Listening to his huge reggae record collection last night, we'd tried smoking some anyway. Better than cigarettes, and my head's still a little...loose. "*Ja-ja be my eyesight.*" Singing that and walking crosstown to the B-way line. It's Burning Spear, he sings with his neck stretched forward like a black goose. "*My way is long, for the road is so foggy foggy.*" You can hear the fog in his voice. My road is so foggy. That means the future is uncertain. Time branches. The music is like garbage underfoot. Beautiful garbage, blowing all up and down the streets of NYC. The graffiti on the subway cars has evolved during the two years I've been in Germany. You can't read the names at all anymore. The wild abstract expressionist "lettering" covers all the windows so you have to just know where to get out. Everyone does know, except the junk-sick stick-thin black man shouting, "Mah *numbuh* come in," shuddering there with empty seats around him, running his fingers through an astral heap of zero-dollar bills. Blank Eddie hovers there in the fluorescent light like a big, cautious fish. "Mah *numbuh* come in!" Crash, roar, crash, roar, crash – we're on Fifteenth Street. Down the stairs uptown, up the stairs downtown. Who needs matter-transmitters when he's got subways? It's teleportation, just crash-roar and everything's different! It's still a sunny February day, a cold day, a street of houses. Down the block there's a liveried chauffeur smoking a spliff outside his dark-blue Buick.

Secret smiles. "We should try Union Square," Eddie says, "I had to wait for someone there this summer and twenty guys must have come up to me." "You think they'll be there today?" "Are you kidding?" There's an interracial cordon of smilers blocking the entrance to Union Park. Heads down, we try to break through. "Pot?" "Powders?" "Black beauties?" I stop on a dime. It's like the New York Stock Exchange here. Futures, pasts and presents. "Let me see it first," I say. "Sure you can see it," a red-faced little dealer says, handing over a tiny manila envelope. Lots of seeds in there. On the street you're glad if there's seeds. "I'll give you four bucks." "Make it four-fifty." "Four." "Okay." I give him a five-dollar bill. Suddenly it is clear that there is no way in hell he is going to give me a dollar back. "*Black* beauties." The next dealer starts in. "Let me do my thing now, man." He's happy and bouncing, a walking endorsement for his pills. "It's a beautiful world, folks. *Black* beauties." Eddie is pulling me away. "I don't let him take pills," he explains to the dealer. "I may be back," I call. We still need papers, and a place to roll. The Lone Star is a block away, I read about Bo Diddley playing there two years ago, before I was exiled to Germany, I want to check it out. "Do you sell cigarette papers?" I ask the bartender. A slim jock, he looks at me like I'm out of my mind. I guess he doesn't like pot-smokers. "No," he says finally, "I don't sell *cigarette papers*." Maybe I've been gone too long. "Give us two Dos Equis," Eddie says. Nobody drinks regular beer in the Village. This is by no means a head-bar at two in the afternoon. It's all... *executives* drinking boilermakers. I peer into my little manila dope envelope. The seeds wink up at me. I haven't been really high in over a year. You ever try scoring in Germany? "I'll make some phone calls," Eddie says and disappears. The Mexican beer is worse than German, worse than American. "Three chilled vodkas straight up!" someone calls. Oh, man. Then Eddie's back. "My friend Dan says we can come over. He's very busy, but he'll give us a jay. He smokes only the *best*." Eddie says this with absolute conviction, his Paul Newman lips compressed to a line inside his Moses beard. Who needs telepathy if you've got telephones? We walk two blocks... all this motion, from here to there... how is it possible? Everything is teleportation! Dan meets us in the hall. We have to look over his shoulders to see inside. Wet paint. "This is Rudy,"

Eddie says. "He's my favorite science fiction writer." True enough, since Eddie never reads. "Eddie's told me about you," Dan tells me with an old pro's warm smile. He hands Eddie a fat spliff. "This stuff is very...resinous. Have a good time with it." The only time I ever scored in Germany was from a Turk in the street. A bar of hard, light-brown "hashish." It wouldn't fluff up or burn right, so I chewed a lot of it. It's funny how you can recognize the taste of camel shit the very first time you encounter it. Almost two years I've been in Germany. I make Eddie give me the reefer as soon as we've walked a block. Two hits and the air has that great clear-gelatin look to it. Communing with space! I can feel the pressure between the buildings, the long trough of the street, the art nouveau complexities trailing my hands...not just space, but *spacetime*! The light is clear and yellow. It's a whole different city again, like taking the subway, crash-roar and *wham* you're in a...new place. I start trying to explain this to Eddie. "You dig how the subway is the same as matter-transformation, moving you around in ordinary space?" He doesn't care. He doesn't *not* care. He just strides along, his clotted welcome-mat of hair behind him. My mouth is still running. "But just now, getting high, everything changed again...as if we had taken a subway. It's *parallel worlds*, you dig. You can walk crosstown, get a subway downtown...you can take an elevator *up*. But dope is like moving in a different dimension. The fourth dimension. We didn't move at all in regular space, but now we're in a different place." "In my building," Eddie says, "This is what somebody scratched in the elevator: THIS IS A BOX THAT CANNOT WALK! SO? YOU?" We cross Avenue A. The blocks are smaller way down here in the East Village. It's a good feeling to know that I'm by no means the first person to walk these sidewalks completely stoned. Eddie has his camera along and stops to take a picture of something on a church. I stand there, like a bodyguard in my long black German overcoat, and old people shuffle around us, anxious of sudden gestures. Stoned and loitering, there's a feeling of being *on the other side*, an alien. Eddie wants to show me a place called Reggae Record Ranch. It's on Seventh Street near Avenue B. A storefront with the windows covered. No way I would ever have found it alone, much less gone in. Good loud Jamaican music in there, highly evolved. There's like no record racks. Just a three meter by four meter floor covered with linoleum patterned like a zebra hide. The light is yellow, gelatinous. A high counter across the back of the room, with a Jamaican behind it talking to two others. They know Eddie. He was cameraman on *Rockers*, a movie sort of like *The Harder They Come*. Eddie was down in Jamaica shooting for months. That's when he became a White Rastafarian. I can't understand what anyone's saying at all, but walk up to the high counter and hold my hand out to the man behind it. He touches my hand. "Garfield." He's wearing a very high-crowned felt hat, sort of a space-dilated derby. It's wooly and a nice pink and gray plaid. There's an X scar on Garfield's nose. I ease back to the wall. There is a record rack after all, and I lean on it, keeping an eye on Eddie, feeling like a gunsel. But, hey, the music is really *good*. The guy across the room is clearly a Jamaican musician. He has the dreadlocks, about ten rings, and a ROCKERS button. We keep making and breaking eye-contact. I've got to say something, just to relieve the pressure. "Who's this record by?" I ask whitely. "Oh this is a round thing some brothers razza jive fa-tazz comin' in you say I mean diggin' it out the burnin' seed in there sha-bazzo wrap in there the burnin' seed you gettin' got . . ." There's more, and while he talks, a big stoned grin crawls out of my mouth. He stops and cracks a slight smile. "You know what I'm talking about?" "Well, yes, I mean generally speaking . . ." Eddie's been conferring with Garfield all this time. Garfield cuts off the record . . . this is Garfield's *disco*, I realize. He puts on . . . but can't be! He's playing "Memo from Turner!" My all-time favorite Jagger song that I've never heard again since I saw *Performance in Berkeley* these ten years gone. I still know the words, I can still see Jagger, there's a light swinging back and forth over his head, and Jagger is dressed like a businessman, leaning across a desk and shaking his finger. I hold my coat out like bat-wings and start dancing. The Rastas watch impassively, more alien than anything any fevered middle-class imagination has ever come up with. The song is over and I ask the guy with the dreadlocks his name. "Richard . . . but they call me Dirty Harry." This is a good parallel world we've hit on. Eddie buys me the Jagger record and a pack of Big Bambú, and we hit the street. "What's it like in Jamaica, Eddie?" "Like in there, but when you walk out the door you're still inside." We hunker down in a sunny doorway and get out my little thumb-sized envelope of street weed. It's full of seed and ashes and rocks and mouse turds...if you really cleaned it, there wouldn't be anything left. We split it in two, and each roll ourselves a big, tapering bomber. There's no rush in the stuff, but it does touch up that initial spacey high like a coat of fresh paint. I puff cautiously at first, waiting for my feet to go PCP-wooden, but it's just harmless roach-weed, we smoke and walk a few blocks, pitch the butts...stoned and clean. Hundreds of Puerto Rican kids are out of school and swarming up and down the short blocks, staring at us, first Anglos they've ever seen here. A man cool and muscular as a snake watches us, unblinking, standing in the doorway of the FAMILY SOCIAL CLUB. "I'm getting uptight, Eddie. Get us out of here." "Okay." But there's no subway, no more dope, no matter-transmission, just step after step in the cold wind, weaving down the street like aliens from NGC 38, the kids look at us with open curiosity, por favor, y'all...God it's cold. I wish I was back in Jamaica, man, with three red suns overhead and a methane rainbow... "Let's get a cab, Eddie." He looks at me unbelievingly. Eddie knows every subway station in Manhattan and I want to spend money on a cab? "I'll be happy to *ride* in a cab, Rudy." "Don't worry, I'll pay." He makes me walk another block first, though, so we can hail a cab on a street that runs uptown. I'm dying. Finally we're in the cab. It's warm and like a kountry kitchen with brick-patterned vinyl paper glued to the back of the front seat. "Do you want to go back to the apartment?" Eddie asks. But I know there are children there, Eddie's two-year-old and a little friend or two, mothers and noise and hassles as if I were back with *my* family. I'm fading, but it's only four o'clock and... "I ought to check out Times Square first." I finger two Reactivins out of my change pocket and swallow them dry. "What was that?" Eddie demands. "It's over-the-counter in Germany. A psychic energizer. It's like for when everything is...*made of wood*. That's a P. D. Ouspensky line." In truth, the Reactivins are little more than caffeine and sugar, but I'm trying to act *bad*. "I better go home," says Eddie. We get out at Times Square, I pay the cab and Eddie catches a subway. I'm standing there on Broadway, looking around with bright, omnivorous interest. There

used to be a peep-house here with some really hot film-loops, but I
can't spot it. But there's plenty else. There's porno in Germany of
course — it's completely legal there, and even the weekly news-
magazines have nudes on their covers...but I've never seen a live sex
show. That's what I'm really looking for here in Times Square, live
sex and a place to take a crap without getting gang-fucked. Right on
42nd Street just east of Broadway is the place I'm looking for, an ex-
movie theater with LIVE LOVE SEX on the marquee. TWELVE BOY-
GIRL SHOWS A DAY. The admission is an utterly reasonable $3.49,
and I scuttle on in. I'm a little nervous going into the bathroom.
There's piss on the floor and heavy breathing in the next stall. I
squeeze out my turd, keeping my feet well back from the space
under the partition, fearful of powerful hands. The theater is huge,
and they're filling in the time between acts with a giant porno movie.
Projected to big-screen size, the 16mm images are milky, translucent. I check out my fellow sex-enthusiasts. Except for one young
couple, who look like their marriage counselor sent them over from
Bayonne, it's all Japanese tourists and sixty-year-old men. And me.
Up on the screen they're just getting into a nifty three-way: a guy
dog-humping the top girl in a female 69 while the girl on the bottom eats his eggs...then click, buzz, the film stops and a spotlight
comes on. There's a bed on the stage, I notice now, it's tilted up
about ten degrees for better viewing and...everyone starts moving
up...will I be able to see? The first row is packed as solid as the
Steelers defensive line, sixty-year-old men slotted in there shoulder-
to-shoulder, *they* know the score. I grab a seat in the second row. The
music comes on and the girl steps out on stage. She's...beautiful! A
Fifth Avenue model, with the perfect curly hairdo and dark lipstick,
cool shades that are dark at the top and light at the bottom...she's
wearing a sort of silk swimsuit or teddy or camisole and *dancing*.
This woman is going to fuck and I can watch her! Her face is expres-
sionless, but her slim ass is dimpling at us, she's casual but not too
casual, excited but not too excited. One song one tit, two songs both
breasts, and then she's *naked* up there, dancing naked with real cunt
hair. I feel like cheering! It's a blow for freedom, it really is. I haven't
felt so uplifted since going to see the Stones at the Buffalo Stadium,
two months before we had to leave the country. Now I'm back at

last, and there's live pussy! She swivels onto the bed and freezes, sitting on the edge toward us with her feet together and drawn up, her
knees spread wide, showing pink. If she wiggled or smiled now it
would be…whorish. But as it is, it's *iconic*, of higher significance,
the real thing! Suddenly a guy comes walking down the aisle in a
bathrobe. He jumps up on the stage. The male lead! He's a wise-ass
greaser with John Travolta hair and a smile that won't quit. She's so
glad to see him, she takes off her sunglasses. He slips off the robe
and gets right down on her split. Like exhibition wrestlers, they
move smoothly from hold to hold. But it's all fun and love. They kiss
and talk when their faces come near each other. They never look at
us. We all keep real quiet, and I, for one, am too fascinated to even
have a hard-on. Later, when I think about it…I'll be hard, but for
now it's a Holy Mystery. I'm too merged in the great Oversoul to
even think of stiffening my bit of stick. Now they've rotated 180
degrees and she's sucking on his big limp cock, taking it all in, right
down to the root, but…we shift uneasily…will he ever get it up? Is
this going to be a *shuck*? Faster than I can follow, she slips around
and seems to sit on his prick…but is it really hard and in her? Or is
it lying limply doggo there, squashed flat by that hard-working juicy
minge? A faster song comes on…it's all disco of course…and they
switch to a new position, with him on top, and now there's no doubt
about it, the guy is stiff. Yes! He's *putting it to her*, and she's into it,
man, the old in-out, they're shaking that bed, her high-heels are digging into his back…He whips it out with a baby spotlight focussed
on him, on his huge distended pecker…he's *spurting*! The guy is
coming, you can see the clotted-arc shadows on his belly … there's
no doubt about it! A sigh of relief goes up. We're all in this together.
What a relief to participate in something so natural and decent in
this twisted world. The equipment still works. I feel like I'm in
church, a little boy again. She licks off his slickery dick and balls,
they kiss, and it's all over. He stands there, smiling his wise-ass
smile. *Stud*. We're all clapping for him, even the girl on the bed,
clapping daintily with a pleasant smile. A sudden pang seizes my
heart. Is this primal couple going to just leave? Are Mommy and
Daddy going to leave me 'cause I saw them making babies? Just walk
backstage and out of my life … after all we've shared? Not yet! He

puts on his robe, a dark-blue karate robe like *I* have, heh, and she wraps herself in the sheet. There *is* no backstage here at LIVE LOVE SEX, they use the projection booth for dressing, it looks like, which means that the star couple, the Mommy and Daddy, are going to walk right past us, right up the movie theater aisle like anyone else! People are lurching to their feet, stumbling out towards the aisle trying to, got to, want to, get a little . . . closer. I get out in the aisle too late. There's a flying wedge of sixty-year-old men between me and the BOY-GIRL, so I give up the chase. I know when I'm outclassed. On the street it's still light, still New York. There's a curious billboard over Times Square, a big round-the-corner Alex Katz mural up there. No writing on it, just pictures of women's faces. Intelligent self-possessed faces, beautiful with Inner Light. Someone's idea of equal time, I guess, the heads up there and the asses down here . . . but the Inner Light is everywhere today, clear White Light. I buy two loose joints at the subway station and get the train up to Eddie's.

—*Appeared in* Journal Wired, *Winter, 1989.*

Journal Wired *was a small SF-related literary magazine published by Andy Watson and Mark V. Zeising. It had no connection with the large magazine called* Wired.

Jerry's Neighbors

This all started back in 1980. I was in Heidelberg at the time, writing science fiction and living off a mathematics grant from the German government. The grant was running out, and the only job I could get back in the U.S. was teaching math at a women's college in Lynchburg, Virginia. I had a vision of a county courthouse, a public square, trees, drinking, party boys, hot women with drawls. At this point I'd never heard of Jerry, but the sound of "Lynchburg" was a bit . . . troubling. I wondered if I should go.

The only older relative around to consult with was my ninety-year-old German grandmother. "Lynchburg," she said thoughtfully. "It's called that because in the old days bad people had to live there, and anyone who wanted to was allowed to shoot them. Pow!" She cackled and pretended to aim a gun. She was getting old.

"Grandma, that's all wrong. Anyway, it's the only job I've been offered. I've got to move back to America."

A week later I came home from my office at the mathematics institute to find my wife looking at a copy of *Life* magazine.

"Look at this, Rudy. Your brother sent it. It's an article about this awful man called Jerry Falwell who lives in Lynchburg." I looked over her shoulder. There was a picture of a fat man in a three-piece suit. Praying on his knees. Nice *Life* photography, with shadows and wrinkles but . . . the guy was clearly some kind of evil demagogue. On the next page he was driving an ATV three-wheeler, chasing one of his guards around his walled estate.

"I don't believe this." My visions of checkers and whiskey in the courthouse park went up in flames. I saw a city of angry robots, pointing out my sins. Jerry denouncing me from the pulpit. The annual Full Gospel Hog Roast, with me on the spit. "I don't believe this is the only job I can get."

The people in Lynchburg looked really strange. The women especially. There were all these fifty-year-old women in lime-green skirts and pink alligator shirts. I couldn't figure out if it was time-warp or space-warp: on the one hand I'd been out of America for the last two horrible years of the Seventies; on the other hand, I'd never lived in a small town in southern Virginia. Turned out it was a little of both.

"Preppy," my ten-year-old daughter told me, after her first week of school. "I want to look preppy. That's what's in, Dad. I want an alligator shirt and a pink corduroy skirt."

"Are you kidding me? That stuff went out in the '50s. I didn't march on the Pentagon so my children could be *preppy*."

"You don't know anything, Daddy. You're *groovy*."

So the people were preps, but so far I didn't see any angry robots. Socially, at least. The week after we bought our house, representatives of four or five sects came by to try and sign me up. Robots for sure but not angry . . . though who knew what lurked inside those bulging Bibles. I heard stories about Jerry Falwell's church sending out guys in vans to drive children to Sunday School. A woman wrote the paper about it. She said the van drivers had lured her children off by promising them snacks and games. A girl from Jerry's college, Liberty Baptist College, a.k.a. LBC, accosted my daughter at a bus stop, asking her if she was saved, and if she loved Jesus, and where she'd go if she *died right now*.

I signed my family up at the Episcopal church. My fellow college teachers thought I was nuts to go to church at all, but I figured it was better to have a cover. Anyway, I'm used to church, I'm the son of a preacher. I believe in God, and even if I don't agree with all the details, it's nice, every few weeks, to sit in a church and have nobody talking about money.

Except at Thomas Roads. Every weekend the paper had a big ad for Thomas Roads Baptist Church, with a picture of "Doctor" Falwell. As a writer, I felt it was incumbent on me to go check the service out. I took my wife and the three kids. My wife kept telling the kids not to give out their names, "or the van will come get you."

Actually the guys at the door were nice enough, maybe not quite Rotary Club material, but trying hard, smiling and flashing their glasses and not fluffing their lines even if I did have a strange look in my eyes.

The only odd treatment they gave us was to have a hard-looking guy in a trench coat follow me in and sit right in front of us, with his hand on a zipped-up leather Bible case. I definitely didn't want him to undo that case and come out blazing. I made no sudden gestures.

The church is basically a theater, with a sloping floor and with seats radiating out from the stage. There are three or four heavy gray TV cameras mounted in the theater; each one has a red light on top that goes on when it's transmitting. Jerry and some other people walk around on the stage, and standing at the back of the stage is the choir.

There was one black person in the church. She was standing in the front row of the choir, right next to the Asian-American woman. The odd thing about the choir was that they didn't really sing. When it was time for a song, a tape recording would come on, and the choir would lip-synch it. Control, control, everything under control.

Jerry talked about all the people who want to stop his ministry. The drug pushers, the Communists, the homosexuals, the abortionists, and the pornographers. I tried to look inconspicuous.

Jerry talked on and on, stressing the point that *they* were against *us*, making the world outside his theater sound vicious and scary. He referred to the service as "this program," and sometimes he broke for a commercial. One of the commercials was for a copy of the entire Bible printed on a microfiche, a little square of plastic.

"It's a good tool for . . . *soul-winning*," smiled Jerry. "A good way to . . . start a conversation." I found myself really wanting a whole Bible printed the size of a postage stamp. How big would the letters be? Could you actually read it with a microscope? And it was *free*, although you were certainly urged to include a prayer offering.

Several times, while the TV stations were running their own commercials, the choir would lip-synch a song or two, and some men would go around and take collection. That impressed my children, the way Jerry took collection over and over, like a parking meter.

The thing that really got me was that there was no gospel and no prayers. At one point Jerry did open up a Bible, and he started in on reading a lesson, but after a verse or two he broke off and said, "Friends, why don't I just summarize this for you; summarize it and share some of my insights with you."

"He can't stand to read it because it isn't something he wrote," my wife whispered to me.

The people in the audience looked just like you'd expect, only more beat up. Honest working people with bad luck and no money. Maybe a drunk in the family, maybe a druggie, maybe a daughter knocked up. Payments behind on everything, the bank wanting to take back the car, no money to go to the doctor and get those lumps checked. If any people needed God's grace, it was these folks right here. And still no prayers; still no Holy Spirit! Then, finally, almost at the end, it came.

"Friends," said Jerry, bowing his head, "Close your eyes and let's join in a moment of prayer." All right! "As you know, our enemies are trying to get this program off the air." Huh? "We're close to bankruptcy, Lord." Then how'd you get so sleek and fat, man? "If we don't get two million dollars by next month, our television ministry must cease. Two million dollars, Lord, two million dollars by next month. Amen."

All those people there, plenty of them hurt and needing something, and all Jerry Falwell could think to help them pray for was two more millions of dollars for himself. Unreal.

In the long run it gets tiring. Just when you think Falwell can never get any more wrong-headed, he tops himself and gets another run in the press. His broadcasts supporting the "Peacekeeper" missile. His circus trial against Larry Flynt. His this, his that. You mostly just live with it. The South is weird. I have a theory, for instance, that Jimmy Carter had the CIA shoot Flynt for having printed a picture of Jimmy's sister, the evangelist Ruth Stapledon. Shortly after the highly publicized plane ride during which Ruth "saved" Flynt, there was an issue of *Hustler* that said, "Inside: Ruth Stapledon Shows Pink" on the cover. The issue was shrink-wrapped, and I didn't buy it, so I'm not sure what kind of picture of the President's sister it was. But a month later, Flynt was shot in the pelvis while traveling in Georgia. Very little effort was made to find the sniper. Is Larry Flynt the Martin Luther King of the '80s? Is Jerry the Hitler?

By almost any objective standard, Jerry Falwell is a racist, a warmonger, and a fascist – but it's hard to make these charges stick. When cornered in an argument, Jerry starts talking about America and God, and he gets that little smile in the corners of his mouth, and people begin to feel that . . . well, at least he's *sincere*. The *sincerity* seems to have a life independent of what he is saying. I often get the feeling that Jerry doesn't really care what he is saying at all – he simply picks as outrageous a position as possible, a position guaranteed to draw news coverage, and then he slathers his oily *sincerity* all over the cameras.

A corollary of his main stock in trade being *sincerity* is that Jerry does appear to be moral and honest in his personal life. His various organizations pull in a lot of money, but it wouldn't be accurate to say that Jerry is using religion to get rich. I doubt if he is very interested in the luxuries that wealth can bring. He's interested, rather, in being famous and powerful. The money his broadcasts make is spent on more broadcasts. His religion might best be thought of as a kind of nonmalignant tumor. It draws in energy which is expended almost entirely on itself. Jerry Falwell raises money so he can afford bigger shows to raise more money.

If I speak of him as nonmalignant, it is because he does not overtly preach violence and hatred. Wrong-headed as his ideas are, Jerry Falwell doesn't have death-squads to wipe out his detractors. He doesn't funnel money to the lunatics who go around murdering abortionists. Demonstrators at his church are not beaten, and people who make fun of Jerry are not hounded out of Lynchburg. After Reagan's landslide re-election, a number of my fellow left-wing friends in other cities expressed a fear that "now Jerry Falwell is going to run the country." "He's already supposed to run Lynchburg." I told them, "And people here can say whatever they want to."

I tested this out in April, 1984, as the following story will demonstrate.

At that time, the head of Jerry's Moral Majority organization was a man named Cal Thomas. (Cal has since stepped down to become a full-time syndicated columnist.) As it happened, Cal Thomas lived about a block from me. I was going through a difficult period in my life just then – I was jobless and broke, I'd just finished writing my tenth book and felt resentful about my lack of recognition, I was smoking pot and drinking too much. The fact that successful, right-wing Cal lived nearby was starting to rankle – not that he knew me.

It was Friday. I walked to the 7-Eleven to get another twelve-pack of beer. On the way back, I saw Cal mowing his lawn. I gave him the finger and yelled:

"Christ sent me here to take you and Jerry out!"

We got into a kind of discussion then. I said that I was a "Christian" myself, a member of St. John's Episcopal church, and that I didn't like him and Falwell to be using Jesus as a club to beat people over the head with.

"Did you learn to give the finger like that at St. John's?" sneered Cal, a tall guy with a mustache.

"No! I learned it from LSD!" I said, by way of invoking the '60s.

Cal wanted to know who I was – I repeated my name several times, and pointed out my house, its red roof visible down the hill.

"I'm the second most famous person in Lynchburg," I cried, "And you don't take account of me!"

I ranted some more, then I went on home, and a little later I was walking over to a friend's house. By then I'd forgotten about talking to Cal. But he hadn't forgotten about me. He was still mowing his lawn, and when he saw me go by he jerked, and turned off his mower and came over and said things to me. I don't remember exactly what. I think he was worried that I might try and do something violent. His wife called out to him from his porch.

"Gay," says Cal to her, "Gay, go in the house and get the gun."

I split fast.

Next day I still thought it was funny, but the day after that – Sunday – I was desperately scared and remorseful. *How much power do the god-pigs have?* I wrote Cal a letter which was basically begging him not to have me assassinated.

Sunday, April 29, 1984

Dear Cal:

I do feel I owe you an apology for having bothered you Friday evening. Obviously, there are some issues on which you and I do not see eye to eye, but you certainly have a right to mow your lawn in peace. A neighborhood is a neighborhood. I promise not to repeat my performance, and I hope that, in the long run, we will be on good terms with each other. You are clearly a man of patience and intelligence, and I really regret having acted the way I did.

Here's one of my books – which may or may not interest you – if you get around to it, please send me one of yours.

All the best,

Rudy Rucker

I put the letter inside a copy of *Infinity and the Mind* – not *The Sex Sphere*, for God's sake, and set it by his door. I was nervous doing this, as Friday he'd intimated that he'd shoot me if I ever stepped on his property again. But I had to get it delivered right away, before the final order to the God-Squad went down!

I hadn't told anyone yet about all this, but now my wife, noticing my furrowed brow, asked what was up. I told her about giving Cal the finger and telling him that everyone in Lynchburg hates him and Jerry.

"Boy, you're stupid, Rudy."

A few days later I got a letter back from Cal:

May 3, 1984

Dear Rudy:

Thank you for your gracious note and the book. I appreciate the spirit in which you wrote the letter.

I must say that this was the most unique introduction I have ever received to anyone!

Enclosed are a couple of my recent newspaper columns. I am now writing for the Los Angeles *Times* Syndicate. I'll give you a copy of my book, *Book Burning*, when I get a chance.

Again, thanks for your note.

Sincerely,

Cal, "Vice Ayatollah"

Which was a real load off my mind. Before the letter, I'd reached the point of paranoia where I was wondering if it wouldn't be wise to go ahead and preemptively firebomb Cal before Jerry's minions could burn down my house and have the police shoot us as we ran out screaming. But this really *isn't* El Salvador here.

Cal's letter is quite classy – it's kind of unnerving, the fact that when you actually get to some super media pig, there is sometimes actually a person there, a person who wears a certain kind of public mask. Not that I particularly like Cal now, or believe anything he writes – but it is interesting to know that he has a certain sense of humor about having worked as Jerry's "Vice Ayatollah."

A few months later, I was talking to the assistant minister of St. John's Episcopal, a gentle and thoughtful man my age whom we knew socially. He said, "Rudy, your name came up the other day in a very strange context. I was talking to Cal Thomas about a student exchange program, and he asked me if I knew you. I said, yes, and then Cal told me that you'd flipped him the bird and told him that Jesus sent you here to fight him, and that everyone at St. John's hates him."

"Well, yeah, I did that. I wish I hadn't. I was pretty drunk."

"Cal asked me if you might have been drinking. I said that it was . . . possible."

"Was he pissed off?"

"It was more that he wanted to figure out . . . what had happened."

—Appeared in Science Fiction Eye, *#2, August 1987.*

I'm glad I don't drink anymore!

Jerry Falwell continues to appear in the news now and then, always advocating the absolute worst possible ideas. He even hates science fiction:

> The decline in American pride, patriotism, and piety can be directly attributed to the extensive reading of so-called 'science-fiction' by our young people. This poisonous rot about creatures not of God's making, societies of 'aliens' without a good Christian among them, and raw sex between unhuman beings with three heads and God alone knows what sort of reproductive apparatus keeps our young people from realizing the true will of God.[50]

---

50. Jerry Falwell, "Can Our Young People Find God in the Pages of Trashy Magazines? Of Course Not!" *Reader's Digest,* Aug. 1985, pp. 152-157.

The Central Teachings of Mysticism

This is not going to be very funny, but I hope it's at least interesting. One reason I like to talk about mysticism is that talking weird gets me high: the air gets like thick yellow jelly, you know, and everyone's part of the jelly-vibe jelly-space jelly-time . . .

All is One. That's the main teaching, that's the so-called secret of life. It's no secret, though. It's a truism that we've all heard dozens of times. The secret teachings are shouted in the streets. *All is One*, what can I do with that? How can I use it in the home? If *that's* the answer, what's the question?

I guess the most basic problem we all have to deal with is death. In Zen monasteries, the entering students are given *koans* to solve. A *koan* is a type of problem unsolvable to the rational mind: What was your face before you were born? This is not a stick. [Holds up a stick.] What shall I call it? Each of us on Earth has a special koan to work on, it's the death-koan, handed out at birth: "Hi, this is the world, you're alive now and it's nice. After awhile you die and it all stops. What are you going to do about it?"

The mystic escapes death by denying that he or she exists as an individual bag of meat. "I am God," is the easiest way to put it, though this doesn't always go over too well. "Hi, I'm God, this is my wife, she's God, too. These are the children, God, God, and . . ." What I have in mind here is that God – or the One, if you want to be more neutral-sounding – what I mean is that God is everywhere and we are all part of God. We are like eyes that God grows to look at each other with.

The word "God" does grate. Organized religion puts a lot of people uptight (we will be passing out the plates soon) and when a lot of us hear that word (get your hands outta there, friend) our first impulse is to find a brick and throw it, or just leave or go to sleep (you're gonna burn for this) . . .

Here's where the second central teaching comes in. All is One, fine. But: *The One is unknowable*. "God" – that's just a noise I'm making up here, a kind of pig-squeal. We don't know God's name, and we never will. The ultimate thing, the fundamental Reality – it's not something the rational mind can tie up in a net of words. I can't really tell you what I'm thinking about. In a way it's pointless to talk about mysticism at all. "If you see God, only piss to mark the spot" – that's a line from a poem I wrote when I was thirty. I was down in the islands, standing on a beach at night. *If you see the Buddha in the road, kill him.*

So here's two teachings: *All is One*, and *The One is unknowable*. The third (and last) teaching is *The One is right here*. You're totally enlightened right now, right as you are. You see God all the time; you can't stop seeing Him. We're all in heaven and there is no hell.

First I claim that all of reality is one single thing, a sort of giant orgasm or something. Then I say that this One is unknowable, but right away I turn around and say that the One is perfectly easy to see, it's everywhere. Do we have a contradiction? How can the mystics say that, on the one hand, God is unknowable, and that, on the other hand, God is everywhere?

People who have a more or less fascist view of religion are perfectly comfortable with the idea of God as something way up there, something unattainable: the Commander in Chief, the Head Technician, our Fearless Leader, the Great Scientist who put all this together. The Church of Christ, Cosmic Programmer. What's God thinking about? Smart stuff, hard stuff, stuff we can never understand. That's the *God is unknowable* teaching. No rational human description can exhaust the riches of the One.

The other side of the coin is that we know the One perfectly well. You can't describe God in any complete way, but God's as much a part of you as your body is. You can know something in an immediate way without knowing it in any kind of analytic way. You don't need to be a geneticist to know how to make babies.

So when mysticism says *The One is unknowable* and then says *The One is right here*, there isn't really a contradiction. It's just that there's two *kinds* of knowing. We can't know the One rationally, but we can know it in an immediate and mystical way. Anyone can go into the temple, but you have to leave your shoes outside. "Temple" stands for a mystical vision of God, and "shoes" stands for conventional ways of talking. You take off your shoes and walk into the temple.

We don't have to go to the Far East to find mystical religion. Christianity is based on the idea that, on the one hand, God is way up there in seventh heaven, and that, on the other hand, Jesus comes down to live in our hearts. It's a strange thing that many of us are more comfortable with Buddhism than we are with Christianity. It's strange, but the reasons are pretty obvious – I mean, imagine if there were a 24-hour-a-day Buddhist Broadcasting TV network:

"Friends, I want to talk to you about *samadhi*. This blessed state of union with the Void – Void being Nothingness, friends – this blessed state was first experienced in a little town near the Ganges River. God brought a man – a *man*, friends, and not a woman – God in His wisdom brought forth this human – a *human*, friends, and not a Communist – God brought to this seeker a vision of the Void. How best might you, in your ignorance, in your sin, in your present debased circumstances, how might you best seek the Void? The Void can be found in your wallet, dear seeker, if only you will send its contents to me . . ."

So you go turn on the radio, man, and instead of music there's some grainy-voiced guy yelling:

". . . hatred. Yes, *hatred*, my fellow enlightened ones, Buddha came to preach hatred. I know this may sound strange to some of you out there in the radio audience, but it's *not* a matter of conjecture. God hates the unbeliever, just as the unbeliever hates *me* . . ."

There is so much negative stuff associated with religion, that many of us would just as soon never talk about God at all. But there's still that death-koan hanging overhead: *life is beautiful, life ends, what can I do?* If I decide not to think about bad stuff like death and loneliness, then I end up spending all my energy on not thinking. I can buy lots of stuff, but every visit to the repair shop is an intimation of mortality. I can get real high, but I always have to come down. And not choosing anything at all is itself a choice.

Mysticism offers a way out. It's really just a simple change of perspective. A person's life is like a design in an endless spacetime tapestry. Molecules weave in and out of your body all the time. Inhale/Exhale; Eat 'n' Excrete. You breathe an atom out, I breathe it in. I say this, you answer that. Atoms, thoughts and energies play back and forth among us. We are linked spacetime patterns, overlapping waves in an endless sea. No one exists in isolation, everyone is part of the Whole. If a person can only take the word "I" to be the Whole, then that "I" is indeed immortal. In the book of Exodus, Moses asks God what His real name is. God answers: "I AM." All is One, *All is One*.

If this were just an abstract idea, then mysticism would not be very important. What makes mysticism important is that you can directly experience the fact that All is One.

I used to read about mysticism and wonder how to score some enlightenment. There's something so slippery about the central teachings – the way the One is supposed to be unspeakable, yet everywhere all the time – it used to really tantalize me. And then finally I started getting glimpses of it, sometimes with chemicals, sometimes for no reason at all. I'd see God, or feel the world synch into full unity, and I'd love it, but whenever I tried to grab onto it, the life would somehow drain out, and I'd just have some dry abstract principle.

After I got so I could occasionally feel that All is One, I started being uptight that I couldn't be there all the time. I bought lots of books by totally enlightened men. Eventually I concluded that no one does stay up there all the time. You can't always be having a shining vision that All is One; you have to do other stuff, like deal with your boss, or fix the car, meaningless social hang-ups, the stuff like walking and eating and breathing. You can't always be staring at the White Light.

But you can. That's the next level, you see. The Light is everywhere, all the time. Being unenlightened is itself a kind of enlightenment. There are no teachings, and there's nothing to learn.

Congratulations, Mary.

— Appeared in Transreal, *WCS Books, 1991.*

In 1982, a friend of ours named Mary Molyneux Abrams had been taking classes at Sweetbriar College so she could get her Bachelor's degree. But then she decided to stop going to school, and her husband said, "Why not give Mary a graduation party anyway?" He made up engraved invitations mentioning me as the commencement speaker. At the party, I handed out mimeographed copies of "The Central Teachings of Mysticism" and read it to the audience of some forty people.

Looking back at this little lecture, I enjoy its flow, but I feel like it's missing something. God isn't just some kind of logic puzzle, God can directly touch your heart. Over the years I've added a fourth and a fifth "teaching." God is Love, *and* God will help you if you ask. *Help you do what? To be less selfish, more loving, less driven, and more serene — to let go and stop trying to run everything.*

Haunted by Phil Dick

My head was in a very bad place in the spring of '82. I often think of life as being like surfing. Ups and downs, manic-depression, all you can really do is ride it out. Hang ten. On the board. Sometimes you fall off, the board hits you in the head, sharp coral comes up, etc. I'd lost my most recent teaching job, my wife and I were fighting, I was singing in a psycho-punk band called the Dead Pigs.

Phil Dick died around then, and I started thinking about him a lot. In May '82 I started working on a post-WWIII book called *Twinks*. Every day, starting out, I'd pray to Phil Dick and ask him for guidance – to some extent I was trying to twink him. "Twink" is a SF word I made up; to "twink" someone means to simulate them internally, to let their spirit take possession of you. The idea is based on my notion that Soul = Software.

Let me explain this concept a bit. Using a computer analogy, we can compare the body to hardware, and the mind to software. The personality, memories, etc., can all, in principle, be coded up to give the individual person's software soul. A powerful enough hardware system can boot and run any given software. Given enough information about another person, you can twink them.

In fall of '82 I got a contract for a nonfiction book called *The Fourth Dimension*, and *Twinks* was set aside. I still thought about Phil Dick a lot. Sometimes, me walking around some tree-lined Lynchburg neighborhood, he would feel very close. I heard I'd been nominated for the first Philip K. Dick award (for my novel *Software*) and I felt I had a good chance of getting it. I begged Phil, or my internal simulation of him, to make sure I would get it. I'd done five SF paperbacks at this point, and was getting zero recognition. I really needed a break.

Later that winter – like in January '83 – Audrey and I and a friend named Henry Vaughan went out to a party at a girl's house in the country. We didn't know too many of the people – they were sort of rednecks, where those days in the South a redneck was a per-

Rudy at the first Phil Dick award
ceremony. (Photo by S. Rucker.)

son with long hair and a scraggly beard. It was mellow, plenty of
weed, loud music, and everyone getting off.

At some point I glanced across the room and in walked Phil Dick.
He didn't say he was Phil Dick, but he looked to be wearing his circa-
1974 body... hair still dark, beard... hell, I don't know what Phil Dick
"really" looks/looked like, but I knew *this was the guy*.

At first I just grinned over at him slyly – like Aphid-Jerry eyeing
"carrier people" in *A Scanner Darkly*. Then, finally, I introduced
myself and drank beer and whisky in the kitchen with him for
awhile. Of course I was too hip to confront him with my knowledge
of his true identity.

The man's cover was that he was in the garbage business. "The
Garbage King of Campbell County." He said he had a fleet of
trucks, and that he'd furnished his entire house with cast-off items
gleaned from the trash-flow.

I steered the conversation around to science fiction, mentioning
my novel *Software*.

"What's it about?"

"It's about robots on the moon. In a way they're black people. The guy who invented them – he's my father – is dying and the robots build him a fake robot body and get his software out of his brain."

"Go on."

"They run the software on a computer, but the computer is big and has to be kept at four degrees Kelvin. It follows him around in a Mr. Frostee truck. There's a big brain-eating scene, too."

"Sounds all right!"

Maybe that was Phil Dick, maybe not. In any case, I got the award, and it did help my career. The award ceremony was a good party, too. First Tom Disch talked, and then Ray Faraday Nelson talked, synchronistically basing his remarks on some stories he'd happened to tell me walking over from dinner – and then I stood on the bar and read a speech which I'd prepared in advance. The speech went like this:

> I'd like to just say a few words about immortality. I have a theory about how artistic immortality works. When you're reading a well-written book, and totally into it, then you are, for those few moments, actually identical with the person who wrote the book. It's my feeling that artistic immortality means that the artist is, however briefly, reborn over and over again. We could express this idea in terms of computers. If you can somehow write down most of your program, then some other person can put this program onto his or her brain and become a simulation of you.
>
> If I say that Phil Dick is not really dead, then this is what I mean: He was such a powerful writer that his works exercise a sort of hypnotic force. Many of us have been Phil Dick for brief flashes, and these flashes will continue as long as there are readers.
>
> Let's push the idea a little harder – that's what SF is all about, after all – pushing ideas out into new territory. Even if there were no more readers, then the Phil Dick persona would still exist. Actually, each of our personalities is immortal, as a sort of permanent possibility of information-processing.
>
> Another push now. Just as each of Phil's works is a coding

of his personality, we might go on to say that sometimes various authors are, as people, examples of the same higher-level archetype. I'd like to think that, on some level, Phil and I are just different instances of the same Platonic form – call it the gonzo-philosopher-SF-writer form, if you like.

One last thought. Up till now I've talked about immortality in very abstract terms. Yet the essence of good SF is the transmutation of abstract ideas into funky fact. If it is at all possible for a spirit to return from the dead, I would imagine that Phil would be the one to do it. Let's keep our eyes open tonight, he may show up.

So hi, Phil, wherever you are, and thanks for everything. Let's party.

Over the next couple of years in Lynchburg, I saw the Garbage King of Campbell County a couple more times at parties. One time we were in a house, a house like a house I often dream about, with a front and a back staircase, and the King and I were on a landing, him and his good-looking wife, and he says, "What was that writer guy you talked about? Philip Jay Dick?" Only then he gave me a sly wink. I was stoned enough at the time to think that the "Jay" was a psychic reference to the fact that the first Dick book I ever owned was *Time Out of Joint*.

I lost track of the Garbage King during the last evil times in Lynchburg, and then all at once it was 1986 and I was a computer scientist in California – more than that, a *hacker* – and I saw Phil again. He was back into the mode of *A Scanner Darkly*.

I first read that book, by the way, in Brighton: SeaCon, 1980, my first SF con, where I met my heroes Ian Watson and Robert Sheckley and sold my manuscript of *White Light* to Virgin Books in the person of Maxim Jakubowsky. I was partying the whole time thanks to following the first Brit I saw go by in lace-up white leather boots, I think his name was Gamma. I sat down next to him and his sleazy buddies and sexy girlfriends and began bragging about how great I was and how they should turn me on. One of them gave me hash and I smoked that for a day and then I couldn't find him for more. I'm all, "Where's Lester?" and they're all, "Lester's gone into the City to get some powdah." I was shocked.

I was in Brighton two nights, staying in an attic flat up near the train station, all the hotels having been full on my arrival overland from Heidelberg. Both mornings I lay in bed leisurely reading *A Scanner Darkly* and wallowing in its greatness. Lester didn't like the book because the ending was, "Too obvious, you know, so against drugs." When it was time for me to go back to the *Mathematisches Institut*, I was on the subway-like Brighton train in time, reading *Scanner Darkly*, the part about Barris and the amphetamine plant, Barris *pausing in his work*, alertly slackful, and me laughing so hard that people are looking over, and the train is inching out of the station and I realize I've left my suitcase on the platform.

I've reread *Scanner* three or four times now. The plot is very intricate and delicate, like the nerves in a vivisected bat. And it's an incredibly sad book, even though it's so funny. Textually, the words "dreary" and "slushed" come back over and over, making a kind of sad oboe music in the background.

You wanna talk short stories, two Dick stories stand out in my mind. "The Golden Man" was the first of his stories I read, as a twelve-year-old, not noticing Phil's name, but pondering that story for years, especially its key concept of being able to see alternate futures. The other story I think of right off the bat is "Explorers We," about men who think they are astronauts landing and then they get killed because they are really Martian invaders.

How I got hold of that particular story was that my Swarthmore roommate, Greg (who appears as the canny Ace Weston in my *Secret of Life*), is now a book dealer, and, knowing my love of Phil (especially after the award), Greg gave me a dead man's set of twenty-three 1950s SF magazines, each containing a story or novelette by Philip K. Dick. I had this great crappy writing office in Lynchburg, with an over-stuffed white vinyl couch, and a bookcase with the Dick mags, and usually I didn't feel like writing much on Mondays or Tuesdays, so then I'd likely lie on the white couch and read one of those old SF magazines. It always encouraged me to see Phil's humble roots.

Now if we pop up the stack we have "Explorers We," we have *Scanner Darkly*, we have the fact that Phil is alive, we have my move to San Jose. The way I found Phil in San Jose involves my friend Dennis. Let's assume you've read one of my *Ware* novels. The character Sta-Hi, also known as Stahn, also known as Stanley Hilary

Mooney, is transreally inspired by a real person: Dennis Poague, occupation freelance mechanic, legal status Blank (like the "Blank Reg" character in *Max Headroom*), long-term resident of San Jose, now residing in Belo Horizonte, Brazil. It was Dennis, also known as Dementex, who showed me the still-living, though terribly methed and bedusted, Philip K. Dick in the fall of 1986.

I met Dennis in the mid-seventies when I was teaching college in upstate New York, a state college in a small town called Geneseo, described as "Bernco" in *White Light*. Dennis's brother Lee was an English professor who lived across the street from us. One day Dennis showed up from California on his way to Europe, acting totally outrageous. He took the cheap red nylon skateboard I'd bought my five-year-old and set to carving and ripping all up and down the steep campus's sidewalks. He had some primo Thai-stick with him, and he gave me one in exchange for some acid someone else had given me – a good trade for me, as I was scared to take acid again anyway, having had my big "ordeal poison" initiation into the Eleusinian mysteries several years earlier. Dennis and I got along very well together, each of us happy to meet such a madman. And for the rest of the time in Geneseo, every half year or so Dennis would orbit through our town and we'd see him. One time he had a whole suitcase full of cheap green pot. It was so bad that he cooked a pound of it into tea. He took the rest of it to the Mardi Gras and got robbed.

When my wife and I moved from Geneseo to Heidelberg for a two-year grant I had, Dennis stayed in touch, sending joints, a hit of acid one time (see my short story "The Jack Kerouac Disembodied School of Poetics"), tapes of the Dr. Demento show, and, best of all, tapes of the people who rode in his cab. He was driving a cab in San Jose – just an unknown Hispanic-sounding California city to me then. The cab tapes were amazing, like of drunk hookers, or of giggly teenage girls, with Dennis's manic, insinuating voice going on and on, "You girls wanna stop and do a bowl? I'm Sta-Hi, live or die, just keep me high, chaos and confusion reign supreme!"

From Heidelberg we moved to Lynchburg, which I always write about as "Killeville," and then I found out where San Jose really is (it's at the southern end of Silicon Valley, which stretches up the Bay peninsula through Palo Alto to San Francisco), and ended up moving here. I hadn't seen Dennis in a few years, and I was a little nervous about it. Finally he called up, and asked me to stop by his apartment in downtown San Jose.

Where he lived wasn't actually a real apartment, it was simply a small room at the head of a flight of stairs in someone's house. Wherever Dennis lives there are always four or five half-assembled cars in the driveway and backyard. He was fixing one or several of these cars in return for being allowed to live there. His room was not much larger than a bed; there were shelves on the wall piled with electronic music equipment, cartons of old *Heavy Metal* magazines, car parts, ragged clothes and hundreds of T-shirts.

"You got no idea how glad I am to see you, Rudy."

I gave him a Xerox of the typescript of *Wetware*, and then Dennis took me downstairs to meet his speed connection, a muscular, shirtless fifty-year-old Filipino called Buffalo Bill. I watched them crush up some crystal, snort it, and begin to jabber about skin-diving for jade boulders as big as cars. Every so often a different woman would come in and disappear into the back room with Buffalo Bill. I sat around and enjoyed the scene. When it was time to go, I opened the wrong door, a door which led down into the basement. Standing there on the basement stairs was a punk in painter's clothes and just below him, staring up at me like out of a cover of the PKDS newsletter, was the real Phil Dick, not too tall, balding with a beard with a white stripe in it, and with the unmistakable aura of a hologram from hell. He and the punk painter were snorting lines of meth off a pocket mirror.

I freaked and closed the door right back up. "Who was that?" I asked Dennis as soon as we got outside. "On the stairs, who were the two guys on the basement stairs?"

"Hell that's just Tommy the painter. His father owns the place. The other guy with him rents the back room by the garage. He doesn't talk much. Just . . ." Dennis made loud piglike snorting noises, the same noise he'd made earlier when I'd asked him what he would do if he really did make a lot of money off jade.

"The other guy, Dennis, that's Phil Dick. You know, the Philip K.

Dick award I got for *Software*? That was him in the basement. He must not really be dead! He's living right here in your building!"

"Why didn't you talk to him?"

"What would I say? But, look, Dennis, do one thing for me. After you read *Wetware*, give it to him. It's dedicated to him, wave? 'For Philip K. Dick, 1928–1982, One must imagine Sisyphus happy.' That's from Camus, see, Sisyphus being the proletarian of the gods, you understand, daily proving that scorn can overcome any fate, rolling another wad of paper up to the top of the same old mountain and letting it blow away, just imagine him happy. Does he seem happy?"

"I'll ask him."

But Dennis never did talk to Phil. Phil got on his motorcycle and left that house for good, right after I did. I saw him in my rearview mirror, right before I turned onto Route 17. He was all in black, idling on the putt, wearing shades, a greasy old biker, calm with meth. Looked to me like he was headed for South San Jose. He never waved.

Is there any meaning in my visions of Phil as Garbage King and Meth Biker? Well, the real meaning is simply that I was interested enough in Phil to imagine seeing him after his too-early death. I've always hoped that when *I'm* gone I'll have fans as obsessive as Phil's fans, people who piece together my letters, fiction, and nonfiction to try and see a soul. As you read this: Am I dead yet?

— Appeared in Transreal, *WCS Books, 1991.*

California New Edge

When my family and I moved to California, one of the first things I did was to visit the City Lights bookstore on Columbus Avenue in San Francisco's North Beach, right across Jack Kerouac Alley from the funky old beatnik bar/cafe called Vesuvio's. I got so excited seeing all the cool books and magazines that I could barely even breathe. One particular magazine that caught my eye on this visit was a huge pink thing with a Ben-Day dot picture that seemed to be a cross between Tim Leary and Art Linkletter. Art Linkletter was the host of a 50's candid-camera TV show called *People Are Funny*, and he authored the book *Kids Say the Darndest Things*. Linkletter's daughter had a mental illness which was compounded by the use of LSD, and she ended up committing suicide by jumping out a window, so Art Linkletter became a prominent spokesperson against psychedelia. So now here's these California weirdos putting out this big pink magazine – which is called *High Frontiers* – and they have Linkletter's face merged with Leary's, and out of the mouth is coming a shaky speech-balloon saying, "Kids do the darndest drugs!" And if that weren't enough, walking across the top of the picture is a drooling three-eared Mickey Mouse holding out the logo of the Central Intelligence Agency. The magazine *High Frontiers* became *Reality Hackers*, which became the magazine *Mondo 2000*, and now I'm co-editing the *Mondo 2000 User's Guide to the New Edge*. Software packages always come with a book that says *User's Guide* on it, even though in the rest of culture, a "user" is usually using drugs. Are people who buy software the same as the people who buy drugs? People are funny!

At first California was hard to get used to. My family and I were coming from a small town in central Virginia, you understand, a place called Lynchburg, the home of that notorious God-pig, Jerry Falwell, always on TV, preaching fear and asking for money. The main thing you notice first about California is how much you have to drive. At first I'd see all these little shopping centers along the highways and I'd be thinking, "Oh, I better come back here sometime and check out those nice stores." It took me awhile to realize that the little shopping centers, the strip malls, were all the same, and that there was no point in going into one except for an instantaneous purchase. In this great American urban mega-suburb, shopping is a parallel, distributed process. Shopping for ordinary things, that is. For special things you need special, nonmall sources.

California drivers aren't usually rude – if there is a necessity to merge, people will pause and wave each other on – but they are pushy. If you don't take advantage of a hole in traffic, someone else will squirm around you to get at the hole. Once, in Santa Cruz, when I paused flounderingly in an intersection in our big old Chevy station wagon, two separate drivers called me an asshole. I was blocking a hole and I was driving an American station wagon with Virginia plates, therefore I was an asshole. I notice a fair amount of standoffishness and impatience among Californians. It's like Californians know that there is the possibility of getting REALLY GOOD STUFF out here, and when they have to settle for something inadequate – like seeing a whale-wagon in the middle of an intersection – they get very miffed. When I first got here, I was so happy to see restaurants that weren't Red Lobsters and Pizza Huts that I was bewildered by all the "Very Best Restaurants" guides I kept seeing in the paper. "Hell," I'd say, "I don't need the VERY BEST. I'm perfectly happy with something that's REASONABLY ADEQUATE." But of course now, after six years here, I don't feel that way anymore. I'm a Californian, and I want the very best all the time!

Some of the first Californians I befriended were fellow science fiction writers. There's few enough SF writers that we're always glad to see each other. The one thing that my new SF friends were most interested in telling me about was Marc Pauline of SRL (Survival Research Labs) and the cool things he did with machines. They knew, of course, that I like machines a lot – my novel *Software* is about the first intelligent robots, and *Wetware* is about the robots using bio-engineering processes to build people like machines. Cyberpunk fiction is really ABOUT the fusion of humans and machines. That's why cyberpunk is a popular literature for this point in time — this is a historical time when computers are TAKING OVER many human functions and when humans are TAKING IN much more machine-processed information. There is a massive human/computer symbiosis developing faster than we can even think about it realistically. Instead of thinking realistically, we can think science-fictionally, and that's how we end up writing cyberpunk near-future science fiction. Cyberpunk is really about the present.

You would think science fiction conventions would be very hip and forward-looking, but often they are dominated by a fannish, lowest-common-denominator, Star Trekkie, joiner kind of a mentality. At times there's even a nostalgic, backwards-looking streak to science fiction gatherings, with ancient writers saying reactionary things like, "The future isn't what it used to be." When the idea of cyberpunk SF first developed, it was very unpopular at SF cons. Along with some of my fellow cyberpunk writers, I was practically booed off the stage for talking about cyberpunk at an SF Con in Austin a few years back. In California, I finally went to a good and intelligent science fiction conference. It was called Sercon (which is SF fan jargon for "serious and constructive"), and was held at the huge old Claremont resort hotel in Berkeley soon after I moved here. All my new San Francisco SF friends were there, and the British SF writer Ian Watson was there, too, and I spent a lot of time hanging out with him and with Faustin Bray and Brian Wallace of Sound Photosynthesis. Faustin and Brian were videotaping everything everybody said, which made us feel smart and important. In the morning the grounds of the Claremont were full of beautiful flower beds and big pastel sculptures, with a warm damp breeze off the bay. Ian Watson and I had lobster ravioli for lunch. This, I felt, was California as I'd dreamed it would be.

Faustin brought me into contact with the editor and the owner of *Mondo 2000*, R. U. Sirius and Queen Mu. R.U. is a pale-skinned puffy-faced individual with very long hair and a goony gap-toothed smile. Mu is fey and spacey, thin, attractive in a toothy Camelot-Kennedy way, also with long hair. They invited me to come and give a "Reality Hackers" speech/reading in a space called Shared Visions on San Pablo Avenue in Oakland down below Berkeley. Before the reading, they gave me and my wife Audrey a good meal at the

"*Mondo* house" – the huge rambling redwood California Craftsman deco pile in the Berkeley hills where *Mondo 2000* is produced. I was nervous about the talk, for which I was billed as a cyberpunk – in my past experience, the public's reaction to cyberpunk had been quite negative. I kept my shades and leather jacket on and read a chapter of my novel *Wetware* in which some people have sex, and one of them turns out to be a robot meat-puppet with a steel rat living in his skull. The audience was about 70 strong, and R.U. and Mu had charged them $10 apiece. And they totally got into what I was talking about. I'd expected them to be snobby arty/literary East Coast types, but they weren't like that at all. They were reality hackers, nuts, flakes, entrepreneurs, trippers, con-men, students, artists, mad engineers – Californians with the native belief that (1) There Is a Better Way, and (2) I Can Do It Myself.

To put it in a clear gelatin capsule for you, I'd say that (1) and (2) are the two beliefs that underlie what *Mondo 2000* calls the New Edge. The way that Big Business or The Pig does things is obviously not the best way; it's intrusive, kludgy, unkind, and not at all what you really want. I mean, look at what they show on TV! Look what the government does with your taxes! How can we make things better? The old political approach is to try and "work within the system," and spend years trying to work your way up to a position of influence so you can finally set things right, only by then you no longer even want to. But now, thanks to high-tech and the breakdown of society, you're free to turn your back on the way "they" do it, whatever it might be, and do it yourself. DIY, as the punkers say. You can make your own literature, your own music, your own television, your own life, and – most important of all – your own reality. There is no reason to believe in or even care about the stale self-serving lies being put out by the media day after dreary day. The world is full of information, and some of it is information YOU NEED TO KNOW, so why waste time on the Spectacle of the politicians and the media?

At my Reality Hackers talk, I finally relaxed enough to take off my mirrorshades and put on my regular glasses, and we all sat in a circle and people did show-and-tell. Someone had a mind machine with earphones playing pulsed sound to match the flickering

A cubic Mandelbrot set. (Image generated by Chaos.)

rhythms in two rings of tiny red light bulbs mounted in goggles that went over your eyes. As soon as I put them on I saw close-ups of the Mandelbrot set, just like the ones I'd been seeing on my new computer. The Mandelbrot set is a mathematical pattern discovered by Benoit Mandelbrot of IBM, the same guy who coined the word "fractals." Fractal shapes have the property that each small part resembles the whole thing. Trees are a kind of fractal, in that the branch of a tree tends to look like a shrunken version of the whole tree, and the sub-branches look like the tree as well, on down through about seven levels. The Mandelbrot set is shaped like big fat warty buttocks with a knobby disk stuck on one side, and with a bumpy stinger sticking out of the disk. If you zoom in on the edges of the Mandelbrot set you find little copies of the butt, warts, disk, and stinger, some of the copies wound around into gnarly spirals, all swathed in diaphanous veils and gauzes of the loveliest imaginable colors. The really *heavy* thing is that the whole endlessly various pattern is based on nothing but repeatedly evaluating a single quadratic equation. A potentially infinite information structure can emerge from one simple equation, if the equation is iteratively coupled to a repetitive computation. And THAT could very well be how the world is made, you dig, a simple rule plus lots and lots of computation. The world's "rule" is the Secret of Life and the world's "computer" is matter – pursuing the analogy another step, the "system software" for the world's "computer" is physics.

My new California physics friend is Nick Herbert. Nick is lean, button-nosed and over fifty, with Ben Franklin spectacles and a fringe of white hair around his bony pate. He holds to the belief that maybe there really IS some laboratory way to build a time-machine or a matter-transmitter or a telepathy-inducer. For all this, Nick is neither a charlatan nor is he a self-deluded nut, meaning that Nick does not LIE about being already able to build these physical devices (as a venture-capitalist-wooing charlatan would), nor does he THINK that he knows how to build them on the basis of some badly flawed or even nonsensical "symbolic proof." Nick is more like a gymnast who decides to spend the rest of his life walking on his hands, just to see how it is to have the world permanently upside-down. I already knew Nick before moving here by his having written me some letters arguing about synchronicity and time travel. When I got out here, he got me invited for a free weekend at Esalen in Big Sur. I'd read about Esalen for years of course, and was really tripped to go there. Nick's scam was that it was a workshop having to do with fringe concepts in Mind and Physics. Esalen has workshops on all kinds of things, and if you're a presenter it's free and if you're a participant it might cost a couple of hundred dollars. While the *Mondo/Reality Hackers* scene felt really happening, the Esalen scene did not. A lot of the other guests from the other workshops seemed very pushy, cold and uptight. They were like unkind Swiss and German tourists into their own personal health, man, I mean like readers of *Self* magazine. Going to Esalen felt like going to visit Thomas Jefferson's house Monticello in Virginia. There used to be something there. The scenery is beautiful. But now it's run for tourists by Park Rangers. At least that's how it struck me that one time, but in all fairness to Esalen, remember that I was then still undergoing the economic and cultural "bends" at moving from hideous Lynchburg to lovely CA. The wealth of Californians annoyed me a lot at first. And the indifference. The hard glossy surfaces of people's character armor. I soon realized that if I was going to make any money at all, I was going to have to retool and become high-tech. I began practicing looking at things – like the rocks and surf off Big Sur, for instance – and trying to believe that THIS TOO was a computer calculation. This was the big mental transformation I was needing to make – to think of everything as a computer – and talking about things like enlightenment or the theory of relativity struck me as a waste of time, dead-horse topics left over from past.

One of the great scientific centers for the study of the mathematical theory of chaos is the University of California at Santa Cruz. Soon after moving here, I had my first opportunity to give a talk to Ralph Abraham's chaos seminar at UC Santa Cruz. Ralph is a ruminative man with a dark beard. He speaks softly, but is somehow rather intimidating. You never feel like interrupting him. He showed me a drawer-full of computer circuit boards and said that he wanted to use computer processes to generate musical output. After my talk, we went to a great Santa Cruz Chinese restaurant called the Oh Mei. The day's special was called "Ants on a Tree," though that's not really what it was, I think it was a zucchini with transparent rice-flour noodles. The talk had been publicly announced, so besides Ralph, me, and his students, a couple of random strangers showed up as well. The next time I saw Ralph he was mostly interested in talking about cosmic historical trends, about the primordial Chaos of myth, the Mother Goddess, way-out things like that. California culture is like an organico-chemical bath with thousands of distinct kinds of macromolecules with open bonding sites. No matter what kind of triple-cis-alpha-desoxy thought probe you might be waving around, you know you'll find minds with receptor sites you can bond to.

Speaking of chemicals, after one of my talks somewhere else, a random stranger walked outside with me and pulled out a paper packet of white powder. "This is a new drug, Rudy. It's like Ecstasy or MDMA. Some people I know made it. They'd be very interested to hear how it affects you." "Wow, thanks." I saved the powder, and was finally unwise and idle enough to eat it one night a month or two later. It made me grind my teeth a lot, and then I got into a phone-calling jag, getting in touch with various weird old-time computer-programming and hacker types whom I hadn't had the nerve to talk to before. Merged on the phone I had the feeling of being jacked into some huge synchronistic Net. But then the full force of the drug hit me, and I sat in the living room feeling crazed and frightened. The next day I was so depressed that I wanted to die — this chemically induced clinical depression being the usual aftereffect of psychedelics on me, and the reason why I very rarely take them. I enjoy READING about people taking psychedelics, and I like to THINK ABOUT the effects they have, but I don't really like to TAKE them, nor would I wholeheartedly recommend them to others. To me the political point of being pro-psychedelic is that this means being AGAINST consensus reality, which I very strongly am. Psychedelics are a kind of objective correlative for being weird and different.

But in the end, for many of us, drugs are a trap. Can computers supplant psychedelics? It's worth a try. With cool graphics and virtual reality we can pursue the dream of the pure non-physical software high. When I first got my computer I still knew very little about programming. The only software that I had was a free Mandelbrot set program someone had given me, and my idea of "hacking" was to reach around to the back of the monitor and randomly change the little switches I found there, but this wasn't exactly a great feat of hacking I could impress my family and friends with. "Look, when I turn this little switch the picture gets different!" No, to do neat things with my machine I needed to understand how its insides worked so I could make up my own switches. Just as you can't write a story without having something to write about, you can't program without having something to program about. But I knew right away what I wanted to program: cellular automata (CA for short), which are parallel computations that turn your screen into self-generating computer graphics movies. In a two-dimensional CA, every pixel on your computer screen is "alive," in that each pixel looks at the colors of its neighboring pixels and adjusts its own color accordingly. This is analogous to the way in which each spot on the surface of a swimming pool is "alive" and sensitive to the neighboring spots. When you throw a piece of redwood bark into a swimming pool, the ripples spread out in perfect uniformity and mathematico-physical precision. How do they know where to go? Because each spot on the water's surface is updating itself in parallel a zillion times a second. The world is a huge parallel computation that has been running for billions of years. The folks putting on this all-encompassing show we live in – they've really got the budget! Even within the small budget of a PC's memory and clock-rate, CAs are a rich environment for letting the computer do weird things. By blending together a succession of CA rules you can, for instance, do something like this: start with a blank rectangle, fill it in with concentric ellipses, break some of the ellipses into globs, arrange the globs into a moving face, grow a detailed skin texture, turn the skin's pores into small beetles that crawl around and chew the picture up, send connecting lines between nearby beetles, bend the lines into paisley shaped loops, and fill the loops with growing fetuses.

I really got into the heart of California computer culture when I started going to the annual hacker's conference held here. The first time, I was invited on the strength of my science fiction, but by then I was already trying to be a hacker, so I brought my machine to the conference to show off what I'd achieved with my cellular automata. It was the most fun I'd ever had. Everyone there seemed happy. They were happy because they could actually DO something. We stayed up all night partying, bullshitting, and hunching over each other's machines. It all began to seem so SIGNIFICANT. The human brain gets along by grouping things into patterns and assigning meanings to them. If you have a nice fast chaotically changing computer graphics program you have lots of things to try and make patterns out of. And, unlike with watching clouds or fire, with a computer you also have the meta-level to play with; meaning that you can stop the process, go in and look at the rules generating it, tweak the rules if you like, then start it up again. And then there's the meta-meta-level, the discourse about what this image in connection with this program MEANS – like do fire and clouds really work this way? Are the thought-patterns in our brains like computer-generated fire and clouds? While my new friends and I were gloating over each others' graphics, other hackers were doing entirely different kinds of crazy stuff. Someone had linked his computer to the public telephone and was talking to Russia using the blank spaces between successive TV screen images going across the satellites. That little bar between frames that you see if your TV loses its vertical hold – that was this guy's Panama Canal to everywhere. And the things in the real world these guys had done! "I wrote the software for the first Versateller machines," someone might say, or, "I wrote this arcade game your kids play," or "my program is used in the carburetor of your car." What really impressed me was that people could play around on machines in their homes and end up affecting the events in the big industrial world. Before hackers it seemed like you needed a factory and an accountant and a bunch of workers before you could actually make something. But in the information economy, you can package it up and ship it out right from your home. Not that all the hackers were only into information. Hacking is an elastic concept – some guy showed up at the conference without paying, and proudly told me that he'd "hacked the hackers conference" – hacking in the sense of finding your way through some hindering thicket. Another told me he was going to hack Death by having his head frozen. Someone else had robot cars that could sense light, little radio-controlled type trucks with no radio-control but instead with a chip that the guy himself had made. The cars liked the edges of shadows, they liked to find a place where they could keep wavering in and out of the light. In this midst of all this fun, I felt a real sense of being engaged in a Great Work, in something like the same way that the workers on the Notre Dame cathedral might have felt.

I often think of Silicon Valley (and other hacking centers) as being like the Île de France in the Middle Ages, a spot where artisans and craftspeople from all over come together to work on the Great Work. It's certainly not a cathedral that we're building here – so what is it? At first I thought the Great Work was artificial life. The idea behind artificial life (called A-life for short) is that what living systems are really doing is moving information around. When living systems reproduce themselves, they are replicating their information. When a living system heads towards some food, it is using information about its environment to improve its situation. A computer virus is alive in a lowdown kind of way: it attaches itself to programs and gets those programs to make copies of it. A higher kind of artificial life might be an electronic ant colony with graphical critters that dart around on the screen and evolve to get better at bumping into the pixels that count as food. Much higher than that might be a program which is able to repair and even improve itself. Higher steps might be programs which not only talk like a person, but which are even able to effectively drive a robot body around in the physical world. And somewhere down the science fictional road might be robots that build robot factories that make new robots. A race of "artificially alive" machines spawned by us – the torch of life passed from carbon on to silicon.

It's an inspiring vision, but is artificial life really the Great Work which hackers are working towards? Isn't the more important goal to make things better for the humans on Earth now instead of for some race of future robots? This line of thought views the Great Work as the achievement of some kind of material paradise on Earth, with comfort and abundance and perfect understanding for all mankind. The watchword here is global network, rather than artificial life. Great high-bandwidth communication links with people talking to each other in virtual reality, instantaneous electronic polling, ten thousand different TV channels, and all good stuff like that. Keeping something this complicated working would take exceptionally good computer programs, of course, and the best kind of program is going to be one that's artificially alive, so in the end the two Great Work images may really merge into one utopian vision.

Utopias have a way of blinding you to the real present, though, so let's draw back from that. Let me tell you about what I saw some REAL machines do. Fellow freestyle SF writer Marc Laidlaw took me and the family to a Survival Research Labs show held under a freeway in San Francisco. It was terrific, a mad swirl of politics and collaged machinery, with a giant flamethrower that seemed continually about to explode, a pile of burning pianos, a giant metal arm poking at the pianos, and so on. After the show, my son and I found a heap of what seemed to be unexploded dynamite – clayey substance packed into an officially printed wrapper saying "FRONT LINE DEMOLITION PURPOSES ONLY", and with a long fuse. My son and I love fireworks. We tried lighting one, but it didn't go off. We were spending the night at the Laidlaws' apartment in Haight-Ashbury. Audrey kept saying that it was too dangerous for us to keep the dynamite, that it was unstable and might go off. After some thought I agreed. So how were we to throw it away? Laidlaw didn't exactly want it in his kitchen trashcan, so he and I went outside to ditch the dynamite. The sidewalks of Haight-Ashbury are crawling with homeless stoners every hour of the night and day, and we didn't want them to get hold of the dynamite, so we couldn't just leave it on the curb. The public trashcans were out of the question, as some Haighties practically LIVE in the trashcans – you throw something in a trashcan and there's a guy inside the can to catch it. Finally we found a church with a metal grating over the entrance. We pushed the dynamite through there out of reach. A few days later I saw an article in the *San Francisco Chronicle* about a rash of "fake dynamite" being found all over the city. It had all been a mind game that was part of the Survival Research Labs show. The show had kept going on for several days, as it were, and the Establishment's Spectacle had been (ever so slightly) taken over and co-opted by Marc Pauline.

The reality is that there is no unifying Great Work, there are just a lot of people here in the pit together, slamming and hacking. Our Great Work is to stay in the pit, to control our own destinies, and to hack what we can of the world. There are no nations in the pit, no us against them, and the Japanese are not our enemies. Recently Audrey and I went to Japan where I was to appear on a cyberspace panel along with hacker Jaron Lanier and some others. Queen Mu of *Mondo 2000* was there as well, as chance would have it. After our talks we were invited to the Gold Disco where a Mr. Takemura was putting on his monthly show. His show is a series of collaged videos he makes, also lighting effects, smoke clouds and scent clouds, and fast acid-house disco. The video show is a mélange consisting of (1) the chaotic pattern you get by pointing a TV camera at a monitor in a feedback loop, the key thing being, as Santa Cruz chaos mathematicians discovered, to have the camera upside down, (2) gay porno films of men kissing and dicks with studs and rings, (3) dolphins and politicians in black and white d) screens from the new *Sim Earth* computer game, (4) SIGGRAPH style computer graphics. Standing with Mr. Takemura and Jaron by the disco control panel, and the Japanese kids dancing like crazy, vogueing, some of them in bathing suits, a geisha off there somewhere, the video projected on seventeen different screens, *Sim Earth* going by, Mr. DataGlove right next to me – I get this really heavy flash that the New Edge really IS happening, it matters to these people here, it is going to happen, and we're all hanging out at the surfin' edge. Right then Mr. T. takes my arm and leads me off to a corner of the room, past the guy in the bathing suit, past the beautiful Japanese girl in the high shorts, and there on a PC monitor is...my own program CA Lab! The "Rug" rule, boiling away, bopping right to the beat as the casual viewer might think, my program running live here in the coolest disco in Tokyo. Hallelujah, my information had made it this far on its own. I'd GOTTEN OVER, as the brothers say.

And that thought sets off the flash that none of us hackers or writers or rappers or samplers or mappers or singers or users of the tech is in it solely for the Great Work – no, us users be here for our own good. We work for the Great Work because the work is fun. The hours are easy and the pay is good. And the product we make is viable. It travels and it gets over. And if you help make a piece of it, then that piece is part of you. You're part of the thang.

Now what exactly IS this Great Work which is taking place on the New Edge? We are not given to truly know WHAT IT IS. The Great Work is like a Mandelbrot Set of which we are the pixels, or even the steps of the computation. The Great Work is like a living body in which you and I are like a cell, or even like a specific chemical process, like an enzyme which copies ten thousand rungs of DNA. The Great Work is so big that nobody alive can even put a name on it. In a few hundred years they can look back and say what it was, but here inside it, nobody can see. It has something to do with people getting more and more mixed up with machines, it has to do with do-it-yourself, it has to do with sampling and collaging, it has to do with the end of the old style of politics. A wave of revolution is sweeping all of Planet Earth. Incredibleness: the Soviet Union is no more. How many more years can it be until the revolution comes back here to the United States, back to where it started? To reduce it to a bumper sticker: "IF THE RUSSIANS CAN GET RID OF THE COMMUNISTS, THE AMERICANS CAN GET RID OF THE REPUBLICANS!" Pass it on. Surely the ever-escalating rape of the environment, the crazy wastage of the "drug war," the warmongering, the elitist selfishness, surely this will someday come to an end – blown away perhaps by the onslaught of total New Edge information? Maybe soon.

Let's follow the Great Work and see.

— *Appeared as "Introduction: On the Edge of the Pacific" in* Mondo 2000: A User's Guide to the New Edge, *HarperCollins, 1992.*

Vision in Yosemite

One long weekend in August, 1992, my son "Tom" and I went backpacking in Yosemite. The trip was utterly wonderful. The first day was Thursday, we got a late unhassled start from San Jose, and drove up to Tuolomne Meadows, getting there about 6:00 PM. We got a Wilderness Pass for free from a ranger-girl in a booth in the parking lot, we'd been worrying about getting the pass, but if you are willing to backpack to at least four miles from the road, you can just walk on in. We've been here in CA for six years, and I used to try and get reservations at the (actually quite shitty, I now realize!) Curry Company campgrounds at Tuolomne Meadows, and there would never be a spot available, even if you called in February for next July. But if you're willing to backpack in with all your food and your tent for at least four miles, why then, brother, you can stay wherever you dang please. Simply treat the wilderness well and leave it as you found it. And now, finally, thanks to the energy of my son, we were able to do it. I used our old frame pack, he used his new internal frame pack, he bought a bunch of dehydrated food and a miniature alcohol stove, we used light old "Pup," the pup-tent we bought the kids in Lynchburg grade school, and we each have a down sleeping bag and cheap sponge-rubber sleeping mat. The High Sierras at last!

So Thursday night, Tom and I are a little worried about how we are going to get four miles off the road before the dusk of 8-9 PM, and also which way we, um, are actually going to be going. "Which trailhead?" the ranger-girl asks. "Do you have any recommendations?" "We're not allowed to recommend." "Which is less crowded?" "This is Yosemite in August." So first we say Cathedral Lake south of Tuolomne and towards Yosemite Valley, and then we change our minds and go back and get the pass changed to Glen Aulin north of Tuolomne, and then as we hike towards Glen Aulin we find the path too used-looking, deep and padded with sand, and what the hey, branch off towards the Young Lakes six miles north and 2,000 feet up.

The Young Lakes trail is deliciously deserted, but there is no way we are going to make it up there before it finishes getting dark. We spot a stream on the map and hike that far, then head up the stream a few hundred yards into genuine wilderness. Reassuringly, there is a fire-ring back in the woods near the stream, we pitch camp there, rapidly and anxiously, as night falls fast. There's a gibbous moon making silvery shadows in the empty woods around us. In the dark, the complicated alcohol stove won't work, but we get a campfire going – it keeps away the spooky moonshadows – heat up some water, mix it with dried Wild Tyme turkey dinner, the water isn't very hot but we are very hungry, we eat dry food mix in puddled spicy water, the fire dies down, we get the food hung from a tree branch with a counter-balance in the prescribed Yosemite bear-bag method (described in detail in our Yosemite guide). We sleep peacefully and wake up alone in the woods, with beautiful riffles of water sliding down the granite bed of the stream.

That day we make it up to Young Lakes, we find an isolated campground with another stream all to ourselves. Reading some info in our Yosemite guidebook, I find that the giant domes of granite that make up these mountains are called "plutons" after Pluto, not the dog but the god of the underworld. The plutons are immense balls of magma that froze up far beneath the surface of the Earth and eventually got pushed upwards. What makes the Yosemite granite so remarkable is that its filled with big chunks of quartz, scattered in like pineapple cubes in a fruitcake.

That night the bears hit us. I knew it was coming, sort of, as I'd hung the food rather low on a comic-book-silhouette of a pine tree right behind the tent. At 4 AM or so I hear the bag hit the ground and give out a great yell of warding-off and sheer terror. I get my shoes on, run outside, the white bag of the food is on the ground, but it's too dark to see the bear, I'm terrified, I yell – obscenities are inadequate in this situation, instead I yell things like YAH – grub up a rock and throw it towards the grunting or gobbling sound of the bear over there in the dark. Tom comes out with our candle lantern and extra candles. He lights a candle on the rock under the bent Donald Duck dead sapling pine that I'd tied the Barks bag to. The candle on the Yosemite pluton looks like something from *The*

Exorcist. This is very creepy. I feel at the torn food bag, "The salami is gone," I cry, "The salami is all gone!" But I hoist the remaining food up to the tip of the sapling again. Meanwhile there is frost on everything. Pup is sagging down to touch us, stiff with ice. In the dark, one waits for the sun to return as one would wait for a return-ing god. Blessed sleep doth knit up the raveled sleeve of care. At seven AM the first ray of sun strikes me getting out of the tent. Not only is Tom's salami safe in the bag, the clean tail end of my half of the salami is in the grass, not dented by bear tooth. Next to it is Tom's Powerbar and his bag of gorp, gorp chewed open, all choco-late gone, then another Powerbar. The two remaining freeze-dried dinners are intact, and so are the dried eggs. Victory! We won! We kept our meat! Actually Tom cared more about the Powerbars than he did about the salami, the salami was just my obsession.

After salami and eggs for breakfast, we left the packs in our camp and did an amazing tour of Ragged Peak Saddle, the Teeth of Death, Quartz Pipe, Hyper Young Lake Above Upper Young Lake, Fresh Bear Shit, Wrong Valley, Compass Reading, Home, The Fort, all quite incredibly Alpine, more Alpine than the Zermatt of today (lacking, *il faut dire*) the Matterhorn and the 15,000 foot peaks. On our map and compass tour, Tom and I peaked at 11,200 feet, on a level with northeastward-stretching sea of High Sierras and with the Cathedral Range to the south. The peak was of plutonic granite that had weathered into spars and disks. Each of us climbed a sepa-rate tooth, instead of having to perhaps muscle the other one aside, both of us wanting to beat the other one, but loving and wanting to defer, but really wanting to beat...We each climbed our own fins. Getting down, I said to Tom, "It was nice that we each had our own peak to be on. Of course mine was just a bit higher, but – "

"*Mine* was higher!"

That night we made our dehydrated Shrimp Cantonese just right with the now highly effective alcohol stove. We had a tiny cooking pan, a flat eating pan and two spoons. Plus two salamis and the bag-gies of gorp and the Powerbars. Our filter-pumper has several pieces: an oddjob porcelain filter that's inside a blue polystyrene bar-rel, a white syringe-like pump, and three soft rubber hoses that run from stream to pump, from pump to filter, and from filter to water-bottle, the removable hoses wedged onto ridged nipples. It's so unwieldy that it takes both of us to use it, but it's a thrill to confidently drink the water from a stream.

We bear-bag the food really well this time, in a position nearly matching the Yosemite guide-mandated dimensions of *12' off the ground, 10' from the trunk, 5' from the branch.* The night before on our Donald Duck tree it had been 7' from the ground with the bent dead pine too spiny to mount. So the bear had reached 7' up in the air and I'd been yelling at him in my T-shirt, glasses, and sandals? Not this night, no thanks, we hung the food high, and the frost didn't even come down and we slept like babies.

Sunday morning at 7 AM I'm up to greet the dear sun. I get dressed in my short-sleeved thick cotton dark-blue-with-snaky-paisley shirt, my tan wool V-neck sweater, my mole-colored knickers with the Velcro fastenings, my cotton-lined nylon defective Polo windbreaker from on sale at N.Y. Macy's, my blue cotton socks and my mountain boots from Zermatt like 20 years ago, 1972, the year Tom was born. He's still fast asleep, I wake him for a second to tell him I'll be back in an hour, like he cares, and I head cross-country up the stream that leads from Lower Young Lake to Middle Young Lake, and then up a grassy ramp to Upper Young Lake. I see one bear-bag on a tree up here, I skirt around it, around another fold in the Valley and here I am alone alone alone, not a sound in the sky, I am here at the shore of a beautiful glacial lake. "Take off your clothes and swim," says a mind voice. I wade in, delicately rupturing virgin sediment, then slump forward into the breast-stroke. The water was acceptably tepid. I rubbed my pits, butt and hair in the water, got into the depth, swam underwater 10 feet deep then surged up in terror tic of potential tentacled death-monster beneath the world of air.

I was born again in that water. I got out and looking at a feldspar-chunked granitic pluton I realized Rocks Are Alive. I'd always drawn a line in the past, sort of a time-scale chauvinist, right, with only plants and animals alive. But now after the Ragged Peaks hike with Tom, where he found an amazing crystal well, a disk that was the surface cross-section of an ancient volcanic heat-tube vent on the side of the plutonic exfoliating granite we'd clumb, and after all the amazing chunky knobs in the speened surfaces, look dude, Rocks Are Alive.

So now I fully had the web vision of Nature. In the past, like everyone, I'd learned to see the plant/animal ecology as a web. And on my own I'd come to think of the air as alive since it is eternally performing a programmable analog vortex computation. But I'd never thought of rock as alive, and now looking at these rocks, these rocks are as alive as college-student Green Party solicitors at your door, these rocks are like down with the program.

I've always known *All is One* in a bloodless intellectual's way but now, bathed in the live pellucid waters of Upper Young Lake, drying off on the cotton lining of my red coat, I saw how very wonderfully and precisely our web of Life doth adorn the curves of Mother Earth. Everything reaching out to each other – the plants the water the rocks the animals the air and even humankind – us not as spoilers but as thinkers, as pattern makers. The plants are pattern makers, too, the rodents peeping and darting are pattern makers…but why and wherefore? What causes and what senses the patterns? I scan and reject my beloved tricks of physics and math – these ideas aren't everything, they're only human beauty, only the ferns and flowers that grow, no, math isn't the answer, math is part of the pattern that is the question: *Why?*

I ponder this down the boulder-rodent-stag-water-air-moss-shrub-grass-soil-filled ramp towards The Fort and our campsite. Here is all this fabulously interlaced organic God-like beauty of Nature and why? I turn and stare at the sun, close my eyes, raise my hands, and

Love

Love is the force that grows the world. Love and beauty. Everything is beautiful because everything loves to be beautiful. All of us in the web of Life love each other, we love to churn out better patterns for the others in the web to love.

God is Love

Tom and I hiked cross-country around Ragged Peak and over the hoof-lands to Dog Dome and the car, I thought I'd lost my keys and then had the joy of finding them in a recess of my pack. We hadn't seen ourselves in mirrors for three days and each of us thought his own self looked terrible in the car mirror but that the other one looked fine. Like you only really criticize your *own* appearance. We drove a quarter-mile to the Curry Tuolomne Grill, Tom ordered two cheeseburgers and salads, I called Audrey, then went back to eat the gnarly burger with my beautiful son.

Next to us is a table of hiker-bums, two women and two men, drinking beer and for some reason selling shoes. Tom and I go to the men's room, a concrete hutch that's cheek-by-jowl with the grubby patio. As I use the urinal I notice on the floor of the closest stall a man's shorts, underwear and T-shirt. The man's foot is visible with a corn plaster on the pinkie and an alarmingly distended vein. Rhythmic grunting. Tom has peed and is washing hands, I say to him, "Don't you think it's pretty unusual to take off all your clothes to take a shit," and laugh, and point at the suspect stall. And now from this angle we can see pink cotton women's panties on the concrete floor as well. It's like a punch line: *All is Love*.

—*Appeared as "Zip.2: All is Love" in*
bOING bOING *#10, fall, 1992.*

Cyberculture in Japan

MAY 28, 1990, MORNING. FIRST SIGHTS.

We came in last night, first sight from the plane a long beach, the edge of Asia, the sand empty and gray, rice paddies lining the rivers, hillknobs sticking out of the paddies like castles, green and misty. The crowd at the airport: the variousness of the Japanese faces. I notice this again downtown later, the diversity of their faces from round to square, and skin color from yellow to pale white. Audrey and I hit the street to walk around the fancy Ginza neighborhood once we've checked into the Hotel Imperial.

An arched stone passage under a train line, barbecue smoke streaming out, people sitting eating and drinking, a TV crew with 12 guys pointing lights at the announcer, who waits poised, then starts screaming crazily and the camera and lights follow as he surges forward into the BBQ crowd and confronts someone. Taxi cabs like cop cars streaming by. It's all so cyberpunk.

We eat sushi and beer, and at some unknown signal half the people there get bowls of soup with clams in it. On the street we get lost, gawking at the huge electric signs. The oddity of seeing story-high electric letters that mean *nothing* to you. Pure form, no content. Burroughs talks about rubes staring up in awe at the crawling neon. It's humiliating to be illiterate.

Driving in from the airport we passed Chiba City on the right, and on the left I saw a building that might have been a motel, with sloping buttress side walls that went right down to the edge of a solidly building-lined canal leading out to the Tokyo Bay, and I thought of *Neuromancer*. There were a DJ man and woman on the radio, she repeatedly giggling madly, then they started a song; Roy Orbison singing "Only the Lonely."

Walking around the Ginza lost that night we see lots of groups of "company-men" in blue suits, some of them quite drunk by end of evening. One particular guy is doing the double-jointed wobbly-knee walk that my father used to call "the camel walk." He's fifty or sixty, gray-haired, leader of his buddies. They're having such fun out on the street, everyone: no one begging or stealing or looking for a fight.

MAY 28, 1990, AFTERNOON. AROUND TOKYO.

Audrey and I were up quite early, and spent about six hours exploring. We sat outside the Kabuki Theater for awhile to rest, and saw construction workers in split-toed cloth boots with rubber soles, good for climbing. "Split-toe" in Japan is like "hard-hat" in the U.S. Women in kimonos were going in and out of the theater, musicians and makeup people. They have the self-confidence of artists with a job.

The imperial palace is in the center of a park with deep-looking moats with slanting stone walls. There are also places where the slanting stone walls just come up from the ground, leaning against embankments. The walls are fascinating because at the edges they use rectangular blocks and towards the center they use huge irregular hexagons, all the blocks fitting together as nicely as soap-bubbles. It's interesting to me to see a transition between rectangular and hexagonal grid arrays, as this relates to a problem connected with the electronic ant farm program I've been working on recently.

We find a lovely green field in the palace park. It is deserted and Japan is so crowded. Maybe Japanese always do the same thing at the same time, so that either they *all* go to the park or *none* do? Or maybe they have too much respect for the Emperor to enter his park. The hedges are trimmed with a peak running lengthwise along the hedge tops, like the tops of a roofs. We hear someone playing or practicing a flute, it sounds Zen and spacey. Hearing that and looking at the pleasing meadow with a few trees and its low ridged hedges I think, "Of course it looks nice, it's arranged according to some transcendental holistic Japanese vision,"...then wonder if maybe I'm reading more into it than is there. The beautiful swooping catenary lines of the stone moat walls going down to the water are certainly by design.

We went to a museum with an art nouveau exhibit; all the other museum-visitors were young women. They look so goody-goody and tidy and sweet. Audrey says that sex is not viewed as sinful in

Japan, maybe that's why the women can be so clean and good, with nothing dirty about sex or the prospect of it to sully them? The women and children are in the shops and museums, and all the men are in the office buildings. After work the men drink and sing in the street and walk funny and go home and start over. Seems like a simple kind of life for either side.

Then we found the main art museum and saw an interesting show on "The Best of Bunten 1905–1917." Turns out Bunten is an acronym for a national art show/contest they had in Japan for awhile, till the artists quarreled so much the shows stopped. The pieces we saw were really interesting. Lots of them were straight copies of impressionist style. Cézanne and Degas and Manet copped composition ideas from Japanese prints, fans, and kimonos – and then the Japanese turned around and copped back impressionist lighting tricks for their own pics. Mirrors of mirrors. There were some wonderful big traditional-style scrolls and screens, too. Some of the screen paintings are done, if you look closely, in a fast loose brush style almost like cartooning, but at a slight distance they look formal and dreamily real. I noticed one beautiful woman guard in the museum, slightly plump – I keep trying to fix mental images of people I can use for Japanese characters in future books.

In the park, there's a woman kneeling, taking a picture of her toddler coming towards her saying "Mama," glancing over at us with such a shy happy look on her Asian secretary's face, not that she was a secretary, she had lipstick and a silk suit. With "Asian secretary" I'm thinking of the weak-chinned long-toothed look that kind of goes with the idea of a gossiping office-girl, a pretty fair number of the women here have that look, with a bright lipstick mouth stuck on like a mouth on Mr. Potato Head, only using a chinless yellow parsnip instead of a potato. In the primo examples of this look, the lips won't quite meet and an asymmetric bit of front tooth is always visible. But *regardless* of what anyone might think of her looks, there she is, the woman in the park, a mother getting her pictures of her toddler, having the nicest kind of simple fun. These people are so alien to me, I see them in a clearer way than the people back home – kind of like the thing with their writing: since I can't read it, I notice its pattern and semiotic weight, like *there* is an advertisement, right on the handle of the subway strap (Audrey noticed that one), and not be caught up in reading the message. Thus with the woman in the park, I have no ability to "read" her appearance and surmise her life (what kind of house, what kind of husband, kinds of opinions, etc. – and one can, or at least thinks one can, surmise all this easily and automatically from people back home), so instead of saying, like, "Oh, there's a yuppie woman with her baby," I just see the ideograph, the form, the woman, the mother getting a picture of her baby's early steps. "Mama," he said, same as us. I could push this further, of course, to get a concept of being around real aliens, though to do that I'd have to imagine not having mothers and children. Much is readable even here in Japan; I know for instance that letters are for expressing words, and I know what a mother is.

We found our way to the subway next, also interesting, two women walking past talking, one of them smiling almost crazily while talking to her friend, pausing to clear throat or wet lips and the smile is completely gone, it's simply part of talking. Audrey figured out the kanji sign for IN is a picture of lambda and a box: walking person + hole. And OUT is a picture of like a double psi and a box: cheering person + hole. You walk in the hole and then you cheer when you get out.

MAY 30, 1990. CYBERSPACE, INTERVIEWS, PACHINKO.
Yesterday was the big work day. In the morning I went to the building that the Ministry of Information uses for their Hightech Art Planning (HARP). These are the guys who paid my plane fare and hotel and gave me righteous bucks to come give a twenty minute talk on the topic of cyberspace.

There was an exhibit of some computers on one floor. I played with one for quite a while. It was a realtime graphics supercomputer called a Titan. It had a simulation of a flag which was made of a grid of points connected by imaginary springs, and with two of the points attached to a flag pole. You could crank up the wind, or change the wind's direction, and see the flag start to ripple and flap. I kept thinking of the Zen story about three monks looking at a flag flapping in the wind. A: "What is moving?" B: "The flag is moving." C: "No, the wind is moving." A: "Ah no, the mind is moving." To keep the flag from looking like a bunch of triangles they used a cool computer-graphics trick called "Gouraud shading." You could rotate the flag too, and as a last touch you could cut one or both of the flag's tethers to the pole and see it blow away, a crumpling wind-carried shape.

We all did presentations on our work, Scott Fisher on work he did at NASA with headmounted displays with one screen for each eye (immersion in virtual reality), in which the view changes as you move your head (realtime controllable viewpoint), and in which you can move an image of your DataGloved hand and do things (user entry into the image). He feels all three features are essential for creating the feeling of being in the artificial world. He used sound instead of tactile feedback, meaning that if you are manipulating, say, a robot arm, there is a sound whose pitch grows as the arm gets nearer to a wall. He spoke of a "3-D window" as a clipped volume containing a different viewpoint; you can reach out and resize a 3-D window. It would be nice to have several 3-D windows to other worlds in the room with me, even better than the old 2-D magic doors of SF.

I missed most of the other presentations because the HARP organizers led me off to do interviews, but another significant flash I got was from Susumu Tachi, who is into telepresence robots. He had a robot like a tricycle with a pair of binoculars sticking up out of the seat, able to swivel back and forth. A user drives the tricycle by wearing goggles and a head mount and using a brake and accelerator pedal. So you see the tricycle going along, turning its pair of eyes this way and that and stopping if someone is in the way. This is an interesting way of separating the problem of hardware and software. You can postpone getting pattern-recognition and judgment programs by letting the control go to a telepresent operator, and meanwhile just get a robot which can mechanically move around and, for instance, pick up objects the way you want it to.

I also got to hear part of Jaron Lanier's talk. Jaron is the hero of virtual reality; his company, VPL, is the first to sell DataGloves and the EyePhones with the two little screens. Jaron is a plump, substance-free hippie with Rasta-style dreadlocks. I sat next to him at the dinner day before yesterday and talked a lot; I ended up defending him when the waitress incredibly started harassing Jaron for having long hair. She's all, "You are woman?" Jaron took it in stride, calmly saying, "She only acts this way to promote a feeling of rowdiness." Two of Jaron's beliefs are, "It's not really a virtual reality unless there're at least two people in it," and, "Sex in cyberspace is a dumb idea: polygons aren't sexy."

In the morning we rehearsed the talks by talking to our translators and seeing if the video stuff worked. For lunch they brought us Styrofoam boxes of Japanese food. My lunch consisted of a *single* shrimp and *two* beans. Really *large* ones though, each bean a kind of giant lima that you squeeze out of its husk, and the shrimp a hefty little dude the size of a thumb. There was also a table full of soft drinks. The first one I tried, nothing came out, it was a "soft drink" of grape jelly. I had some Pocari Sweat instead. Who is Pocari and why are we drinking his sweat?

My talk went well, I had a video of my CA Lab cellular automata software showing behind me, and I talked about artificial life, about robot evolution, and about growing artificial life in cyberspace. It was an easy, painless talk. Doing a bunch of interviews was part of the gig, too.

One of my interviews was by a skin magazine called *Goro*, all their questions were about sex and drugs, like, "Do you feel pornography is a driving force for high tech?" I played along, "Of course. The same human thrill-seeking which makes sex and drugs important is a big factor in seeking out astonishing computer graphics." I  asked about the "soapland" sex places I'd read of in the guidebook, places where, it says, a woman soaps you all over, *using parts of her own body to soap you with* (I assume soapy boobs and soapy pubic hair), they were surprised I knew of it. They asked what I and my fellow Americans thought of the Japanese, and first I said, "Cool and strange," and they were happy, and then I said, "In the USA, many think of Japan as an anthill," and they looked upset. I was sorry I'd said that – over here I'm quickly getting into the concept of "*wa*," the common happiness and agreement. One aspect of *wa* is that whether or not I thought we had time to squeeze in yet another interview, they always said, "Yes we must do it."

Interviews I had: (1) A music magazine with all Japanese writing on its cover except *New Age Total Magazine*, though perhaps the name is *Rock Land,* which phrase appears several times on the table of contents. This interview was conducted by a guy who had been active in getting *The Secret of Life* published in Japanese, which I'd never even known happened. (2) *Goro*, as mentioned. (3) *ASCII*, a computer magazine. I remembered near the end of the interview that my friend Bill Buckley writes a column for them. "Buckley and I smoke marijuana together at hackers' conferences," I told them truthfully, though mischievously. (4) Yesterday evening with *Hayakawa's SF Magazine*. This was by my Japanese SF translator, a nice guy called Hiroshi. (5) and (6) Today by two more computer magazines, *Log In* and *Eye Com*. The guy who asked questions for both of them had some quite complicated fantasies about artificial realities. "In Sim City artificial world, would you rather be the mayor or the Sim?" He had the idea of *becoming* an artificial reality in which networkers live, any of them able at any time to, e.g., stop your heart. Another of his ideas was that you could shuffle your direct reality with someone else's, taking in their reality as an artificial reality. If you did this very often, like ten times a second, you would effectively be living as them and as you. If you speeded up the shuffle rate and brought in more and more people, then everyone would be the same metaperson. A catch is that you probably couldn't effectively even walk with all that shuffling. He gave me a wad of yen worth about $70 at the end of the interview! (7) Then a TV taped interview for NHK TV. This interview had interesting, well-thought-out questions, like, "How can artificial reality help children learn?" and several about ideas of cyberspace and mathenautics as a new frontier with an excitement more relevant to us than the somewhat boring and used-up stuff of space-travel. I really got into all this and laid it on thick, especially since the translator was the same charming woman, Ryoko Shinzaki, who had simultaneous-translated my speech. She was quite small when she stood up, but she had a beautifully symmetric face, with eyes that turned into semicircle slits when she smiled, also a nobly straight nose and a big upper lip. I got so interested in watching her talking that I would hardly hear what she said. (8) Then a stupid interview with someone who said he was a massage person who worked with HARP and mainly wanted to explain his theories of massage. I told him my gums hurt, and he pushed his knuckle into my hand until I said my gums felt okay. (9) Finally a magazine called *Diamond Executive* with a guy who actually understood no English, but would nod and look so much like a promising executive that you felt he was on your wavelength, only then the translator would take three minutes to tell him what you said.

The *Diamond Executive*'s translator was an expatriate American woman. I met several other people like her, Westerners who'd established themselves in niches of the Japanese culture. They all seemed to have a somewhat hangdog and dispirited air.

At the reception after the HARP stuff, there was a whole table covered with glasses of whiskey on ice, God how I hated to leave that room! Standing there talking to the guys, two of them managers of HARP (at least seven people were introduced to me as *the* manager of HARP), and the guys are so fucking drunk they can hardly stand up, yet they give off no vibe of USA-style shame for their altered state.

We had supper with my science fiction guys from Hayakawa Publishing, Inc. As well as publishing *Hawakawa SF Magazine*, they're the biggest SF book publisher in Japan, and have, incredibly, all of my books in print. If only I were so well-loved in the U.S. We ate as a party of 6 people in a basement French restaurant, some of the best French food I ever had, and then all five others start smoking, unbelievable, smoke and drink aren't evil here and people aren't embarrassed about sex, what a country.

Hiroshi the translator was a really good guy, I was tired but insisted on doing the interview after dinner to get it over with, up on the third floor with the Hayakawa offices – the French restaurant we had supper in turned out to be owned by Hayakawa, is in the basement of the same building. Propped my feet up on the sill of a huge open window, four- and five-story Tokyo buildings outside, the night and the street, talking about my various careers. The electroshock excitement of the computer graphic world is one thing, the thoughtful artfulness of writing another, the clarifying formulas and occasional revelations of math a third, and the humble public service of teaching is an underlying fourth.

This morning Audrey and I went to a shrine at Asakusa, on the way came up from the subway looking for breakfast, bought cheese rolls, but then where to eat? I ate mine on the street, but I wouldn't do it again; if you eat in public, Japanese look at you like you're taking a dump on the sidewalk. At the shrine there were zillions of school children, all in white shirts, so cute, group after group coming up to us, "May I speak with you?" to practice their English. At the shrine there was a shiny brass Buddha to one side, with a slot for money. You put money in the slot and then rub a certain part of Buddha, and then rub the same part of you, to heal. I tried it on my cheek over the gum where I've had the unbelievable, unrelenting pain ever since I had a bunch of back teeth pulled two weeks ago; recently I've been scraping agonized gum away to chip off spiky dead jawbone frags, and stirring up incredible endless torture of nerves up and down neck and deep into inner ear. The bone pieces are like having a three-dimensional Mandelbrot set pushed through my gum one cross-section at a time.[51]

We had a disgusting lunch in a badly chosen restaurant. Many Japanese restaurants display plastic models of the food they serve; I ordered from the plastic displays, but erred and ended up with a potty of utterly tasteless tofu custard, and a salad of cold noodles topped with 2 maraschino cherries and slices of scrambled eggs. Yum! Actually it had a single tempura shrimp on it, the come-on. Two women in kimonos were there eating, one of them our age, delicately pincering bits, her complex cheek muscles working. The waitress had hair over her face and a cheesy dumbbell mouth with the upper lip literally vertical at the ends where it met the lower lip.

I played pachinko, you put a few bucks in a machine and get a basket of ball bearings, and then dump them in a hopper and they are rapid-fired into a steep, nearly vertical playboard studded with nails and with high-scoring input hoppers here and there, and a big zero-score hopper at the bottom. Your control over it is via a knob that affects the speed with which the successive balls are launched up into the board. A special hopper guarded by two kneeling space-men figures opened up on my machine, and I held the knob at the right position for many balls to stream in there. More and more pay-off balls came out into a basket under the machine – there's a slot-machine aspect to it, and you get paid off with extra balls – finally I

51. See http://www.mathcs.sjsu.edu/faculty/rucker/cubic_mandel.htm for some images of cubic Mandelbrot sets.

had a whole shoebox full of balls, many more than the 700 yen worth I'd started with. Audrey and I took the box of balls back to a woman in an apron, she had the stubby sticking-out curly bob so popular here, she poured the zillion balls into a counting machine and gave me a piece of paper and gestured towards some cigarettes and candies. "Can I get money?" I said, pointing towards some coins in my hand. She nods and gives me some lighter-flints with the brand name "MONY." Like what are these good for? This is *money*? I start to complain, then she gets another girl to watch the counter while she leads me out of the parlor, out of the chrome and the whooping sound effects, into the street, down an alley to the right, down a smaller alley to the left, walking rapidly in front of me, aproned, walking with a rocking motion, walking so fast I can barely keep up and Audrey is a block behind me, she stops finally and points to the door under a horizontal red sign with writing on it, I go in, there is a tiny window at waist level, wood, I put the MONY lighter flints in there, and a hand passes out 2200 yen! Three to one payoff, all right! I asked my Japanese contacts about it later, they said, yes it is always lighter flints, and it would be illegal for the payoff to be inside the pachinko parlor proper, but this way is all right.

On the subway riding back, looking at the faces across from us, I see one old guy with a face all folded, the upper eyelids folded over the lower lids, the mouth folded shut, huge eyebrows, skinny skinny legs, he made me think of my pictures of old idol D. T. Suzuki in his *What is Zen?* book. Next to the old guy I see a succession of younger guys, one replacing the other stop by stop, the flow of life through the different bodies of man, each of them so individual and various, each life unique.

MAY 31, 1990. THE GOLD DISCO.

Yesterday evening we went to the Gold Disco, a multi-story building that looks like a shitty warehouse from the outside, down under a freeway by the river, guests of the same Mr. Takemura who was the organizer and panel-discussion leader for the HARP Cyberspace Symposium. He is a man who looks and behaves something like our San Francisco SF friend Richard Kadrey, kind of a maven, hiply up on all the latest. I first met Takemura when Allison Kennedy of

Mondo 2000 put him onto me in SF, he was doing an article for a Japanese magazine called *Excentric*, a *Mondo*-type publication with features on all the weirdos in a different given area each issue. He photogged me in front of the San Francisco Masonic headquarters in my red sweater, had me in the mag with Dr. Tim Leary of course, and mind-blown John Lilly, and Marc Pauline, who puts on the great Survival Research Labs fire-breathing renegade robot events, also Steve Beck, a friend of Allison's who does computer graphic acid videos and talks about using electric fields to stimulate phosphene visions in the closed eye, which process he calls "virtual light."

Here in Tokyo Mr. Takemura is quite a heavy dude it seems, and he does a monthly "show" at the Gold Disco. His show is a series of collaged videos he makes, also lighting effects, smoke clouds and scent clouds, and fast acid-house disco. The Gold Disco building has a traditional Japanese restaurant on an upper floor, we went there first, it was an airy room open at the sides to the sky (though it developed, on closer inspection that this "outdoors" was an artificial reality, was really a black painted ceiling with brisk ventilation, and that there was another story above ours!) Audrey and I were quite hungry, having skipped supper till now (9:00 PM) as Mr. Takemura's friend Kumiko had assured us it would be "traditional" Japanese food, which Audrey and I imagined as being banquet-like. Jaron Lanier was there, also Steve Beck and Allison Kennedy, also two friends of Jaron's, also Audrey's cousin Zsolt and his wife Helga. Zsolt grew up in Budapest with Audrey, now he's turned German and he's here in the employ of Bayer doing chemical engineering of rubber. Various Japanese companies have licenses to use Bayer's secret ways of making rubber, and Zsolt oversees some of that.

We're eating in a tatami room, meaning you sit on the ground with a tiny lacquered TV-dinner tray in front of you. First a waitress in a really great kimono and obi crawls around taking orders, and then there appears a geisha in the center of the floor/table, sitting there like a center-piece, simpering a bit and fanning herself, answering a few questions which we Westerners put through Kumiko, me and Audrey too appalled however to ask anything. Completely white face and red lips, all kinds of plastic and cloth in her hair, major kimono silk, etc. "She's not actually a geisha,"

Kumiko explains, "She is younger, she is a maiko, this is a young girl of 15 to 20 who has not mastered the necessary skills of singing or storytelling or music to be a geisha, she will in fact most likely not become a geisha, her purpose here is really to find a man who will take care of all her needs." And keep her as mistress, it goes without saying. She's plain and looks sad, and makes me feel so uncomfortable, she's like the goat tethered as bait for the T. Rex in *Jurassic Park*. Then all of a sudden we have to run downstairs to be photographed by Japan's most famous society photog, in front of the Gold Disco, all of us, the Gold Disco supposedly the hottest place in Tokyo these days, just like Andy Warhol or something man, outrageous, and we're just people after all, we glittery ones, then it's back upstairs and *whew* we have a new maiko, and this one is cute and *loud*, asking questions and saying things. And here's the food. A plate with a spiral tree snail, perhaps not dead, three whole salted shrimp each the size of a toenail clipping, and a small piece of what I take to be tuna, but is, on biting, a slice of some fish's long strip of roe, all egg-crunchy. Now the second course comes, two rice balls for me – *ba-ru*, the loud geisha explains, making a throwing motion, meaning "ball," and then putting her hands up to her mouth "gobble gobble," she's a regular bad-ass teenager under the paint, and three crab claw tips for Audrey, who thought to ask for them. Not much food but lots of sake.

Then it's downstairs to see Mr. Takemura's show, first Lanier and I go down, then a bit later Audrey – who'd been waiting around in the hope of more food – is led down with the others by the loud junior geisha, who starts dancing, what a sight to see her in the disco, it made me feel so much better for her to be there amidst the incredibly various throng. For me the best thing of all in the disco was that, incredibly, they had a computer monitor set into the wall with CA Lab running on it, showing my high-speed "Rug" rule.

Later we went up one floor to the so-called Love Sex Club, a lovers' retreat with big banquette/bed seats and a bar decorated with skeletons, skulls, and, dig this, bottles of clear alcohol, each containing an entire gecko, a really *big* gecko, barely fitting in the liter bottle man, not just some insignificant tequila worm here. According to Steve and Allison, who'd already tried it a few days before, this is an incredibly powerful aphrodisiac. Audrey and I split a glass of it, as do Zsolt and his wife. And soon thereafter we all go home to bed. Dot, dot, dot.

So today I'm clear of all my interviews and duties, though it took some running around to find a new hotel. We'd been in the luxury Hotel Imperial and now found, thanks to connections of HARP, a more affordable room in Ginza Dai-ichi Hotel, which is a surprisingly large step down in the direction of the proverbial coffin hotel. The window is like a bus window with rounded corners, the bathroom is made of one single piece of plastic and is tiny, but for now it's home. At first I'd tried calling hotels – our prepaid Imperial reservation ran out today, along with HARP's responsibility towards us – but all were full, but cute roundeyed roundmouthed plumpcheeked Mr. Fujino of HARP helped us out one last bit by finding this.

We were thinking of taking a train to Nikko, but just things like eating are hard enough. We did have a good lunch today, in the basement of the Ginza Style Department Store at Audrey's urging. In the store we first went up to the roof and looked at their bonsai, they had one pine for something like ten thousand dollars, it was especially valuable because it leaned way over and half of its trunk was like rotted away. There was a thick-gnarled azalea for nine thousand bucks, though the flowers on it seemed, to my mind, to ruin the effect of the scale. The department store was full of recorded voices, women's voices talking, Audrey said, in the voice of a Good Doll, a sing-song almost lisping voice. We sampled some of the many available things to taste in the gourmet food-shop in the second sublevel basement, hideous fishy wads and tortured slimy vegetables. After awhile I was laughing so hard at the gnarl of it all that I couldn't stop. My lunch was good except that the soup reeked of mildew. Traced the cause finally to some thick limp strands of fungus(?), maybe they get the spores of mildew and nurture it like a bonsai until it's a stalk the size of a carrot and then they slice that up and soak it in gecko juice or something and they put that in your soup. Once the offending strands were pincered out and banished to the furthest corner of the table, the meal was all right.

JUNE I, 1990, MORNING. SHINJUKU.

Morning, it's raining cats and dogs outside, Audrey is cheerful. Cozy in our tiny room.

Yesterday afternoon we went to Shinjuku. They had lots of pachinko places. I realize now that the machines are not separate entities, there is a vast common pool of pachinko balls behind the stuck-together rows of machines. Proof is that to buy new balls you put coins in a slot shared by your machine and the next machine, the balls don't come from one machine or the other, they come from the common ball space. How apt a symbol of the Japanese flowing out of their offices and through their subways, the pachinko balls, each ball by the way with a character on it, invisible unless you pick it up and peer closely to see the character scratched on. When you're through playing, there is a sink with towels near the door to wash off your hands. We walked through a neighborhood where I'd expected to see sex shops, but with Japanese reticence there was no way to tell which might be sex, or if you could tell, no way to tell what lay inside. Well, there *was* one obvious place – it had a big statue of a gorilla in boxer shorts with stars and stripes and an English sign saying, "This is the sex place." Gorilla in shorts is the typical USA male sex-tourist in their minds no doubt. Mostly Shinjuku was like a boardwalk with games, etc. There was a thin old-fashioned alley with a hundred tiny yakatori (skewered meat) places, we squeezed into one, with like a 5 foot ceiling, had a couple of beers and some skewers, a man helped us translate, "What kind you want? Tongue? Liver? Kidney?" "Uh...are those all the choices?" Then we went to an eighth floor bar called Gibson – I'd imagined maybe it was a cyberpunk theme bar as I'd heard some people use the phrase "Gibson literature" for "cyberpunk," but that's not what it was, it was just another of the zillion places selling whiskey and pickled veggies. We wrote postcards while the place filled up with office-workers in suits. When we got outside the Shinjuku lights were on, the big signs, awesome as the Ginza, but harder to see with all the train stations in the way. One particularly unusual light is a big 3-D cage of bars with neon tubes in every direction. A surface of illumination moved through the cage this way and that and then more and more of the bars came on to make a big chaotic 3-D knot of light.

Beautiful people on the subway, a schoolgirl with a big round chin, her lips always parted in a half smile, all of the women with the lusterless black hair and a few strands of bangs. Heart-stopping symmetries in these young faces, another girl with a slightly rough complexion carrying a basket of arranged flowers, pressing her offering into a corner away from the subway wind.

JUNE 1, 1990, AFTERNOON.
THE KABUKI THEATER, MOMOTARO.
Leaving the hotel for Shinjuku yesterday afternoon I decided, once we were a block or two away, that I should go back and leave my sweater, and then made a wrong turn and blundered around in circles for half an hour, finally giving up and keeping the sweater and with difficulty finding my way back to waiting Audrey. Our first night here we had to take a cab just to find our way back to our hotel. Amazing how difficult it is to orient with *no street names*. Some of the larger streets have names, but the names are "all the same" and "impossible to remember," especially since it is very rare that the name, if there is a name, is written out in Western letters. And you can't orient very well by landmarks since the buildings are mostly gray concrete boxes, or by signs, as the signs are crazy scribbles. Seeing some country-yokel type Japanese guys in our hotel I wondered how *they* ever find anything, and it occurred to me that they must simply ask instructions every block or so. The Japanese always seem ready to help each other, there are, for instance, so many staff always in restaurants and stores, like two or three times as many as back home – reminiscent also of the way there were like seven different guys working as "manager of HARP." The Japanese overemploy so that everyone can get lots of help and service, they give it to each other and they get it back. Generalities, perhaps false, but it's fun to try and see patterns here. One of the mysteries guidebooks and more experienced visitors mention is that there are effectively no usable addresses, houses in a district being numbered according to the order in which they were built, and many of the streets really not having any name at all. How can such a system work? It works if you think in terms of moving along like an (here's that impolitic word again!) *ant*, rubbing feelers with the ants you encounter, getting bits of info as you need

them. Given the city as a hive-mind extended in space and time, you
need only keep asking it where you are and how to get where you are
going, and it will tell you. You just feel-feel-feel your haptic way. As
opposed to the can-do Western approach where you get a map and
fix your coordinates and set out like Vasco da Gama, or like an instru-
ment-navigating airplane pilot, and reckon your way to your goal, all
by yourself, not asking for any help.

At breakfast on the 15th floor there were two halves, Japanese
breakfast half where you could get "rice set" including rice, boiled
fish, miso soup, pickled vegetables, or American half where you get
eggs. We opted for egg. The music in the Japanese half was a recording of a cuckoo, on the American side, Muzak. Great mushroom
omelet, though. Looking out the window through the Saturday
morning rain, we could see into a building with a many-desked
office. The guys in there were doing calisthenics together, just like
Japanese workers are so often rumored to do. It's healthy, natch, and
perhaps a way of bonding – "we all did the same motions at the
start of work."

In the morning paper, I read that one of the biggest gangs in
Japan, their like Mafia, is called Yamaguchi-gumi. Such a sweet-
sounding name for a gang…like the Little Kidders.

The National Kabuki Theater is in the Ginza, so we walked up
there to see if we could get in. Good fortune. They had an 11:00 AM
matinee with easily-bought inexpensive tickets to sit in the highest
(4th floor) seats. And a booth selling boxed lunches! Audrey got two
octagonal wood boxes with sushi in them, even though we weren't
hungry, the box appeal was irresistible. So there we were in the highest row, with Japanese all around us. There's a really pronounced
dearth of other Westerners here – often as not there are in fact no
others in sight (save at American breakfasts). Incredible, really, the
depth of U.S. ignorance of Japan – before coming here I didn't
even know the name of any of the parts or sights of Tokyo. Anyway,
up in the highest row of the Kabuki we sit, looking down at the not-
really-so-distant curtain which has two flying cranes sewn on, and
numerous bamboo trunks, pictures of them I mean, very Japanese
style, beams overhead with some slight decoration on them and
light wallpaper with a meandering parallelogram design. Rows of

red paper lanterns here and there on the sides. Then it starts. There were four scenes with men, a boy, and two "women," though in kabuki the women are played by men, who are called "onnagata," as opposed to "tachiyaku," who act male roles. It's such a sexist society the women can't even be actresses, man, it's wife or geisha and nothing else. The kabuki was like theater, not like opera, with no singing, although if a group laughed, they'd kind of chorus the laughing, and in the big emotional scene after her son is murdered, the mother's sobs were like, Audrey said, an aria. I opened my box lunch and ate of it, also drinking of my canned soft drink: Oolong Tea. The box was covered with paper with large elliptical pastel polka dots. The best food in it was a little sweet yellow rubbery dough cup holding a sushi of rice and salmon eggs. Another good thing was a single stray green pea. At the peak of the kabuki play's action (it lasted an hour in all, though if we'd stayed there would have been a whole second number of dance) the younger brother goes and shakes the older brother, who is lying in bed asleep. The older brother jumps out of bed, knifes the younger brother in the stomach, delivers a speech (probably about why it is "right" to be doing this, the prick), and then knifes him again, killing him, and bringing on the mother's "aria." Last time anyone wakes *that* guy up.

The scenery was a really authentic-looking Japanese house, so much better than, for instance, the "Japanese" set in the production of M. Butterfly we saw in SF last winter. It was just so fuckin' authentic. Another cool thing was that, Macbeth-like, the climax is taking place during a storm, and they had really good thunder sounds that I could tell came from an incredibly experienced Japanese thunder master shaking a big piece of special kabuki thunder metal, as opposed to playing a track on some sound-effects CD. Good lightning effects against the house's translucent windows too. One last interesting feature were the "kakegoe," which are special shouts and whoops which certain audience members give at crucial moments, like when an actor first comes on they might shout his name, or at the end of a scene they shout something, but never shout at a wrong or intrusive time, of course, being into the wa and the Zen and the group mind as they are. "You go on and yell something," I whispered to Audrey, and next time somebody yelled like KAGU-WA, after the mother did her aria, Audrey yelled KAGU-WA too. Later, telling Audrey's cousin Zsolt about it, I exaggerate and say that Audrey stood up and yelled "right on!" in the middle of silence.

We took the subway up to Akihabara, which is supposed to be this big electronics market, but couldn't find any action near the subway stop. Saw a man on a bicycle delivering takeout food, which was a tray held up on one hand with a covered dish and, get this, two covered dishes of *soup*. Soup on a tray on a bicycle. The dish covers were like the top of an oatmeal box, i.e. a disk with a half-inch of cylinder sticking out, looked like black leather, like a dice-cup.

So got back on the Hibiya Line to Ueno Station, where there's a godzillion people in the street. Saw a guy buy a dose from a "One Cup" sake machine and chug it, this right outside the pachinko parlor where I lost another five bucks. They even sell fifths of whiskey in the vending machines, I'm not kidding. My initial pachinko win seems to have been a fluke. Looking at the balls in this place, I realize they all have the same character on them, a number 7 in this case, so maybe in each place there is a like cattle-brand symbol on their balls so you can be found out if you sneak in your own balls. Before, I'd thought it was a different symbol on each ball, like names. We went into Ueno park, and saw a lovely Shinto shrine, someone playing nice flute off in the trees, people pulling a cord hanging down in front of the temple to rattle a bell up in the eaves, a way of getting the notice of the gods. Like the other temples, this had a "backwards" swastika on it, oriented in effect so that it was "rolling" to the right. I remember from my childhood year of boarding-school in Germany a kid saying, "*die Hackenkreuz rollt links,*" a wiry, high-cheekboned kid with a deep, bossy voice, he was also the source of the rule, "*die Kaffemuehle dreht rechts,*" which was used to determine the order of play in card and board games, "the coffeemill turns to the right."

A group of schoolboys stopped us in the park with the same "May I speak with you" English-practicing routine that schoolgirls had pulled on us in Asakusa. More bizarrely, a team of three twenty-year-olds stopped us, one with a video camera, one with a mike, and one (a woman) holding a placard with four cartoons of incidents in the life of Momotaro who is, they assured us, a well known Japanese character. They told us the action in the first and third frames and we were to fill in descriptions of what happened in the second and fourth frames. In the first frame Momotaro is born, his father found him when he cut open a peach. (Hiroshi later tells me that "momo" means "peach" and "taro" means "first born son.") In the second frame two demons steal money from the parents. In the third frame Momotaro and his three friends – a dog, a monkey, and a crane – sail to the island of the two demons. In the fourth the monkey and the dog kill the two demons while Momotaro and his dog look on, and his parents bow to him. Then they gave us two postcards and they didn't ask for money or try to get *anything* from us, though of course they had videoed our answerings. Was it an art project, a sociology study? Will I ever know?

Anyway we went across the street to the Tokyo National Museum, and went into the main building. They had a bunch of 7th Century Buddha statues, then some 13th Century ones, then a room of "enlightenment instruments" that depressingly reminded me of *auugh* dental tools (last night's gum-cutting only made it hurt more today, of course), things with prongs on the end to pluck out evil, then there was a room with some really great looking pipes, like dope pipes with real long stems decorated amazingly, one finned, one polka-dotted, then a room with helmets, one in the "unusual hairstyle" fashion, with a fake ponytail and mustache of like boar's hair – what biker wouldn't want to have that! – then some sword blades, then a door that went out in the back yard, and we could read the Japanese for it, the three characters were the lambda, the double psi, and the square: IN OUT MOUTH. Then there was a room with old firemen's clothes, one with a really cool demon face on it I tried to sketch. Back outside we walked through a neighborhood with nothing but motorcycle things: new and used cycles, tires, leathers (Japanese motorcycle leathers, man, is that kinky or what?), then got the subway back "home."

On the subway there was a teenage boy, and Audrey said seeing him made her miss our son Tom. For a fact Tom has the same skin color as the boy, and the boy's lips and hands looked like Tom's too. It's funny to be so old, or such a parent, that now teenage boys seem cute and touching. Got a couple of beers from a sidewalk machine, came up to the room to write, wrote this down, and now I'll move back up into that stuff they call real time.

JUNE 1, 1990, 'ROUND MIDNITE. DINNER WITH HIROSHI.
'Twas a most mellow and emotionally salubrious fest with my translator Hiroshi Sakuma and his wife Miyuki (Me + You + Key, she explained). Hiroshi came into the city and took us out to his neighborhood by cab (an unbelievably high cab fare, which he paid alone) where we ate at his favorite restaurant. "It's low tech," he kept saying. He's been eating there every Saturday night for 10 years, he and Miyuki, the little building was a country house someone took apart, no nails involved!, and brought spang into Tokyo. There was a bar there with folks eating at it, a short bar, and a tatami room, and our room, with benches, and that was the size of it. The place is called Kappa-home, the kappa being an imaginary beast of Japanese legend.

Miyuki is a modest wife with a tentative smile; she met Hiroshi at an SF convention when he was at the University of Tokyo and she in high school. He has a ponytail, like the Kabuki guys, traditional though uncommon these days. The historical oscillation of ponytails in and out of fashion in Eastern and Western cultures. The ponytailed men in the Kabuki had seemed to have the tops of their heads in front of the ponytail shaved, though on looking closer, I'd noticed that one of them actually had a cloth cover on the front of his head that only made it look shaved. Audrey hadn't noticed the cloth and insisted the guy had really been shaved. We asked Hiroshi and Miyuki about it. Turns out an old-time ponytailed merchant might wear a cloth over the front of his head instead of shaving it, but if it's a colored cloth it means you are a *pimp*. Was the guy in the Kabuki this morning supposed to be a pimp? I'll never know.

The food was outrageously wonderful, the freshest most incredible raw seafood you can imagine, including whole, raw, sweet-tasting squid, and some mysterious white slices of...what? Hiroshi explains, "This is the liver of a kind of fish. It tastes like cheese. The fish lives very deep in the sea; he is so large and jelly-like that you cannot hold him in your hands. The fishermen hang him upside down and the liver falls out of his mouth." Kind o' sets your mouth to waterin' don't it? Audrey liked the liver and the squids a lot. Two other good things were the tempura eggplant and the raw abalone.

Before we started the sake, the server-woman brought out a big

Rudy and Sylvia in Japan, 1990.

tray with lots of little stoneware cups, all different, and you pick the
sake cup you want. Hiroshi's cup was a silver one brought special to
him as a regular client. The sake came from a big white cask with a
big ideogram on it.

About the food, Hiroshi said: "We've been eating exactly this for
500 years." The Kappa-home seemed very together, the people
happy and relaxed. A seventy-year-old lady at the bar was drinking
and eating, and I instantly imagined her USA counterpart as some
shrill, bleached crone of a barfly.

Hiroshi was proud of his translations of the neologisms in *Software*
and *Wetware*. He coined the word "*kune-kune*" to stand for "wiggly,"
for "stuzzy" he invented "*rin-rin*," and for "wavy" he used "*nami*" — as
in tsunami. "How's the surf, dude?" "Nami, dude. Way rin-rin."

JUNE 5, 1990. THE BIG BUDDHA.

Sunday, cousin Zsolt and wife Helga took us sightseeing, we got the
train down to Kamakura to see a Zen monastery and the Daibutsu
(Great Buddha). The monastery was woodsy, be-templed, tourist-
thronged. I saw one monk-type guy, with just the great huge grin
you'd hope for. I felt some inklings of peace there, looking at a hill-

side, at a little Zen shrine, at a perfect arrangement of a flower and a few weeds, feeling once again the unity of all things, the loss of body outline, me a jelly pattern in a sea of sensation.

The Daibutsu is about sixty feet tall, he was cast in bronze pieces and assembled about 1300. In 1495 a tsunami came a kilometer inland and trashed his temple, but he's still there. You can go inside him, he has big doors for air in his back. His head has knobs on it standing for hair. His expression is a marvel of disengaged compassion.

Our last night in the hotel room, I found two pay-TV channels of Japanese porno. I remember Martin Gardner telling me that the Japanese don't allow depiction of pubic hair, so what they do in the porno movies is to usually "pixelize" the crotches, meaning that within a disk area, the image is broken into large squares with each square the average of its component pixels. Another, less frequent trick is to shine a bright spotlight on the crotch so that the area "burns out" white in the video. One of the videos was a fake TV show, with the announcers going down on each other, etc. So odd to realize Japanese act *this way*, too, even the little mask-faced women in their beige suits with the big white lacy collars. After watching for awhile, Audrey was asleep, and I went out and got a late-night bowl of noodles across the street, great noodles, though with the loathsome fungus strips in it like in the department store soup. I asked the counter people and they told me the hideous mildew strips are "namma" which is *bamboo!* not fungus at all. They were a great crew of guys, the noodlers, kind of like a WWII platoon in a movie, with a kid that all the old ones talked to, a bony guy with radar-dish ears, a plump weak-chinned one with a mustache, and a busy cook in the back.

The last thing in Tokyo Monday morning, Audrey shopped, and I took a subway to the Tokyo Tower, a truly cheesy copy of the Eiffel Tower, with none of the Eiffel's mass or heart-lifting scale. You take an elevator up 150 meters, and get out, and there is a fish tank with one poor big black carp in it. A fish in a tank in a tower 150 meters above the ground. In my final ride in the subway I'm tired of being the different one, the carp, and I'm glad to be going back home to California, back to being a fish in my home sea.

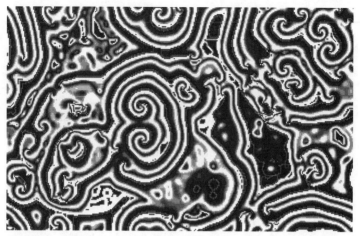

A Belousov-Zhabotinsky CA rule called "Hodge." (Generated by Cellab.)

AUGUST 8, 1993. HELLO KITTY.

Three years later we went to Japan again, this time on a kind of tour organized by a Tokyo publicity agency called Humanmedia, who lined up a bunch of lectures, magazine interviews, and bookstore signings, all of them for pay – enough so that as well as Audrey, I could bring our eighteen-year-old daughter Ida along on the trip too.

The biggest attraction for me was that CA Lab was part of an art show called "A-Life World" at the Tokyo International Arts Museum. CA Lab was nicely installed on ten color laptops resting on a line of music stands, each laptop running a different cellular automaton rule. Some of the rules showed organic pulsing scrolls, some showed tiny scuttling gliders, some showed slowly boiling colors. It was great to see it there.

The museum was out in a suburban part of Tokyo, and before my talk, I had an hour to kill. Right past the museum was a giant building the size of a baseball stadium, only sealed up, and with fanciful towers on it. "That's Sanrio Puroland," Yoko had explained to me. "They are the makers of Hello Kitty. It's a place for children. Like Disneyland."

Hello Kitty is the groovy little mouthless cat that you see drawn on so many Japanese children's knapsacks and stationary. In recent years she's gotten pretty popular in the U.S. as well. She's so *kawai* (Japanese for "cute"). The strange thing is that, as far as I could find out, there are no Hello Kitty cartoons or comic books. Hello Kitty is simply an icon, like a smiley face.

Outside the Sanrio Puroland, I was drawn in by the crowd's excitement and couldn't stop myself from going it, even though it cost the equivalent of thirty dollars. But I knew it was my journalistic duty to investigate.

Inside the huge sealed building it smelled like the bodies of thousands of people – worse, it smelled like diapers. Lots of toddlers. I was the only Westerner. The guards waved me forward, and I went into a huge dark hall.

There was amplified music, unbelievably loud, playing saccharine disco-type tunes, with many words in English. "Party in Puroland, everybody party!" Down on the floor below were people in costumes marching around and around in the circle of an endless parade. One of them was dressed like Hello Kitty. I couldn't pause to look at first, as young guards in white gloves kept waving me on. I wound up and down flight after flight of undulating stairs, with all the guardrails lined by parents holding young children.

Finally I found a stopping place down near the floor. In the middle of the floor was a central structure like a giant redwood, bedizened with lights, smoke machines, and mechanical bubble blowers. The colored lights glistened on the bubbles in the thick air as the disco roared. "Party in Puroland!" Hello Kitty was twenty feet from me, and next to her was a girl in gold bathing suit and cape, smiling and dancing. But... if this was like Disneyland, where were the rides?

I stumbled off down an empty hall that led away from the spectacle. Behind glass cases were sculptures of laughing trees making candy. And here were a cluster of candy stores, and stores selling Hello Kitty products. I felt sorry for the parents leading their children around in the hideous saccharine din of this virtual reality gone wrong.

I made it back out into the fresh air and walked back to the "A-Life World" show. After the stench and noise and visual assault of Puroland, I couldn't look at the weird A-life videos anymore. But the realtime computer simulations were still okay. They were really alive, they had their gnarl and sex and death.

That evening, Mr. Arima, Mr. Onouchi, and Mr. Takahashi treated us to a great dinner in a Roppongi restaurant. These were the guys from Humanmedia organizing my gigs. Mr. Arima delivers one of his rare English sentences, "Mr. Onouchi is a heavy drinker." Mr. Onouchi snaps, "I don't think so," and a minute later knocks the sake bottle off the table. Mr. Arima's hair is wavy from a perm, and there are white cat hairs on his green suit. Sometimes he wears gray pants with white lines on them. When you talk to him, his lips purse out, and if he smiles, one dancing front tooth is at an angle. His oval-lensed wire glasses slide down on his nose. He's cute and touching. The dinner featured a soup called Frofuki Daikon, or steambath radish.

After dinner, Audrey, Ida and I walked around; this is the hippie part of town, the only place you see Westerners. On a big video screen over the street there is the music video of Billy Idol's song "Cyberpunk." In front of us, men in white gloves are digging a ditch and putting up little flashing lights. Billy's chest bursts open and shows wires. The men in white gloves gesture, waving on the passersby.

AUGUST 9, 1993. SHAPE CULTURE.

The next gig was in Osaka, home of my then-favorite band Shonen Knife, not that we saw them. Once a *Mondo 2000* interviewer asked Shonen Knife if they were like Hello Kitty, and the answer was, "No, Hello Kitty has no mouth. We have big mouth, we are *loud*."

My talk was for something called the Society of Shape Culture, which turned out to be just what they sounded like: people interested in unusual shapes. They were big buffs on the fourth dimension. They wanted to know what shape I was hoping to see when I programmed my Boppers program to show artificial flocks of birds, and that was, really, the right question, as it was exactly the beautiful living scarf shape of a flock that I'd wanted to see so much that I slogged through all that code.

I used my color laptop at all of my Japanese demos, showing up with my "axe" and plugging in to whatever kind of display amp they had. At the Shape Culture demo there was a nice big projection screen, but it was keyed to work off a computer in a back room, and

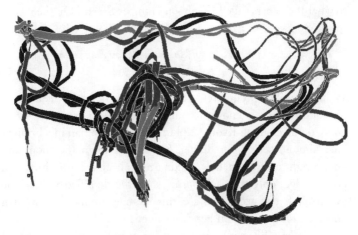

A simulated flock of birds. (Image generated by Boppers.)

when I wanted to change my images, I had to leave the dais and go into the back room, still talking over my remote mike.

After the Shape Culture talk, we all sat around a table made of five pushed-together tables and drank beer and ate sushi that they brought. There was a Buddhist monk yelling about the fourth dimension and showing off his wire models of some polytope, he had four of them and said one was point-centered, one line-centered, one face-centered, and one solid-centered. Nobody could understand the details, but the shapes were great. Another was an origami master. Another a maker of paper hyperspace models. Many of them interested in mysticism. It was a wonderful feeling, a magical afternoon.

Everyone introduced themselves after we'd been eating and drinking for awhile at the Shape Culture luncheon. A heavy student with thick glasses says, "I am a graduate student and have not discovered anything yet." He smiles and rubs his hands as vigorously as if he were washing them. "But I want to!"

AUGUST 10, 1993. DINNER IN KYOTO.
We move on to Kyoto for a signing in a bookstore. The evening of the first day in Kyoto we have the best dinner of all. It's raining due

to what the papers called "Typhoon Number Seven." On the way to the dinner, we see a haiku out the taxi window:

In Kyoto a woman in a green kimono walks on clogs in the typhoon rain.

We use new-bought umbrellas to wind down the back streets to the restaurant which is known to our host Mr. Mori from his having gone to university in Kyoto. A plumpish juicy woman in a brilliant blue kimono serves our dinner. She comes in to the room and kneels right away, somehow making me, pig that I am, think of a porno video, only this isn't porno, she's the dignified wife of the owner/chef. I'm excited to see this strange, immaculate woman kneel. She has a mole on her face somewhere. Her lipstick is fresh and bright red. She smiles and speaks to us in English. She is proud of the room we are eating in, her husband the cook is also a carpenter, he built this room, the air smells like incense from the fresh wood. On one wall is paper printed in clouds from a 16th Century woodblock. Mr. Arima and Mr. Mori order hot and cold sake, plus an endless stream of big Sapporo beers. The cold sake comes in beautiful glass bottles that are shaped like two spherical bulbs, the top one smaller than the bottom one. The glass bottles sit in chipped ice and have vines around them. The hot sake is in raku. You always have to pour for other people instead of taking for yourself. Ida keeps Mr. Arima's glass full and starts giggling. Mr. Arima eventually leaves to go to the bathroom. When you go to the bathroom you put on special shared slippers that are out in the hall, toilet slippers. Ida and I have a running joke that one of us is going to goof up and come back into our shoeless tatami dinner room wearing the toilet-slippers with two meters of toilet paper trailing from the heel.

AUGUST 11, 1993. FEVER POWERFUL.
Outside our hotel in Kyoto is a pachinko parlor designed like a classic Greek temple, the archetypal house shape: a nearly cubical box with a single peaked roof. It is all glass, and the roof is broken into squares with colored lights that march across in patterns.

One of the pachinko games has a little video screen that shows a

girl who eats a fruit and gets big and strong and then the words
FEVER POWERFUL appear across her. The name of the machine is
Fever Powerful. On the top of the machine is a picture of Fever
Powerful on her back, arching her pelvis up, with her boobs sticking
out, she looks like she's fucking.

AUGUST 13, 1993. ZEN ROCK GARDEN.
Back in Tokyo, we hit a high point, a visit to the most famous Zen
rock garden of them all, Ryoanji, raked gravel with fifteen rocks
grouped something like:

    2   2
      5   3
              3

Ida saw an ant on the edge near us, then I saw a dragonfly landing on
the other end, and then later, alone, I saw a skinny Japanese lizard
crawl under the biggest rock of the 5 group. The world's most
enlightened lizard. To put my head into the head of that lizard –
this is a durable enlightenment trick that the rock garden has now
given me, this is something that I am bringing home with me to mix
into my visions, a life as the skinny lizard under the Zen garden
rock. There seemed to be quite a space under the big rock, it looked
like a lizard-sized cave, plenty of room in there.

The rock garden was up against a wood building, an empty Zen
temple with three empty rooms with tatami mats on the floor and
faded ancient Zen landscape paintings on paper leaning *no big deal*
against the walls. Around the corner from the rock garden was
some moss with diverse mushrooms under trees, around the next
corner was more moss and bamboo and a fountain trickling
through a bamboo pipe into a round stone with a square hole in
the middle. The four Japanese characters on the fountain said "I
only learn to be contented." Audrey liked the fountain best, she
bought a little metal copy of it. Getting up from looking at the
rock garden for the third time I had a line of sight through the
plain wood temple to see Audrey stepping barefoot down to the
fountain and washing her hands, and then stepping up onto the

old rubbed wood temple floor and moving her body in such a perfectly Zen and perfectly Audrey way, I saw the cuteness and wonder of her motion. "Yes, I'm stepping up from the fountain onto the smooth wood deck. This is me! Me the exclamation mark, me the same as ye."

The garden has been there for maybe six hundred years. People only started noticing it in the 1930s. The clay walls around the garden have a messy fucked-up pattern, with one piece of wall quite different from the others. The Japanese like asymmetry.

After the rock garden we had lunch in a Zen teahouse near the rock garden, two Zen monks there eating also, big Japanese guys with burr haircuts and gray robes; the lunch was a pot of warm water with slabs of tofu, and strainers to fish your slabs out to put in a little pot that you pour soy sauce into. Some veggies on the side: a few beans, a piece of eggplant, a pickled pepper. We sat on cushions on the tatami mat floor by a slid-open paper door, outside the door a little pondlet with miniature trees and big carp in the pond. One of the carp jumped halfway out of the water. "Did you see that?" I ask Ida. "Yes!" says Ida. "That right there happening was a haiku!" We all felt very happy and high.

AUGUST 15, 1993. THE JAL WARNING FILM.

Back in Tokyo for a last day, in the morning through a hotel door I heard the sound of a woman's voice in sexual ecstasy. "*Hai, hai, hai, hai!*" In the breakfast room, the couples look like high school students. "*Hai*" means "Yes."

We make one last run to the Ginza. In the basement of the Tokyo department store, a plump girl leans over her soba noodle soup. A single noodle dangles from her lips, swaying as she sucks it in.

Everywhere there are the voices of the "Good Dolls," the breathless childlike voices of the Japanese advice women. The best Good Dolls run the elevators in person in the department stores. Their motions are a beautiful dance, with their white gloves they make the virtual moves of pulling the doors open. We're tired of the voices of the Good Dolls, even in our last bus to the airport to leave Japan there is a Good Doll voice. It's like in the movie *Alien* when Sigourney Weaver escapes into a lifeboat ship...and there's an alien in it with her. What if when I get my car at the airport back in SF there's a Good Doll voice in it?

On the plane back: the eager violence of the unfolding inflatable slide that pops out of the airplane in the instructional video JAL shows us. When we near the shores of Californee, JAL shows a short film about AIDS and a long film about drugs. Close shot on an apple. A big syringe injects narcotics into the apple. Close on a Japanese girl lying on her stomach on a towel at the beach. A hand moves into frame holding the apple. English translation of the voiceover: "They may ask you if you want to have fun or if you want to have a good time. They will not mention drugs. They will offer you something that looks harmless, but it is drugs."

When I got to my car at the airport it looked wonderful.

"I'm Rudy's," it said so I could hear it. "I'm Rudy's car. The old red Acura."

"You?" I said. "It's you? Thank you, my dear faithful hound. Thank you for having continued to exist. We have been in Asia for very long."

"Get in and drive me home," said the car. "And next week you and me are going to start commuting to work again."

—Appeared in Transreal, *WCS Books, 1991*
and in Axcess, *#8, Summer 1994.*

The Manual of Evasion

JANUARY 7, 1994. EN ROUTE TO PORTUGAL.

No clear idea what day of the week it is, I'm still in the holiday "broken clock all gone" mode of vacation. Times like this is when it really pays off to be an academic. I don't have to go back to work for almost three more weeks.

I'm on my way to Portugal, to be filmed by some guy who got a grant from the city of Lisbon to make a movie about Lisbon. Edgar Pera. The negotiations were all with his producer, Catarina Santos. Edgar's read some of my books in Portuguese and decided to have me be in his movie, also the SF-and-conspiracy writer Robert Anton Wilson and the psychedelic prophet Terence McKenna. Edgar must be quite a character, judging from his taste in literature, but you never know with Europeans. Catarina wrote me to ask me my sizes for costumes. The movie may be fictional rather than the expected documentary, I don't know. She called again just before I left, and I asked her what the costumes were, and she didn't want to tell me. "It's better if it's a surprise." So the theory I've been promulgating to my friends and family is that I'm going to Portugal to be filmed dressed as a giant chicken scratching at the ground with my feet.

My dog Arf has been scratching the ground like crazy recently, I think it releases musk from glands by his dewlaps. I've been studying him in preparation for my role. If Edgar asks me to improvise, that's what I can do. The first thing I'll say will be, "Do you have a chicken costume I can wear?" My face showing inside the huge, open beak. Foghorn Leghorn. A wobbling featherduster wired to my padded fanny. Or, worse, the handle stuck up my naked butt. But, hey, don't laugh, they're paying me all expenses plus a nice fee.

JANUARY 8, 1994. AIRPORT HASSLES.

It's 29 hours later and I'm still in an airport. Newark was iced in, and my flight from Dulles was cancelled. I spent the night in the Dulles

Hyatt in D.C., and I went back to Dulles pretty early in the morning today. Now I'm at JFK in New York.

I had interesting dreams last night, I was in this half-awake kind of state worrying about when to get up, and started dreaming quite lucidly, knowing I was dreaming, and dreamed endless variations on the hotel room. And sometimes something would come and grab me or attack me, and I realized this time that those things are also me, they are projected by me, everything in the dream is a projection of me, so I'd like *grab* the imp on my shoulder and squeeze and merge with him, and have a whirlpool kind of feeling. Very unusual. The fact that I watched *Indiana Jones and the Temple of Doom* on TV in bed just before sleep helped the dreams too, no doubt.

Here in N.Y., the tree branches are all covered with thick coats of ice. There's been an ice storm, which is why it took me 24 hours longer to get here. I have a boarding pass for TAP (Air Portugal); here's hoping it takes off in an hour like it's supposed to. Bad sign: it doesn't have a gate listed yet, and all the other planes do. My suitcase got away from me at Dulles yesterday, too, so I've been wearing these clothes for two days now, and slept in the shirt as well. Supposedly it will catch up with me or I with it in Lisbon. If I ever get there.

Okay, we are on the plane now. I have a window seat and the plane is completely full. This is going to be rough. Nobody on the plane seems to speak English at all. The loudspeaker is playing the Lettermen singing Christmas carols. A big fat stoic lady next to me in all black and with big purse and coat and shopping bags that she doesn't want to put in the overhead. Her face is covered with warts, warts on warts like a fractal. Her arm is sticking way into my space. It's a good thing they're paying me to do this.

JANUARY 9, 1994. LISBON, TERENCE MCKENNA.

As it turned out, the plane sat on the ground for 2 hours before taking off. While we were sitting there, Robert Anton Wilson got put on the plane, his connection had been late. I said hi to him; he looked pretty stressed, his face taut, red and masklike. Later he told me that he's 62 and has high blood pressure. He also has post-polio syndrome, which makes him walk unsteadily.

When we got to Lisbon, it turned out that *both* our suitcases were lost. It took a long time to give info to the baggage people, and when we finally got out of the airport there was *surprise* nobody there to meet us. So there I was, 36 hours after starting out from D.C. (where I'd made a stopover to visit my ailing Pop), with my suitcase gone, no clue what to do, and old Bob Wilson on my hands – he prefers "Bob" to "Robert." He was starting to really lose it, obsessively complaining about everything, like that he wouldn't have his medicine, and me falling unwillingly into the role of chirpy cheerer-upper that I'd just finished doing with Pop on the way out here. Wilson looks a bit like Pop, actually: he has white hair and beard. I told Wilson, "Don't be so surprised they didn't manage to meet us. I mean these are people who invited Rucker, Wilson and McKenna to be in their movie. These people have got to be nuts! These people are fucked up! It's like... how long would you wait for Queen Mu to meet you at an airport?" We had a voice and fax phone numbers for Catarina Santos, but she wasn't answering her phone, nor did she have a message machine.

So Bob Wilson and I asked the tourism counter to recommend a hotel, and we got a cab to their recommended Hotel Nacional, a depressingly anonymous place in the business district, new, soulless, with a lobby of stone polished to a fierce tombstone glare; it didn't seem as if anyone else at all was staying there. Wilson and I lay down for naps in our separate rooms. My heart was doing funny things lying there, palpitations you might call it, my poor overstressed heart fluttering at my chest. I got up in the early afternoon, and Wilson was still asleep. Fine.

The sidewalks of Lisbon are mosaics made of miniature cobble-stones, extremely slippery in the winter rain, mostly white, but with black swirly symmetric Belusov-Zhabotinsky patterns every so often. In the less traveled areas, grass grows verdant in the multiple mosaic cracks.

I found a small funicular railway and rode it up to the Barrio Alto, a neighborhood of old houses with laundry hanging out. The walls were crumbly stucco washed over with colors. It must be glorious on a sunny day. And there are tiles everywhere. The Moorish influence. I missed having Audrey here to show it to. I saw a little park with a nice-smelling cedar that had been trained to grow out over a circular overhead trellis – some beams up in the air making a hundred foot-diameter disk with the branches of the cedar sprawling atop them. Old men underneath playing cards at little tables. Very quaint. I could see out over the city from one spot in the Barrio Alto – these view spots are called *miradouros* – could see Teja River (called the *Tagus* in English, no doubt a British idea like using *Leghorn* for the city *Livorno* in Italy or, for that matter, *Lisbon* instead of *Lisboa*) and I could see the big landmark: the Castelo de São Jorge (the tilde over the letter *a* in *São* means to pronounce it like *Saoung*, cognate to Saint).

As it was Sunday, most things were closed, but I did stop in at one hole-in-the-wall cafe for a 150$00 escudo glass of beer. (The Portuguese use the $ sign for a decimal point.) The exchange rate is about 160 escudos to a dollar, so that means the beer was about ninety cents. Not that it was a big one by any means, it was a strange crippled-looking little glass. This humble cafe is beautifully appointed – tiled walls and a real wrought-iron lamp high on the wall, it's the kind of place that would be full of yuppies in Germany or the U.S., but here it's full of Mediterranean men, short guys with lined faces and thin lips, guys whom in California you'd be more likely to see in the parking lot of 7-11 than in a cafe. Portugal is *their* country!

I also stopped in at a cafe next to a movie theater and had a *Pizza a Atum*. *Tuna* in English is *Atun* in Spanish, and *Atum* in Portuguese. Because the cafe was next to a movie theater on a Sunday, it held two darling little groups of mother and children. How I love seeing women with their children, it is so wonderful to see the happy cute big-cheeked ice cream-eating kids, and the loving tender mothers, the mothers albeit a bit frayed and distraught due the pressures of raising said kids – as were Audrey and I during those three-kid-travelling-circus years of yore, raising Sorrel, Tom and Ida. The Holy Family, the divine and darling herd.

When I got back to the Hotel Nacional it was nearly evening. The good news when I got back was that Catarina Santos was on the phone just then looking for me. I'd sent her a fax when I got up from my nap. Catarina had been assigned to meet us at the Lisbon airport, which has an exit and a traffic that looked (to me anyway) comparable in size and complexity to the airport of, say, Lynchburg,

Virginia. It's pretty hard to miss someone at that exit, but Catarina had missed us, and had even given a frantic "Your father is missing!" call to son Tom, back in Los Perros, at 2 AM California time, which made me want to kill her.

Waiting for Catarina to come to the hotel, Wilson and I had a few drinks, then slept a couple more hours, and then she showed up looking much cuter than expected at about quarter of ten. And trailed by none other than Terence McKenna.

Catarina is *une jolie laide* (a beautiful ugly), a woman with such lively complicated features that you love to watch her. She has large, highly animated lips which are often drawn twitchingly up to her nose for this or that badger/gopher face of mockery or emphasis. She has a cracking, charming voice because she smokes cigarettes all the time, like all of the people here. When she met us, she was dressed all in black with a miniskirt and a black leather coat. Terence was glued to her like a limpet, apparently they were having an affair. I didn't envy him, as she's a sulker and a manipulator. But she was always fun to watch; her face was like a circus.

It turned out that Terence had gotten to Lisbon three days earlier than Wilson and me, and was angling to stay three days longer. He's divorced, unemployed, and was eager to stretch out the gig.

Terence is a person who grows on you. He's a tall skinny guy, about six feet and 160 pounds, with kind of a gold-prospector face, meaning a chin up near his nose as if he didn't have teeth, and loads of whiskers in no particular pattern covering most of his phiz. His eyes are large, thoughtful and brown. His forehead is low; I'd say the guy's whole face is about half the height of a standard horse-faced soap-actor's visage. He has a head like a cheerfully scrunched fist. He looks a little like what you get when you put two dots of ink for eyes on your index finger's bottom knuckle and bounce the knuckle up and down over your thumb with a handkerchief wrapped around your hand to make a kind of puppet. (Sorry, Terence, I'm exaggerating!)

So Bob Wilson and I went out for dinner with Terence and Catarina and Edgar Pera, the director of the movie, which is called *The Manual of Evasion: LX94*. LX stands for Lisbon, or an alternate Lisbon, and the production is funded by the city of Lisbon in honor of a year-long festival of the arts called Lisbon '94. We went to a place near the water, near the Rio Teja, at ten o'clock at night, a typical or even early time for dinner in Lisboa, quite a shock for someone with my supper-at-six upbringing. I had some beautiful olives and salt cod *seviche* as appetizer, then grilled cod, cod cooked in milk, and cod with beans and shrimps.

Edgar is a handsome man with short dark hair, a Mediterranean/Moorish face with full features and a lovely round chin with dark stubble. He often shrugs and makes self-deprecating gestures, like, "Who cares!" or "Don't ask me!" or "For God's sake relax!", blowing out air and shaking his head.

The best part of the day was that we took our backpacks (no luggage yet, guys!) out of the cold, shiny Hotel Nacional after dinner and brought them to the four star York House.[52] This is where our employers, the Companhia de Filmes Principe Real, had meant to put us up all along. And it is a terrific four star hotel, all in wood and tile and ceramic. Edgar said that during World War Two, the York House was a meeting-place and hang-out for spies. According to Wilson, who refers to the movie *Casablanca*, Lisbon was a big hang-out for spies in WWII.

I should mention that on the way to dinner, and on the way back to the hotel, we got high in the car smoking hash. (Not mine! I don't remember whose!) Walking up the three gardened flights from the street to the York House, the spy house, high on hash in Lisbon, well it felt pretty cool.

As we checked in, Wilson started a big fight because the clerk wanted to keep his passport overnight; I evaded, and went on to my bed.

JANUARY 10, 1994. FILMING ON THE RIVER.
I was awakened by a liveried man knocking on my door to bring a tray of breakfast at 7:30 AM. Rolls, butter, apricot jelly, and a pot of coffee and a pot of hot milk. It was delicious; the butter was like a different substance from the butter I get in the U.S. – it was so fragrant and healthy-tasting. Outside it was raining.

I phoned TAP (Bob Wilson's interpretation of the Air Portugal

52. York House Residencia, Rua das Janelas Verdes 32-1, 1200 Lisboa.

acronym was now "Take Another Plane"), and there was no news about my suitcase. It seemed that TAP's origination airport for the NYC/Lisbon flight alternates between JFK and Newark. So my bag was 48 hours out of phase. I put on the same clothes for the fourth (!!!!) day in a row.

A woman showed up at the hotel to put make-up on me and Bob and Terence. Catarina and some film-crew people were there with a bunch of clothes, but they figured my overcoat and beret looked fine. They were fresh out of giant chicken suits, even though I did repeatedly ask for one. Bob was wearing a white T-shirt and a camel's hair coat, and they made him put on something black, which pissed him off.

There was a yacht waiting for us by a monument to the Great Navigators (a big theme in Lisbon!). It belonged to the production company, or to one of the company's contacts. The rain cleared up and the sun came out. Seeing Edgar and all his lively hip crew, I began to realize just how serious a gig this was. I mean, these guys had big heavy-duty 35 mm cameras, not to mention any number of Hi-8 video cams.

We got on the boat and motored around the wide Rio Teja for awhile, being filmed answering questions about time. The questions were posed by Carlos, a TV reporter who was playing a reporter. Bob, Terence, and I were cast as the Shaman, the Neuro-Magician, and the Master of Chaos. (They use X for CH in Portugal, so actually, we were the Xaman, the Neuro-Magician, and the Master of Xaos.) I was kind of stiff and like jockeying for position, worried the others would talk more than me, but eventually I got a good rap or two on film, talking about my idea that we are like eyes which God grows to look at himself with − God being thus like a giant snail or mollusk that extrudes eyestalks.

Later I actually got to see this shot onscreen in the rushes. The camera angle was low so that my head was like sticking up from behind the dome of the boat's binnacle (compass enclosure), and I was raising up my arms to simulate eyestalks, the arms at different heights and my hands cupped as if holding eye-spheres. Right above and behind me was the great suspension bridge over the Rio Teja. This bridge looks just like the Golden Gate bridge, and was built by the long-term dictator Salazar, but is called the April 25 bridge in honor of the date of the 1974 revolution. In the shot, my hands stuck up above the lines of the bridge. Much as I liked this shot, it didn't make it into the finished film.

The technology of the filming, which I didn't understand at first, was that the video cameras would be on most or all of the time, but the heavy-duty 35 mm cameras would only be on for occasional bursts of three minutes. A three-minute role of 35 mm film costs $300, and another $200 for processing. Given Edgar's finite budget for the film, he is sparing with the 35 mm, preferring to wait and wait around until finally there is a feeling that all is ripe and the key scene can be shot – almost always in one take with no repeat. The final film may include some footage from the videos to pad out or vary upon the 35 mm. For editing, everything is transferred first to video tape and then to a digital format called AVI. The edit is done by using the AVI files on a computer, much as if one were word-processing a bunch of documents. Once you have all the snips and splices figured out digitally, you print out a spec sheet, and the lab does the snipping and splicing for you.

Eventually the boat docked on the other side of the Rio Teja. They filmed us arriving – the idea of the movie is that there are Saboteurs who are changing the speed of time in various parts of Lisbon, and that they are being helped by the Xaman, the Neuro-Magician, and the Master of Xaos.

We went up the hill to have lunch in a small town with a name something like Alameda. I waited with Carlos in a square, and noticed a woman filling up big plastic pitchers at a fountain. "I can't believe that woman has to haul water to her house," I said. Carlos answered, "You have to understand that Portugal is the end of Europe and the beginning of the third world."

We went into an unprepossessing place for lunch, and sat at a long table. I sat next to Michael, a guy who seemed like a Frenchman with good English, but who turned out to be a longtime expatriate New Yorker who's acquired a French accent. He lives in Paris in an apartment above, of all places, the Procope, the brasserie where dear Audrey and I had dinner on our 25th anniversary in Paris in 1992! *Voltaire* used to hang there. Michael is a very talkative, dynamic guy, typically wearing a jump-suit with a zillion zippers. He has a shock of black hair and a long nose. Michael is the cameraman for *The Manual of Evasion*. For lunch I was served a Portuguese mixed meat plate with part of a pig's leg, some blood sausage, some lard sausage, some beans, pot-roast, potatoes, cabbage and, lo and behold, a pig's ear. We had red, white, and "green" wine, this being a tart slightly effervescent white wine.

After lunch we went to shoot film in a winery. The idea was that this is where the Xaman, the Neuro-Magician, and the Master of Xaos were meeting the Saboteurs. I got in a couple of good raps about transrealism and the Central Teachings of Mysticism. For a long time we sat at a huge picnic table covered with wine bottles, some open, sitting there, and pretending to be getting drunk. It was up to us how much we actually drank, and when they needed to reshoot a scene, they'd empty out our glasses into a pitcher so that the actresses could refill them. It was weird to have an infinite amount of wine in front of me – a moment I'll remember during thirsty times. I kind of held back on the drinking lest I do something stupid. The actresses were a fat lively blonde woman named Suzy, and a cute actress called Ana, who was also acting in a Pirandello play.

Terence was quite funny, saying things like, "Gentlemen, the question on the floor is *what is reality?*," and then going into all sorts of raps about time-machines. He has this idea that logically we can't see a time-machine before one is invented (because as soon as we see a time-machine, then we can copy it and invent one). So as soon as the first time-machine *is* invented (which will happen, according to Terence, in 2012), then time-machines from all down the future will show up, and the arrival of all this novelty at once will cause some kind of information explosion. It's fun to hear him talk about time-machines with that same wild, unschooled excitement that I had about them as a teenager.

The river had gotten rough, so we drove back to the hotel instead of taking the boat. When we got back, my suitcase was finally there! I took a shower and changed my shirt three times in a row. My four-day underwear could have been cut into squares and sold to dysmenorrheic women needing hormone therapy. I had dinner alone in the hotel dining room, sitting at a table near the kitchen. I had a great fish soup, and feeling casual in the European ambience just said, "Can I have another?" and they brought me another, and then a shrimp and endive salad, and then a nutcake of ground hazelnuts. A perfect meal.

In bed I turned on the TV, and saw a Portuguese news story about how six people on a yacht had drowned in the Rio Teje today!

JANUARY 11, 1994. THE OBSERVATORY. "TIME FLIES."
The next morning Catarina drove Bob, Terence, and me to an astronomical observatory for the day's shooting. Bob was in a foul, sulky mood.

The observatory was a lovely pastel yellow classic mansion sitting in a small botanical garden in the misty rain. The Portuguese used to have lots of colonies: Goa in India, Angola and Mozambique in Africa, Brazil in South America, the Cape Verde islands in the Pacific, and the island of Timor near Indonesia. They have the same latitude as San Francisco, so exotic plants from the former colonies can flourish in their botanical gardens. Terence is something of a botanist due to his researches into psychedelic plants, and he told me that one of the big trees was a dragon's-blood tree from the Mid-East. Its red sap is used for incense.

Walking out alone into the rainy garden later in the day, I thought of the phrase from Sartre's *La Nausée* which I quote in my *The Secret of Life*: "I went into the garden and the garden smiled at me."

On this day's shooting there were three actresses and two actors as well as Terence, Bob and me. The funniest actor was called Duarte Barrilaro Ruas; he looked like Bela Lugosi with slicked back hair, lab coat, and a pasted-on goatee. He had a huge mouth, and liked to do crazy laughs.

For filming us they were making us go up on a creaking lacquered-wood ladder – like a library bookcase ladder – to get near the eyepiece of this huge telescope, a telescope with a big lens at one end and a little lens at the other end, the traditional idea of a telescope in other words, and not some newfangled thing with a mirror. The place was trippy and rundown but still actually functioning. The telescope was in a giant cylindrical room with the traditional penislike slit-silo-dome on top. A rotating slit. There was a bal-

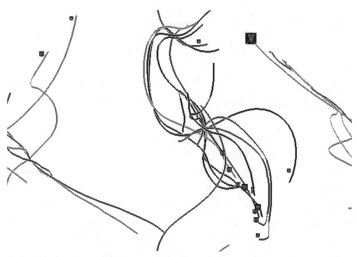

A simulated swarm of flies. (Image generated by Boppers.)

cony/catwalk all around the edge up high, with windows looking out on this part of Lisboa.

An actress called Margarida Marinho had lunch at a table with Edgar, Bob and me. She was such a funny actress; I'd been watching her pretending to be an astronomer adjusting a telescope during the morning's shooting. It really taught me something about acting to watch her seemingly endless free flow of improvisations of gesture; different ways of twiddling the dials, looking surprised, moving about, and so on. They were doing shots with us standing on a kind of ladder next to a huge brass telescope.

After lunch one of the guys ran up to me with this ice cream-cone shaped cigarette and said, "Rudy, would you like some psyche-delic? This is tobacco with hashish." And we all smoked some of that and the afternoon got funnier. Bob Wilson cheered up a bit, but then was cranky again, and when I said enthusiastically, "We're going up on the wobbly observing ladder to be filmed again," he said, "I don't like to see sadism in a man," and I said, after a minute or two of it sinking in, "I didn't mean to sound sadistic, I was just trying be cheerful," and then Terence chimed in, "I hate to think of all the atrocities that have been committed under the name of trying to be cheerful." Well that moment was bum, but much else was wavy during this stony afternoon.

I noticed that rain leaked in through the windows on the high room circling balcony, and that there was crumbled-off window-glazing on the sills, and there were lots of little flies there, breeding in the water or something, funny little baby Portuguese flies, and I got into this rap, rehearsing it to whomever would listen, that the insects were *timeflies*, which relates, you wave, to Zeno's Second Paradox of Motion: "Time flies like an arrow, but at each instant there is no time, so how does the arrow move?" And relates further to the classic automatic language translation program which translated "Time flies like an arrow," into Russian and back into English, yielding: "Insects which live on sundials enjoy eating arrows." And, most weightless fact of all, the arrow which the timeflies enjoy eating is *Zeno's* arrow!

In the milling around, I happened to walk up the stairs behind Durte and Juanne, a striking woman who turned out to be a professional model, aged 19. You could tell she was a model from the way she held herself, posing so perfectly. Before I'd grasped that she was a model, she'd just seemed kind of bland and skinny, but once I thought of her as a *model*, she seemed very attractive. She was wearing thick-soled sexy boots and tight leather pants, oh my. I filmed her a little with my own video camera. And then they filmed a big scene of me and Terence talking on the room-circling balcony, and Juanne was supposed to turn a big crank on the wall next to me as I talked, and I'd been flirting with her a little, and she said, "In the scene, I will bump you, yes?" And I said yes, so then she kept bumping me with her leather butt while I was talking – what thrills these sporadic contacts sent through me! I tried to *act* a little, and show reactions to the bumps. Finally in fact I pulled out my handkerchief and started polishing her bent leather butt – much to the filmed outrage of Terence who was just then holding forth to me about liberating oneself by pursuing the erotic element of life, and, noticing my polishing of Juanne's butt, complained that I wasn't listening to him. Another of my favorite moments that didn't appear in the film – ah, the heartbreak of being an actor.

My clowning was greatly to the amusement of a hip young guy

called Daryl Pappas, moved to Portugal from L. A., who was taking publicity still photos for the film. When we finished shooting, he was hitting on Juanne. "Are you a virgin?" Juanne: "I'm saving myself for God." Daryl: "Well, I'm him!" Juanne: "No, God has no head." Heavy. Juanne's way of showing heightened sexual interest was to chew her gum a bit faster.

Back at the hotel, I had a few drinks in the hotel bar with Bob. He cheers right up when he's having drinks or drugs. It would be fun to write an SF story together sometime, he's an incredible fount of knowledge with an idiosyncratic worldview. A little later, I had dinner at the hotel with Edgar, his wife Marguerite, Terence, Catarina, Bob, and Michael. I had dried fish appetizer (swordfish and lox), some duck breast in a delicious Madeira sauce, and a lot of drinks.

JANUARY 12, 1994. AROUND LISBON, THE ALFAMA.
I slept late, till 10:30, and woke feeling like shit. In the morning we went out to shoot on location in Lisbon. Terence was friendly and full of gossip about all the *Mondo 2000* people on the way over.

Our first shot was in a giant free-standing outdoor seven-story elevator that goes down a cliff into the shopping district, known as Beixa. I talked a lot to Carlos, he was explaining a headline I saw about a man named Xanana being arrested. What a cool first name. He's a Portuguese-speaking resident of East Timor who is leading a rebellion against the Indonesian government, which took over Timor about seventeen years ago. The Portuguese are on the side of the rebels, but according to Carlos the U.S. has been on the side of the Indonesian oppressors. Then we walked down the Beixa main street to the dock where the ships used to arrive, the caravals. According to Terence, the king's men would be right there to take the valuables from the ships as they landed.

Speaking of first names that begin with an "X," Terence told a story about going into the Amazon and taking a weird drug with some short brown natives, and how after about an hour, he's looking at them, at their eyes that were "black and glittering like a cockroach's" (Terence's quote from William Burroughs), and starts wondering if his new friend Xlotl is going to kill him. Xanana and Xlotl. "How do you spell Xanana?" "Like banana with an x." Xanana and Xlotl are going into my new book *Freeware* for sure as surfer limpware moldies; flickercladding dudes infested by psychedelic camote fungus.

Then we drove to Edgar's studio and had lunch in a dive next to it. I had two whole grilled fish, quite good, though dangerously bony. If I'd eaten them as fast as I normally like to eat, I would have choked to death.

Inside Edgar's studio was the "Time Lab," an amazing set with lots of clocks going at all different speeds, and a smoke machine, and colored lights, and dials and meters and big weird gears to roll back and forth and make strange shadows. The set was in the shape of a cylinder, so that standing inside it, the cameraman could pan, and never pass a wall-corner, giving the effect of the lab's being huge, even though it was only about twenty or thirty feet across.

Edgar would frequently argue with Michael the cameraman about how to do a shot; Michael was quite knowledgeable about how to shoot a scene – it's like the cameraman gets the picture, and it's more the director's job to put the pieces of picture together. There was some conflict because, as Edgar later told me, he likes to not be like a dictator, he feels that if he lets situations evolve spontaneously, people do better work for him. And Michael, feeling the power-vacuum, kept trying to start bossing, but Edgar – when push came to shove – wouldn't let him. Michael felt that the movie was being shot too slowly, while Edgar felt that it was better to wait until everything was right before shooting a scene.

So we waited about four or five hours until everything was right, and then shot our last scene in the Time Lab. I cranked up my adrenaline by singing some songs for the actors – they videoed me doing my Dead Pigs version of "Duke of Earl." Bob had a tantrum just before this scene about his clothes – they made him take off his camel's hair coat and white T-shirt again, so as to match his other scenes – and he kind of did his best to spoil the scene by complaining about his clothes in the scene instead of talking about time; so this scene didn't make it into the movie either. And then Bob had a tantrum about getting our checks from Catarina. A difficult man, but a genius, able to quote page after page of Pound, Joyce, Shakespeare, the last words of Dutch Schultz, you name it. But egomaniacal much more than me. I had some fun in the scene anyway by wav-

ing around a giant wrench and starting a mad scientist laughing jag
which Durte got into.

By now it was eight, and Edgar had invited us to his house for supper at ten, so I killed an hour or so walking around the neighborhood
of his studio. This was the Alfama neighborhood, the old Moorish
part of town. It was one of the most amazing experiences. Built all of
tiles and cobblestones and stucco on a steep hill, the district has alleys
and staircases leading every which way. It reminded me of Escher's
engravings of Maltese hill towns, or of his pictures of cities with
ambiguous perspectives. To make it the more completely Escher-like,
many of the buildings are entirely covered with tiles that are patterned
in arabesques, or in *trompe l'oeil* designs. It was one of the most exciting strolls I've ever taken, and the more enjoyable after a day of being
cooped up with all the film crew's (and especially Bob's) personalities.

When I got back from my marvelous walk, they were through
shooting, and I rode over to Edgar's house with him. It was me,
Edgar, Marguerite, Edgar's friend Pedro and his wife Lourdes,
Durte, Carlos, then Catarina and her production higher-up Marie-
Juana (loved the name!), also Terence and Bob. Dinner was served at
– get this – 11:15 PM. And nobody thought this was particularly
late! It's sure not Louisville, Kentucky.

Before dinner, Edgar said something to me in his sincere way
that really made me happy. "Everybody loves you. All of us on the
movie." That felt so good. He was very satisfied with my work for his
film. I'd made a point of mentioning his plot line several times during the filming, which will be a help in trying to make the movie feel
like a coherent whole.

Dinner was pot-roast with a nice pureed carrot sauce. During
dessert, one of the guests passed around tobacco and hash jays. It
was like the '70s again – nicely dressed lively young people having
some civilized tokes together after a fancy dinner at home. I haven't
seen anything like that in the U.S. for 20 years. Maybe I travel in the
wrong circles – or is it that Americans really have gotten more
puritanical? Or maybe it's that my friends and I are all middle-aged.

After dinner, we watched some rushes on Edgar's TV – mostly
of Terence, as the rushes lag two days behind. There were some
really funny scenes with Terence; he has a golden tongue. "You are

such a great talker," I exclaimed to Terence, and he answered, "It's the only skill I have. If it weren't for that ability, I'd be sleeping under a bridge." Another time I heard him introduce himself to someone saying, "I'm a criminal and a bullshit artist." Not a pretentious guy. I hope some of my scenes come out well – the one with the eyestalks looked promising, and there ought to be more. And I hope there's some good ones of Bob, too. After watching all the rushes of Terence we were both wishing there was more of us.

Some of the movie is shot in speeded-up time, like there's a love scene in a factory. The love scene was a panic, it was like Chaplin in *Modern Times.*

With any luck, *The Manual of Evasion* might be a psychotronic classic of cinema. Or at least a highly respected work of surrealist film. It's supposed to be about 55 minutes long. Edgar's trick was to have some of the action take place in front of landmarks of Lisbon, so that the City of Lisbon will be satisfied that the movie is "about" the city – even though it is science fiction. Terence came up with a rant how all great cities are transtemporal and transspatial, and that Lisbon has a bridge like San Francisco's. And in one of my scenes, I made the point that if you go across the Golden Gate bridge and look at San Francisco, the ocean is on your right, but if you go across the April 25 bridge and look at Lisbon, the ocean is on your left, implying that Lisbon is a mirror-image of San Francisco . . .

I liked acting. It was a big adrenaline rush; you'd know when your scene was coming, and you'd get ready for it, trying to think of what you'd say and what mood you'd project, and then it comes, and it's over in a flash. Once the company applauded after I did a scene ranting about time, chaos and temperature (as per request), and it felt wonderful. You get this big ego boost right back; it's addictive, a true fix. After their scenes everyone is trembly and smoking cigarettes. Another great thing was to be working in a group instead of working all alone, as I do when I write.

This was really a terrific trip. I did something interesting and creative, managed to party without ending up feeling like I made a fool of myself, and forgot completely about my usual life. I can't believe I'm going to have to go back to work.

—*Appeared as "Zip.5 The Manual of Evasion"*
in bOING bOING. *#13, Spring, 1994.*

Memories of Arf

In September of 1981 we were living in Lynchburg, Virginia. Audrey and I were in our thirties; Sorrel was twelve, Tom was nine, Ida was six. We decided we wanted a family dog, partly as a present for Ida's seventh birthday.

We looked in the classified ads and found an ad: *Free Puppies*. I called and got directions and the place was in the boonies north of Lynchburg. We had to drive on smaller and smaller roads to get there; it was a farm, with lots of bare red dirt. The farmer's dog had done *it* with two different males and had given birth to a litter of six puppies on July 3, 1981, though later we always like to say that it had been the Fourth of July.

Five of the puppies were black and shorthaired, one was orange and white and had long hair. He liked to lie on his back when you petted him; the farmwife liked him best, she said she always brought him inside to pet while she watched TV. We all practiced petting him, and he eagerly rolled over on his back to offer us his stomach. The farmer gave him to us. On the drive home we agreed to name our new puppy Arf, a.k.a. Arfie.

At first I thought we'd keep him in a box down in the basement, but he whined so pitifully that the children got him promoted to the kitchen. We all took turns walking him around the little neighborhood streets of Lynchburg. A lifelong characteristic of Arf's soon became evident: he didn't like to come when you called him. At all. Ever. Although, according to Sorrel, if you squatted down very low and clapped he was likely to come a-runnin'.

We had a big house, and Arf spent a lot of time inside with us. There was a wide pie slice-shaped step where the carpeted staircase turned: that was Arf's special spot. He could sit there and be aware of whatever was going on upstairs or down.

I did start trying to make Arf spend more time outside after our first Christmas together. We had a bunch of houseguests and everyone was slipping pieces of turkey and country ham to Arf, and during the night he got very sick, from both ends, in lots of different places all over the house. I asked our guest Eddie if he'd heard anything during the night, and he said, "He was scampering around – and squealing."

Arf didn't learn how to bark until he was about six months old, and he never became a big barker. Occasionally he would stand out in the yard barking into the night with all the other distant dogs the way they like to do, "Here I am! Here I am! Here I am!" But he wouldn't bark at friends, just at menacing strangers – especially if we were picnicking in the woods, where it really helped to have him defend us, what with rural Virginia's many crazed rednecks. But mostly, Arf would only bark to let us know he wanted something, like to be let in or let out or taken along on an outing.

One of our neighbors put out a doghouse for the trash one day, and I brought it home, probably on the kids' wagon. I put the doghouse in our open garage so that Arf could sometimes sleep outside. I was always trying to get him to be outside more – I was, after all, allergic to him, as I am to all hairy animals – but it was kind of a losing battle. Arf learned how to open the back screen door by hitting it with his paw. "He's so bright it's frightening," we liked to say, though actually Arf was only bright at things that served his immediate purposes, and not always then.

Two stories about Arf's doghouse. Across the street we had a bachelor lady with a small female chow dog. The little chow got loose one day and was rumored to be in our doghouse with Arf. When the bachelor lady heard what was going on, she came over in a fury and yanked Arf out by the scruff of his neck – even though the chow was already elsewhere. The other doghouse story had to do with a four-year-old girl who lived next door to us. She was a grubby brat who wouldn't learn how to talk properly. She would point and grunt for things she wanted. She wasn't retarded, she was just spoiled and lazy. Her two big sisters played with our kids quite a bit. One day she crawled into Arf's doghouse, and her father came and got her out and spanked her. My children, her sisters and I were in paradise.

As well as his special stair-step and his doghouse, Arf liked to spend a lot of time under our front porch. This was a four-foot-high space about forty feet long, with bare red dirt on the ground. Arf liked it in there because it was cool and shady in the summer, and he could dig up the ground as much as he liked without getting scolded. The children liked it under there too, for about the same reasons. Arf dug himself several large crater-like depressions to lie in, and Tom liked to fill these pits up with water from the hose so that there would be a really good supply of mud. Later we had a discarded mattress that made its way under the porch, and Ida would sometimes try to camp out down there with her friend Lalla – until they would get scared and mosquito-bitten and come inside.

One problem with Arf being outside a lot was that he would roam all over the neighborhood, and into neighborhoods further and further beyond. He liked to explore, sniff other dogs' old pee-marks, and make his own pee-marks. And of course if there was a female dog in heat, he wanted to go there. "Arfie ran away 'cause a girl dog had heat," as Ida would put it.

And run away he did, hundreds of times. Not that he was ever *lost* – if we waited a few hours, or at most a day, he would always come home, sometimes looking a bit exhausted and wrung-out. We never found out for sure if he successfully fathered any puppies, although some Lynchburg friends claim they see Arf lookalikes to this day. I hope so.

Once we saw Arf doing *it* with a poodle in front of our garage. It was surprising how little time it took, maybe forty seconds. But those interludes were of key importance to Arf, and it was more or less impossible to keep him from roaming. Especially in the springtime, he'd sniff at the air in a certain way, and you knew that he was going to make a break for it.

The problem with Arf's roaming was that Lynchburg had dog-catchers who rounded up stray dogs. Sometimes they would phone us up, and sometimes they would bring him home to us and give us a ticket. Sometimes they would just take him in to the pound. I actually had to go to court over Arf's tickets one time. A dogcatcher came and testified. I had my new short punk haircut and the judge had long blow-dried '70s hair. It was like the hair had reversed from the '60s.

Arf didn't just roam because he was looking for dogs in heat, he also roamed because he liked to follow the kids to school. Tom and Ida used to walk five blocks to Garland-Rhodes Elementary School, and Arf liked to follow them every day. The kids would die of embarrassment when Arf would manage to get inside the school and go tearing down the halls looking for them, with his feet skidding and kids running after him and teachers yelling. Tom and Ida said they would sit stiffly at their desks, pretending they didn't know Arf at all. We had a friend with a fenced yard right by the school, and sometimes he would get Arf and keep him out of trouble until the kids got out of school.

When Tom started taking the bus to middle school, about three miles away, Arf figured out how to follow the school bus. It's hard to see how he could have done it, but he did. This opened up a whole new spectrum of neighborhoods for Arf to explore.

One joyful time Arf tricked the dogcatcher in one of those new neighborhoods. The dogcatcher phoned Audrey to say that he had Arf and that she should come get the dog and accept a ticket, but when Audrey got there the dogcatcher was holding a collar and no dog. Because of *habeas corpus*, he couldn't give Audrey a ticket! Audrey brought the collar home, and there was Arf on the porch.

This seemed like a good development. I spent some time trying to teach Arf that he should always run away from the dogcatcher. We sat down together in the driveway, and I moved two little rocks around on the ground to stand for Arf and the dogcatcher. "Dog-catcher come. Arf run away! Dogcatcher bad. Arf run away!" Arf almost looked like he understood, but then he started sniffing at my hands to see if there was food in them.

In general, Arf failed all official IQ tests with flying colors. We had a hall separated from our living room by a glass door. If the glass door was closed, you could get to the hall by going out the other end of the living room and around the back of the stairs. So one night after eating roast chicken for dinner, the kids took Arf into the living room and I put the platter with the chicken carcass on the floor in the hall right behind the closed glass door. Arf could see and smell the chicken, and he wanted it very much. He scratched and scratched at the glass door. "Come on, Arf," the kids told him, running out of the living room and around the stairs to appear in the hall with the chicken. "Come on around!" Arf stayed right at the glass door whining. Eventually Audrey and Sorrel said we were

Arf on the James River. (Photo by R. Rucker.)

being too mean to Arf, and he ended up getting the chicken in his dish on the back porch. So, in a way, he won.

Arf never succeeded at things by acting human, he succeeded by keeping on being Arf. He would insist on his way of doing things, and eventually we and the rest of the world would give in.

The children loved to spend time petting Arf. "I like confiding with Arf when the world seems against me," as Tom put it. "He's always soft," said Sorrel, "He's fluffy!" "If you're ever sitting on the ground, Arf comes up and sticks his nose in your face to see what you're doing," observed Ida. "The nerve!" Audrey liked taking him for walks, she was proud of what a cute puppy he was, and of how everyone would comment on him. She particularly admired his high-held feathery tail; she liked to call him "Plume." And she relied on him to defend the house when I wasn't around.

I could always count on Arf to come on hikes with me, even if nobody else in the family wanted to come. One day in particular I remember, everyone was mad at me, and I floated down the James River alone with Arf in a rubber raft. That day, for some reason he spent a lot of time sitting like a person, with his butt down, and with his back leaning against the fat ring of the raft. I guess the thin rubber bottom of the raft was too unsettling. I took my favorite photograph of Arf that day, a profile shot of him staring off across the water, with his ears cocked and his eyes alert. He had a long, handsome muzzle with a beautiful black nose.

That little day-trip I took with Arf was part of the inspiration for my novel *The Hollow Earth*, which is about a much longer journey, set in the 1840s. Arf played a supporting character under his own name. I want to copy out some of my Arf descriptions from *The Hollow Earth*, as they're a good store of things I wrote about him.

At the beginning of the book, Mason Reynolds is about to leave his farm near Lynchburg, Virginia, along with his slave Otha.

> Arf got excited and started barking. He had the noble profile and the feathery legs of a retriever. His legs and ruff where white, but his head and body had the tawny coloring of a collie. I'd grown up talking to him like a person. He had a way of moving his eyebrows and his feathery tail so expressively that I often felt he understood me. Now in the farmyard, his tail and eyes were merry as he pumped his barks skyward.

Later I came to always refer to Arf as orange, rather than tan or tawny. I in fact got quite obsessive about this, and started telling people, "I defy you to say that Arf is not orange." Finally someone did defy me: when I picked up Arf's body this week, they said he was a red and white collie-mix, while we'd always called him an orange and white collie/beagle. Picked up his body? Yes, this is an elegy.

Speaking of Arf's orangeness, there was a phrase I always meant to build up into a children's story: "And there in the middle of the Christmas parade was a confused little collie-beagle dog with an orange saddle on his back." In *The Hollow Earth*, Mason tries to leave Arf behind, but "Arf slipped out the gate after us, his tail held demurely down. I scolded him, and he cringed, but he kept right on coming." Which is completely typical of Arf. He follows Mason with a vengeance: to the center of the Earth and back. A few scenes later, Mason and Otha get in trouble and are running from the sheriff. They hide in a boat at the wharf.

> Arf stood up on the wharf staring down at us. "Come on," I hissed. "Come on down here, Arf." He snuffled and backed

off. I lunged and got hold of the loose skin of his neck. Man's best friend had to let out a yelp, of course, which set off hallos from the sheriff's torch gang.

Arf had a knack for refusing to cooperate when you needed it the most. Like when we were moving to California and he was howling in the parking lot outside the motel and we tried to sneak him up the stairs to our motel room of course he had to get his toe stepped on and yelp at the top of his lungs. In *The Hollow Earth*, Mason and Otha get to Richmond where they split up. Arf follows Otha, but soon he ends up back with Mason.

> At the sound of my voice, a dog came rushing out of the alley by the Whig building and jumped on me. He was white-legged with a tan head and body. He pushed his feet into my stomach and stretched his head up toward my face. His feathery tail was beating a mile a minute. It took me a minute to understand that it was my dear old Arf. "Arfie! What are you doing here, Arfie boy?" Arf licked and whined and rolled on his back. I knelt down and petted him for a long time. He lay there squirming, with his front paws folded over like a dead rabbit's. When I stopped petting him, he sprang up and shook his head vigorously. The way he shook his head was to stick it far forward and then to rotate it back and forth so fast that his ears slapped like the wings of a pigeon taking flight. The head shake was Arf's way of punctuating his changes of moods. Now that we were through greeting, it was time for something else. He stood there next to me with his tongue lolling out.

There were so many enjoyable things about Arf. The noise he made when drinking water was a particular wonder. He made the water sound so liquid and delicious. Ida and I used to like to get near the water dish and gloat over the noise of his drinking.

I had a favorite line I liked to use about Arf's name: "*He's so smart he can say his own name, and he's so famous all the other dogs talk about him.*"

I used this line on hundreds of people over the years. I'd dole the two jokes out cautiously; if the person didn't get the first one, I wouldn't try the second one. Almost anyone will come up and talk to you if you have a dog, particularly a noble handsome hound like Arf, orange-and-white old Arfie perhaps at ease on his back, his black lip line looking particularly winsome. I'd often see that winsome lip line when Arf would lie on his side and let me brush and curry him, perhaps cleaning his ears. He calmly soaked up any attention we'd give him.

When we moved to California from Lynchburg in 1986, Arf came with us. I thought a little of leaving Arf behind, but by then he was a member of the family. He, for one, wanted to make absolutely sure he wasn't left behind, and the whole time we were packing the Ryder van he was jumping in and out of it. On the drive out, Arf rode with me in the van every day plus each day one of the kids; they took turns. Audrey rode in our purple whale station wagon with the other two kids. One thing Ida and I noticed was that Arf would stand up whenever we passed a pasture with cows. He was effectively imitating a cow. He was so bright it was frightening. We started calling him the cow-detector.

Arf did something memorable after the Loma Prieta earthquake of 1989. The hardest-hit buildings in our town of Los Perros were only two blocks from our house; two of them were restaurants. A few days after the earthquake I was walking Arf on a leash downtown and a city worker said, "There's that dog!" to his partner, who chimed in, "That's some dog." They went on to tell me that the day of the quake, while they had been cutting off the gas and electricity in one of the ruined restaurants, they'd seen Arf come trotting in, take – get this – a bucket of bacon out of the gaping 'fridge, bite the bucket's handle in his mouth, carry the bucket out behind the ruined building, and there wolf down as much of the bacon as he could hold, i.e. all of it. Arf was, in other words, a looter. This wasn't the only time that people would recognize Arf downtown; it wasn't unusual to hear people say, not always in a friendly fashion, "There's that dog."

Arf's habit of running away got more and more troublesome in California. Although there were no dogcatchers patrolling the streets, the area we lived in was much more urban, with many more people, and they would often assume that Arf was lost, and phone us up about him. Busybodies. In the California years I must have gone to pick up Arf fifty or even a hundred times. Arf never looked apologetic, he simply took my taxi-service as his due. Some of the people would be real priss-pots, trying to lecture me – as if I had any control over this godlike avatar of a dog.

Only once, back in Lynchburg, did I try smacking Arf when picking him up – that time it was a dogcatcher who had him, and he told me not to smack Arf or he'd give me *two* tickets. "He can't help it, sir. That's the way he's made." It was useless to reason with Arf. He was so bright it was frightening. But, again, he was only bright about things that *he* wanted to do. If you threw a stick or a ball, he would just look at you. If you tried again, holding the stick out to him, he'd sniff at it to make sure it wasn't food, then watch you throw it again. And then look away.

Eventually I had to start keeping Arf penned up on our deck all day, or leashed in the driveway. In order to exercise him without having to get calls from busybodies, I took to jogging with him every day. It was great for my fitness; I started calling Arf my personal trainer. One thing he liked to do a lot when we were jogging was to npak (pronounced *en*-pack). "Npak" was a Sorrel-invented expression for Nose, Pivot, Arfie Kick. The origin of this was a Sorrel-drawn three frame broadside she put on our fridge in about 1982 in Lynchburg:

HOW TO SHOW PEOPLE YOU'RE WAY *WAY* TOO
GOOD FOR 'EM. (1) Nose. Point your nose up in the air.
(2) Pivot. Turn on your heel. (3) Arfie Kick. Scrape your feet
backwards, one at a time, trying to toss up dirt or gravel
towards the victim.

The older he got, the more Arfie loved to npak. I think it would release musk from glands by his dewlaps. Arf and I often jogged up the hill to a local winery with a fountain in front of it. Arf would always stop at the fountain and lap up some of the water. He was a complete creature of habit; he always had to drink for a while, step down, step back up, and drink some more. It was such a beautiful spot with Arf there; I always meant to bring my camera and take a picture: a redwood trunk on the left and a palm growing out of the ground on the right; the fountain in the middle, a pool of water lovely green with algae and a plashing trickle of water being forever pumped out of a wine-barrel. I'd think of a woodland animal at a spring, my animal drinking his water, and in the background would be a meadow lit with the California sun and overhead the bright blue California sky.

In the last few months of his life, Arf went deaf. He got more and more like an old person, everything always had to be the same. Grazing new-grown grass-blades, peeing at special places, drinking from the vile water-dish outside Gwen's Hair Salon, crapping on the bridge to Los Perros, shaking his head over and over and over, chewing himself endlessly, and if he sensed a car might slow down for him, he always made a point of getting in front of it. I would get kind of tired of him. But going out in nature with him was always good.

One sunny day in December, 1994, Tom and I went up into some hilly wilderness behind our house and sat in the middle of manzanita chaparral for a long time with happy lolling-tongue Arf hanging around in the vicinity, and then we pushed on over the hill to some entirely new terrain, a steep near-cliff that dropped down the back, covered with native plants; we three worked our way down it like – we imagined – divers dropping down off the continental shelf, we went down a few hundred feet and sat there with Arf, we three boys, perfectly dog-happy, me watching for ages a cloud of gnats over a manzanita bush, marveling at how the strange attractor of the gnat swarm would form over and over in the heat plume over the manzanita. When the wind would blow the gnats out of the attractor, they'd hang down off to the side of the bush in the wind-shadow, and then when the breeze died down, they'd work their way back up into the plume to where they knew the others would meet, Tom and I discussing this a little bit. At our side, Arf's relaxed Nature face was inhumanly beautiful. Dear Arf.

The way Arf finally died was that he figured out a way to escape from the deck where we always penned him up. I'm still not sure exactly how he was doing it, maybe he was squeezing under the railing and jumping down to the ground. On January 31, 1995, Arf broke out and ran away, and while he was deafly crossing a Los Perros street a car hit him in the head and killed him. He was thirteen and a half.

I used a pick and shovel to dig a four-foot-deep grave in our backyard, the deepest hole I've ever dug. There's a lot of big rocks underground. Having lost both my parents in the last couple of years, it felt kind of cathartic to be digging a grave. I got Arf's body from the Humane Society and laid him down on the grass next to the grave. I cried a lot. Arf looked about the same, except his tongue was hanging out and one eye was open and one eye was closed, like a dead creature in a cartoon. His fur was as orange as ever. I clipped off some bits of the fur, and then I put him down in the hole. Audrey and I threw some wildflowers from the yard down in there with him, and then I filled the hole up. We went inside and listened to "Old Blue," a song by The Byrds about losing your dog: "Bye bye, Blue. You good dog, you."

— *Unpublished. Written February, 1995.*

Island Notes

TONGA

We took Reno Air to LA, Air New Zealand to Honolulu, and Royal Tongan Air to Nuku'alofa, the largest city in Tonga. We had to wait four hours, midnight to 4 AM, in the Honolulu airport. The whole trip took about twenty-four hours door to door. We skipped July 16, 1996, or only got a couple of hours of it, because of the dateline.

The Honolulu air terminal buildings were open to the breeze. We lay down to rest on a smooth concrete bench under some huge tropical plants, just outside the terminal building. Yodeling Hawaiian music played softly. I stared at the leaves tossing in the gentle breeze, thinking about chaotic motion.

The Tongans use fans woven of palm, handheld fans with feathery fringed edges that shed off vortices. A vortex is like a boulder. You hit a boulder and it breaks into smaller rocks; shock a vortex and is decomposes into a passel of smaller vortices. You can't just make the vector curl disappear anymore than you can get rid of matter.

I was annoyed by the voices of the drunk New Zealanders, the Kiwis. They sounded so aggressive, so plucky, so manfully squaring their little shoulders for the next obstacle to be fox-terriered through.

Duty Free Liquor = Kiwi Cultural Center.

A giant clam with crenellated shell lay on the bottom. Rising up off the side of it was a bumpy staghorn coral. The clam and coral made a wonderfully unbalanced composition, something nobody would ever think of designing, yet something with a beautiful inner logic. One single fish lived in the branches of the coral.

I found a giant lofa bean. I felt a little guilty about making off with the giant bean, and tried to hide it in the knapsack, but it wouldn't fit completely; it peeked out at the top. In a snack bar I put my hat on the knapsack and the waitress thought the pack, bean and hat were a baby. Odd, that. Audrey took the backpack to the post office.

Rudy and the lofa bean. (Photo by S. Rucker.)

"That bean is getting us into trouble," she said when she came back.

"What do you mean?"

"A woman asked me where I'd gotten it."

"Was she mad we took it?"

"No, she just wanted to know where we got it, so she could find one. She said it was used for Tongan ceremonies."

"I stole the ceremonial bean?"

At the hotel desk the girl told me that, "If you let it ripen and get brown, the lofa bean seeds can be used for – dancing." I surmised that she meant castanets.

"What a beautiful green color our lofa bean is, Audrey." Audrey was tired of talking about the bean, so I began riffing to renew her interest. I wondered out loud if it might be the larva on an alien centipede. After all, the bean's vine had seemed to hang down from nowhere. Like Jack and the Beanstalk.

"What if it splits open and eats my brain tonight, Audrey?"

"It would get a small meal."

The elevator in the Foreign Ministry building had a marble floor.

It was the only elevator in Tonga, and it was manned by a man in a tie and a blue serge skirt.

"Hello," I said.

"*Malo e lelei*," said the elevator operator. "You must learn to say hello in the Tongan way. *Malo e lelei.*"

On the way up to the hill where we would find the bean − this was "Mt." Talau (131 meters high) − we encountered an old man walking down the dirt street. His shirt had several buttons missing, many of his teeth were missing as well, and he was carrying a small aluminum tub holding a big steak of fish flesh. He struck up a conversation with us, talking about his sister in California. His name was Lata Toumolupe. He invited us into his house to look at his shells. We took off our shoes, sat on his couch, and he brought out his treasure, his little plastic bag with tied handles and some paper in it wrapped around his shells. Such shiny nice shells, like he'd gathered them and played with them for years. I took a big whelk, two brown cowries and two tooth cowries.

"It was so touching, him offering us his treasure," said Audrey outside. "You should send him something nice."

View from the porch. A volcano in the distance, a papaya tree, other trees with little fruits like lanterns, translucent and green when young, red when ripe. Inside is a black matte octagonal seed. The waves beat, little waves, more like lapping. The waves lap. Wind today. Lassitude, we nap all the time. So relaxing here.

I walked from our hotel to the village of Toula on the Vava'u island in Tonga today, went past the palm-frond huts, up a little hill with a graveyard, down the hill to the sea and rocky beach. Brittle sea stars were everywhere on the shallowly covered rocks, most with two or three arms in a hidey-hole and the other arms out snaking around. "Thank you, God," I thought. "Thank you for making the world."

Coming back through the graveyard, I saw a thin young woman with a pack of children working on a grave; sweeping it with a stick broom and burning the rubbish in a small fire. The woman made a gesture I hadn't seen yet in Tonga. The woman held her hand palm up, slightly cupped, with the fingers stiff and outspread and then flipped the hand down towards me, a bit as if sowing seed. The gesture definitely meant go away, rather than come here.

As I walked back down the hill into the village, the children came after me, friendly and laughing, three or four girls and a boy. I asked them to catch a pig, but they wouldn't. The boy, about four, had fun poking my backpack with a long, rather sharp stick. The girls asked my name and had me spell it for them and then they danced around me saying, "Rudy, Rudy, Rudy." Wow, I thought, that's me. I'm really here. It felt almost like being awake in a dream.

The town of Neifu under the moon, with the barking dogs, the grunting pigs.

FIJI

Now we're near Vuna village, on Taveuni Island in Fiji. Diving today on the deep outer wall of the Vuna reef. It felt like being on the steep slope of a mountain. Over and over, looking ahead, I'd barely notice something disappearing. I think it's feathery polyps pulling themselves *zip!* back into hidey-holes in the coral. They're almost like that old idea of mine about there being very fast forms of life that you never quite see, or only see as a flicker from the corner of your eye.

A pig tusk. Beach shells with cockroaches in them. A pocketful of baby acorns. A triton shell. Coral. Giant clam shells. A reef pearl.

It was pouring rain. I sat in the large common room of Susie's Plantation. Coconut palms. Orchids. Dark red ginger flowers. Orange flowers. The locals laughing and talking out in the kitchen. Such peace.

A lion fish. Red and black fins, long. They turn white from the tip inward when hassled. The clown fish live in anemones, and swim out of them at you. The anemone is pinkish, tan, fleshy. The tips are darker ball shapes. At first I thought the clown fish were friendly, but it turned out they were territorial, being aggressive. Looking closely at some of the larger ones, I could see that they have rows of jagged sharp teeth top and bottom inside their clown smile. I thought of the line from Dylan's "Like a Rolling Stone," "You never saw the frowns on the jugglers and the clowns/ as they did *tricks* for you."

Snorkeling across acres of soft coral today, all alone, like exploring a new planet. The soft coral was fat and chubby and changed from clump to clump. It was like turning a parameter in a fractal generator and seeing a series of shapes. Pale purple, lavender.

Three teenage Fijian kids took Audrey and me to see some lava tubes. These were horizontal tunnels just underground. One of the boys carried a big machete. Audrey started joking nervously about cannibalism. "Yes, eat white people," said the boy.

We took a long bus ride around Taveuni to the Bouma waterfall. The bus was Indian-made, a SHREEDHAR MOTORS product. The virgin forest by the second Bouma waterfall seemed like rain forest, though another tourist termed it "low jungle." All the trees had lianas on them (a liana being a climbing woody tropical vine), and epiphytes (a plant such as a tropical orchid which grows on another plant upon which it depends for mechanical support but not for nutrients). Life upon life upon life. Like a reef! A place where there's so many ambient nutrients available that all you really need is an anchor spot. So you attach yourself to others. A granny cottage in Silicon Valley.

The lower Bouma waterfall is a high cascade, maybe 100 feet, going into a pool. It's not huge. I swam out into it, as I approached the 20 foot wide shower I felt fear – the cascade seemed pretty strong and I couldn't see through it. The location of the heaviest part of the waterfall shower wandered about as a chaotic orbit on a strange attractor. The heaviest part of the torrent was almost too much, really hard, and it pushed me under. Where the waterfall hit, the water was so agitated and foamy that you could hardly float in it. Dense mist was rising up. I swam through the core three times, thinking of a hole to the Hollow Earth.

Story idea about the Christmas tree worms. "It's a combination of the two most perfect forms," said Onar. "The triangle and the helix." Tiny little balls were forming on the altered Christmas tree worms, silvery little spheres like glass mirror-balls. "*Edem mutata resurgitur*," continued Onar. "Do you know it? The inscription on the tomb of Archimedes, beneath a drawing of a logarithmic spiral. The same, yet altered, I am reborn. Now imagine a quaternionic spiral. That's the Christmas tree worm."

A little piece of coral with a tiny zebra-striped angelfish. Fish of a heart-stopping, mouth-watering neon blue. Fish-shaped fish. Like an aquarium, but untransportable.

Diving at Yellow Tunnel, a reef in the Somosomo Straits off

Taveuni in Fiji. The guide drew a chalkboard picture. The little Fijian guide Lui swam ahead across the top of the reef, using his hands on the coral. I swam after him as if into a gale-force wind. Kicking as hard as I could, an inch above the reef surface. Lui went further and I gave up, drifting back.

THE BIG ISLAND OF HAWAII

We're staying near the Kilauea volcano crater. The former lake of fire-boiling lava is cold and black now, a dead hole. The fresh, live lava is far away, and they say that where the fresh lava hits the water it makes "hydromagmatic explosions." Great phrase.

I struck off walking across a lava field today, walking across a series of layered old flows trying to get to where that fresh, hot lava hits the sea, but it was too far. I turned back after 2 miles. Getting dizzy in the sun − it was like a great asphalt parking lot, but not flat, the surface wavy as the ocean and in spots with big domes like bubbles, cracked and shattered at the tops. Guidebook sez: "The undulating pa'hoehoe looks like a frozen sea." *Pa'hoehoe* is the name for smooth lava, as opposed to the bumpy clinker kind that's called *a'a*.

In the big pa'hoehoe field, the newer lava was iridescent, some pieces reticulated in white. Smooth glob shapes, ruffle shapes, some tossed up and twisted like frozen splashes, and rope shapes with twisting small ripples around them, fractal style. The colors were the dull greens and purples of raku pottery.

All around the park are steam vents or "fumeroles," fields of them, the sulfuretted steam rising up in the dawn light. Holes in the ground, round deep. It reminds me of Avernus, the underworld in Vergil's *Aeneid*, of how Aeneas sets a bowl of fresh blood by the hole so he can talk to some wraiths. His ancestors.

I went back to the fumeroles at twilight, the sun low in the sky. Tall pink grasses. Orchids growing like wheat − purple and white flowers. The sun making stripes in the steam above the fumeroles. Spirits issuing forth, each plume the size of a man or woman, drifting, twisting, torn apart by a vagrant breeze, then forming itself again in the calm. My parents. Close up the steam was humid as over a steam grate in the city. The little "sulfur flowers" around the holes, masses of pale yellow crystals.

Today we saw a flower the size of a face-mask – like for anes-
thesia. One *thick* white petal and one stamen the size of a banana.
Maybe you stick the stamen down your throat like a gag, while
inhaling – to be transported down a steam-vent. And there were
bright pink flowers blooming down a bud like birds of paradise and
the stem was like a gooseneck lamp.

Now we're at the Kona shore, there's a lot of petroglyphs here –
they're ancient designs scratched into rocks. I got a book about
them, it talks about the glyphs being in places where there is a lot of
power or *mana*. We walked to an isolated petroglyph field in Pukao,
a field of smooth *pa'hoehoe*, cracked like the tiles of a turtle shell and
covered with petroglyphs, many of them with their heads towards
Mauna Kea.

The men on the rock are perhaps projections of the artists, like
shadows. I could visualize the 14th Century Hawaiians jumping up
in the air, looking at their shadows, drawing that kind of design. A
spooky place – now overgrown with introduced *kiawe* (mesquite)
thorn trees – back then it was just lava. Much *mana*. Scary, a little.

There was an odd line at the bottom of the sign at the petroglyph
field:

"Those who defile or mistreat the petroglyphs must bear the
emotional, physical and spiritual consequences for those and those
around them – we can take no responsibility for these effects."

Nevertheless I tiptoed among the petroglyphs with my shoes off
– in my socks – to get a better photo, and felt like I was trespass-
ing, that I had intruded. A bit later, dizzy from the August sun, I
branched off on a mistaken path in the woods, and the crisscrossing
shadows of the *kiawe* branches became as petroglyph men, all over
the ground, twisting at odd extra-dimensional angles like a square
coming up out of Flatland, threatening, nay *pursuing* me, intent on
extracting a terrible vengeance for my defilement of their field.

Writing this, I hear a knock on my hotel room door. Peer out
through the peephole. A petroglyph is in the hallway!

The jellyfish warning sign at the hotel beach: a big rectangle with
a yellow background divided in two by a wavy black water line, a
black struggling figure in the water with pointed arms and legs, one
arm raised in despair, and all around it are glyphs of jellyfish. The

glyphs are hump-bumps with dangling wiggly stuff, they're like question marks with elongated wriggly tails, like brains 'n' spines.

Two-tank scuba dive off the beach in Puako this morning. It was good. There was an eel garden seventy feet down by the drop-off of the continental shelf. There were about a hundred eels, silvery green, each with its tail tucked in the smooth white sand, and floating erect, wobbling this way and that. A few eels were swimming around free, adjusting their position. They had long slit mouths partly open. Behind them was a huge form slowly moving, a leviathan of the deeps. The sense of mystery, of hugeness.

I told my dive guide about my idea for a petroglyph story. I suggested that the petroglyph knocking at my character's hotel-room door could be grooved into space, a 4-D bump. Analogous to a Flatland petroglyph which is a 3-D bump in the surface of their 2-D space. The light would warp around the 4-D space curvature of the petroglyph's lines. The guide said, "Is it *all* the petroglyphs that are after the guy or just *one* of them in particular? Maybe he has to get a second petroglyph to help him fight the first one? Maybe the first one was from a burial site. The helper-petroglyph might be a turtle."

The incipient nitrogen narcosis of the dive made everything slow and stony. It made me really want to get high. But trace it through – then I'd want a drink. I'd come down. I'd want more. There'd be no end to it. No, instead of *getting* high, I can *be* high.

I was talking to a fellow clean-and-sober type here who said some interesting things. A surfer. He said you have to be fully into your program for sobriety, be really *standing* on it, like on a board. He also said that we're ninety percent God, just like we're ninety percent water. There's only this little bit of us that's our ego.

KAUAI

I drew all the time instead of writing on this trip. The illos for *Saucer Wisdom*. Yesterday I took a last snorkel. A *humuhumunukunukua-pua'a* fish darted in to a hole in the reef to hide. I was wearing my diving gloves, so I poked my finger in and touched him. He *grunted* really loud, a lot of times, each time I'd touch him. "Unk-unk-unk. Unk unk." My totem fish. *Pua'a* means *pig*, referring either to the fish's nose or to the noise he makes, or both.

Saw a turtle resting on the bottom.

Staghorn finger coral head, full of damselfish and wrasses. The coral like a brain, the fish like thoughts in the brain.

— Unpublished.
Handwritten travel notes made in Tonga and Fiji, July 15 through
August 6, 1996; on the big island of Hawaii, July 28 through
August 5, 1997; and on the way back from Kauai, June 21, 1998.

In Search of Bruegel

AUGUST 28, 1998.

ON THE PLANE FROM SAN FRANCISCO TO GENEVA.
I'm flying alone, Audrey went a few days earlier so as to spend a few extra days with her family. It's almost night.

The landscape of clouds below us is like a hugely plowed field. It's odd that there's no organism that will ever *learn* the shapes of this particular cloud landscape, the geodesics of its surfaces, its crannies and its nooks. It's completely temporary and in some sense *without purpose*. Are the clouds random? Yes and no. The furrowed shapes are repetitive, they are the patterns of a chaotic attractor. So not random overall. But, yes, they are random in their small details.

Then the clouds break up and I can see the night-lit cities of the Bay area. What lovely luminous jellyfish of night. The shapes are built from pinpoints of three kinds of lamp: blue arclights, pink sodium vapor lights, and ordinary incandescent bulbs. Dizzying to think of all the human lives down there doing Friday night: suppers, conversations, parties, sex and TV, TV, TV.

SEPTEMBER 3, 1998. MUSÉE ARIANA.
Finally tomorrow we get to really start our vacation. We've been visiting Audrey's father here. The view out his window is of huge old trees. Oaks, beeches, pines. The chaotic purposeful motion of the beech branches. Like seaweed.

Now I'm in the Ariana Museum of Ceramics. In the Middle Ages, forks only had one tine. A fork like that was called a "pique de table." In the 1600s they started having *two* tines. It's like time travel, looking at this stuff. And here's a bouillon bowl, from Nyon, 1790, glazed to look like knotty pine paneling.

The Ariana Museum is in an old villa with the floor cut out of the second floor so that the main part of the ground floor rises up two stories. There is a mezzanine around the edge of this space with an amazing set of eighteen marble columns holding up the barrel-vaulted ceiling. Very odd, twisty, Baroque columns. I've seen this space before and always wanted to come back here to figure out if the columns are all different or not. At first glance it looks as if they are, but now today I find out for sure.

I assign the letters A through R to the eighteen columns and walk slowly around the mezzanine noting each column's characteristics. The columns are single fat worms, or braids of up to four worms, and the braids twist either clockwise or counterclockwise from bottom to top, making from three to eight full twists between bottom and top. Another distinguishing feature is that the component worms of the columns can be either smooth or grooved.

I have a lot of fun analyzing all this, it's math in action, the coding up of some pattern by a few numbers, and eventually I've learned that of the eighteen columns, seven are twisted clockwise, ten counterclockwise, and one is not twisted at all. Fourteen of the columns are distinct, and four of them are copies of others. If the four copies had only been mirror-reversed then all could have been different, sigh.

The spacing of the duplicated pairs has no obvious rhyme or reason to them. If you label the columns A through R, then the pairs are: AM, BP, DL, HN, and IO.

Wandering around some more, I see several examples of the huge porcelain stoves called *poêles*. One of them reaches all the way to the ceiling. A few years back I smoked DMT for the first and last time. It was an unbelievable nightmare (my usual reaction to psychedelics!) and the most malignant demon in my hallucinations was, of all things, just such a *poêle* stove – I'd recently seen one at John Walker's house in Lignieres, Switzerland. That hallucination later made its way into *The Hacker and the Ants* – I used it both in a "dark dream" freakout scene and in a robot ant attack scene, the ants had a nest in the *poêle*. Even in the sober light of day, the Ariana's gigundo *poêle* scares me, no logical reason why.

Out in the park I see a man with a pipe and a furled umbrella gathering up hazelnuts. A giant bell, a gift from Japan, hangs there, I gong it, and it resonates for more than a minute. A deep humming noise that rises and falls.

SEPTEMBER 4, 1998. FRACTALS AND PAINT.

This is our N[th] honeymoon. Yee-haw. Audrey is next to me happily writing out a $/franc conversion table. Comfortable seats on a fast train. Audrey's stepmother packed us a good lunch: cheese, tomatoes, radishes, chocolate, grapes. We bought a peasant bread.

Yesterday I happened across the hotel where my parents, my brother and I stayed when I came to Geneva to marry Audrey in 1967. I looked into the hotel. I seem to see my spectral parents in the breakfast nook.

I took a ride on a lake boat from Nyon to Geneva the other day, past the Eaux Vives park where we had our wedding lunch. Talk about spectral. I think more than half of the people who were at that lunch are dead now, these 31 years gone. When I was young I saw myself as the unique protagonist of a hero-epic. Time goes by, and now life is more like a chain, a rolling wheel of human seasons, the old trees falling and the saplings coming up.

I have a mental game I like to play, of thinking of my life as a single cosmic year, and of then viewing my current age as a particular date in this cosmic year. It's the old notion of childhood as spring, youth as summer, middle age as fall, and old age as winter. But, being a mathematician, I like to quantify it. To work out the correspondences, I need to decide on how many actual years I'm likely to live. It's convenient for this to be a multiple of twelve; when I was younger, seventy-two used to seem like a reasonable length of life, but these days eighty-four is looking a lot more reasonable to me. So, okay, if my "life-year" is eighty-four years, then each "life-month" is seven years. This means that my current age of fifty-two is equal to, um, seven and a half months, and seven and a half months from the beginning of the life-year is *August 15*. This time of year, in fact. Early harvest. I still have some time.

I talked to Audrey about the idea that as you age, your worldview gets broader. "And then it narrows back down," she reminded me — for, yes, for all four of our parents, when they got old the scope seemed to close down to the most immediate needs of their bodies.

In Geneva, Audrey and I went to see an exhibit of 19th Century Swiss painting at the Musée Rath, a cute little shrine of a Beaux-Arts building on Place Neuve between the opera and the park that includes the university. I noticed one artist in particular: Robert Zünd, 1827–1909. He did these huge canvases of woodlands, with seemingly every leaf in place. He works down to a much lower level of detail than most painters. Yet, like any other painter, even Zünd hits a bottom level where it's just little crusts of paint. The trick painters use is, at some level or other, to replace the fractality of nature by the physical fractality of paint and canvas. The ancient "As Above, So Below" principle in painting. By practice, a painter perhaps learns to approximate a given target fractal dimension by paint that is handled or manipulated in a certain way. Scumbling. A clever artist can do this at a relatively high level and not bother with so much work as another, and still somehow capture the impression of the scene.

When I took the lake boat and it passed under the Lake Geneva fountain called the *Jet d'Eau* I saw such interesting shapes. The sun was behind the fountain, so I saw shadows where the water was thicker. The water came down in big drapes like the drapes in waterfalls.

SEPTEMBER 6, 1998.
PARIS, SEA POTATO, GRAND GUIGNOL, BRANCUSI.
I'm in a tabac/café alone, about to get breakfast, Audrey is in the hotel doing her hair. A few doors down is the entrance to the Place des Vosges – an amazing 18th Century square. Like stepping into a tinted architectural etching on some genteel wall. But the fountains are alive – four of them – and the plane trees are green and chaotic, albeit trimmed into long multi-trunked rectangular prisms. It feels like really good virtual reality – note how a familiarity with VR makes one appreciate real reality the more.

Yesterday we had a great – though kind of disgusting – dinner at La Bar des Huîtres. The "plateau géant," about $60, with regular oysters, round oysters, cherrystone clams, big shrimp, tiny shrimp that you eat in the shell, a big crab cut in half, two little crabs that you pick at like *you're* the crustacean, tiny black snail periwinkles, bigger spiral shell things (whelks?), long razor clams and – *la pièce de résistance* – a "violet" or "patate de mer" (sea potato) which is a tough black thing cut in half, leather on the outside, then an inch of cartilaginous pearly white material, and in the middle the part that I ate, God help me, a beige-yellow mass a bit like sea urchin roe, attached to the thick hide by ligaments and membranes that I severed with some difficulty, finally freeing a soft mass the size of my little finger. Was it eggs? stomach? milt? brain? − whatever, I cut it in half and had it in two mouthfuls. It tasted intensely of the sea, of the fresh sea not the rotten sea, a tang of salt and iodine, like getting blindsided by a wave and sent tumbling over the falls in whitewater surf. I thought uneasily about the sea potato − and about the one bad sewage-reeking oyster I got − for the rest of the evening, my unease compounded by three unwisely consumed balls of ice cream.

Yesterday we went to see a puppet show at Rond Point on Champs Elysées. Such a pitifully small theatre − so humble next to, say, the Opéra de Paris. The puppet theater was called a "guignolet," it was the size of a child's playhouse, an old little thing with "M. P. Guentleur, 1818" painted on it. Seated on four benches upon the park sand in attendance were some ten children with their mothers, and Audrey and I − me the only man other than an employee of the enterprise who sat on the back bench to help initiate the correct shouted responses. The chief puppeteer was an attractive, somewhat roughskinned young woman wearing a bowler hat at an angle. She had a loose pullover that was askew, baring one shoulder and a black silk bra strap. Ah Paris! Before the show, this woman walked out to the little knee-high gate ringing a handbell, to admit the mothers, children, Audrey and me, 16 francs apiece, there was one baby in a carriage who I think got in free. We sat on the little benches, she welcomed us, then disappeared into the little playhouse with its faded red velvet curtains. She told us to call for "Guignol" to make him come out. Wonderful.

I never knew that "Grand Guignol" puppetry was *about* a puppet named Guignol. The man on the back bench called "Guignol" a few times and the children took it up. Eventually, Guignol came out − he wasn't hook-nosed like Punch, as I'd expected, he was a fairly ordinary-looking man in a green frock coat. His wife was Madelon − with a wonderfully high, squeaky puppet voice − and his son was Guillaume. Eventually he got down to the basics of hitting a policeman puppet with a stout, freshly cut and trimmed stick. A cudgel.

Later we go see a bunch of Brancusi sculptures set up in a mock-up of his studio, "just as he left it," except the walls are glass, we walk around looking into the four rooms. The floors are bare, there's nothing present except one or two hundred of Brancusi's sculptures, he kept the studio this way, he *lived* somewhere else, used the studio to show his work to guests and customers, like a gallery.

Imagine if the model of Brancusi's studio had "him" in it, an actor or an android, oblivious to the viewers, arranging things, working a little, maybe fabricating yet another "Bird in Flight." The android Brancusi would of course eventually get out of control.

Afterwards there's music in the street – a diva's voice singing operatically from a tape store. Endless flowing tones. Across the way a woman sits, her leopard scarf fluttering in the wind. Like the flowing music, like the shapes of Brancusi, like the years that swallowed Brancusi's eighty-year life and flow on, leaving his shapes, his cast-off shells.

SEPTEMBER 12, 1998. LONDON MUSEUMS.
In London first we stayed at a YMCA with endless alienating empty halls leading from our tiny wind-rattled room to athlete's-foot-floor hideous-porcelain-bowl-shit-stain copious-pubic-hair bathrooms, it was so gnarly we switched hotels for the second night, me out at dawn trying eight places till I found one that wasn't full or $450 a night.

We were in the Bloomsbury district, around the corner from the British Museum, with its great Egyptian and Greek sculptures. The British were among the very first to rip off, plunder, and loot the cradle of civilization, back in the sun-never-sets days of the British Empire. The Egyptian holdings of the British Museum make the stuff in the Met in NYC look like the broken shit left on the floor after the burglars got away.

I had a lot of uneasy feelings about the loot, in other words. But there were some great pieces. A granite Rameses 2, 1270 BC from Thebes. So calm and beautiful, such a wonderful smooth curve in the cheek at the corner of this mouth – yet, really, how different is this Rameses from a plastic sculpture of the hamburger icon Big Boy?

There was a beautiful queen – Amenophis – and her husband. Really clear lines along the edges of their lips; I could grasp that Egyptians are Africans, black people. Amenophis's husband looked like Lightin' Hopkins.

I saw the best panel of hieroglyphics ever, so clear, so deeply incised. Yet – *mystery* – couldn't find the panel the next day, although the hall was rather small.

Outside we saw a classic cameras store with lots of old Leicas, I wandered in, and "What can I tempt you with, sir?" asked the proprietor. So polite, the British. The place was in "Pied Bull Yard," a courtyard, and in there was a pub, "Truckles of Pied Bull Yard."

I wander into a park near the Embankment tube stop near Trafalgar Square. There are blue-and-white-striped lawn chairs with, mostly, bums in them. I lie in one for awhile, it's free. My legs are giving out from day after day of pounding the pavement. The lawn chairs billow chaotically in the breeze. Chaos is everywhere, if you have the eyes to see it.

In the National Gallery, I find a good painting by Peter Bruegel the Elder, *The Adoration of the Magi* of 1564. The signature says BRVEGEL MDLXIII. How clear and fresh the canvas is. The three kings are in a triangle of gaze, each looking at a gift held by one of the other kings. Balthazar looks like Jimi Hendrix at the Monterey Pop festival. He has a beautiful pointed-toe red boot. Fringed chamois leather cape. His gift is a gold ship called a "nef." It holds a green enameled shell, and within the shell is a tiny live monkey.

The gallery note by the picture says that Bruegel put soldiers in his pictures because for most of his life the Netherlands were occupied by Spanish soldiers. This touch makes it seem so *real*. Makes me want to write Bruegel's life. The rainy Flemish day.

Mary looks like a hot number: full lips. A guy whispers in Joseph's ear. Either it's about the gifts or he's saying "You're a cuckold." Joseph looks undisturbed.

In the background are a bunch of interesting characters. A scholarly fellow with glasses. Joseph's accountant? One of the soldiers is a classic, pie-eyed fool. Next to him is a fat guy like the oyster man at our market.

There's a second, small Bruegel too, a grisaille of *Christ and the Woman Taken in Adultery*. Jesus is writing in the sand. "DIE SONDER SUND IST / DIE…" This is the beginning of the Flemish for "Let he who is without sin cast the first stone." The picture is signed

BRUEGEL MDLXV. Kind of incredible to see Bruegel's signature. The picture is small, I have trouble looking at it well. This story it illustrates was said to be a favorite among Protestants, another heavy historical touch, to know that the Protestant reformation and the Catholic Counter-Reformation were raging through the Lowlands.

Getting into the subway the next day, Audrey got ahead of me and she got on and the door closed me off. A door that had a slanting section at the top, like a greenhouse. Audrey looked so excited behind the door, like a tropical bird, kind of gleeful and triumphant. She waited for me at the target stop, Picadilly Circus. On the British "tube" subway trains, the dangling hand grips are coiled springs with black Bakelite bulbs.

SEPTEMBER 13, 1998. CAMBRIDGE, MY A-LIFE TALK.
So now we've been to London and came to Cambridge for the Digital Biota 2 Conference, the guys who paid our airfare. It's Sunday night, the conference is over. I gave a good talk this morning, trying to make two points: (1) the *Ware* series is a thought experiment about artificial life, and (2) A-life can have soul because God is everywhere. And I ran my CAPOW continuous-valued cellular automata screensaver as a background behind me, showing oozing colored computational liquids.

Actually I stood in the projection beam a lot, I like to feel the CAs on my body, but probably it would have been better to stand to one side. In the light of the computer projector, I always think of Tim Leary onstage in NYC with big oil-drop light-show images on him as he gives a group "Guided Trip." In my talk I mentioned that I'd told Audrey I kind of wanted to take my clothes off so I could feel the CAs on my bare skin, but she'd said she didn't think it was a good idea. What she really said was, "Now that you're not drunk and stoned, why act like you *are*?"

SEPTEMBER 16, 1998. EDINBURGH.
Up at the Edinburgh Castle today, there was a stained glass window knight standing on a knotted shape and Audrey thought it was a bagpipe, but it was a dragon, coiled Celtically. I love the ambiguity between dragons and bagpipes.

What a spooky town. Halloween-like. Such flinty hard gray brick walls, with spectral spires and steeples poking up at the crests of the craggy hills and at the ends of the long, dwindling avenues. *Dr. Jekyll and Mr. Hyde* was set in Edinburgh.

Lovely faces the British have, all so fair and clear-skinned and crisp-featured. Why was I against British things for so long? I was a fool. It's nice here. Easy to talk the language. Everyone polite.

The Scots really *are* frugal. Scrooge McDuck and Lord Quackly's castle. In our hotel room, there's a slot in the wall where you put your room key, and when you take the key out to leave, all the power to the room is cut off. It's handy for rebooting the timed bathroom vent-fan.

My legs are very tired. In a big landscape my legs are like − I often think − a spermatozoon tail beating. And now the beating grows pained and feeble.

SEPTEMBER 21, 1998. ANTWERP. BRUEGEL.
We're in Antwerp now. I've had breakfast and taken a walk. I got a book about Bruegel by Keith Roberts in Edinburgh and have been reading it. I've decided to make Peter Bruegel the Elder my focus for this trip. I'd kind of like to write a historical novel about him. After Antwerp, while Audrey makes another stop in Geneva, I'll hit Brussels and Vienna. Vienna has the Kunsthistorisches Museum where so many Bruegel paintings live. There's several in Brussels as well.

There's some pictures by Bruegel's sons in Antwerp. Peter the Younger copied a lot of his paintings, but Jan struck off on his own topics. He painted flowers, for instance. Jan was fat and rich, a friend of Rubens, a good dresser, they called him "Velvet" Bruegel. The Rubens religious art has huge mannerist human figures.

I keep looking for parallels between myself and Bruegel. Me as a novelist and nonfiction writer, him as a painter and engraver. His paintings never made it into churches as altarpieces because they were satirical (e.g. a man who won't help Christ carry His cross is wearing a rosary) and often vulgar (with people shitting and pissing). He possibly came from a peasant background, but as an adult he was a cultured man. (Kentuckian = peasant!) He worked a lot with the tension between his overall landscape or theme (cf. plot or science concept) and the specific individuality of his people. Later in life Bruegel started to paint increasingly large and detailed human figures, akin to a writer beginning to use stronger, more fully developed characters. Bruegel prided himself on drawing sketches from life; a bit like the transreal notion of working real settings and people into your art.

Walking around inside the big Antwerp cathedral today. Christ, but religious art makes me want to puke after awhile. So vapid and unreal and knuckled-under to the fat-bellied powers of the Church. Might Bruegel have felt this way?

In the streets of Antwerp, I'm thinking that the genes walking around me are the same genes that Bruegel was surrounded by. Like a little pond of fish. It's been four hundred fifty years, about fifteen generations.

The people here so far have seemed a bit rapacious and unfriendly. They speak Flemish, which is really the same language as Dutch. The museum in Antwerp that has the one Bruegel (the *Mad Meg* of 1564) is closed for renovation. The streets stink of sewer gas; it must be hard to drain here in the wet lowlands. In the morning when we stepped out into the square with the huge cathedral, there was a twentyish boy running along screaming. His hair was soaked with dried and fresh bright red blood. Some of his friends were trying to catch him. He wasn't so much screaming as squealing. When we walked by the renovation-closed museum a bald old man stopped and stared at us all the way down the block. Very surreal.

But I'm a baby to be complaining. Here's a list of some things to be grateful for. I'm not working. I have a sexy, loving wife. I can afford this big trip. We have a good hotel room in the heart of town. I have a new research topic (Bruegel) which I'm excited about. I finished writing *Realware*. I'm sober. It's a sunny day. I'm healthy. I just ate a great Belgian endive *(witloof)* salad with Roquefort cheese. I have good shoes. I have a nice new shirt and a new vest from Scotland. I found a cybercafe where I can check my email. The world exists and I'm alive.

SEPTEMBER 22, 1998.
BRUSSELS. BRUEGEL; I BECOME HIM.
Audrey's on the train for Geneva now, and I'm alone till I see her again in three or four days. I miss her, but it's exciting to be alone.

Well, actually it feels rootless and mortal, I feel like a piece of dust drifting around. But what adventure.

I'm getting the night train, fourteen hours to Vienna, so I have the day to kill here in Brussels. In the train station a sign warns to look out for *zakkenrollers*, which is Flemish for "pickpockets." I checked my bags in at the station and visited the six Bruegels in the Belgian Royal Museum of Fine Arts.

1) *The Adoration of the Magi.* 1556. A tempera on canvas, an early work in poor condition.

2) *Landscape with the Fall of Icarus.* 1557? Several versions exist, and this may be a copy. Heavily retouched in any case.

3) *The Fall of the Rebel Angels.* 1562. A Boschian work, complete with lobster-demons.

4) *Yawning Man.* 1563. A miniature, of questionable provenance.

5) *Winter Landscape with Skaters and Bird Trap.* 1565. One of Bruegel's most copied pictures. The birds are so full of character.

6) *The Numbering at Bethlehem.* 1566. A Bible scene set in a winter Flemish village. A masterpiece.

Brussels is French-speaking, unlike Antwerp, which was Flemish-speaking. In Antwerp people repeatedly started talking to me in Flemish. I *look* Flemish! "These are my people," I kept telling Audrey. There is a well-known ancient Flemish family of harpsichord makers called *Ruckers*. I always thought the Bosch and Bruegel faces looked like mine, e.g. the drunk man in *The Peasant Dance*. From now on, when anyone asks what kind of name Rucker is, I'll say Flemish! It's not German after all. Indeed, when I lived in Germany, the name Rucker was quite unfamiliar to them, and they often spelled it Rocker.

In Antwerp yesterday, a really pretty, tall, Bruegel-faced young woman with dark hair and a baby stroller asked me, in Flemish, what time it was. She could have been Mayken Coecke van Aelst, Bruegel's wife!

I just visited the house of Bruegel's granddaughter – and possibly his house as well – in the Marolles district of Brussels on a street called Hoogstraat, just a few blocks down from the Notre

Dame de la Chapelle, which is where Peter and Mayken were married in 1563, and where Peter was buried in 1569. If he lived in that house, how local and touching. Six short blocks down Hoogstraat from the church to his house. I lit a candle by his grave marker, knelt and prayed – for what? Oh, to say "Hi" to Bruegel, and that I'm thinking about him and might try and write about him.

I wrote this up over an omelet in a sidewalk cafe in Brussels. While I was writing, a man begged me for money, he had the gentlest smile, his hat held out, I shook my head, continuing to write, and he said "C'est l'article important..." and wandered off – what if it was Bruegel I just refused?

I then walked a block, and sat down for a dessert in a different cafe. I saw one of those European women who make me think of a big '50s populuxe American car – the plump lips and strong teeth like a grille, the Bezier curve cheeks, the thick bob of dyed blonde hair, huge knockers under a tight silky chartreuse woman top, skin bronzed from studio tan. She was two cafes down. Very snobby-looking. Now she's gone, I missed seeing her walk by because I was distracted by my outrageously delicious Belgian dessert, a cylinder of cream and meringue covered with chocolate shavings. Never mind about any populuxe Euro woman, dessert is readily attainable, even for a fifty-two-year-old man.

I'm going back to the museum to look at some engravings (I think) that I requested at the Cabinet des Estampes of the museum. I asked for *La Cuisine Maigre*, *La Cuisine Grasse*, and *L'Homme à la Recherche de Lui Même*. *Thin Man*, *Fat Man*, and me.

So I went and did that. Actual fucking Bruegel drawings had been engraved and printed by Hieronymous Cock in 15-whatever and I was sitting there looking at them and even touching one with the tip of my finger. They gave me four different versions (states? editions?) of the *Man in Search of Himself*. He's labeled *Elck* (everyman) and holds up a lantern to peer inside a barrel, the goof.

After the engravings there was almost no time and I ran back up to the Bruegel paintings. I felt such *sorrow* leaving them, especially *The Numbering at Bethlehem*. "Goodbye, I love you." The other painters of the time are muddy and dumb. Bruegel is clear, intelligent. I was almost in tears leaving the museum.

I ducked into a museum of musical instruments hoping to see a 16th

Century Flemish bagpipe — they had lots of bagpipes there, but only from the 19th and 20th C, and none from Flanders. I would suppose the leather sack would rot away over the years, but some 16th C nozzles could have survived. The thing I *did* see in the music museum was a "virginal" — a keyboard instrument like a rectangular box on legs — made by Andreas Ruckers, Antwerp 1620. My ancestor Peter Rucker came to America in 1690, twelve generations ago. The Andreas Ruckers virginal appears in a painting by Vermeer. They had a print of the painting right next to the instrument. The "s" at the end of "Ruckers" means nothing, it's common in the Lowlands to put an "s" after the name of the son, in fact Bruegel's name is spelled "Bruegels" in one document. Since I'm Flemish, maybe Bruegel and I are related! After today, I feel a spark of him alive in me and will fan it more.

Late in the afternoon, I get the Brussels subway to the train station to catch the night train to Vienna to visit Bruegel's twelve pictures there. And on the subway I get into my SF trip that Bruegel's alive inside me, looking through my eyes. I've "twinked" him as I used to say — this being the word I made up to mean thinking or praying or somehow summoning up a replica-model of another person in your own head. And I'm looking with Bruegel eyes at the subway platform. The diabolical magic moving stairs, is this hell? Yet the people look the same, albeit very strangely clothed. The sight of a train so odd — is it a dragon? The columns holding up the roof look thin and strange. A girl is sitting and singing — beautifully — for money and for the second time I deny a beggar, though the Bruegel inside me wants to go over to her, she's the only living lovely thing in this human ants-nest subway dungeon.

I follow signs for the train station — supposedly reachable from the subway stop — and end up in half-finished construction (there's a lot of that in Belgium, they seem to be slackers). The sun is setting, light on a glass building, no sign of green, just metal and stone and glass and asphalt and for a minute I'm so into being Bruegel that I'm utterly lost and confused.

So then I have to push Bruegel down so I can find my train, get my suitcase out of baggage claim, change some money to pay for that, look out for zakkenrollers, etc. And finally I'm up on the platform and — for Bruegel — fill my fountain pen from a bottle of ink

I carry in my suitcase. Bruegel is interested in the fountain pen of course. I take out a paper and try to draw a few faces I'd seen, in particular the face of a new Mayken I saw, she sat across from me in the Metro, sweet mouth intelligent eyes, and where is *my* Mayken-Audrey now – I'm such a piece of dust.

SEPTEMBER 23, 1998. VIENNA.

I took the overnight train here yesterday. It was good, I slept quite well. Just talked to Audrey on the phone; she's frazzled, she can't find a hotel for us in Venice, I suggest she come meet me in Vienna, though she's also thinking of Verona. All "V" cities all of a sudden. Vienna is nice, I wouldn't mind spending extra time here.

I saw twelve Bruegels this morning! Among them are his greatest works; he only did about two dozen major paintings. The Hapsburg Emperor Rudolf II was a great art collector, and his older brother Archduke Ernst was the governor of the Netherlands. They acquired all the Bruegels they could find by 1600.

1) *The Battle Between Carnival and Lent.* 1559.
2) *Children's Games.* 1560.
3) *The Suicide of King Saul.* 1562.
4) *The Tower of Babel.* 1563.
5) *The Procession to Calvary.* 1564.
6) *The Gloomy Day.* 1565.
7) *Return of the Herd.* 1565.
8) *The Hunters in the Snow.* 1565.
9) *The Conversion of St. Paul.* 1567.
10) *The Peasant Wedding.* 1568.
11) *The Peasant Dance.* 1568.
12) *The Peasant and the Birdnester.* 1568.

The Procession to Calvary is particularly interesting because on the right edge there's a portrait in profile of a man that's believed to be Bruegel himself. He has long hair, a beard and a long straight nose; he's not a fat peasant at all. He looks a little like Dennis Hopper in *Easy Rider*, only kind and gentle instead of tense and crazed. It's incredible to see Bruegel right there, calm and serious, staring at Christ carrying his cross.

The net impact of so many masterpieces in one room is over-whelming, so much so that I kind of short out. The paintings in Brussels were easier to approach, the place was all but deserted and there was a feeling of having them to myself. The pictures here aren't so easy to see. Some are glassed-over, some are blocked by two artist women who are painting strong-smelling oil copies of their own, there are big tour-groups, there is a rope that if you lean over it a beeper goes off, the light seems dim, my legs are so very tired. My "sperm tail" legs can barely beat anymore.

In any case, the world looks fine now, I just had a big meal: spaet-zle, salad and some schnitzels of Steinpilz mushrooms. Pretty good, though I hadn't been expecting deep-fried when it said the mush-rooms were "gebacken" (sounds more like "baked") but, hey, this is Vienna, where they fucking bread 'n' fry anything, even a dog or a cat or the cook's penis. Like the way Egyptians would mummify anything that chanced to pass by – there's a mummy of a fish in the Rosicrucian museum in San Jose.

Outside I see the truck of a butcher or caterer with *Göd* on the back, would be a great heavy metal band name. And then I happen upon what looks like a circus, set up in a tent in front of a very fancy white stone building, the city hall. It turns out to be intermission at the circus, people are drinking champagne, and I blend into the crowd and wan-der in for the second act. It's called the Circus Roncalli, and it's awe-some. They have a clown with a traditional pointed hat and spangle suit with high shoulders and everything velvet, just like in a Fellini movie. And then there's a skinny performer in red tights and with red cones glued all over himself, big cones, so prickly, and he gets on slack wire and makes a weird bird noise and jiggles back and forth so hyper and funny. I'd like to see that again. What an unexpected treat.

SEPTEMBER 25, 1998.

VIENNA. LEARNING ABOUT BRUEGEL.

I'm stoked about Bruegel. I'm learning so much about him. In the Vienna Kunsthistorisches Museum, there are pictures by his father-in-law and his sons and his grandson and his friends, I can start to get the context.

The end of his life was clouded by the Spanish who were being real pricks. They controlled the Netherlands which was Holland and Belgium. It was the time when the Protestants split off from the Roman Catholic Church. There was a political thing about Spain being Roman Catholic and occupying the Netherlands, who were kind of Protestant. They hung a lot of people. Bruegel was mainly a humanist, he cared about people, not so much about the religious labels. He didn't like seeing people get hanged. Bruegel died in his early forties. He was ill for the last year of his life, we know he didn't die suddenly because before that he was painting really fast, turning out his masterworks, and then suddenly there were no paintings for a year and then he was buried. At the time some Spanish soldiers were perhaps quartered in his house. He made some really mocking drawings that he had his wife Mayken burn so she wouldn't get in trouble. Mayken was the daughter of a man and woman who both were artists in Antwerp, Bruegel started out as her father's apprentice. I could go on about this stuff for a long time...and hopefully I will.

SEPTEMBER 26, 1998. VIENNA. AUDREY IS HERE.
Audrey showed up yesterday, it's nice to have my big canary back singing in the room. Another sunny day. Yesterday shopped a little, doing bower bird getting the nest ready to welcome his mate. I got snacks for her, and a present, concert and circus tickets, and tidied up the room. From my actions one would deduce that I've missed the woman.

I've been to see the Bruegels every day − 3 days so far − and am learning more and more. I have a lot of notes. I always carry a folded-in-four piece of paper in my back pocket to write on.

I'm excited about the idea of writing a novel about Bruegel. There actually *is* already a kind of novel about Bruegel's life.[53] It's pretty good, but it leaves me plenty of room to work in. Bruegel's a big guy.

---

53. Claude-Henri Rocquet, *Bruegel or the Workshop of Dreams*, (University of Chicago Press, Chicago 1991). Originally published in French by Denoël in 1987. Another relevant novel is Marguerite Yourcenar, *The Abyss*, (Farrar Strauss and Giroux, New York 1976), which gives a good picture of the Netherlands in the 16ᵗʰ Century. *The Abyss* is the life story of an alchemist named Zeno, rather than being about painters.

Rudy in Vienna.
(Photo by S. Rucker.)

SEPTEMBER 29, 1998.
VIENNA TO SIENA. AUTUMN AT THE CIRCUS.
So now we're finally moving into Italy. I was like a fly with my feet
caught, pleasantly, in the sweet whipped cream – the *Schlag* – of
Vienna the Zuckerbäcker (Sugarbaker = confectioner) city. Six days.

Four days I visited the big B. in the Kunsthistorisches Museum.
One day the museum was closed and one day I was too tired. *So*
tired, my legs and body are. The fifteen hour train trip comes as a
welcome rest.

Now the train is going through "Bruegel's Alps" as I think of them
now, the mountains at the top of Italy that he traveled through in
1554. Imagine B's reactions to seeing the Alps. "The land – it rises up
high high into the air!" The blue ranges of the more distant hills, the
low gray clouds. I try to imagine more remarks by B: "And in places,
the rock bones show through the green flesh of the hills." "The plane
of the world is tilted." "The hills rising up like waves in water."

The other day in Vienna, there was a strange moment – Audrey and I went to the Circus Roncalli on Sunday afternoon, it was lovely, so full of color and laughter and love. And then we came outside and there was a chill in the air, and some low gray clouds — though still with blue showing through — and some of the leaves on the tree were yellow and it was like all of a sudden it was fall, and it had come perhaps gradually and we'd been too busy playing to notice, it had been summer when we left home, but now we'd stayed away so long that it was fall, us off in a distant city, a feeling of having stayed away longer than I'd realized, and a feeling, too, that in the great "year" of my life it's fall. It turned to fall while we were at the circus.

As we come into Italy, I'm scared. On the other hand, it's nice to hear two women chattering in Italian on the train. They seem like parrots. As soon as we're in their home country, the waiters on the train become surly and rude.

SEPTEMBER 30, SIENA. THE HOTEL GARDEN.

We did about sixteen hours door-to-door travel yesterday and landed in a hotel called Villa Scacciapensieri. The name isn't someone's surname, no, it means "scratch [out] thought" or relax, and also is the Italian name for the time-wasting mouth-harp, which is the logo of the hotel. It's further outside the town than I'd expected, kind of in a suburb by a busy road, though with a nice view of the Chianti hills and a lovely big flowering garden outside our window.

I just had a good breakfast of Italian coffee and rolls. The room has nice tile floors and old, rustic-type furniture, quite elegant. It looks like another sunny day. I hope I don't walk too much. Going biking might be good. The hotel has bikes you can borrow.

I have an irritable tendency to want to complain about things like the traffic noise from the nearby road, but this seems unworthy and ungrateful. The very act of being on a vacation sets up — at least in me — an expectation of achieving some kind of perfection. A *striving*. When really I should be *relaxing*. I need to remind myself over and over that perfection is not a reasonable, attainable goal that I can be happy in pursuing. Instead my goal must be serenity, acceptance and love. It's only me in only this same worldly world. Just as at home, beautiful things and moments are found not everywhere, but as gems set here and there, never-quite-predictable glints in the fabric of ordinary life. Yes, yes. It's nice sitting here in the sun writing this, my legs up, Audrey just inside having breakfast, a bird fluttering in a corner of a vineyard below.

OCTOBER I, 1998. SIENA. WOMEN WALKING. LANDSCAPE.
Observing tourists, I note that Japanese women don't move their hips when they walk. They kind of stomp along like Frankenstein. At the other extreme, looking at an Italian TV show about models (our room has a TV), I realize that the secret of the way models walk is that they cross their legs at each step. This exaggerates the hip motion and keeps a tapered silhouette for their body.

Siena makes me think of Bruegel landscapes. The successive scrims of the hills, bluer in the distance. The surface of the Earth here is like a restless sea. Looking at Sienese art, I note the crisp way the faces stand out in the 13th Century icons.

Humanity is everywhere, like fish in a reef, like flowers in a field, all with the same powers of visualization and planning.

The olive trees are shoots from centuries-old trunk stubs. The stubs are covered with thick green moss, and the dirt around the trunks is plowed, probably to keep the weeds down.

The Tuscan hills. The chestnuts, oaks with acorns, porcini mushrooms and wild pigs – all fit together in a musky, nutty whole.

OCTOBER 2, 1998. BIKE RIDE, JESUS.
This morning I borrowed a mountain bike from the Villa Scacciapensieri and rode out into some of the Chianti hills. I had a lovely view of Siena from one mountaintop winery. I kept thinking about Bruegel. A few peasants were visible working the fields, six of them even picking the big sweet dark Chianti grapes, the peasants dressed in light blue cotton overalls and using red plastic buckets. And I was thinking about Chris Langton, what he said in his talk at the Digital Biota 2 conference in Cambridge, it went something like this.

> It's all biology, folks: our cities, this projector, and even that damned computer. Our artifacts are things that we grow – no different than seashells or termite mounds.

To think of man not as some mistaken invader, and of machines not as some blight upon Nature – it's a comforting, integrated, *Bruegelian* world view.

On my bike ride I stopped in a big church on a hilltop and was struck by thoughts of God. "I made all of this," He seemed to say. It's all biology, all part of a whole, the divine Light in each and every fiber of everything there is. Looking at yet another painting of Christ being lowered from the cross, I'm thinking, "All *right* already, I *will* let this into my heart." Remembering solemn, hip, wise, noble Bruegel staring, hands folded, at Christ with the cross in *The Procession to Calvary* – what does the Christ story mean? God is universal, yet Christ is just a man. His story means Love and Compassion and Trust God. Even if you get crucified, the Passion Story tells us, God can still save you, can still raise you from the dead.

I recall the song Roger used to sing on the Parrish steps back at Swarthmore:

> I walked into a church one day
> While travelin' on my way
> I gave my heart to Jesus there
> He's comin' back to Earth again
> To save us from our sin
> And if you would believe in Him
> He'll take you 'way where there's no fear.

OCTOBER 5, 1998. ROMAN GLADIATORS.
We're in Rome, it's raining, it's Monday and the museums are closed. I go to the Forum and to the Colosseum and there are Italians dressed up like gladiators outside the Colosseum. They have red togas and those brush hats. Very funny, lively guys, trying to get three bucks from each person who takes their picture, threatening everyone with plastic swords. Fierce punks, actually. Not so different after two thousand years.

OCTOBER 6, 1998.
ROME. BOOK INTERVIEW, CAPITOLINE MUSEUM.
Today I did a booklength interview for Sante DiRenzo publishing – it'll be a *thin* book, DiRenzo puts out slim volumes of modern

thinkers' ideas, for university students, mostly. I have an uneasy feeling I ego-tripped too much, talking mostly about my *life*, as opposed to *ideas*. Well, I can fix it up in proofs, chainsaw in some stuff from *Seek!*

After the interview I went to the Capitoline Museum on the Campidoglio Hill. A great hall of busts in one room. The whole museum in glorious disorder, so Italian. No labels on anything other than the occasional engraved Latin ones. Cow skulls are a big motif in the friezes. Myoor! There was a bust of a guy called Massimino. "Little Max."

In the room of busts I saw one on the top shelf that was – I swear – the deceased California sculptor Robert Arneson, who so loved to make classical busts of himself. Yes, it was Arneson, looking quiet and sneaky, his eyes fixed on a corner up by the ceiling, his mouth tight, pulled to one side as if holding in a laugh and saying – oh – maybe, "I beat them all. I'm immortal. Ain't death a bitch?"

The Roman noses on the busts so long and straight, like columns. And always a pulpy, twisted sensual little mouth.

I touched the penis of Aristedes of Smyrna and got scolded by a guard.

People crowded into a gallery – the live heads looking at the stone head. Really, how very much more interesting are the live ones. Yet we look at the stone ones.

"Hi, I'm Ken and this is Barb." The American couple next to us at the pizzeria full of bus tourists.

OCTOBER 7, 1998. ROME. GALLERIA BORGHESE.
The great Gian Lorenzo Bernini has a sculpture of the victory of truth, says he wants to show "columns, obelisks, and mausoleums destroyed by Time," that's Rome. He didn't finish that part, though, just has Truth, who looks like some mountain girl hippie peaking on acid.

The Galleria Borghese is largely filled with paintings and sculptures of rich pricks, ward-heelers. The complete bullshit bankruptcy of religious art peaks in Titian with his Play-Doh people.

Looking at Bernini's *Rape of Persephone* and seeing real people around it, I have to think that the real people are more important. So why am I looking at the statue? Why did I stand in line to see it?

Well, people go away, but the art is always the same. It's a still center-point.

Cardinal Scipio Borghese, called Scip for short, built this gallery. Bernini did two busts of him, the first had a crack in the marble, so Bernini copied it in three feverish days.

When they were excavating near the Termini, they found a Roman statue of an *ermafrodito* or hermaphrodite, a guy half on his stomach, his butt invitingly pointed at you, his small and stiff dick laid out in front of him so cute, and he has some nice small boobs. Cardinal Scip flipped for this sculpture, natch, and had Bernini make a *pillow* and a *mattress* for it! Outta marble, you wave, with all the skillful Bernini touches to make the stone look soft and real. A number of stubborn stains on that ermafrodito, though.

OCTOBER 8, 1998.
ROME TO NAPLES. LANDSCAPE, MUSEO NAZIONALE.
I had breakfast with a boy, a "ragazzo" named Roberto, one of my fans, a physics student in Rome. He had a list of big questions for me, like I used to have for Gödel, and indeed he said, "I'm 21, I feel like you visiting Gödel, there is a similar ratio." A nice thought, though I'm certainly no King Kurt.

I'm taking the train alone to Naples for a day. Looking out the train window. The beauty of the sky today. Low fluffy clouds, almost touching the ground, but well separated, with a goodly amount of watery blue sky to see – like spring. But, no, it's fall, isn't it. The clouds are low and close enough to be noticeably three-dimensional, like weightless thickets in the air. Ravishing. The heart-blooming feeling of soft clouds and streaks of light rain. Roberto said, "I have never traveled, but I am sure that nowhere is the sky so beautiful as in Rome."

I spend the day visiting two Bruegels in the Museo or Galleria Nazionale in the Capodimonte park of Naples. Hard to find the two Bruegels in the endless galleries. The unbelievable richness of the collection. The unfriendly jabbering Italians and their insane trove of art. Nobody but nobody is in there except the Italian guards. It feels like a high school late in the afternoon after almost everyone's gone home, just a small clique of people left, a clique I'm not in. The

Bruegels are such a sudden oasis of intelligence in this wilderness of schlock and shit. Yes, of all the paintings in the enormous Museo Nazionale in Naples, only the Bruegels – *The Misanthrope* and *The Parable of the Blind* – only these seem to have something to say.

The Misanthrope is on cloth. There's vertical oval patches of water damage along the left half. It's scraped near the top center right. Signed BRVEGEL 1568, the year before he died.

It strikes me to think of this as Bruegel's last self-portrait. Admittedly the line of the nose doesn't match the line of the nose in *Procession to Calvary*. But the beard and the folded hands remind me of the Bruegel likeness in *Procession to Calvary*. I have the feeling that when he painted this he knew he was mortally ill. The Misanthrope is headed to the left, into death, with mushrooms growing under the rotten trees. Shrooms = decay.

It has this caption, in a really weird script:

> Om dat de Vierelt is soe ongetru
> Daer om gha ic in den ru.
> [In literal English:]
> For that the World is so untrue
> There fore go I in the sorrow.

The "in den ru" is squeezed together. It hits me *wow*, that *I'm* Ru! In a synchronistic sense, perhaps Bruegel is saying he will go "in den ru" meaning "into a book by Rudy Rucker!" Well, it's a pleasant fantasy anyhow. Too bad the Misanthrope doesn't look a little happier about it.

This picture and *The Parable of the Blind* right next to it have the same milky gray sky and dun Earth. Winter. A depressing pair. Bruegel knew he was dying.

I had a very nice lunch in the museum cafe, great vegetables. "Contorni" they call vegetables in Italy. These were Naples style with garlic and hot peppers, four kinds: mushrooms, chicory, spinach, and some other green.

Leaving the Naples museum, I think "Sigh, goodbye Bruegel, goodbye Europe."

Riding back to Rome on the train, the clouds are lit from behind, the sun down west over the Mediterranean. Fields with streams, irrigation ditches, ponds, fens. Now and then the orange-edged clouds can be seen reflected in a patch of ruffled green water – exquisite. A line of pines (cypress?), their green tops blended into one worm, their bare trunks twisting down like legs.

OCTOBER 9, 1998. ON THE PLANE FROM ROME TO SF.
So all right, we're on the way home. I'm ready. Let the hemorrhage of money stop. No more snotty waiters! Good clean food! Hello comfortable bed! Time to go back to being a producer instead of a consumer.

Out the window is Greenland. Whipped cream snow with sharp-ridged peaks sticking out here and there; mountains buried up to their necks in ice and snow.

It's a big world.

— *Unpublished. Handwritten travel notes, fall, 1998.*

Part III: Art

A Transrealist Manifesto

In this piece I would like to advocate a style of SF-writing that I call transrealism. Transrealism is not so much a type of SF as it is a type of avant-garde literature. I feel that transrealism is the only valid approach to literature at this point in history.

The transrealist writes about immediate perceptions in a fantastic way. Any literature which is not about actual reality is weak and enervated. But the genre of straight realism is all burnt out. Who needs more straight novels? The tools of fantasy and SF offer a means to thicken and intensify realistic fiction. By using fantastic devices it is actually possible to manipulate subtext. The familiar tools of SF — time travel, antigravity, alternate worlds, telepathy, etc. — are in fact symbolic of archetypal modes of perception. Time travel is memory, flight is enlightenment, alternate worlds symbolize the great variety of individual world-views, and telepathy stands for the ability to communicate fully. This is the "trans" aspect. The "realism" aspect has to do with the fact that a valid work of art should deal with the world the way it actually is. Transrealism tries to treat not only immediate reality, but also the higher reality in which life is embedded.

The characters should be based on actual people. What makes standard genre fiction so insipid is that the characters are so obviously puppets of the author's will. Actions become predictable, and in dialogue it is difficult to tell which character is supposed to be talking. In real life, the people you meet almost never say what you want or expect them to. From long and bruising contact, you carry simulations of your acquaintances around in your head. These simulations are imposed on you from without; they do not react to imagined situations as you might desire. By letting these simulations run your characters, you can avoid turning out mechanical wish-fulfillments. It is essential that the characters be in some sense out of control, as are real people — for what can anyone learn by reading about made-up people?

In a transrealist novel, the author usually appears as an actual character, or his or her personality is divided among several characters. On the face of it, this sounds egotistical. But I would argue that to use oneself as a character is not really egotistical. It is a simple necessity. If, indeed, you are writing about immediate perceptions, then what point of view other than your own is possible? It is far more egotistical to use an idealized version of yourself, a fantasy-self, and have this para-self wreak its will on a pack of pliant slaves. The transrealist protagonist is not presented as some super-person. A transrealist protagonist is just as neurotic and ineffectual as we each know ourselves to be.

The transrealist artist cannot predict the finished form of his or her work. The transrealist novel grows organically, like life itself. The author can only choose characters and setting, introduce this or that particular fantastic element, and aim for certain key scenes. Ideally, a transrealist novel is written in obscurity, and without an outline. If the author knows precisely how his or her book will develop, then the reader will divine this. A predictable book is of no interest. Nevertheless, the book must be coherent. Granted, life does not often make sense. But people will not read a book which has no plot. And a book with no readers is not a fully effective work of art. A successful novel of any sort should drag the reader through it. How is it possible to write such a book without an outline? The analogy is to the drawing of a maze. In drawing a maze, one has a start (characters and setting) and certain goals (key scenes). A good maze forces the tracer past all the goals in a coherent way. When you draw a maze, you start out with a certain path, but leave a lot of gaps where other paths can hook back in. In writing a coherent transrealist novel, you include a number of unexplained happenings throughout the text. Things that you don't know the reason for. Later you bend strands of the ramifying narrative back to hook into these nodes. If no node is available for a given strand-loop, you go back and write a node in (cf. erasing a piece of wall in the maze). Although reading is linear, writing is not.

Transrealism is a revolutionary art form. A major tool in mass thought control is the myth of consensus reality. Hand in hand with this myth goes the notion of a "normal person."

There are no normal people – just look at your relatives, the people that you are in a position to know best. They're all weird at some level below the surface. Yet conventional fiction very commonly shows us normal people in a normal world. As long as you labor under the feeling that you are the only weirdo, then you feel weak and apologetic. You're eager to go along with the establishment, and a bit frightened to make waves – lest you be found out. Actual people are weird and unpredictable, this is why it is so important to use them as characters instead of the impossibly good and bad paperdolls of mass culture.

The idea of breaking down consensus reality is even more important. This is where the tools of SF are particularly useful. Each mind is a reality unto itself. As long as people can be tricked into believing the reality of the 6:30 news, they can be herded about like sheep. The "president" threatens us with "nuclear war," and driven frantic by the fear of "death" we rush out to "buy consumer goods." When in fact, what really happens is that you turn off the TV, eat something, and go for a walk, with infinitely many thoughts and perceptions mingling with infinitely many inputs.

There will always be a place for the escape-literature of genre SF. But there is no reason to let this severely limited and reactionary mode condition all our writing. Transrealism is the path to a truly artistic SF.

—*Appeared in* The Bulletin of the Science Fiction Writers of America, *#82, winter, 1983.*

What SF Writers Want

I think some of the appeal of SF comes from its association with the old idea of the Magic Wish. Any number of fairy tales deal with a hero (humble woodcutter, poor fisherman, disinherited princess) who gets into a situation where he or she is free to ask for any wish at all, with assurance that the wish will be granted. Reading such a tale, the reader inevitably wonders, "What would *I* wish for?" It's pleasant to fantasize about having such great power; and thinking about this also provides an interesting projective psychological test.

Some SF stories hinge on the traditional Magic Wish situation – the appearance of a machine (= magic object) or an alien (= magic being) who will grant the main character's wishes. But more often, the story takes place *after* the wish has been made...by whom? By the author.

What I mean here is that, in writing a book, an SF writer is in a position of being able to get any Magic Wish desired. If you want time travel in your book...no problem. If you want flying, telepathy, size-change, etc., then you, as SF writer, can have it – not in the real world, of course, but in the artificial, written world into which you project your thoughts.

To make my point quite clear, let me recall a conversation I once had with a friend in Lynchburg. "Wouldn't it be great," my friend was saying, "if there were a machine that could bring into existence any universe you wanted, with any kinds of special powers. A machine that could call up your favorite universe, and then send you there." "There is such a machine," I answered. "It's called a typewriter."

Okay. So the point I want to start from here is the notion that, in creating a novelistic work, the writer is basically in a position of being able to have any wish whatsoever granted.

What kinds of things do we, as SF writers, tend to wish for? What sorts of possibilities seem so attractive to us that we are willing to spend the months necessary to bring them into the pseudoreality of a polished book? What kinds of needs underlie the wishes we make?

In discussing this, my basic assumption is that the driving force behind our SF wishes is a desire to find a situation wherein one might be happy...whatever "happy" might mean for any particular writer.

There are, of course, a variety of very ordinary ways to wish for happiness: wealth, sexual attractiveness, political power, athletic prowess, sophistication, etc. I'm not going to be too interested in these types of wishes here – because such wishes are not peculiar to the artform of SF. Any number of standard paperback wish-fulfillments deal with characters whom the author has wished into such lower-chakra delights.

No, the kind of wishes I want to think about here are the weird ones – wishes that have essentially no chance of coming true – wishes that are really worth asking for.

I can think of four major categories of SF wishes, each with several subcategories:

1) *Travel.*
    (1.1) Space travel. (1.2) Time travel.
    (1.3) Changing size scale. (1.4) Travel to other universes.
2) *Psychic powers.*
    (2.1) Telepathy. (2.2) Telekinesis.
3) *Self-change.*
    (3.1) Immortality. (3.2) Intelligence increase.
    (3.3) Shape-shifting.
4) *Aliens.*
    (4.1) Robots. (4.2) Saucer aliens.

Let's look at these notions one at a time.

1) *Travel.* Your position relative to the universe can perhaps be specified in terms of four basic parameters: (1.1) space-location, (1.2) time-location, (1.3) your size, and (1.4) which universe you're actually in. Our powers to alter these parameters are very limited. Although it is possible to change space-location, this is hard and slow work. We travel in time, but only in one direction, and only at one fixed speed. In the course of a lifetime, our size changes, but only to a

small extent. And jumping back and forth between parallel universes is a power no one even pretends to have. Let's say a bit about the ways in which science fiction undertakes to alter each of these four stubborn parameters.

(1.1) *Space travel.* Faster-than-light drives, matter transmission, and teleportation are all devices designed to annihilate the obdurate distances of space. One might almost say that these kinds of hyper-jumping devices turn space into time. You no longer worry about how far something is, you just ask when you should show up.

Would happiness finally be mine if I could break the fetters of space? I visualize a kind of push-button phone dial set into my car's dashboard, and imagine that by punching in the right sequence of digits I can get *anywhere*. (Actually, the very first SF story I ever read was a Little Golden Book called *The Magic Bus*. I read it in the second grade. The Bus had just one special button on the dash, and each push on the button would take the happily tripping crew to a new *randomly selected* locale. Of course – ah, if only it were still so easy – everyone got home to Mom in time for supper and bed.) That would be fun, but would it be enough? And what is enough, anyway?

In terms of the Earth, power over space is already, in a weak sense, ours. If it matters enough to you, you can actually travel any-where on Earth – it's not instantaneous, using cars and planes, but you do get there in a few days. Even easier, by using a telephone, you can actually project part of yourself (ears and voice) to any place where there's someone to talk to. But these weak forms of Earth-bound space travel are the domain of travel writing and investigative journalism, not of SF.

Hyperjumping across space would be especially useful for travel to other planetary civilizations. One underlying appeal in changing planets would be the ability to totally skip out on all of one's imme-diate problems, the ability to get out of a bad situation. "Color me gone," as some soldiers reportedly said, getting on the plane that would take them away from Viet Nam and back to the U.S. "I'm out of here, man, I'm going back to the *world*." Jumping to a far-distant planet would involve an escape from real life, and certainly SF is, to some extent, a literature of escape.

(1.2) *Time travel.* I once asked Robert Silverberg why time travel has fascinated him so much over the years. He said that he felt the desire to go back and make good all of one's major life-errors and past mistakes. I tend to look at this a little more positively – I think a good reason for wanting to go back to the past is the desire to re-experience the happy times that one has had. The recovery of lost youth, the revisiting of dead loved ones.

A desire to time travel to an era before one's birth probably comes out of a different set of needs than does a desire to travel back to earlier stages of one's own life. People often talk about the paradoxes involved in going back to kill their ancestors – this gets into the territory of parricide and matricide. And a sublimated desire for suicide informs the tales about directly killing one's past self. Other time travel stories talk about going back to watch one's parents meeting – I would imagine that this desire has something to do with the old Freudian concept of witnessing the "primal scene."

What about time travel to the future? This comes, I would hazard, out of a desire for immortality. To *still be here*, long after your chronological death.

To a lesser extent than with space, we have some slight power over time: each day you live through brings you one day further into the future, and going to sleep is a way of making the future come "sooner." And one of the appeals of marijuana is that it can make time seem to pass slower, making the future come "later." And of course, a session of intensely focused recollection can make the past briefly seem alive. (Thus Proust, thus psychoanalysis.)

As with power over space, we must question whether power over time is really enough to wish for. Eventually, both of these powers simply boil down to having a special sort of "car" which enables you to jump here and there, checking out weirder and weirder scenes.

(1.3) *Changing size scale*. Without having to actually travel through space or time, one could see entirely new vistas simply by shrinking to the size of a microbe. Alternatively, one might try growing to the size of a galaxy.

One problem with getting very big is that you might accidentally crush the Earth, and have nothing to come back to. I prefer the idea of shrinking. What need in me does this speak to? On a sexual level, the notion of getting very small is probably related to an Oedipal desire to return to the peaceful and ultra-sexual environment of the womb. On a social level, getting small connotes the idea of being so low-profile as to be unhassled by the brutal machineries of law and fame. Economically speaking, being small suggests independence – if I were the size of a thumb, my food bills would be miniscule. A single can of beer would be more than the equivalent of a full keg!

I would like to be able to get as small as I liked, whenever I wanted to. But would it be enough? Would I be happy then? Probably not. After a week or so, it would get as old as anything else.

(1.4) *Travel to other universes.* In a way, all three of the powers just mentioned are special instances of being able to jump into a different universe. Most of what was said about space travel applies here. Of course, travel to alternate universes can also be taken in a very broad sense which includes travel into higher-dimensional spaces and the like.

One's place in the world seems to be fixed by such factors as income and ability – in another world, things might be so much more pleasant. Rich people and poor people live in different worlds – on a crude level, winning a state lottery can act as a ticket to a different universe. A dose of a psychedelic drug can, of course, accomplish an equally dramatic (but temporary) transportal – this is one reason why people take them.

The drug issue raises the fact that the universe is not entirely objective. To a large extent, the way your world seems is conditioned by the way you feel about it. Keep in mind that I think the driving force behind all of the SF travel-wishes is a desire to find a place/time/size/universe in which to be happy. Rather than asking for a *different* world, one might equally well ask for a way to enjoy *this* world.

2) *Psychic powers.* Travel is only the first category of SF wishes. Psychic power is the second of the four main categories mentioned above. What might we take to be the main types of SF psychic-power wishes? Let's try these: (2.1) telepathy, and (2.2) telekinesis.

(2.1) *Telepathy.* Supposedly, God can see everything at once – God is omniscient. Telepathy is a type of omniscience, particularly if we imagine it as extended to include clairvoyance. It would defi-

Seek!

nitely be pleasant to know everything – to be plugged totally into the cosmos as a whole. I *guess* it would be pleasant – actually, it might get boring. The omniscient gods of our myths and religions do seem a bit restless.

On a more personal level, I think of telepathy as standing for a situation where you are in perfect accord and communion with someone else. This often happens when one is alone with a good friend or a loved one. These moments are, I would hazard, as close to real happiness as one ever gets. The desire for telepathy is basically a desire for love and understanding.

Of course, what one often sees in SF telepathy stories is the hero or heroine being overwhelmed by the inputs from everyone else's minds. You want to understand the people you love – the others you'd just as soon not know about.

As with the case of space travel, telepathy is a faculty that we already, to some extent, have. By talking or by writing, I am able to get someone to share my state of mind; by listening or by reading, I can learn to understand others. Maybe we already have enough telepathy as it is.

(2.2) *Telekinesis.* Not only is God omniscient, S/He is omnipotent. Given a really strong telekinetic (also known as psychokinetic or PK) ability, you would be, in effect, able to control anything going on in the world.

This power appeals to me very little. I don't want to control the world – I just want to enjoy it. I don't need to run it, it's doing a decent job by itself. Of course, a person with less self-doubt might find PK very attractive.

As with telepathy, I might also point out that we already have PK in a limited form. I stare fixedly at the cigarettes on my desk. I concentrate. Moments later a lit cigarette is in my mouth! (Does the fact that, by sheer force of will, I caused my material hand to pick up the cigarettes and light one make my feat less surprising?)

There is one special sort of telekinesis that I do find very appealing. This is the ability to levitate. All my life I have dreamed of flying – as far as I'm concerned, the ability to fly is right up there with the ability to shrink.

But what is so special about flying? Flying involves being high off

the ground, and most everyone likes the metaphor of being high –
in the sense of euphoria, elation, and freedom from worry. Rising
above the mundane. Freud used to claim that flying dreams have
some connection with sex, and I suppose that a good act of sexual
intercourse does feel something like flying. And of course, flying
would provide some of the same benefits that teleportation would,
as discussed under (1.1) above.

3) *Self change.* Under this vaguely titled category, I include: (3.1)
immortality, (3.2) intelligence increase, and (3.3) shape-shifting, or
the ability to change the shape of one's body.

(3.1) *Immortality.* This is a key wish. As soon as we are born, we
are presented with what I have elsewhere called the fundamental
koan: "Hi, you're alive now, isn't it nice? Some day it will all stop and
you will be dead. What are you going to do about it?" The fear of
death is up there with the need for love as one of the really basic
human drives.

One problem with immortality might be that you would at some
point get bored. I've occasionally been so depressed that I've thought
to myself, "Death is the only thing that makes life bearable," meaning
that if I thought I was going to have to be here forever, I just
wouldn't be able to stand it. (Though if you couldn't die, and you
couldn't stand it, what could you do? Not a bad premise for an SF
story . . .)

There are various sorts of immortality, short of the real thing,
that we do comfort ourselves with. Let me list them, as I've thought
about this a lot:

(3.1.1) Genetic immortality. If you have children, then your
    DNA code will still be around, even after you die. Later
    descendants may look and/or act like you – which means
    that the pattern you call "me" will still be, to some extent,
    present in the world.

(3.1.2) Artistic immortality. A human being consists (at least)
    of hardware (= the body) plus software (= the ideas). In
    creating a work of art, you code up some of your software.
    A person reading one of your books is something like a
    computer running a program that you wrote. As long as

the person is looking at your book and thinking along the lines which the book suggests, then that person is, in some degree, a simulation of you, the author.

(3.1.3) Social immortality. Even if you have no children and leave no works of art, you will still, in the course of your life, have contributed in various ways to the society in which you found yourself. Perhaps you were a teacher, and you affected some students. Perhaps you sold clothes, and you influenced what people wore. Even if you had no direct influences, you were, to some extent, a product of the society that you lived in, and so long as this society continues to exist you still have a slight kind of immortality in that the society will continue to produce people somewhat like you.

(3.1.4) Racial immortality. This is similar to (3.1.1) and (3.1.3); similar to (3.1.1) if one takes cousins into account, similar to (3.1.3) if one views the human race as a single large society.

(3.1.5) Spacetime immortality. This perception of immortality hinges on the viewpoint that time is not really passing. Past-present-future all co-exist in a single four dimensional "block universe." Today (May 14, 1984) will always exist, outside of time, and thus I will always exist as well.

(3.1.6) Mathematical immortality. It is abstractly possible to imagine coding my body and brain up by a very large array of numbers. This is analogous to the way in which extremely complex computer programs are embodied in machine-language patterns of zeroes and ones. The numerical description of me may in fact be infinite – no matter. The main thing is that this numerical coding can be represented as a mathematical set. And the Platonic school of the foundations of mathematics teaches that mathematical sets exist independently of the physical world. Therefore, long after I am dead, I will still have a permanent existence as a mathematical possibility.

(3.1.7) Mystical immortality. At the most profound level, I do not feel myself to be just my body, or just my mind. I feel, at this deepest level, that I am simply a part of the One, a facet of the Absolute. The disappearance of my body will mean only that the ever-changing One has changed its form a bit.

(3.1.8) Religious immortality. Who knows – maybe we do have souls that God will take care of. This belief is in some ways like the idea of mathematical immortality. When the good thief asked Jesus to "Remember me," perhaps he meant it more literally than is usually realized.

(3.2) *Intelligence increase.* The idea of having a vastly increased intelligence is certainly attractive – particularly to people who already take pleasure in the life of the mind. One difficulty in writing SF about vastly increased intelligence is that it is hard for us to imagine – or to write about – what that would involve.

What does the wish for more intelligence really mean? It is somehow akin to the wish to be much bigger in size – a wish to include more of the universe in one's scope of comprehension.

Pushed to the maximum, a desire for increased intelligence is a desire for omniscience or perhaps a wish to know the Secret of Life. What would it be like to know the Secret of Life? Somehow I have the image of an orgasm that goes on and on, a never-ending torrent of blinding enlightenment. It sounds nice, but we do need contrasts to be able to perceive.

(3.3) *Shape-shifting.* One form of this wish is analogous to the intellectual's wish for more intelligence. An athletically-inclined person might naturally wish to be a world-class athlete; and a physically attractive person might wish to be a Hollywood star. In each case, it's a matter of wanting to be better at what one already does well. We might also include here a compassionate person's desire to be saintly, and an artist's desire to be truly great.

Why should we want to be the *best*? The drive for excellence seems to be wired in way down there – it's good for the race, within limits.

The kind of shape-shifting I really had in mind here, though, was things like *turning into a dog*. You could really get a lot of slack if you could totally change your appearance at will. For me, this one is right up there with flying and shrinking: the ability to change my body at will. It would be so interesting to see the world through a dog's eyes, or through another kind of person's eyes.

What need is this one coming from? Wanting a diversity of experience, I guess. A desire to break out of the personality-mold inflicted on me by my specific body's appearance and habits.

4) *Aliens*. By aliens, I mean two kinds of beings: (4.1) robots, and (4.2) saucer aliens.

(4.1) *Robots*. Intelligent robots will be very exciting – if we're ever able to evolve them. One aspect is that if we can bring intelligent life into being, then we will better understand what we ourselves are like. Another angle that appeals to me is that, given intelligent robots, it would be possible to program one to be just like me, so that I would then have yet another type of immortality to access.

In some ways, we think of robots as being like the ideal sorts of people that don't really exist. The notion of a happy, obedient, intelligent slave, for instance. Given human nature, no such human slave is possible. But still we hope to build a machine like this. Such hopes are, no doubt, doomed for disappointment. A machine smart enough to act human will be unlikely to settle for slavery.

Another thing that makes robots attractive is the notion that they might always be rational. People are so rarely rational – but why is this? Not because we wouldn't *like* to be rational. The real reason is that the world is so complex, one's data are so slight, and so many decisions are required. Full rationality is, in a formal sense, impossible for us – and it will, I fear, be impossible for the robots as well.

There's another SF tradition of writing about computer brains; here instead of intelligent robots, the vision is of a very large computer brain which is seemingly very wise and just. It is as if we humans might be hoping to build the God-the-Father whom we fear no longer exists. In most such stories the god-computer turns out to be evil, either like a cruel dictatorship or like a blandly uncaring bureaucracy. But this leads us out of the domain of things that writers *wish for*.

(4.2) *Saucer aliens*. I loosely use the phrase "saucer aliens" to include any kind of creatures that might show up on Earth, either from space, from underground, or from another dimension.

In C. G. Jung's classic book on UFO's, he makes the point that, in popular mythology, saucer aliens play much the same role that angels did in the Middle Ages.[54] There is a hope that no matter how evil and messed up things might get on Earth, there are still some higher forces who might step in and fix everything. The UFO aliens are, perhaps, replacements for the gods we miss, or for our parents who have grown old and weak.

Another very important strand in thinking about saucer aliens is the element of sexual attraction. A key element to sexual attraction is the idea of *otherness*. An alien stands for something wholly outside of yourself that is, perhaps, willing to get close to you anyway. This drive is probably hard-wired into us for purposes of exogamy: it's genetically unwise to mate with people so similar to you that they might be your cousins.

It is interesting in this context to note how some rock-groups try to give an impression of being aliens.

Of course, Earth is already full of aliens – other races, other sexes, other backgrounds. By constantly striving to broaden one's circle of understanding, one can begin to see the world in a variety of ways.

So – those are some of the things that SF writers want. Undoubtedly, I've left out some important types of SF wishes, and it may be that some other pattern of classifying SF dreams is more enlightening. One thing that I do find surprising is that it is at all possible to begin a project of this nature. When one first comes to SF, there is a feeling of unlimited possibility – what is startling is how few basic SF themes there really are. As indicated, I think most of our favorite themes appeal to us for reasons that are psychological.

As long as I'm whipped up into this taxonomic mania for system-izing things, let me suggest that the psychology of human behavior is based upon avoiding Three Bad Things, and upon seeking Three Good Things that are the respective opposites of the Bad Things.

The Three Bad Things might be called Jail, Madness, and Death – and the Three Good Things would be Change, Slack, and Love.[55]
—*Appeared in* The Bulletin of the Science Fiction
Writers of America, *#87, Spring, 1985.*

---

54. C. G. *Jung, Flying Saucers: A Modern Myth of Things Seen in the Skies*, Princeton University Press, Princeton 1958. See my *Saucer Wisdom* for further discussion.

55. I mean "Jail" here in the sense of any kind of imprisonment or dulling routine, and I mean "Slack" in the sense of serenity and inner peace.

What Is Cyberpunk?

'Proximately, "cyberpunk" is a word coined by Gardner Dozois to describe the fiction of William Gibson. Gibson's novel *Neuromancer* won the science fiction equivalent of the Triple Crown in 1985: the Hugo, the Nebula, and the Phil Dick award. Obviously, a lot of SF writers would like to be doing whatever Gibson is doing right. At the 1985 National SF Convention in Austin there was a panel called "Cyberpunk." From left to right, the panelists were me, John Shirley, Bruce Sterling, a nameless "moderator," Lew Shiner, Pat Cadigan, and Greg Bear. Gibson couldn't make it; he was camping in Canada, and the audience was a bit disappointed to have to settle for pretenders to his crown. Sterling, author of the excellent *Schismatrix*, got a good laugh by announcing, "Gibson couldn't make it today, he's in Switzerland getting his blood changed." Talking about cyberpunk without Gibson there made us all a little uncomfortable, and I thought of a passage in *Gravity's Rainbow*, the quintessential cyberpunk masterpiece:

> On Slothrop's table is an old newspaper that appears to be in Spanish. It is open to a peculiar political cartoon of a line of middle-aged men wearing dresses and wigs, inside the police station where a cop is holding a loaf of white . . . no it's a baby, with a label on its diaper sez la revolucion . . . oh, they're all claiming the infant revolution as their own, all these politicians bickering like a bunch of putative mothers . . .[56]

SF convention panels normally consist of a few professional writers and editors telling old stories and deflecting serious questions with one-liners. Usually the moderator is a semi-professional, overwrought at being in public with so many SF icons, but bent on explaining his or her ideas about the panel topic which he or she has chosen. The pros try to keep the mike away from the moderator.

56. Thomas Pynchon, *Gravity's Rainbow*, Viking, New York 1973, p. 263.

The audience watches with the raptness of children gazing at television, and everyone has a good time. It's a warm bath, a love-in. The cyberpunk panel was different. The panelists were crayfishing, the subnormal moderator came on like a raving jackal, and the audience, at least to my eyes, began taking on the look of a lynch mob. Here I'm finally asked to join a literary movement and everyone hates us before I can open my mouth?

What is it about *punk*?

Back in the '60s — now safe and cozy under a twenty-year blanket of consensus history — the basic social division was straight vs. hip, right vs. left, pigs 'n' freaks, feds 'n' heads. Spiro Agnew vs. Timothy Leary. It was a clear, simple gap that sparked and sputtered like a high-voltage carbon arc. The country was as close to civil war as it's been in modern times. News commentators sometimes speak of this as a negative thing — burning cities, correct revolutionary actions, police riots — but there was a lot of energy there. Sixties people think of the old tension as "good" in somewhat the same way that '40s people look back on the energy of WWII as "good."

A simple dichotomy. But during the '70s times got tough, and all the '60s people got older. Madison Avenue turned hip into *product*. Businessmen got hot-tubs; and they weren't necessarily faking — I know a number of present-day businessmen who are regular old-time acidheads, but…you've got to get the bread to send your kids to college, right? The gap between hip and straight is still there, but it's faded, the jags have rubbed off.

If you're young, you want to come up with something new — that's how the race grows. Some '80s youngsters may want to be straights — our country will always need sports fans and prison guards — but the smart ones, the ones who ask hard questions, the same kids who would have been hippies in the '60s — these people needed some kind of stance that would bug *all* old people. Thus punk.

I used to live in the boonies, and LP records were my contact to what was happening. The only good music in the '70s was Zappa, and even he was getting old. I'll never forget the excitement of the first punk records — the New York Dolls, Lou Reed, Patti Smith, Elvis Costello, and then…the Clash. Of course that was all eight years ago (which, these exponential days, is a long time). It keeps mutating. Now I listen to the Ramones, Detox, and the Butthole Surfers. "Yes, the Butthole Surfers." Doesn't that tell you more than, "Yes, the *New Yorker*?"

The real charm of punk is that stupid hippies dislike it as much as do stupid rednecks. "What's the matter with them? What do they want?" Anyone who was ever a hippie for the right reasons – a hatred of conformity and a desire to break through to higher realities – is likely to appreciate and enjoy the punks. But a lot of basically conventional people slid through the '70s thinking of themselves as avant-garde, when in fact they were brain-dead. What's good about punk is that it makes all of us question our comfortable assumptions and attitudes. Wait...look at that last sentence, and you can see I'm forty. How complacently I slip the "us" in there – trying to coopt the revolution. How *Life* magazine of me, how plastic, how bullshit. What's good about punk is that it's *fast and dense*. It has a lot of information. Which brings us to "cyber."

What is Cybernetics?

It's the title of an incomprehensible book by Norbert Weiner, mainly. Claude Shannon, the Bell Labs inventor of information theory, encouraged Weiner to use the word "cybernetics" because "No one knows what it means, Norbert, which will always put you at an advantage in an argument." More seriously, if I talk about "cyber," I really want to talk about the modern concept of information.

Mathematics can be thought of as based on five concepts: Number, Space, Logic, Infinity, and Information. The age of Number was the Middle Ages, with their nitpicking lists of sins and layers of heaven. Space was the Renaissance, with perspective and the printing press spreading copies out. Logic was the Industrial Revolution, with great steam engines chugging away like syllogistic inferences. Infinity was Modern Times, with quantum mechanics and LSD. Now we're starting on Information. The computers are here, the cybernetic revolution is over.

What is information? Shannon measured information in "bits." If someone answers a single yes-or-no question, they are giving you one bit of information. Two yes/no questions are two bits. Two bits is enough to distinguish among four possibilities: *00, 01, 10,* and *11.* The game of Twenty Questions is based on the asker being able to get twenty bits of information out of the answerer. Twenty bits distinguishes among 220 possibilities — about a million. For Shannon, the more possible answers there are, the greater is the information. He estimated written English as carrying about seven bits per word, meaning that if a random word is excised from a text, you can usually guess it by asking seven yes-or-no questions. "Is it a noun?" "Does it begin with one of the letters A through L?" "Is it used elsewhere on this page?" "Is it *cat*?" In a crap genre book, generated by a low-complexity intelligence with a very short runtime, the information per word is going to be low, maybe as low as three or four bits. In a high-complexity work the information per word will be higher.

Two mathematicians named Chaitin (IBM) and Kolmogorov (USSR) improved Shannon's notion of information to this: the information in a pattern P is equal to the length of the shortest computer program that can generate P. This quantity, also known as *algorithmic complexity*, can be defined quite precisely and rigorously. If I find a certain SF novel about cats in outer space stupid and boring, it may not just be that I don't like cats. It may be that the book really *is* stupid and boring, as can be witnessed by the fact that the book has a very low information-theoretic complexity.

The point of all this is *that a pattern's information level is a quantity that is absolute and not relative.* The pattern can be a book, a record album, or a person's conversation. If I say something is boring, it's not just my cruelty speaking. It's objective fact. Something either has a lot of information or it doesn't. And if it doesn't have much information, it's a waste of time.

Now you can see where cyber and punk tie together to make cyberpunk. If you value information the most, then you don't care about convention. It's not, "Who do you know?"; it's "How fast are you? How dense?" It's not, "Do you talk like my old friends?"; it's "What do you have to say?" It's not, "Is this comfortable?"; it's "Is this interesting?"

Some cyberpunk fiction characters wear punk fashions. This is fine for now, though in the long run it's not the point. As punk becomes familiar, its information-content goes down. The essence of cyberpunk fiction, as I see it, is that it is concerned with information. The concern exists on several levels. On the objective level, a cyberpunk work will often talk about computers, software, chips, information, etc. And on the higher level which I was talking about above, a cyberpunk work will try to reach a high level of information-theoretic complexity.

High complexity does not, I should point out, mean hard to read. Shannon has shown that any channel, such as easy-to-read writing, admits of efficient encoding schemes. Inefficient writers waste a lot of page-space in posing, repeating clichés, and telling stupid jokes. If you really have some information to communicate, you can do it in a simple, colloquial way. The hard part is getting the information, building up the complexity levels in your brain. Thus one sees cyberpunks reading a lot: a lot of science, and a lot of fiction. Raising the level.

So what I'm talking about with "cyberpunk" is something like this: literate SF that's easy to read, has a lot of information, and talks about the new thoughtforms that are coming out of the computer revolution. Is "cyberpunk" a good word for this? Sure. It's easy to remember, and it makes you think. It's an example of efficient encoding. And the association with punks is fine with me. I'm proud to be a cyberpunk.

POSTSCRIPT TO "WHAT IS CYBERPUNK?"
After I published this essay, a reader pointed out a flaw in my reasoning, to wit:

> If complexity is to be the measure of something's value as a
> piece of cyberized art, then a phone book is "better" than a
> novel, because the phone book's randomness gives it a higher
> complexity. Recall that "the algorithmic complexity of the
> message M" can be defined as "the length of the shortest
> program P which generates the message M," (or it can be
> defined as "the difficulty of guessing what the message M
> says").

The objection is valid, but I have a good answer. My answer is that I should have spoken of measuring a text's information by its *logical depth* rather than by its *algorithmic complexity*. Let me explain what this means.

There are two sorts of extremes of complexity: the "crystal" and the "gas." A crystal-like information structure is something like a string of a million letter A's. The program for such a message is very short: "print one million A's." So such a message has low complexity. A gas-like information structure is something like a totally random string R of a million letters. The program for such a message is very long: "print the string R." (The lengthy contents of R must be listed for the program that writes it out.)

Let me pause and make a point that we'll need three paragraphs down from here. To run either the "crystal" or the "gas" program takes about the same amount of time. In either case the computer doesn't have to do much work. For the "crystal string," it just prints a million A's, for the "gas string" it just keeps copying out the million letters of the string R as specified in the program. Each program takes only about a million steps. (Well, maybe the "gas" program takes two million, but for our purposes one million and two million are about the same size. The point is that they're both a lot less than, say, a billion or a sextillion.)

Now note that interesting objects such as living organisms – or cyberpunk SF novels – seem to lie midway between crystal and gas. They're organized, but not regimented. They're disorderly but not completely fucked up. How best to characterize them? It turns out that these desirable objects have the property of having a relatively *low complexity*, but that actually *computing them takes a lot of work*.

To make this precise, we need to introduce a second dimension of information measure. This is the concept of *logical depth* (or simply "depth" for short). The "depth of a message M" is equal to the "*amount of computation* that it takes to generate M from its shortest program P." A structure with a *high depth* may have a short "explanation" or starting program, but it takes a lot of steps to get from the starting assumptions to the final object. Put differently, if you run a high depth process on a computer, it takes a lot of computer time to reach the final result.[57]

Now as was pointed out three paragraphs above, a gas and a crys-

57. The notion of logical depth was invented by Charles H. Bennett; see for instance his paper "How to Define Complexity in Physics, and Why" in W. H. Zurek, ed., *Complexity, Entropy and the Physics of Information*, Addison-Wesley, Reading 1989. I also discuss Bennett's ideas in my book *Mind Tools*.

tal both have low depth – they result from simple computations. But I claim that a living object – such as an oak tree – is characterized by having a relatively low complexity and a high depth. Why? An oak tree has a *low algorithmic complexity* because the gene code in its acorn is like a compact program. And the mature oak has a *high logical depth* because of the large number of biocybernetic steps taken during its decades-long growth. We think of an organism's growth as a kind of computation which works out the implications inherent in its DNA.

The wonderful music of the Ramones is a good example of a message with low complexity and high depth. Think in terms of Garage Music. Some guys get a really easy tune – like "Louie, Louie," – and they play it and replay it every Friday, and whenever else they can practice. And after a year, they really play an incredible "Louie, Louie." It's gotten *deep*. On the other hand, a simple note-for-note plagiarism of the Kingsmen's "Louie, Louie" has a low depth – it derives quickly from the Kingsmen program.

Books like *Neuromancer* and *Schismatrix* have a low-complexity/high-depth feel to them. I think it's reasonable to think of them as logically deep, because what the authors have done is to start with some fairly standard SF notions – robots, weird drugs, space colonies – and to then think and think about these notions until the final product is very highly exfoliated.

At this point it begins to look like I'm just saying that good books read as if they've been through a lot of rewrites, which is not such hot news. Still, I do think there is something to this – to the Garage Music notion of SF, if you will – the basic thesis being that right now a good way to be writing SF is to keep going back to the beat old clichés, back to the robots and the brain-eaters and the starships, and to reinvent the field just from that, by thinking harder and harder about what it can do. Maybe you don't really have to be a "punk" to be stoned, unemployable, and/or stubborn enough to spend enough time in that garage.

In reading fine cyberpunk literature, it's the realness and the tactility of the scene that really matters. In the old *Mad* magazine – and again in the underground comix of the '60s – what was great was all the little things to look at in the frames, the so-called "eyeball kicks." It takes time to work out all the little touches, and that is where we see logical depth, a.k.a. craftsmanship.

Sociologically, the real point of inventing "movements" is to attract attention. At the most, a label like "cyberpunk" can serve only to get people to read the work of individual authors, and at that point the authors are on their own, as usual.

But still…the concept of cyberpunk is energizing. There are other quite different styles of SF, for instance the *transrealist* style epitomized by Phil Dick. For a transrealist, SF is a type of autobiography. I was happy, writing *Wetware*, to get away from the transrealism of my book *The Secret of Life* and go for the dense eyeball kicks of cyberpunk.

Cyberpunk suggests, once again, that SF really can be about the world and not just about the author's mind. For me, the best thing about cyberpunk is that it taught me how to enjoy shopping malls, which used to terrify me. Now I just pretend that the whole thing is two miles below the moon's surface, and that half the people's right-brains have been eaten by roboticized steel rats. And suddenly it's *interesting* again.

—Appeared in REM, *#3, February, 1986.*

REM was a zine published by that Charles Platt. I added the Postscript to the article in response to a letter from a reader, so I suppose the Postscript must have appeared in issue #4.

The Mondo 2000 *editors latched onto my phrase "How fast are you? How dense?" and used it in their ad campaigns and on some of their T-shirts.*

Cyberpunk Lives!

William Gibson, Bruce Sterling, John Shirley and I grew up under the spell of beatnik literature. And somehow we got the opportunity to start our very own cultural and artistic movement: cyberpunk.

I remember meeting Allen Ginsberg at someone's house in Boulder, Colorado, 1983. "Allen," I gushed, "I always wanted to be like one of the beats. What was the secret? How did you guys get so much ink?" "Fine writing," said Allen. I pressed further: "Will you give me your blessing?" "Bless you," he said and slapped his cupped hand down on my scalp, sending a sheet of energy cascading down my shoulders to trickle into my chakras.

The canonical beat writers are four in number: Jack Kerouac, Allen Ginsberg, Gregory Corso, and William Burroughs. Taken as I am with the concept of a beat/cyberpunk correlation, I occasionally muse over who matches whom.

Kerouac is the most wonderful writer among the beats, and surely the one who sold the most books. Gibson is a natural fit for this role. He writes like an angel, and everyone knows his name. Without Kerouac there would have been no beat movement, without Gibson there would be no cyberpunk.

Ginsberg is the most political and most engaged – here I think of Sterling. At the beginning of cyberpunk, it was Bruce who was the indefatigable pamphleteer and consciousness-raiser with his *Cheap Truth* zine. His *Mirrorshades* anthology defined cyberpunk in many minds. Like Ginsberg, Sterling continues to roam the planet, making guest-lectures and writing up reports on what he finds. Of the beats and the cyberpunks, it is Ginsberg and Sterling whom one sees most often on television.

Not so well-known as the other beats, Corso is a poet with a keen ear for ecstatic strophes and ranting invective. Corso also has the cachet, the bonus, of being the only one of the four still alive. A reasonable match for the dark, zany and strangely healthy John Shirley.

For myself, as the oldest of the cyberpunks, I claim the role of Burroughs, with his wise, dry voice of hallucinatory erudition and his rank, frank humor.

But but but – Gibson doesn't center his books upon himself, like Kerouac did. And Sterling writes about future technology, not about mystical perceptions of everyday reality. And Shirley is a novelist, not a poet. And I'm a professor, not a junkie. And cyberpunk isn't really mainstream literature, is it? Perhaps my comparing the cyberpunks to the beats is like the sad but true tale of Jacqueline Susanne comparing herself and Harold Robbins to the Lost Generation writers. "I'm the Fitzgerald of the group and Harold's the Hemingway..." Ow!

And, hmm, what about Lew Shiner? Well, he can be John Clellon Holmes, the beat who drifted from the movement after his book, *Go*.

Okay, my analogy is just a Procrustean mind-game, a little wise-acreing for the swing of thought, something to get this essay rolling and with a generous dose of self-aggrandizement thrown in. Why not? Onward.

What I want to do here is to go into specific comments about three cyberpunk novels, and to gloat over some of the good bits with you. The books happened to come out within about a month of each other in 1996. It felt like getting letters from home.

William Gibson, *Idoru*, G. P. Putnam's, New York 1996.
Bruce Sterling, *Holy Fire*, Bantam Books, New York 1996.
John Shirley, *Silicon Embrace*, Mark V. Ziesing Books,
    Shingletown CA 1996.

Like his *Virtual Light*, William Gibson's novel *Idoru* has two main characters, a young man and a young woman, with the narrative told from their alternating points of view. The girl is a teenage fan of a rock musician named Rez, and the boy is a technician hired by Rez's managers because he has "a peculiar knack for data-collection architectures." In a more traditional kind of fiction, this structure would be a setup for a happy boy-meets-girl ending, but that's not what happens in *Virtual Light* or in *Idoru*. None of the characters are really out for romance. Except for Rez.

The *Idoru* of the title is an artificial woman who exists as a holographic projection generated by a largish portable computer. Rez – Rozzer to his friends – is in love with her. "Man," says Rez's blind drummer at a dinner party, "Rozzer's sittin' down there makin' eyes at a big aluminum thermos bottle." The drummer's synthetic eyes don't register holograms; he sees through to the core of the idoru hardware.

The first mention of Rez and his partner Lo is in this sentence describing the bedroom of Chia Pet McKenzie, the teenage fan: "The wall opposite Chia's bed was decorated with a six-by-six laser blowup of the cover of Lo Rez Skyline, their first album." In a subtly associative way, this image evokes the now-famous first sentence of Gibson's smash first novel, *Neuromancer*, "Over the port, the sky was the color of television." Kind of the same, no? Gibson's so smart, he's playing with deep structure.

Chia is worried about Rez's rumored infatuation with the idoru, and she flies to Japan to try and bring him to his senses. Half of the chapters are from Chia's point of view; Gibson has somehow mastered the knack of writing the thoughts of teenage girls, their enthusiasms, their slang. One of the words Chia uses is "meshback." A meshback is what we currently call a redneck, a low-income person who wears unfashionable clothes and whose thoughts are completely controlled by lowest-common-denominator media manipulation. The name comes from – the meshbacked high-hat gimmie caps that meshbacks like to wear. A great new word like this jumps right off the page and into your daily language. I can't wait for the next opportunity to say, "Oh wow, let's get out of this place, it's totally full of meshbacks."

Speaking of great new words, Chia hooks up with a Japanese Lo/Rez fan club member who happens to mention that her brother is an *otaku*. Chia's automatic translator renders "otaku" as "pathological-techno-fetishist-with-social-deficit." Chia gets the picture instantly. "It's a *boy* thing, right? The otaku guys at my last school were into, like, plastic anime babes, military simulations, and trivia. Bigtime into trivia."

Idoru is set in the same future as *Virtual Light*, and some of the tone is the same as well. We're so far into the future here that characters are totally lacking some of the basic knowledge we take for granted, e.g. the meaning of the swastika. There is "...a fast-food franchise called California Reich, its trademark a stylized stainless-steel palm tree against one of those twisted-cross things like the meshbacks had drawn on their hands in her class on European history." Bill knows meshbacks!

The boy character in *Idoru* is named Laney; he's a little strange because he was given an experimental drug called 5-SB as a child, not that he likes to admit it, due to the long-term sociopathic effects it's reported to have − 5-SB "...makes folks want to stalk and kill politicians..." When quizzed about it, Laney suggests that maybe he'd only had a placebo. "You don't mistake 5-SB for any placebo, son, but I think you know that." A perfect Burroughs touch, crowned by the fact that the main somatic side-effect of 5-SB is this: "In his mouth a taste of rotten metal."

Idoru continues to touch up Gibson's vision of cyberspace, which is now becoming a fairly definite science fictional setting, something as standardized as the lunar colony domes and the generation starships of '50s and '60s SF. Today's cyberspace is a huge, shared virtual reality which individual users can enter via small computers that they carry with them. Certain parts of cyberspace are difficult to enter, as they contain valuable information. You may encounter other users in cyberspace, and you may also encounter artificially alive software agents.

Although today's World Wide Web is somewhat conspicuously lacking the effortless speed and virtual reality immersion of science fictional cyberspace, the Web's difference from SF cyberspace is now only one of degree. Looking back, it's hard to remember how radically new an idea this was when Gibson first wrote about it, lo these fifteen or so years gone. To a significant degree, the reputability of cyberpunk rests on this one visionary extrapolation. Jules Verne may have predicted the submarine, but William Gibson envisioned the explosive growth of the Web.

So it's a special delight to see our Founding Father adding new touches to his vision. Here's a funny description of something Chia sees while in cyberspace with an otaku boy.

> Something chimed. She glanced at the door, which was
> mapped in a particularly phoney-looking wood-grain effect,

and saw a small white rectangle slide under the door. And keep sliding, straight toward her, across the floor, to vanish under the sleeping ledge. She looked down in time to see it rise, at exactly the same rate, up the edge of the striped mattress and over, coming to a halt when it was in optimum position to be read... It said 'Ku Klux Klan Kollectibles,' and then some letters and numbers that didn't look like any kind of address she knew.

Another chime. She looked at the door in time to see a gray blur scoot from under it. Flat, whirling, fast. It was on the white rectangle now, something like the shadow of a crab or a spider, two-dimensional and multi-legged. It swallowed it, shot for the door...

"What were those things?" Chia asked...

"An advertisement... and a sub-program that offered criticism."

"It didn't offer criticism; it ate it."

"Perhaps the person who wrote the sub-program dislikes advertising. Many do. Or dislikes the advertiser..."

Idoru has several hooks to *Virtual Light*, and can be thought of as the second in a new series of Gibson novels. *Idoru*'s ending promises more to come. It seems like Rez and his supernally intelligent "software dolly wank toy" are going to find a way to reproduce, perhaps biologically. With just a little DNA nanomanipulation it could be done. Although predicting the final somatic effect of a change in a fertilized egg's DNA is a rather radically difficult problem in the analysis of algorithms, I'm sure that the child will turn out most wonderfully hale and gnarly.

Here's a toast to the alchemical marriage of man and machine!

John Shirley's *Silicon Embrace* is so strange and shaggy a magpie's nest that it must needs be published by a smaller press.

Someone unfamiliar with the field might expect that science fiction novels would tend to be about the kinds of weird science you see in mass media such as TV shows and supermarket tabloids. You might expect, in other words, that there would be a lot of SF novels about aliens and UFOs. In point of fact, most SF writers are too persnickety to want to write about the repetitious fever dreams of the mass public mind.

In *Silicon Embrace*, Shirley boldly goes where few writers have gone before, and gets right down to nuts-and-bolts UFOlogy, complete with the canonical little aliens. "It was a Grey, the classic Grey described in close encounters, an alien...with improportionately big oval eyes of whiteless onyx, and something that might have been a nose, and the slit of a mouth, and no hair, and holes for ears . . ." But this is not going to turn into some cloying, conning UFO-nut miracle tale. Shirley's aliens aren't devils and they're not Disneyland mummers in shiny masks. They're businessmen, and they like to smoke cigarettes, which make them terribly intoxicated.

One of the more satisfying aspects of the hit movie *Independence Day* was the way in which it incarnated and elaborated our tabloid myth about the Roswell UFO that allegedly crashed and was preserved by government agencies – who performed an alien autopsy and who have a few alien pilots in suspended animation. *Silicon Embrace* delivers the same thrill, but in a more artistic way. Here's that government-owned UFO: "There was a frightening smell about the saucer, though Farraday could smell nothing...It was as if the saucer gave out an irritating sound, though it was soundless; it was as if it glared a painful light into his eyes, but it glowed not at all."

The book has lots of other threads besides the aliens. For some of the first hundred pages, Shirley goes off on a fairly bloody tangent, perhaps the effect of his having spent so much time in the airless, flickering caves of Hollywood, where troglodyte producers mistake sentimental violence for deeper truth. But soon, thankfully, Shirley's violence busts out of this box and exfoliates into the bizarro territory of underground comix and Grande Guignol:

> Anja opened the back of the van, and...pressed channel 7 on
> the remote clipped to her jacket; responding instantly, Sol
> came roaring out and sank his teeth into Noseless's neck...
> and in a few minutes more Sol had pulled his head right off.
> Anja patted her ex boyfriend on the head as Sol knelt over the
> body, shaking, mouth streaming blood. "Good boy. Good boy."

Sol has a chip in his neck, you wave.

As well as the Grey aliens, *Silicon Embrace* features a higher, nobler kind of alien, a crystalline life-form known as the Meta, one of the Metas' avatars is a traditional lab-built mutant creature known as a land octopus or prairie squid. "It looked like an independently motile scrotum with human eyes and the legs of a human toddler interspersed with octopal tentacles," and it speaks in a sweet, ingratiating voice. Later we learn that the humble prairie squid is in fact none other than a resurrected form of that greatest Meta alien of all, our Savior Jesus Christ of Nazareth. Yes, *Him*. "Crucified, this time, in disfigurement; in the dislocated shape of a land octopus. Jesus in a prairie squid. Christ in a cephaloped." Here an extra element of deep funniness derives from the fact that the "prairie squid" is an icon of the Church of the SubGenius, a half-serious mock religion in which John Shirley is a high-ranking official.

And − told you this book was shaggy − there's even some mystical physics. Here's a rant from a guy called the Street Sleeper, telling about his mad-scientist friend the Middle Man.

> "Okay, lemme see: There's a subatomic particle called the IAMton. Physicists, they speculate about it, but the Middle Man knows. He was a cutting-edge hot shot at Stanford. He isolated the IAMton, using a wetware subatomic scanner that re-created the thing in his natural cerebral imaging equipment, and when he did, it spoke to him. It spoke to him! Can you fade that? A subatomic particle that tells you, Yeah! You found me!... Actually, see, it was all the IAMtons on the fucking planet that spoke to him, in the local macro-octave. Spoke to him through the group of 'em he had contained in the tokomak field and scanned with the electron microscope interfaced with his wetware. You know?"

Yeah, I know, John. This is music to my ears, man. This totally makes sense. As Shirley puts it, "Science Fiction, see, is humanity's way of warning, readying itself; it's what goes on under the racial Rapid Eye movement."

One final gem of wisdom. "The universe is alive, but it is not 'God.' And...it is not friendly. Nor unfriendly. However, we do not wish to make these distinctions with the American public." Too true.

Daringly set in the late twenty-first century − well, hey, the twentieth century's all done! − Bruce Sterling's *Holy Fire* is about

Bruce Sterling in 1983. (Photo by R. Rucker.)

an extremely old woman who gets a radical rejuvenation treatment and becomes a beautiful twenty-year-old. Due to this
extreme change in her body she is no longer human in the old
sense of the word; she's post-human. Other SF writers have come
up against the task Sterling faces here, how to depict people after
technology has made them into superhumans; I would say that no
other writer has ever succeeded so well. Here's one of Sterling's
statements about post-humans: "Machines just flitted through
the fabric of the universe like a fit through the brain of God, and
in their wake people stopped being people. But people didn't stop
going on."

In person and in his journalistic writing, Sterling is loud and
Texan, but in his novels he is the most thoughtful and civilized of
men. In *Holy Fire* he transforms himself into this wide-eyed rejuve-
nated old lady and takes us on a tour of marvels, a *wanderjahr* in
Europe in search of the holy fire of artistic creativity.

She arrived at the airport. The black tarmac was full of
glowing airplanes. They had a lovely way of flexing their

> wings and simply jumping into the chill night air when they
> wanted to take off. You could see people moving inside the
> airplanes because the hulls were gossamer. Some people had
> clicked on their reading lights but a lot of the people onboard
> were just slouching back into their beanbags and enjoying the
> night sky through the fuselage.

When science fiction performs so clear and attractive a feat of envisioning the future, it's like a blueprint that you feel like working to instantiate.

Instantiate, by the way, is an object-oriented-computer-programming word that, in Sterling's hands, means "to turn a software description into a physical object." Such as a goddess sculpture derived from studies of the attention statistics of eye-tracked men looking at women "...what we got here is basically a pretty good replica of something that a Paleolithic guy might have whittled out of mammoth tusk. You start messing with archetypal forms and this sort of thing turns up just like clockwork." This pleasing suggestion of cosmic order contains a subtle nod to the notion of a chaotic attractor.

Science fiction sometimes gets humorous effects by extrapolating present-day things into heady overkill. Here's what espresso machines might evolve into:

> The bartender was studying an instruction screen and
> repairing a minor valve on an enormously ramified tincture
> set. The tincture set stretched the length of the mahogany
> bar, weighed four or five tons, and looked as if its refinery
> products could demolish a city block.

The obverse of this technique is to have future people look back on our current ways of doing things. "That's antique analog music. There wasn't much vertical color to the sound back in those days. The instruments were made of wood and animal organs." Or here's a 21C person deploring the obsolete habit of reading.

> "It's awful, a terrible habit! In virtuality at least you get to
> interact! Even with television you at least have to use visual
> processing centers and parse real dialogue with your ears!

Really, reading is so bad for you, it destroys your eyes and
hurts your posture and makes you fat."

Like all the cyberpunks, Sterling loves to write. He can become con-
tagiously intoxicated with the sheer joy of fabulous description, as in
this limning of a cyberspace landscape:

Rising in the horizon-warped virtual distance was a mist-
shrouded Chinese crag, a towering digital stalagmite with the
subtle monochromatics of sumi-e ink painting. Some
spaceless and frankly noneuclidean distance from it, an
enormous bubbled structure like a thunderhead, gleaming
like veined black marble but conveying a weird impression of
glassy gassiness, or maybe it was gassy glassiness . . .

Wouldn't you like to go there? You can, thanks to this lo-res VR
device you're holding, it's called a printed page . . .

Sterling is an energetic tinkerer, and he drops in nice little
touches everywhere. What looks like a ring on a man's finger is "a little strip of dark fur. Thick-clustered brown fur rooted in a ring-
shaped circlet of [the man's] flesh." Two people riding on a train ring
for a waiter from the dining-car and here's the response:

A giant crab came picking its way along the ceiling of the
train car. It was made of bone and chitin and peacock feathers
and gut and piano wire. It had ten very long multijointed legs
and little rubber-ball feet on hooked steel ankles. A serving
platter was attached with suckers to the top of its flat freckled
carapace . . . It surveyed them with a circlet of baby blue eyes
like a giant clam's. "Oui monsieur?"

This crab is a purely surreal and Dadaist assemblage, quite worthy of
Kurt Schwitters or Max Ernst. The wonder of science fiction is that,
with a bit of care, you can paste together just about anything and it
will walk and talk and make you smile.

Near the end of the book, the heroine encounters the ultimate art
medium.

It was like smart clay. It reacted to her touch with
unmistakable enthusiasm . . . indescribably active, like a poem

becoming a jigsaw. The stuff was boiling over with machine intelligence. Somehow more alive than flesh; it grew beneath her questing fingers like a Bach sonata. Matter made virtual. Real dreams.

Such is the stuff that science fiction is made of.

So, okay, those were the three new cyberpunk novels of 1996. Let's compare and contrast. What are some of the things they have in common other than the use of cyberspace?

One of the main cyberpunk themes is the fusion of humans and machines, and you can certainly find that here. In *Idoru* a man wants to marry a computer program, in *Holy Fire* machine-medicine essentially gives people new bodies. There is less of the machine in *Silicon Embrace*, though there is that remote-controlled guy with the chip in his head.

Another cyberpunk theme is a desire for a mystical union with higher consciousness, this kind of quest being a kind of side-effect of the acidhead '60s which all of us went through. Contact with higher intelligence is the key theme of *Silicon Embrace*, though in *Idoru* it is present only obliquely, as part of the idoru's appeal. *Holy Fire* ends with a thought-provoking pantheistic sequence where a human has actually turned his own *self* into an all pervading Nature god, with "every flower, every caterpillar genetically wired for sound."

Cyberpunk usually takes a close look at the media; this is an SF tradition that goes pack to Frederic Pohl and Norman Spinrad. *Holy Fire* goes pretty light on the media, but in *Idoru*, the main villain is the media as exemplified by an outfit called Slitscan. "Slitscan was descended from 'reality' programming and the network tabloids . . ., but it resembled them no more than some large, swift bipedal carnivore resembled its sluggish, shallow-dwelling ancestors." One of the heroines of *Silicon Embrace* is Black Betty, a media terrorist who manages to jam the State's transmissions.

He watched the videotape, the few seconds of a former President yammering with a good approximation of sincerity in his State of the Union address – and then Black Betty stepping into the shot; stepping her video-persona into the

former President's restricted public space; taking public space
back from authority, giving it back to the public, the Public
personified by Betty. Tall and lean and smiling from a
crystallized inner confidence…she seemed to…stare at the
president from within his Personal Space: a rudeness, a
solecism become a political statement."

In terms of optimism/pessimism about the future, *Holy Fire* is very
optimistic, *Silicon Embrace* very pessimistic, and *Idoru* somewhere in
the middle. In terms of political outlook, *Silicon Embrace* is explicitly
radical, *Idoru* is apolitical, and *Holy Fire* is – well – Republican?
In *Holy Fire*, the world is run by old people, by the gerontocracy, and
this is not necessarily presented as a bad thing, it's simply presented
as the reality of that future.

Above and beyond the themes and attitudes, the single common
thing about these three books is style. All are hip, all are funny, all
are written by real people about the real world around us.

After all the good ink I've just given my peers, I can't resist slipping you a taste of my *Freeware*, which came out a few months after
the books discussed here.

So here's shirtless Willy under the star-spangled Florida sky
with eighty pounds of moldie [named Ulam] for his shoes and
pants, scuffing across the cracked concrete of the JFK spaceport
pad. The great concrete apron was broken up by a widely
spaced grid of drainage ditches, and the spaceport buildings
were dark. It occurred to Willy that he was very hungry.

There was a roar and blaze in the sky above. The *Selena* was
coming down. Close, too close. The nearest ditch was so far he
wouldn't make it in time, Willy thought, but once he started
running, Ulam kicked in and superamplified his strides,
cushioning on the landing and flexing on the take-offs. They
sprinted a quarter mile in under twenty seconds and threw
themselves into the coolness of the ditch, lowering down into
the funky brackish water. The juddering yellow flame of the
great ship's ion beams reflected off the ripples around them. A
hot wind of noise blasted loud and louder; then all was still.

[A crowd of angry locals appears and attacks the ship.]

There was a fusillade of gun-shots and needler blasts, and then the mob surged towards the *Selena*, blazing away at the ship as they advanced.

Their bullets pinged off the titaniplast hull like pebbles off galvanized steel; the needlers' laser-rays kicked up harmless glow-spots of zzzt. The *Selena* shifted uneasily on her hydraulic tripod legs.

"Her hold bears a rich cargo of moldie-flesh," came Ulam's calm, eldritch voice in Willy's head. "Ten metric tons of chipmold-infected imipolex, surely to be worth a king's ransom once this substance's virtues become known. This cargo is why Fern flew the *Selena* here for ISDN. I tell you, the flesher rabble attacks the *Selena* at their own peril. Although the imipolex is highly flammable, it has a low-grade default intelligence and will not hesitate to punish those who would harm it."

When the first people tried to climb aboard the *Selena*, the ship unexpectedly rose up on her telescoping tripod legs and lumbered away. As the ship slowly lurched along, great gouts of imipolex streamed out of hatches in her bottom. The *Selena* looked like a defecating animal, like a threatened ungainly beast voiding its bowels in flight – like a frightened penguin leaving a splatter trail of krilly shit. Except that the *Selena*'s shit was dividing itself up into big slugs that were crawling away towards the mangroves and ditches as fast as they could hump, which was plenty fast.

Of course someone in the mob quickly figured out that the you could burn the imipolex shit slugs, and a lot of the slugs started going up in crazy flames and oily, unbelievably foul-smelling smoke. The smoke had a strange, disorienting effect; as soon as Willy caught a whiff of it, his ears started buzzing and the objects around him took on a jellied, peyote solidity.

Now the burning slugs turned on their tormentors, engulfing them like psychedelic kamikaze napalm. There was great screaming from the victims, screams that were weirdly, hideously ecstatic. And then the mob's few survivors had fled, and the rest of the slugs had wormed off into the flickering night. Willy and Ulam split the scene as well.[58]

Cyberpunk lives!

—Appeared as "Letters From Home" in
The New York Review of Science Fiction, *#113, January 1998.*

58. *Freeware*, pp. 154-156.

Interview with Ivan Stang

Ivan Stang is the High Scribe and co-founder of the Church of the SubGenius, a kind of dadaist religion that centers around the iconic image of a '50s-style pipe-smoking man named "Bob." Attracted by some small zine ads promising *slack*, I myself joined the Church of the SubGenius in 1982. It cost me a dollar to get hold of the classic *SubGenius Pamphlet #1*, and soon after that, Stang ordained me by mail in exchange for copies of some of my books.[59]

Over the years I've met Stang (not his real name) in person a few times, which is always a great experience. He's a true media artist and wonderfully intelligent force against all things pink – "pink" being a SubGenius word for all the dumb, repressive and soulless aspects of our society.

Stang started our telephone interview with a disclaimer.

Stang: Don't interview me. The article should be about the Church of the SubGenius, not about me. I'm just a part of the Church, though perhaps the hardest working part. I want to keep it clear that "Bob" comes first, not me.

RR: I often feel a lack in my life these days, Ivan. Can "Bob" actually fill the hunger for religion?

Stang: No, he can't. For that you need, "Yoko and me." As Charlie Manson used to say, "I trust the only one who's left to trust...me."

RR: One thing that makes me not take "Bob" completely seri-

---

59. The amazing *SubGenius Pamphlet #1* is *still* available by sending one dollar to "the sacred box number" of the SubGenius Foundation, PO BOX 140306, Dallas, TX 75214. Or you can view the *Pamphlet* for free on the Web at http://www.subgenius. com. There's lots of other goodies at this site; one can, for instance, access Stang's taped "Hour of Slack" radio shows via online streaming audio. Two other good sources of information are the SubGenius Foundation books: *The Book of the SubGenius*, Simon and Schuster, New York 1987, and *Revelation X*, Fireside, New York 1994.

A cellular automaton rule called "Bob." (Image generated by Cellab.)

ously is that when I'm in a hospital thinking I might die, I feel more like praying to Jesus than to "Bob."

Stang: There's nothing wrong with repenting on your death bed. It's all a "just in case" thing anyway. Pray to Jesus just in case there's an afterlife. Pray to "Bob" just in case there's an X-day and the saucers come to kill all the normals.

RR: When is X-day?

Stang: July 5, 1998, 7 o'clock in the morning at the International Date Line. California will be the last ruptured. You can watch X-day on TV for nearly a full day before it hits you. Watching X-day in progress may be "Bob's" biggest test of faith. You may not like what you see. You may feel like burning your Church of the SubGenius membership card.

We're not going to end up like the Jehovah's Witnesses who are always predicting the end of the world and making fools of themselves. We have several outs. We may end up having to have a big X-day party every year.[60]

60. When the Earth didn't come to an end on July 5, 1998, Stang's assembled followers tarred and feathered him, using *pink* feathers. Stang now explains that his prediction was a simple mix-up: he happened to read the paper with the X-day date *upside down*, and the true year of "Bob's" coming will be 8661! In the meantime, X-day is still celebrated every year.

RR: What about the Church's new book, *Revelation X*?

Stang: Our first book, *The Book of the SubGenius*, showed the glory that is "Bob." It had more sheer bullshit than the *Book of Mormon*. But *Revelation X* shows the danger that is "Bob." Thanks to our art director Paul Mavrides, it's really really sick, it's like a Jehovah's Witness comic book.

RR: What have you been doing this summer?

Stang: I did a wedding in Chicago on the beach, a classic hippie wedding. Then I was in two SubGenius events, Portland and Seattle X-day celebrations, both awful, both controlled by local fans and done not the way we would have done it. Then I went to Dragoncon in Atlanta, which was great, a science fiction convention, they paid me and brought in Philo Drummond and his Zappaesque band The Swinging Love Corpses. They had Janor Hypercleats there to preach. And Susie the Floozie. She's our latest woman SubGenius preacher and she's great. She's an ex-stripper.

RR: Did you fuck her?

Stang: (Outraged.) I haven't fucked her and I wouldn't. I'm married, and if I did I wouldn't tell you. I have hefted her tits though, her bare nekkid tits, they're all any guy could ask for. She preaches about her personal experiences with Connie Dobbs, "Bob"'s primary wife. After Dragoncon, I went to a pagan event, they say it's the biggest pagan gathering in the country. It's called Starwood, it's held in far western rural New York. Tim Leary and Terence McKenna and Robert Anton Wilson have all been there. I run across them all the time. The drug addled philosophers; they always bum cigarettes from me. I smoke Merits except now I just quit. At Starwood I was on with Dr. Legume of Philadelphia and Reverend Bleepo Abernathy of New York City. It was broadcast live on FM.

RR: Were you stoned?

Stang: (Increasingly testy.) I never fool with cheap conspiracy street drugs when I'm working. After the show that's a whole different thing. The kind of things I end up taking are still legal. Toad venom and Hawaiian woodrose and San Pedro cactus. I took some of that at Starwood. It's an aphrodisiac, like yohimbine. Instant hard-on. Of course my wife wasn't there, so I had to sit in my tent and beat off.

RR: Describe your childhood and adolescence.

Stang: Well. I'd say the main aspects were my Mammy and Pappy and the Three Stooges and Bugs Bunny. This was a barely middle-class Fort Worth neighborhood and if you saw a black person or a Mexican that was a big deal, it was something you'd tell your friends about. I had pretty much of a rationalist upbringing. My parents quit going to church when the preacher told them they shouldn't drink. I got pretty good grades, read monster comics and read H.G. Wells. I even drew comics, but when I was twelve I burned all these comics because we were moving to a new town (Dallas) and I wasn't going to be weird anymore. I decided I was going to be normal. Luckily it didn't take.

RR: Something must have happened in high school?

Stang: I'd been making movies since I was ten. By the time I got to high school I started winning awards for these claymation films I'd made. I was already a celebrity and a has-been by the time I was twenty. I'd won these awards all over the world.

What really happened in high school – I hit puberty at the age of five – I was really ready for female companionship, but my parents put me in a private school that was all male. All I could do was beat off and make violent horror movies. And then I was going to be the next Orson Welles, and I started doing like really weird art films. About the age of sixteen I switched from being a nice dutiful boy to being a bad hippie.

RR: That sounds like drugs.

Stang: Well yeah. I took LSD before I'd ever even tried a beer. That's what definitely what took me away from the monster movies and into art films. Plus about that time Frank Zappa appeared and Jimi Hendrix, and I discovered R. Crumb and underground comix. My main ambition for a time was to be accepted by these guys who do underground comix. That's one of the only goals I've achieved. By the time I was 26 I was married and struggling in sweatshop companies doing cheesy business films. But I had written that first SubGenius pamphlet which as far as I'm concerned was equal to doing *Citizen Kane*. The first place I sent that thing was the underground comix publishers. The owners threw them out, but two of the artists fished copies out of the trash can, Paul Mavrides at Ripoff Press and Jay Kinney at Last Gasp. Those two guys were a big help.

They were the first professional artist types I knew.

I was not actually an outcast in high school. I was a friend to the outcast but I was in pretty tight with the in-crowd. Did you ever see that movie *Dazed and Confused*? I could just as well say go see that movie, that was my high school years. As long as you were one of the dopers you were okay. I was like the class beat poet.

I'll tell you what, though. There's no question to me that if I had gotten laid a little earlier in life there wouldn't have been a Church of the SubGenius.

RR: How did you meet your wife?

Stang: I needed a girl to act in a 16 mm film I was doing and she was in the drama club at her school. She was an older woman; she was a senior and I was just a sophomore. We ended up going to the same college together, to University of Texas at Austin. I was only there a year, and then I went to SMU and flunked out because I was making *World of the Future*.

RR: That movie showed you dressed like a crazed crying clown and shooting up speed.

Stang: That was fake. If you look closely it was a big beer can with a spike that slid up inside it. I never did do that, shoot up hard drugs. Compared to my friends I was real straight. Most of my high school friends are dead from drug overdoses. It's a real shame. Only the hardy SubGeniuses survived.

RR: How often have you really seen "Bob"?

Stang: The only time I've ever seen him was when he got shot in San Francisco. I never get invited to those parties where people see him. Philo always says, well the guest list was full. "Bob" owes me quite a bit of money. This check's been in the mail for fifteen years now. If it's in his best interest to meet you then he'll meet you. But frankly, I'm scared shitless of the guy. What might be good for him may not be good for you.

RR: What are the Church's teachings in a nutshell?

Stang: Fuck the normals and get all the slack you can.

RR: How do you get away with being so weird all the time for so many years?

Stang: I have a wife and a color television and they both work.

—*Appeared in Frauenfelder, Sinclair, Branwyn, Eds.,*
The Happy Mutant Handbook, *Riverhead Books, 1995.*

Special Effects: Kit-Bashing the Cosmic Matte

What with Al Gore's data superhighway initiative, the *Time* magazine cover on cyberpunk, the new HDTV standard, the *Wild Palms* miniseries, and the computer-generated dinosaurs of *Jurassic Park* – well, it starts to feel like computer reality is finally here.

Why do so many of us care so much? What is the big attraction of things like networking, virtual worlds, artificial life and cyberspace? I think we want computer reality because we want to transcend the mundane.

City-dwellers tire of the panhandlers and the crowds. Country-dwellers tire of the rednecks and the isolation. Commuters have to commute. If only we could get out of our flesh and crawl inside the computers, maybe then we could have it all – we could be safe, in the thick of the action, and capable of travelling at the speed of light!

I remember in the early '60s reading a paperback science fiction book called *The Joy Makers*.[61] It was about some futuristic humanoid hedonists who lived their whole lives in jellied capsules, intravenously fed, with their brains wired into pleasure-buzzers and communication networks. I remember the disgusting image of a burst-open pod with a twitching larval hedonist lying in a melting pool of slime.

In a '90s cyberpunk novel, a hedonist would not end up this way. He or she would long since have turned his or her twitching larval body into a computer program that could be uploaded to any suitable host machine. What is it that we want to transcend? The body, old sport; the flesh, old bean.

But for now, just about the only creatures who really do live as silicon-pure computer data bases are the dinosaurs of this summer's smash hit *Jurassic Park*. They inhabit computers at George Lucas's Industrial Light and Magic in Marin County, California. And no, those nasty dinos are not idle, no indeed. They're busy evolving

61. See the quote and the reference in "Four Kinds of Cyberspace."

themselves into new colors and shapes so that they can perform in another live action movie: *The Flintstones.*

Shortly before the release of *Jurassic,* I spent some time hanging around ILM, trying to get a feel for what's happening at the interface between the old analog world and the new digital realties.

The visual production unit of ILM is disguised as a series of non-descript garages and office buildings. The main entrance bears a misleadingly bland sign that says something like "THE GLOVER COMPANY. OPTICAL RESEARCH LAB." When the *Star Wars* craze was at its peak, fans and nuts made nuisances of themselves trying to penetrate to the source of the world they'd fallen in love with. One demented seeker even got run over by a car. To this day, ILM is pulled-back and security conscious.

Inside ILM, things are busy and happy. Model makers, computer hackers, animators, and film technicians work in teams to provide the extra zing for many of Hollywood's biggest films.

In making any film, the producers try to shoot as much of it as possible with actors, sets, props, backdrops, and people in costumes. It's up to companies like ILM to enhance the master film by adding the missing pieces: the chrome robots, the spacewar dogfights, the cosmic backgrounds, the melting flesh.

The traditional method of doing this is to build scale models and paint mattes of the missing pieces – a *matte* being a large, detailed painting, often on glass with part of it left transparent so that a moving film image can be set into the gap. Films of the models and mattes are made, and these model films are then layered onto the master film by a process called optical compositing.

How does optical compositing work? If you're doing something like, say, adding spaceships to a sky background, you might film your model ships and project these model films onto a big screen that is showing a film of the actors beneath the sky. Then you film the combined images directly from the big screen.

If there are only one or two elements to add to a scene, optical compositing is quite cost-effective. But scenes like a space-battle or a dinosaur stampede can involve dozens of different models, each of which needs to have its image added as a separate step.

To get around the problems of optical compositing, ILM and

Kodak jointly developed a machine which can turn a frame of film into about twenty megabytes of digital information. In a fine example of industrial altruism (or buck-passing), Kodak calls it the "ILM scanner," and ILM calls it the "Kodak scanner." It's a bulky device that looks like a workbench with lenses on top and computers underneath.

The point of scanning film images into digital form is that it then becomes much easier to cut and paste the images together. Each part of the process is perfectly reversible, and you can undo old things without harming newer additions. Optical compositing is giving way to digital compositing.

And once you have the ability to turn your movie film into digital images, the entire range of digital processes becomes accessible to you. It's easy to erase the guy-wires that are used to make a truck fall over in the right direction, for instance. And, most radically, you can add in computer-generated images that are not of any physical model at all. Let one byte of a computer into your tent, and it drags all of cyberspace in there with you.

Computer animation was used to a limited extent for the water snake alien of *The Abyss* and for the chrome-skinned robot of *Terminator 2*. When it came time to create the dinosaurs for *Jurassic Park*, the computer graphics faction at ILM decided it was time to go digital in a big way.

"We began planning for *Jurassic* in December, 1991," says Mark Dippé, an ILM Visual Effects Supervisor who is a strong advocate of computer animation. "There was a question of should we use computer animation or should we use latex puppets over metal armatures, along with men in rubber suits and some big hydraulically-driven arms. The problem is, you can only shoot a hydraulically-driven device from one angle. And a man in a suit moves wrong. And a puppet can't readily roll on its back if the armature is on its left hip. There's limitations from the physical things. And when you want a herd of animals – are you going to build five hundred rubber models?"

Dippé and his group modeled their first virtual dinosaurs by measuring some dinosaur sculptures. The resulting numbers were used to create computer meshes: assemblages of mathematical triangles in three-dimensional virtual space. Next came the problem of writing programs to move the meshes around in a realistic way. "We had to communicate their massiveness," says Dippé. "What do they notice, what are they afraid of, are they wary? We shot photos of each other acting out the dinosaur roles. We played with little puppets. The others still weren't sure. But I knew this was the opportunity. And in spring of 1992 we had the deal. The computer animation team has about twelve people, and they're shifting us into every arena."

Adding computer animations to a movie involves four steps: modeling, animating, rendering, and compositing. A *model* is a three-dimensional static model of an object – like a wireframe dinosaur. In *animation*, you set some keyframe positions you want the thing to be in, and have the computer smoothly fill in the positions between. *Rendering* converts the computer's three-dimensional model of the camera, the lights, the objects and their surface textures into a two-dimensional image. *Compositing* is combining your rendered image with the film of the background, with the matte paintings, and with the film of the actors. A typical shot involves doing this for a couple of hundred frames.

The old "animatronix" approach to positioning a model was to have the model be a foam-and-latex creature built over a hinged metal armature with lots of little motors. A wire or a radio control would connect the motors to a puppeteer. But, points out ILM programmer Eric Enderton, "As soon as you have a data link like the radio control, you can replace either end by a computer." Using this insight, the computer animation group built a skeletal data-dino which they could move around to change the position of virtual dinosaur skeletons inside the computer. The data-dino acts like a mouse, or like a DataGlove. The skeleton on the screen emulates whatever pose the data-dino is in.

Once the virtual dinosaur skeletons could be positioned at will, there came the question of the dinosaurs' muscles. Mark Dippé says, "We attached models of muscles to the dinosaur bones, and then we assigned one guy to be the muscle expert for each dinosaur. The muscle expert had to program a complex procedural system of relationships between the muscles and the angles of the joints. The shoulder, for instance, affects a lot of the muscles. And if one of the muscles doesn't swell dramatically enough, we use a secondary set of muscle controls called *bulgers*."

At the rendering stage, the material of the dinosaurs' skins was taken into account. What kind of colors and textures go into the tiny triangles of the moving wireframe computer meshes? "Part of the game is image complexity," says Enderton. "And on a computer you have to work for everything. One trick is to bring real world information into the computer. You can scan in actual skin textures. But we had to do more. The dinosaurs' skin was a big deal."

"We finally ended up building a three-dimensional paint system called *Viewpaint*," adds Mark Dippé. "You get a three-dimensional computer model, and spray some paint onto it. Then you turn the model and the paint turns with it, and then you paint some more." In addition to colors, the "paints" which Viewpaint can apply include such subtle things as shininess, dirtiness, bumpiness, and the patterns of a dinosaur's scaly skin. As a final touch, the skin textures were subtly roughened with computer-generated chaos to give them the indefinable level of detail that characterizes images of the real world.

This seems like an unbelievable amount of work for one movie but, as Dippé happily points out, "All the dinosaur technology can be used again for *The Flintstones*. The dinosaurs are vicious in *Jurassic Park*, they have to kill to exist. But in *The Flintstones* they're like people, they're pets, they complain, the escalator is a dinosaur in a hamster wheel, they're more anthropmorphized. But the techniques are the same. And it doesn't just have to be dinosaurs. We can do all forms of animals now. And superheroes are okay, too."

What next? Enderton says, "The holy grail is to do a believable human in clothes – a human with cloth and hair. This is hard because you know exactly how a human is supposed to move, reflect light, and behave. You're never seen a live dinosaur, which was an advantage for *Jurassic*."

The success of digital compositing and of the computer animations for *Jurassic Park* has set off a small upheaval within ILM. The tinkers in the creature shop and the model shop feel threatened. "I liked working on a stage with lights, making something to look real," recalls Jeff Mann, former head of the model shop, and now Director of Production Operations, which creates digital mattes. "There's a camaraderie in the production aspect; you have a common goal to make it real. We worked for ten years to make the process flow smoothly, and it seems weird to suddenly do it all on one work station. The change to work stations is happening so fast – it's like the Richter scale. It's stressful for a fair number of the model builders. ILM is trying to retrain the optical compositors as digital compositors, and to teach some of the model builders to use the tools of the computer to build computer models. Some will be able to adapt, some will get to keep building models, and some will go do something else."

But models are not going to fade out overnight. Even in *Jurassic Park*, the old-style rubber models were used for many scenes – such as the one where the T. Rex attacks the car. For each shot, it's a question of which technique will get the job done for the least money in the fastest time. Despite ILM's recent alliance with the Silicon Graphics computer company to form a Joint Environment for Digital Imaging (JEDI!), convincingly realistic computer animations are still very expensive. As Dippé puts it, "A movie like *Terminator 2* or *Jurassic* is like building the pyramids."

The model builders refer to their creations as "gags." They're like elaborate practical jokes, in a way, things that can fool your naked eye. They're fun to be around.

An example. As I was touring the creature shop with Mark Dippé and the ILM publicist Miles Perkins, Mark suddenly said, "Hey, Rudy, look at this!"

I walked over and Mark pulled back a sheet to reveal a tortured rubber man on an operating table. Leaning over him was a rubber alien wielding something that looked like dental apparatus. Suddenly the tortured man began to move and twitch. I screamed. The *gag* was a hidden cable leading to a control in Miles's hands. This was great. I thought about Jeff Mann's wondering if working on a work station could ever be as much fun as handling real models.

While I was in the creature shop, Miles mentioned to me that the main stash of old models and creatures is in the ILM archives, located at Skywalker Ranch, a half hour deeper into Marin County. I had an instant mental image of the great hall where the crated-up Ark of the Covenant gets stored at the end of *Raiders of the Lost Ark*. I knew I had to go.

Several days later, I drive with ILM head publicist Lisa van Cleef up a misty winding valley towards the California coast. The Skywalker Ranch includes George Lucas's offices, a sound studio, and guest quarters for visiting ILM customers – such as Steven Spielberg. Everything is California-perfect, like the best weekend retreat you can imagine. The sound studio has a small vineyard in its front yard, a gift to George Lucas from Francis Ford Coppola. There's even a small fire department and a small working ranch with a few dozen cows – these features were mandated by Marin County before they'd approve the construction of Skywalker *Ranch*. Since the cows aren't *really* there for ranching, I guess they're actors of a kind.

There are three or four men busy working on models in the archive building, and one of them, Don Bies, acts as my guide. "You've come at a really good time," he tells me. "We're just restoring the *Star Wars* models to send them on tour to some museums in Japan." Here in the archives the model builders are happy, and the work stations are far away.

The first gag that catches my eye is a baggy humanoid shape, orange with green spots, rubbery, with a hula skirt bedizened with electronic parts, and with a face sporting a three foot snout with red-lipsticked lips on the end. "That's Sy Snootles, the singer from the band that plays in Jabba the Hut's castle in *The Return of the Jedi*," Don tells me. I pick up a handgrip connected to a cable that leads into the figure's back. When I squeeze the grip, Sy's lips purse.

Right next to Sy Snootles is Darth Vader's costume. The cryptic alien writing on the little control panels on his chest is Hebrew. "Not many people realize that Darth Vader is Jewish," smiles Don. "Notice also that he's clean. Darth Vader and the robot C3PO are the only shiny things in the *Star Wars* universe. Everything else there is grungy."

We turn next to a yard-long spaceship model. "We wanted to make this the shape of an outboard motor that's been rocked up out of the water," says Don. "For the details we used a technique we call kit-bashing. We include a lot of pieces from standard model kits. See that there, it's the conning tower of a submarine, and here's the hull of a destroyer ship, and this down here is the front of a jet plane, and up here is part of a helicopter." This kit-bashed spaceship is a reality collage. The computer graphics animators scan textures from things, but the model makers break up and reassemble real objects.

"Where's R2D2?" I ask. He's always been my favorite.

Don points, and I turn to see a whole herd of R2D2's in a far corner. There are eleven of him. Why so many? Because when *Star Wars* was filmed, the science of radio-controlled machines was quite primitive, and it was easier to build a different R2D2 for each of the different things he was supposed to be able to do: turn his head, roll, fall to pieces, and so on. Each R2D2 has a big "holographic projector lens" near his top. The lenses look familiar because... they're those movable nozzle lights that airplanes used to have over the passenger seats. "And those slots along his side are from coin-operated vending machines," Don adds. It's kit-bashing in a higher, more industrial way.

Now we come to the gilded Ark of the Covenant itself, resting beside a busted-open wood crate. Stenciled on the crate is *"Eigentum des Deutsches Reich,"* with a swastika. I really *am* in the *Raiders of the Lost Ark* warehouse, and now, yes, Don opens a cabinet and he pulls out the matte painting of the *Raiders* warehouse scene, a giant sheet of glass with piles and piles of boxes fading into the painterly distances, and with an irregular trapezoid of clear glass where the image of the moving warehouseman was projected for optical compositing.

The ceiling struts in the matte painting seem to match the struts in the archive room, and when I go back outside and the foggy beauty of this hidden valley spreads out before me, it's hard for me not to believe, for a moment, that I am looking at an even huger matte painting.

And then the wind and the movement of the light remind me that this is real, this is where I live. In the mist a big bird circles on great, fingered wings, and I'm filled with joy at being alive in a world where I can dig into the details, just as I am, without a work station.

Standing there bathed in the real world's full-body sensory input, the efforts of computer reality seemed fiddling and paltry. The world has been running a massively parallel computation for billions of years, after all; how can we even dream of trying to make our machines catch up?

But we do keep pursuing the impossible dream of computer reality anyway; we keep on trying to digitally kit-bash the cosmic matte. It's one of the human race's ways of blooming – like science or like art. And in a funny way, thinking about computer realities gives you a greater appreciation for the real thing you get to walk around in.

— *Appeared as "Use Your Illusion: Kit-Bashing the Cosmic Matte,"*
in Wired, *September 1993.*

Art in Amsterdam

JULY 23, 1994. VAN GOGH AND PERPLEXING POULTRY.
Ida met up with us in Amsterdam, she's in Europe herself this summer. We rode the canal bus to the museum district and hit the Van
Gogh Museum right away; it was great. My favorite four pictures
were from June/July 1890, right before he shot himself. If you could
paint like that, how could you want to die? Maybe it was unbearable
to be that great? It's tough being a great artist, yes it is. The Vincent
I got into the most was one of a mansion or castle at twilight. What
he does with the brushwork is to completely shape the strokes to the
subject of that part of the picture. In the grass the strokes are quick
parallel vertical lines. On the sunset horizon there is a stack of parallel orange strokes, a pile of light. And, ah, in the big trees the strokes
are Perplexing Poultry puzzle pieces, they are like an M. C. Escher
tessellation yes they are, with leaf, branch, sky, sun colors tiled in,
light and dark leaves, man I have got to use this in *Freeware*, this is
what the Perplexing Poultry philtre is *for*, man, to make the world
look like the mature work of Vincent Van Gogh.[62]

As well as thinking of Vincent's brushwork in terms of the Poultry, I also, since Ida was there, thought of it in terms of a hyena tearing a piece of meat in half by whipping its head around in crazy-
eights. This being a rap that Ida and I got into watching a nature
show once – how a hyena that's bitten onto something big (possibly

---

62. The mathematician Roger Penrose has shown that the plane can be tiled in a
non-repeating way with two funny-shaped tiles that he sometimes draws as a skinny
chicken and a fat dodo bird. These are his "Perplexing Poultry." It used to be possible
to buy puzzle-sets of Perplexing Poultry from a British company, Pentaplex, which
can be found on the Web at http://www.pentaplex.com. The ordering links at this
site are dead, so I'm not sure if the puzzles are still available. Perplexing Poultry also
play a role in my novel *Freeware*, where one of the characters develops a "philtre"
which is a kind of program you can use to make everything around you look as if it
were made of three-dimensional Perplexing Poultry.

Penrose's Perplexing Poultry.

even an entire ruminant), will lash its head around in a kind of figure-eight pattern to tear loose a bite of flesh. And Ida and I got into doing that to each other's shoulders, or *threatening* to do it, and getting into the very wild and hyper motion of your head that goes with it. We called this motion "crazy eight." So looking at Vincent's last pictures, I found my head moving around in those loops, imagining how it would be to tear into that kind of painting — if you could do it.

JULY 24, 1994. EDWARD KEINHOLZ'S *BARNEY'S BEANERY.*

This morning I saw the most wonderful work of art I have experienced in years. *Barney's Beanery* by Edward Keinholz in the modern art museum here behind the Van Gogh museum.

A dumpster, painted silver, with some slight, direct set-up instructions consisting of the circled letters A, B, and C, along with a few crooked lines, and arrows directed at holes in the substance of the dumpster, holes through which power and information were making their way.

By the door into the dumpster is a newspaper stand with headline KIDS KILL KIDS: VIETNAM, dated, I believe, August 28, 1964. Inside is the model of a diner, with the Righteous Brothers singing "You've Lost that Loving Feeling," on a tape over a crackle and gabble of conversation and dishes, at first I wonder "what are they going to play next," and slowly I realize it is always the same song by the Righteous Brothers, and then, later, I realize that it is in fact always the same verse and chorus of "You've Lost that Loving Feeling." There are lots of people inside the place, it's full like a full bar/beanery late at night in August in 1964. I find my way down the diner aisle. I am light and huge, I am the ghost of Summer 1994, thirty years later than the world of Barney's Beanery.

The reason I feel big is, I realize, that all the people are about five-sixths normal size. The beer bottle on the waiter's tray at the back must be, come to think of it, a pony-size bottle, as it has a very bogus label: Lowenbrau from Zurich, Switzerland? In any case, everyone and every detail of chair bar table sign bottle plate, every detail is consistently at the same subhuman scale. About five sixths or three fourths, between that, maybe four sevenths, maybe the golden proportion, the golden Keinholz *Barney's Beanery* proportion long may it wave.

So I enter the Beanery and push back my way to the back, knowing Audrey will slowly follow me just as if we were invading a real Beanery. The weird thing, everybody in here has a clock for their face. Why? "You've Lost that Loving Feeling" I'm grasping that this one chorus loop is *it*.

On the shelf at head level behind the bar are lettered drink specials. Towards the back is a sign saying something like "All Visitors of Barney's Beanery Must Order An Amount Exceeding 35 Cents." And pasted to the sign with scotch tape is a quarter and a dime. Running down from the coins along the wall is a ballpoint line and arrow pointing to a guy with his face down on the side on the table top, except his head seems to be a large vacuum tube. (How '60s, a head that is a vacuum tube. How 19th Century, the idea that everyone's head is a clock, a clock with hands.)

So then Audrey and I worked our way back out, sharing a tender lingering-feeling moment by the Barney's Beanery dial payphone near the door, and then Ida went in there alone real fast, emerging not obviously impressed, at least not impressed enough to be patient with my grandiose exegesis of *Barney's Beanery*.

"It's a moment in time," I told Ida. "Wouldn't it be cool if all of the people's face-clocks in there had the same time?"

"Yeah, *duh*," snaps Ida, "They're all set to ten-ten."

"Oh," I say, and decide I've got to go back in to check this and other details. So later after we've seen all the great stuff on the upper floor, and the women are in the card shop or hanging out in the vast building-high open spaces, I *run* downstairs and *dart* around all the wambling other tourists who are about to maybe see this work, and get alone back into the Beanery and run to the back corner where the music is the loudest and I am the farthest from the unending reality of this working life. It's the same chorus, the same emotion that wells up in me at hearing that chorus wells up again...and again...and again...this is my college years, this Beanery is like a great wild college drinking and diner night. It's as if while staggering around in that world Ed Keinholz had a special moment, not so much more wonderful than any other moments, but still a wonderful moment, and he like mentally photographed it so that he could reproduce it at a golden ratio of scale in a dumpster-sized box with input lines labeled A B and C for wonderfully simple '60s analog technology of power and audio.

Now I finally look sharply at the clock faces of the people and Ida is right, it's ten ten over and over for ever and ever.

— *Unpublished. Written July 1994.*

Pieter Bruegel's *Peasant Dance*

I've loved Bruegel for a long time. When I was thirteen, my parents sent me away from Kentucky to live with my grandmother for a year in Germany. She was a wonderful old woman. To teach me German, she helped me read and reread a fairy tale about a child that falls down a well and finds another world down at the bottom, an apt image for a parallel world such as, e.g., Germany relative to Kentucky. To further educate me, Grandma showed me *Das Bruegel Buch*, a book of Bruegel's paintings. I was particularly impressed by the apocalyptic Boschian painting *The Triumph of Death,* with its armies of skeletons. "This is cool," I remember thinking while looking at that picture. "This is like science fiction." I was also naively pleased with Bruegel's hundred-in-one pictures like *Netherlandish Proverbs.* In later years I became more fond of Bruegel's mature, non-seething paintings such as *Peasant Dance.* Thanks to their deep, detailed pictorial space, these paintings look into worlds that are very large.

I think of Bruegel's paintings as being like novels, so filled are they with character, incident, narrative and landscape. I feel a pang of sorrow when I stop looking at one of Bruegel's pictures, just like when I finish reading the last page of a great novel. I don't want to leave, I don't want it to be over, I want to stay in that world. How far into the world of a painting or a novel can you get?

In each, the information has a kind of fractal structure. I would define a fractal as something that has this property: when you look twice as hard at a fractal, you see three times as much. Language is fractal with words suggesting words suggesting words, while paintings are fractal with their details within details within details. A basic problem is that in either case only a limited amount of information is really being given. Fractal nature has an essentially infinite precision, but a novel or a painting is radically finite.

How finite? It depends. A significant difference between paintings and novels is that when you get a printed copy of a novel you get *all* of

Peter Bruegel's *Peasant Dance*.
(Photo © Kunsthistorisches
Museum Vienna)

the available information: all the letters of all the words of the text. But when you get a reproduction of a painting, you are settling for a degraded semblance of the original. Given that a painting is a non-digital object, it's not even clear how much information really would be needed to perfectly specify the image. This is a real problem when you want to get deeper and deeper into a detailed image such as a Bruegel.

At this stage in human technology there's no replacement for going to a museum to look at the original of some beloved masterwork – although, sadly, the very fact of being in a museum involves its own distractions, of standing in a public space watched over by museum guards, with your schedule subject to opening and closing times and your senses impinged upon by the other tourists.

Over the years I've made a point of visiting as many Bruegel paintings as possible. The world's richest trove of Bruegels is in the Kunsthistorisches Museum in Vienna; they hang together in a single high-ceilinged room. I well remember the sensation I get going into this divine: a feeling of great urgency. Each picture is filled with individual specific people, places and things, all presented as the most delightful visual forms: the arabesque two-dimensional curves, the sensual massings of three-dimensional shapes, and the scumbled color fields. One of my favorite paintings there is *Peasant Dance*.

Before going into detail about *Peasant Dance*, I want to add a detail about detail. I always have a certain disappointment when I get an extremely close look at a beloved painting, either by seeing it in person or by looking at a magnified view of some small section. At a certain level of enlargement, the painterly illusion goes away and all you see are brushstrokes. Blow up a small figure's face and instead of pores, you see daubs of paint. The same thing is true of novels. If, for instance, you flip through a book and carefully read all the descriptions of some one favorite character, you'll notice a certain mechanical element: certain identifier phrases and attributes occur over and over. These fictional "brushstrokes" are used by authors to give their fictional people an air of persistent existence. The seeming reality of a novel or a painting is an artful construct that only pops into focus at a certain distance. It is only the cosmic fractal of real life which allows for endless zooming.

Peasant Dance, also known as *Peasant Kermis*, is one of Bruegel's last paintings, completed a year or two before his death at about age 44 in 1569. What do we see?

A little dirt road through a village beneath a gray sky; there's leaves on some trees but it doesn't feel like summer; I'd say it's spring. Gray sky and muddy buildings, a small town. Some people dancing in the middle ground. In the foreground are two main groups, one on the left, one on the right. On the left is a bagpiper with a drunk man watching him from a few inches away. On the right, a couple is running into the canvas from outside the frame, they're late, they're hurrying, their attention is focused ahead of them on the dancers and probably on some food and drink back there to the left. The man is hard-faced and black-toothed, his run is already breaking into a bit of a dance, he has a spoon tucked into his hat. The woman he tows behind him is too busy hurrying to dance, she seems a pale-faced unlovely goose with room for but one thought at a time in her head.

I always think of Jack Kerouac when I look at the drunk man watching the bagpiper, of the *On The Road* passages about Jack and Neal digging jazz, "Blow man, blow!" And I cringe a bit, remembering the times I used to be like this myself: crowding up to a guitar-playing friend and fixating on his performance, "gloating over it," as Jack says in *Visions of Cody*, thick-tongue-edly urging the musician on, lost in the inebriate's self-centered feeling of creating ("realizing" by observing!) the air-vibrations and the sight trails of the soundy scene around. Meanwhile the musician is playing on, his small eyes fixed on the distance, he's putting the music out there, grateful perhaps for the accolades of his drunken acolyte. After all, unheard sound is hardly music at all, any more than an unseen picture is a painting, or an unread text a novel – communication is one of art's several vital organs.

Instead of identifying with the man staring at the musician I can – with equal discomfiture – project myself onto the man running into the picture from the right, the guy arriving late at a party, trying to get into the swing of things, to be one of the revelers right away. "Hey, I'm cool too!" His face is a mask of harsh, naked desire. The man's redneck appearance and the dirt of the street puts me powerfully in mind of the years I've spent living in small towns, hungry for the distraction of my communities' small, puttering festivals. Though, really, so universal is the *Peasant Dance* that the image overlays equally well onto the hippest scenes imaginable. Entertainment and the entertainees.

Let's look some more. At the table on the left are some *seriously* fucked up guys, they almost look like they might be blind and/or deaf. Blind to logic and deaf to reason, in any case. That odd, upside-down white shape on the table is, according to one commentator, a drinking glass that you can't set down (you have to chug it all), though another thinks it might be a dice-cup. Behind them are some fat lovers, behind the lovers is a shy guy watching the dancers, behind him are a man and woman in a tug of war at an inn-door — think he wants her to come out and dance, unless maybe she wants him to come in and fuck? Still further back is a man dressed in red and yellow fool's motley. What a scene! Way far back, partly glimpsed, are more and more people and what looks like the tops of booths selling stuff — it's a *kermis*, a street fair. In the middle ground two couples dance. Of the lefthand middle ground couple, the man seems ecstatically, or soddenly, involved in the dance; the woman is calm, happy, maybe a bit glazed around the eyes. She's having a good time dancing. The righthand couple seem uptight, athletic, intent on executing some specific step.

A final grouping of note is the two mutually absorbed girl children standing real short in the left foreground. Looking closer, you can see that the larger girl is probably teaching the smaller girl to dance. Her face is exactly the face of a mothering big sister, and the little one's face is perfectly that of a wondering toddler. The little one has a jingle bell pinned on her sleeve, perhaps so as not to get lost. The pair of girls are tender and heartening — how eager we humans are to grow, to teach, to learn.

I've been working on this essay for a week now, and something that begins to strike me, coming back over and over to the *Peasant Wedding*, is how the image is always the same. Everyone frozen there forever in time, with the trees against the sky making their beautiful shapes. A day like any day, yet a day that lasts forever.

It's nice that the picture waits up for me. But of course it's never quite the same picture. You never step into the same river twice — if only because you're never the same "you" again. Each time I look at the picture again I find something new to think about.

How wonderful it would be to write a novel as rich as a painting by Bruegel — a masterwork that achieves the illusion of containing a cosmos. It's a goal to live for.

—Appeared in World Art. #13, *spring, 1997.*

Dates of Composition

TITLE	DATE WRITTEN
Drugs and Live Sex	Spring, 1980
The Central Teachings of Mysticism	December, 1982
A Transrealist Manifesto	Winter, 1983
Jerry's Neighbors	May, 1984
What SF Writers Want	Spring, 1985
What Is Cyberpunk?	February, 1986
Haunted by Phil Dick	Fall, 1986
Welcome to Silicon Valley	Summer, 1988
Cellular Automata	May, 1989
Cyberculture in Japan	June, 1990 and Fall, 1993
Four Kinds of Cyberspace	Summer, 1991
Vision in Yosemite	August, 1992
Mr. Nanotechnology	December, 1992
Coming to California	January, 1992
Special Effects:	
Kit-Bashing the Cosmic Matte	May, 1993
Life and Artificial Life	July, 1993
The Manual of Evasion	January, 1994
Interview with Ivan Stang	Summer 1994
Fab! Inside Chip Fabrication Plants	June, 1994
Hacking Code	July, 1994
Art in Amsterdam	July, 1994
Tech Notes Towards a Cyberpunk Novel	July 1994
Memories of Arf	February, 1995
Goodbye Big Bang	April, 1995
A Brief History of Computers	Summer, 1996
A New Golden Age of Calculation	Fall, 1996
Cyberpunk Lives!	November, 1996
Pieter Bruegel's *Peasant Dance*	December, 1996
Island Notes	1996, 1997, 1998

Bibliography

Asterisks indicate the books that are out of print. I've included ordering information for the small press books.

TWENTY BOOKS

Realware, novel, Avon Books (to appear 2000).

Saucer Wisdom, novel/nonfiction, Tor Books (to appear 1999).

Seek!, selected nonfiction, Four Walls Eight Windows, 1999.

Freeware, novel, Avon Books 1997.

*The Hacker and the Ants, novel, Avon Books 1994.

Transreal!, fiction and nonfiction collection, WCS Books 1991. (Order from http://www.cambrianpubs.com/Rucker/)

*The Hollow Earth, novel, William Morrow and Co. 1990, Avon Books 1992.

All the Visions, memoir, Ocean View Books, 1991. (Order from Ocean View Books, Box 102650, Denver CO 80250.)

Wetware, novel, Avon Books 1988, Avon Books 1997.

Mind Tools, nonfiction, Houghton Mifflin 1987.

*The Secret of Life, novel, Bluejay Books 1985.

*Master of Space and Time, novel, Bluejay Books 1984, Baen Books 1985.

The Fourth Dimension, nonfiction, Houghton Mifflin 1984.

*The Sex Sphere, novel, Ace Books 1983.

*The Fifty-Seventh Franz Kafka, story collection, Ace Books 1983.

Software, novel, Ace Books 1982, Avon Books 1987, Avon Books 1997.

Infinity and the Mind, nonfiction, Birkhäuser 1982, Bantam 1983, Princeton University Press, 1995.

White Light, novel, Ace Books 1980, Wired Books 1997.

*Spacetime Donuts, novel, Ace Books 1981.

Geometry, Relativity and the Fourth Dimension, nonfiction, Dover 1977.

BOOKS EDITED

Mondo 2000: A User's Guide to the New Edge, edited with Queen Mu and R.U. Sirius. HarperCollins, 1992.

Semiotext(e) SF, edited with Peter Lamborn Wilson and Robert Anton Wilson. Autonomedia 1989. (Order from Autonomedia, 55 S. 11th St., Brooklyn, NY 11211-0568.)

Mathenauts: Tales of Mathematical Wonder. Arbor House, 1987.

Speculations on the Fourth Dimension: Selected Writings of Charles Howard Hinton. Dover, 1983.

SOFTWARE

I've worked on a number of software packages. All of them are now available for free download from my Web site http://www.mathcs.sjsu.edu/faculty/rucker. All programs are for machines running Microsoft *Windows* (any version of *Windows* will do).

CAPOW. Software for simulating 1-D and 2-D continuous valued cellular automata, 1994-1998. Written by Rudy Rucker and his students.

Hypercube98. Software for visualizing solid and wireframe four-dimensional hypercubes. Written by Farideh Dormishian and Rudy Rucker.

Boppers: First published as *Artificial Life Lab*, Waite Group, 1993. By Rudy Rucker.

James Gleick's CHAOS: The Software. A DOS program that runs under *Windows*. Written by James Gleick, Josh Gordon, Rudy Rucker and John Walker. Autodesk, 1990.

Cellab. Originally released as *CA Lab: Rudy Rucker's Cellular Automata Laboratory*. Written by Rudy Rucker and John Walker. Autodesk 1989.